Teacher Development
in Higher Education

Routledge Research in Education

For a full list of titles in this series, please visit www.routledge.com

56 **International Case Studies of Dyslexia**
Edited by Peggy L. Anderson and Regine Meier-Hedde

57 **Schooling and the Making of Citizens in the Long Nineteenth Century**
Comparative Visions
Edited by Daniel Tröhler, Thomas S. Popkewitz and David F. Labaree

58 **Islamic Education and Indoctrination**
The Case in Indonesia
Charlene Tan

59 **Beyond Binaries in Education Research**
Edited by Warren Midgley, Mark A. Tyler, Patrick Alan Danaher and Alison Mander

60 **Picturebooks, Pedagogy and Philosophy**
Joanna Haynes and Karin Murris

61 **Personal Epistemology and Teacher Education**
Edited by Jo Brownlee, Gregory Schraw and Donna Berthelsen

62 **Teacher Learning that Matters**
International Perspectives
Edited by Mary Kooy and Klaas van Veen

63 **Pedagogy of Multiliteracies**
Rewriting Goldilocks
Heather Lotherington

64 **Intersectionality and "Race" in Education**
Edited by Kalwant Bhopal and John Preston

65 **The Politics of Education**
Challenging Multiculturalism
Edited by Christos Kassimeris and Marios Vryonides

66 **Whiteness and Teacher Education**
Edie White

67 **Multidisciplinary Approaches to Educational Research**
Case Studies from Europe and the Developing World
Edited by Sadaf Rizvi

68 **Postcolonial Perspectives on Global Citizenship Education**
Edited by Vanessa de Oliveira Andreotti and Lynn Mario T. M. De Souza

69 **Education in the Black Diaspora**
Perspectives, Challenges, and Prospects
Edited by Kassie Freeman and Ethan Johnson

70 **Gender, Race, and the Politics of Role Modelling**
The Influence of Male Teachers
Wayne Martino and Goli Rezai-Rashti

71 **Educating for Diversity and Social Justice**
Amanda Keddie

72 **Considering Trilingual Education**
Kathryn Henn-Reinke

73 **Commitment, Character, and Citizenship**
Religious Education in Liberal Democracy
Edited by Hanan A. Alexander and Ayman K. Agbaria

74 **Adolescent Literacies in a Multicultural Context**
Edited by Alister Cumming

75 **Participation, Facilitation, and Mediation**
Children and Young People in Their Social Contexts
Edited by Claudio Baraldi and Vittorio Iervese

76 **The Politics of Knowledge in Education**
Elizabeth Rata

77 **Neoliberalism, Pedagogy and Human Development**
Exploring Time, Mediation and Collectivity in Contemporary Schools
Michalis Kontopodis

78 **Resourcing Early Learners**
New Networks, New Actors
Sue Nichols, Jennifer Rowsell, Helen Nixon and Sophia Rainbird

79 **Educating for Peace in a Time of "Permanent War"**
Are Schools Part of the Solution or the Problem?
Edited by Paul R. Carr and Brad J. Porfilio

80 **The Politics of Teacher Professional Development**
Policy, Research and Practice
Ian Hardy

81 **Working-Class Minority Students' Routes to Higher Education**
Roberta Espinoza

82 **Education, Indigenous Knowledge, and Development in the Global South**
Contesting Knowledges for a Sustainable Future
Anders Breidlid

83 **Teacher Development in Higher Education**
Existing Programs, Program Impact, and Future Trends
Edited by Eszter Simon and Gabriela Pleschová

Teacher Development in Higher Education

Existing Programs, Program Impact, and Future Trends

Edited by Eszter Simon
and Gabriela Pleschová

NEW YORK   LONDON

First published 2013
by Routledge
711 Third Avenue, New York, NY 10017

Simultaneously published in the UK
by Routledge
2 Park Square, Milton Park, Abingdon, Oxon OX14 4RN

*Routledge is an imprint of the Taylor & Francis Group,
an informa business*

© 2013 Taylor & Francis

The right of the editors to be identified as the authors of the editorial material, and of the authors for their individual chapters, has been asserted in accordance with sections 77 and 78 of the Copyright, Designs and Patents Act 1988.

Library of Congress Cataloging-in-Publication Data
    Teacher development in higher education : existing programs, program impact, and future trends / edited by Eszter Simon, Gabriela Pleschová.
        p. cm. — (Routledge research in education ; 83)
    Includes bibliographical references and index.
    1.   College teachers—Training of—Cross-cultural studies.   I. Simon, Eszter.   II. Pleschová, Gabriela.
    LB1738.T43 2012
    378.1'2—dc23
    2012009977

ISBN: 978-0-415-50266-5 (hbk)
ISBN: 978-0-203-09682-6 (ebk)

Typeset in Sabon
by IBT Global.

Printed and bound in the United States of America on sustainably sourced paper by IBT Global.

Contents

List of Figures   xi
List of Tables   xiii
Acknowledgments   xv

1   **What We Know and Fail to Know about
    the Impact of Teacher Development**   1
    GABRIELA PLESCHOVÁ AND ESZTER SIMON

**PART I
Training for What?
Instructional Development for Graduate Students**

2   **Preparing Doctoral Students for a Teaching Career:
    The Case of an International University
    with a History of Regional Engagement**   19
    JOANNA RENC-ROE AND TATIANA YARKOVA

3   **Graduate Student Teacher-Training Courses,
    Job Placement, and Teaching Awards in the United States**   34
    JOHN ISHIYAMA, ALEXANDRA COLE, ANGELA D. NICHOLS,
    KERSTIN HAMANN, AND KIMBERLY MEALY

4   **The Impact of Training on Teacher Effectiveness:
    Canadian Practices and Policies**   53
    CHRISTOPHER KNAPPER

PART II
Using Programme Assessments to Improve Programme Design

5   Mentorship in Teacher-Training:
A Preliminary Review of a Professional Development
Programme for Tertiary Teachers in Singapore   71
HUANG HOON CHNG AND ALAN SOONG SWEE KIT

6   Combining International Experience with
the Local Context: Designing and Improving
Instructional Development in a Post-Soviet Setting   86
MARI KARM, MARVI REMMIK, AND ANU HAAMER

7   Institutional Factors in Re-Designing an Accredited Continuing
Professional Development Course in Northern Ireland   105
VICKY DAVIES AND SARAH MAGUIRE

PART III
Top-Down Determinants of Success in Instructional
Development Programmes

8   The Emerging European Higher Education Area:
Implications for Instructional Development   129
KATHLEEN M. QUINLAN AND ERKKI BERNDTSON

9   Teacher Development Programmes:
National Policies Enabling Local Impact in Ireland   151
JENNIFER MURPHY

10 The Influence of the Research Philosophy and
Pedagogical Management Decisions of the University of
Helsinki on University Teaching: A Longitudinal Study   170
ANNE NEVGI

11 The Impact of UK University Teaching
Programmes on Lecturers' Assessment Practice:
A Case for Pedagogical Action Research   191
LIN S. NORTON, BILL NORTON, AND LEE SHANNON

PART IV
Theorizing about Instructional Development

12 How Effects from Teacher-Training of Academic
    Teachers Propagate into the Meso Level and Beyond   213
    TORGNY ROXÅ AND KATARINA MÅRTENSSON

13 Instructional Development for University Teachers:
    Causes of Impact and Practical Implications   234
    ANN STES AND PETER VAN PETEGEM

14 Evaluating the Impact of University
    Teaching Development Programmes:
    Methodologies that Ask Why there is an Impact   257
    KEITH TRIGWELL

15 Creating Successful Teacher Development Programmes   274
    ESZTER SIMON AND GABRIELA PLESCHOVÁ

    Contributors   299
    Index   307

Figures

7.1   Relationships of an SPD Framework to other university systems and processes.   109

7.2   Internal and external factors for development of the new PgCHEP.   114

7.3   University of Ulster teaching and learning strategy: aims and objectives.   115

7.4.   Illustration of normal progression for a newly appointed member of academic staff—Route A.   119

7.5   Illustration of normal progression for a member of staff taking a course for CPD purposes—Route B.   119

10.1   Organisational structure of support for pedagogical development in faculties at the University of Helsinki.   177

12.1   The micro, meso, and macro levels with semi-autonomous knowledge networks clearly visible at the meso level.   226

13.1   Framework for analysing the impact of the instructional development programme at the University of Antwerp.   239

13.2   Framework for analysing the impact of instructional development including the lessons learnt on the basis of the University of Antwerp programme.   250

Tables

3.1 Coefficient Estimates and Collinearity Statistics for Dependent Variable (PhDs Placed over Total Number of PhD Degrees Granted 1999–2007)   39

3.2 Coefficient Estimates and Collinearity Statistics for Dependent Variable (PhDs Placed over Total Number of PhD Degrees Granted 1999–2007) for PhD Programmes Not in Top Forty on Hix Index   40

3.3 Coefficient Estimates and Collinearity Statistics for Dependent Variable (PhDs Placed at Non-PhD-granting Departments over Total Number of PhD Degrees Granted 1990–2007) for PhD Programmes Not in Top Forty on Hix Index   40

3.4 Awards at all Universities   43

3.5 Awards at Non-Research 1 Universities   44

3.6 Comparing Teaching-Award Rankings and Other Rankings Based on Reputation, Citations, and PhD Production   46

3.7 Teaching-Awards Rankings Compared to Overall Rankings of Graduate Departments   48

3.8 Summary of Different Graduate Programmes   49

5.1 The Value of the Teaching Practicum   79

5.2 Importance of Mentorship in the Teaching Practicum   82

6.1 Outcomes and Contents of Basic Teaching Skills Course in the Context of Higher Education Environments   94

7.1 UK PSF Standard Descriptors One and Two   107

9.1 Theory and Practical Modules Offered in Certificate Programmes   156

9.2 UCD Structure of Accredited Programmes in Teaching and Learning   157

9.3 Academic Professional Development Modules for Postgraduate Students (Five ECTS)   158

9.4 Key Learning Objectives of Diploma Courses   159

10.1 Curriculum for the Programme of University Pedagogy (Sixty ECTS) at the University of Helsinki 175

13.1 Levels of Outcome as Distinguished in the Current Research 236

14.1 Relations between Completion of Grad Cert in University Teaching and Receipt of University Teaching Awards 267

14.2 Teaching Reward Recipients from Facilities for Whom the Grad Cert Is Compulsory/Voluntary and Who Have Completed/Not Completed the Programme 268

15.1 Factors Discussed in This Book That Are Proven to Have a Positive Impact on Instructional Development Programmes 278

15.2 Levels of Analysis and the Outcomes of Instructional Development Programmes with Examples from the Literature 280

Acknowledgments

The editors would like to acknowledge support from several institutions and individuals that made the publication of this book possible.

Between March 18 and 20, 2010, the European Science Foundation (ESF) held an exploratory workshop entitled *The Impact of Training for Teachers in Higher Education* in Bratislava, Slovakia, during which many of the contributors of this book presented their papers. This workshop allowed for experience from existing teacher development programmes to be drawn together, and also facilitated the outline of directions for further research in this area. The European Science Foundation funded the workshop and covered part of the cost of publishing this book.

The publication of this book would not have been possible without support from the European Social Fund through a project carried out by the Institute of Physics of the Slovak Academy of Sciences. This project, which is being realized between 2010 and 2013, aims at reviewing the results of various teacher development programmes. Based on this review, a program for beginner university teachers is being introduced in Slovakia, and the effects of this programme are being evaluated.

The original idea for this book came from Bob Reinalda, whose guidance and encouragement have been invaluable, especially in the early stages of the book's preparation. We also wish to thank Graham Gibbs for his support and advice during the preparation of the workshop. Furthermore, we are indebted to Keith Trigwell for his trust and support and we are grateful to all workshop participants for their creative ideas and active participation. In closing, one of the editors (GP) would like to thank her husband for his work as the project manager and for his long-standing support, which were of utmost importance in the realization of this project.

This publication was supported by the European Union and the European Social Fund.

Modern education for the knowledge-based society/Project is co-financed from EU resources.

1 What We Know and Fail to Know about the Impact of Teacher Development

Gabriela Pleschová and Eszter Simon

FACTORS PLACING TEACHER DEVELOPMENT ON THE POLITICAL AGENDA

During the last decade, governments in most developed countries have aimed to increase the numbers of university graduates and to improve the quality of university education as means to maintain or to increase countries' growth and competitiveness. Yet, while educational expansion and structural changes, in particular relating to the Bologna Process (Reinalda and Kulesza 2006) have brought about improvements for students, they have not necessarily done so for faculty members who are in charge of teaching. Many professors are worried that institutional requirements brought about by the Bologna Process, such as paying greater attention to learners' needs, offering more flexible learning paths, or varied assessment techniques, will consume much of their time and thus negatively affect their research (Reichert and Tauch 2005, 38). Accordingly, many faculty members consider teaching enhancement courses as one of many bureaucratic demands on their time (Gibbs 1989, 58–59). At the same time, the characteristics of the teaching faculties are changing as graduate teaching assistants and doctoral students are increasingly being employed to teach. Indeed, many of them will replace the current "baby boom" generation of scholars, who will retire in coming years.

Some countries, most notably the UK, Ireland, Belgium, and the Nordic states, have responded to these challenges by paying closer attention to teacher development.[1] Centres and networks have been created and restructured to implement teacher development courses for higher education (HE) practitioners, starting from a certificate level, through to diploma and master's level courses. On a wider institutional level, the Higher Education Academy and the Staff and Development Association and the Heads of Educational Development Group were established in the UK, while the National Academy for the Integration of Research, Teaching and Learning was created in Ireland, in addition to a Network of Educational Developers in Sweden and to the Higher Education Research and Development Society for Australasia.

Especially in Anglo-Saxon countries, educational development has come into the mainstream as an important field of practice for any teacher. It has also integrated university management, amounting, for example, to the creation of positions of hierarchical importance such as that of the vice-president or vice-chancellor for teaching and learning at the University of Sydney (Prosser and Barrie 2003, 194), and of similar positions at the University of Nottingham and Open University, to name a few. Entities offering educational development are gradually being recognized for the importance of the service that they offer. In Europe and in Australia, in particular, their role is not only to research learning, teaching, and development but also to engage in curriculum development and to become involved with quality assurance (Knapper 2010, 3). In some countries like the UK, educational development is increasingly seen as playing a strategic role, as staff members at educational units are being engaged in designing university strategies for quality education (Gosling 2009, 9).

Some teacher development programmes already have a history of serving teachers and their students, and it is important to know what they have achieved. Baume (2003, 89–90) summarizes three main sets of practical reasons as to why staff and educational development programmes should be evaluated: first, to determine whether the programme has fulfilled its aims, second, to propose strategies for improving the programme, and third, to understand the reasons for the programme's effects, successes, and failures. Also, exposure to evidence showing that such programmes are successful in enhancing the quality of teaching could motivate those teachers who are hesitant to undertake them.

THE STATE OF RESEARCH ON THE IMPACT OF TEACHER DEVELOPMENT

In spite of increased attention to instructional development, not enough is yet known on its effects. Little has been done to systematically measure the results of many programmes that were established in the 1990s or earlier. Gosling (2001) sent a questionnaire to fifty-three heads of educational development units in the UK to map their work in much detail. The survey revealed that only a few units were required to systematically evaluate the impact of their activities, while many of them reported having used questionnaires or feedback tools to assess certain activities, and some had hired external evaluators. This is consistent with Kreber and Brook's (2001) findings in Canada, which concluded that the evaluation of teacher development programmes often relied on inference measures including the extent of students' participation and satisfaction. A number of authors (Coffey and Gibbs 2000; Eggins and Macdonald 2003; Smith 2004) presented arguments along the same lines: that debate about faculty development goes on in the absence of evidence on its effects.

Since the end of the 1990s, much more has been done to evaluate the effects of teacher development programmes. Unfortunately, many studies suffer methodological weaknesses. Because of the volume and varying quality of studies that are currently available on this topic, studies included in this literature review were selected carefully. Studies were included either on the basis of having made major advancements in scholarly knowledge on the effects of instructional development, or because they can serve as illustrative examples of particular research methods. Preference was also given to those studies which were methodologically strongest. In the review of existing research presented in this book, areas of consensus or near-consensus, areas of disagreement or debate as well as gaps in knowledge have been identified (Knopf 2006). In the presentation of these studies below, ideas and findings are related to each study's particular methodology, allowing the reader to understand possible limitations of the methods used and how these may have influenced the results obtained (see Boote and Beile 2005, 8). A different review of published literature on the results of instructional development can be found in Trigwell's chapter in this book.

Areas of Disagreement or Debate: Which Research Methods to Use?

An important proportion of studies that attempt to measure the effects of teacher-training courses are informed solely by the opinions of those educators who went through them. For example, between 2000 and 2003, Donnelly (2006) studied the self-perception of change in teaching practice by lecturers who received a postgraduate certificate on HE teaching and learning from the Dublin Institute of Technology. Her respondents indicated that training transformed their teaching practice, because it increased their reflection on their own teaching methods, allowed them to learn about and introduce new teaching strategies, improved their focus on the design and delivery of classes, and increased their confidence about learning and teaching, among other things. Using a similar method, MacDonald (2001) examined the results of a model that has been evolving at Monash University and Swinburne University in Australia for the professional development of teaching staff. The author concluded that the Teaching Community Approach[2] had brought about remarkable changes in teachers' understanding of their role, as well as in their teaching skills and, most importantly, in their enthusiasm for teaching.

Unfortunately, there are certain noticeable weaknesses in the methodology used for conducting these studies. Above all, their results are solely based on self-assessments from teachers, which were collected either through interviews or questionnaires. Because of this, the validity of findings by Donnelly (2006) and MacDonald (2001) that teacher development programmes yielded positive impacts is limited.

Coffey and Gibbs (2000) and Gibbs and Coffey (2004) took these studies a step further by undertaking quantitative research that was centred on students' opinion on their instructors' teaching. In their first study, the authors collected and analysed data from 302 matched pairs of student responses providing feedback on seventy-two teachers from nine institutions in the UK. Later, they conducted an extensive study at twenty-two universities in eight countries. However, the study's methodology showed important limitations. Indeed, while researchers found that teachers having undergone training received the best ratings from their students, they could not attribute these positive results to development programmes themselves, or state whether other factors, for example teachers' institutions, had brought about these results.

Norton et al. (2005) examined the effects of teacher development programmes using a quantitative survey that was informed by teachers' opinions. The authors analyzed questionnaires from two groups of university teachers from one British institution, the first of which was composed by fifty teachers who had taken a programme on teaching and learning in HE, and the second of which was made up of twenty-two teachers who had not undergone training. Contrarily to studies by Donnelly (2006) and MacDonald (2001), this study did not ask teachers how they felt they changed as a result of teacher development programmes. Instead, the study compared the beliefs and intentions of two groups of teachers, with the assumption that those having undergone training would view teaching as the facilitation of learning, rather than as simple transmission of knowledge. Studies have confirmed that the way instructors understand teaching is critical in informing their actual teaching practice (Prosser and Trigwell 1999). Therefore this is a valid method for examining effects of teacher-training.

In their study, Postareff, Lindblom-Ylänne, and Nevgi (2007) used both qualitative and quantitative methods. The authors examined the impact of pedagogical training on teachers' approaches to teaching and on their beliefs of self-efficacy. Two hundred teachers from two HE institutions in Finland were divided into four groups according to the extent to which they had undergone teacher-training—from not having gone through any programme at all, to having completed one year or more of such training. The researchers used the Approaches to Teaching Inventory with an additional questionnaire measuring motivational strategies and they also interviewed seventy-five of these teachers. This study advanced the research method by including several control groups; however, it did not consider teachers' practice or students' learning.

Studies by Stes, Coertjens, and Van Petegem (2010) and Stes et al. (2011a, 2011b) combine quantitative and qualitative methods to compare the effects on trained teachers with a control group that had not undergone training. Moreover, they tested teachers' capacities before and after having undergone training to assess the effectiveness of teacher development programmes. Aside from this, the researchers considered the link between the performance of individual students and the extent to which their teachers had gone through a teacher development programme in assessing these programmes' impact.

Indeed, there are many challenges in controlling all possible variables when conducting such research. The methods used in this study were quite rigorous, and so the results obtained raised important considerations on the limitations of quantitative methods. Quantitative methods only allow researchers to receive answers to predefined questions; and these questions cannot be modified or added to. Also, when using quantitative methods, informants have little opportunity to express their own perceptions on what they find to be important.

Ho (1998, 2000) used a research design similar to Stes, Coertjens, and Van Petegem (2010) and Stes et al. (2011a, 2011b); however, she traced the impact of teacher development on both teachers and their students. Ho interviewed twenty-one participants of a programme at the University of Hong Kong before and after completing the programme, and analysed teachers' reflective diaries. Quantitative data were collected from these teachers' students over a two-year period, and four teachers who had never undergone a teacher development programme were included as a control group. Contrary to studies conducted by Stes et al. (2011a, 2011b), Ho measured the impact of the training programme on students two years after it was completed, rather than after three months.

Similar studies that examine the impact of training in the longer term are, however, rare. In 2007 Stes, Clement, and Van Petegem found that two years after finishing the programme, respondents still referred to the programme as a means of explaining changes in their day-to-day teaching practice. However, in this study these results were solely derived from teachers' self-assessments, and the impact on students was not examined (Stes, Clement, and Van Petegem 2007).

Examples of research mentioned earlier illustrate that studies which go further than to rely on teachers' self-assessments face severe obstacles in terms of their design. Their samples are small, because only a relatively small number of teachers usually participate in a given training programme at a time. Moreover, samples are based on the self-selection of participants because participation in research, just like participation in teacher development programmes, is voluntary. As these programmes are relatively new, they are often weak at supporting teachers in implementing newly developed knowledge and skills in practice. This makes it difficult to measure the programme effectiveness in terms of student learning (Stes et al. 2010).

Researchers try to overcome these obstacles in different ways. Some conduct interviews with directors of schools and mentors to gather information about teachers' behaviour (Smith 2004), while others rely on materials produced by teachers having gone through the programme, such as portfolios (McLean and Bullard 2000; Groom and Maunonen-Eskelinen 2006) or their letters to the programme team (Smith 2004). Some use a combination of these methods of data collection to obtain a more comprehensive picture (Smith 2004). This is consistent with Berk's recommendation to use more objective strategies to measure programme effects, including, among others, peer-to-peer class observations, student interviews, student performance assessments, alumni and employer ratings as well as teaching scholarship and teaching awards (Berk 2005). Even if some measures can be difficult to carry out, including alumni and employer ratings, others can be carried out quite feasibly, for example peer-to-peer class observations or teacher assessments on the difference in students' results in relation to changes in their own teaching.

Areas of Consensus or Near-Consensus: Teacher Development Programmes Yield Positive Impacts

Most publications that measure factors beyond teachers' self-assessment suggest that instructional development programmes yield positive effects. According to a study by Gibbs and Coffey (2000), students' ratings of their teachers, as part of the Student Evaluation of Educational Quality (SEEQ) questionnaire, showed considerable improvements in scores on four of the six scales for teachers having gone through one semester of two- and three-semester-long training programmes. These four scales included learning, enthusiasm, organisation, and rapport with students. In a larger study, the authors detected a range of positive changes in teachers in the training group and in their students, and a contrasting lack of change, or even negative change, in untrained teachers from a control group. In teachers having undergone training, the main positive change identified was that these teachers increasingly adopted a student-centred approach, which encouraged students' taking a deeper approach to learning, and ultimately improved the quality of student learning outcomes. Also, researchers found evidence of numerous improved aspects of educators' teaching as judged by students, such as better group interaction, genuine interest in individual students, or an improved ability to contrast the implications of different theories (Gibbs and Coffey 2004). However, as with other studies, authors could not attribute this change solely to the fact of having gone through a development programme.

Ho (1998, 2000) reports on the effects of a programme that engages teachers in the processes of self-awareness and self-reflection through four half-day sessions. This programme exposes teachers to alternative conceptions of teaching and encourages them to build up a commitment to change. Research has revealed that two thirds of instructors who held a teaching-focused conception of teaching changed in the desired direction, that is to say, a student-focused view on teaching. All these lecturers received better student ratings on their teaching performance in the year following the programme, and most of them also facilitated significant improvement in their students' approach to learning.

The results of research by Postareff, Lindblom-Ylänne, and Nevgi (2007) indicate that pedagogical training had an effect on their conceptualization of their role as teachers, on their approach to teaching towards one that is more student-centred, as well as on teachers' self-efficacy beliefs. Contrary to results from Ho (1998, 2000), the positive effect was only observed in teachers who had completed one year or more of teacher-training. According to the authors, this is perhaps because the programme is a process that initially challenges teachers' conceptions and can bring about dissonance and insecurity in teachers. Indeed, it may take time for teachers' conceptions to be reorganized and for them to adopt and apply a renewed, comprehensive, and student-focused approach to their teaching.

This correlates with the findings of Shannon, Twale, and Moore (1998), who researched quality of teaching in teaching assistants (TAs) at Auburn University in the U.S. They found that the only type of training that produced a significant effect on the effectiveness of teaching was an undergraduate degree in education. Indeed, TAs having completed an undergraduate degree in education were rated as more effective by their students, and they also rated themselves more favourably, likely because this type of training is more thorough than the brief introductory sessions that are usually offered to TAs by university departments.

In contrast to these studies, Stes, Coertjens, and Van Petegem (2010) and Stes et al. (2011a, 2011b) found that the University of Antwerp's year-long teacher development programme produced relatively small effects on teacher's teaching abilities, as well as on students' perceptions of their learning environment, and on students' learning outcomes. While this study's qualitative data suggested that the programme brought about a significant impact on instructors' teaching abilities in relation to a control group, its quantitative data did not show statistically significant differences between the two groups. Also, when investigating the effects of the programme on students' perceptions, Stes et al. (2011b) found that, on average, differences in the perception of students on the same teacher were larger than perceptions of students on different teachers. The authors concluded that several factors could have interfered with the results obtained, for example, certain characteristics of teachers in the control group, the fact that programme aims are defined by its organisers rather than being co-formulated with participating teachers in relation to their needs, or because a programme fails to take into account the variations in students' approaches to learning, among other things (Stes et al. 2011b, 18).

Gaps in Knowledge: Factors Determining Success in Teacher Development, Levels of Impact of Teacher Development, and Evidence from Elsewhere

Even if it is agreed upon that certain teacher development programmes bring about positive change, our knowledge of the factors that influence the success of instructional development in HE, and on the conditions under which they do so, remains limited. According to what we know today, it seems more meaningful to study what makes programmes successful rather than to study whether programmes bring about an impact or not.

Aside from programme length, programme content was identified as a factor that is likely to influence programme effectiveness. According to studies on training offered to new academic staff in Australia and in the U.S. (Boice 1992; Martin and Ramsden 1994), programmes that integrate both ideas about how students learn and how assessment and teaching affect students' learning, as well as practical teaching exercises and discussions on teaching methods and theory, are more effective at improving teachers' teaching abilities than programmes that solely focus on teaching skills.

At the same time, teachers surveyed at Open University, UK, found that non-formal and social learning experiences were more important for their educational development than were formal courses (Knight, Tait, and Yorke 2006). In this study, the authors spoke to 2,401 part-time teachers and received online feedback from 248 full-time staff from the UK's Open University. When asked about their preferences on how to improve their teaching, a significant number of respondents emphasized the importance of "social learning," or learning through consulting with others. The authors thus recommended complementing formal, event-based development activities with, for example, components allowing for the accompaniment of colleagues in various departments and teams in their everyday praxis (Knight, Tait, and Yorke 2006). Again, however, this article only built on teachers' perceptions and preferences, rather than showing which learning practices had important impacts on their teaching capacities. Therefore, the validity of these findings is somehow limited.

Despite not being empirically confirmed, certain other factors are mentioned in the literature as influencing the success of teacher development programmes. These have to do with the teachers' context, for example, their discipline, departments and schools, professional networks, and mentors. When examining the determinants of an impact, it may also be meaningful to control for such variables as gender, prior teaching experience, and so on.

Most existing studies concentrate solely on the effects of teacher development on participant teachers and/or their students. However, for any impact to take place, changes at other levels are desirable and perhaps even necessary, for example, at the department level, at the institutional level, as well as at the national and international levels. One study by Olsson and

Roxå (2008) examines these changes at different levels, by describing how a teacher reward system introduced by the Faculty of Engineering at Lund University, in Sweden, had an impact at the policy level within the faculty, and how decisions made have a noticeable influence on the behaviour of individual staff members.

Similarly, the self-assessments that were completed by the participants of a one-year teacher development programme at the University of Antwerp showed that years after the programme's completion, a certain impact was felt at the institutional level, too. Researchers could not, however, detect any relationship between the strength of the impact on individuals and the extent to which they felt compelled to introduce change at the institutional level (Stes, Clement, and Van Petegem 2007).

Perhaps more importantly, there is a disagreement or inconsistency in the literature as to which conceptual framework categorizes outcome variables in a way that is best suited to measure impact. Bauer et al. (1999) and Hannah and Lester (2009) differentiate outcomes at the micro, meso, and macro levels. More popular is Guskey's (2000) categorization that differentiates between five levels of analysis: (i) academics' reaction to the development programme, (ii) academics' conceptual change, (iii) academics' behavioural change, (iv) organisational support and changes, (v) changes in student learning.

Other categorizations (e.g., Levinson-Rose and Menges 1981) use similar terms. Most recently, Stes et al. (2010) adapted Fitzpatrick's (1994) model, which differentiates between impact on students, teachers, and institutions. At the student level, they considered both changes in learning, for example, changes in attitudes, concepts, knowledge and skills, and changes in behaviour. The most significant changes perceived by students were their perceptions of their learning environment, their approaches to studying as well as their learning outcomes.

It is difficult to make generalizations as to which factors bring about programme success, however, because large differences exist between different programmes. Indeed, programmes differ in their purpose, as well as in their target audience. While some programmes evaluate their results quite rigorously and claim to have positive effects, it is not clear which elements of teacher development programmes are most effective, either in changing teacher attitudes and behaviour and/or in improving student learning.

Finally, the vast majority of published literature on the results of instructional development, including both research articles and many edited volumes, is generated either by Anglo-Saxon countries, Nordic countries, or in Belgium (Gibbs 1989; Evans and Abbott 1999; Blackwell and Blackmore 2003; Eggins and Macdonald 2003; Kahn and Baume 2004). Because different institutions' programmes are designed to respond to specific local contexts and their particular needs, further studies generating knowledge on the impact of more programmes can improve our general understanding of the determinants of success and the levels of impact of teacher development programmes.

In closing, while a number of studies were published on the impact of teacher-training, important gaps still exist in the literature. The gaps in our knowledge include, among others:

- The methodological weakness of numerous studies that attempt to measure the results of educational development programmes (including failure to compare posttest data with pretest data, reliance on self-assessments rather than on more objective evidence, lack of a control group with whom to compare results, overreliance on single sources of information, lack of evidence on long-term results);
- Conflicting findings from existing studies;
- Little evidence concerning what *elements* of teacher development programmes are most effective;
- Less attention paid to different levels of impact than effects on the individual teacher—for example, impact on students, on institutions and beyond;
- Lack of evidence on the effect of academic development programmes outside of Anglo-Saxon countries, Belgium, and Nordic countries.

PURPOSE OF THIS BOOK AND THE CHALLENGES IT ADDRESSES

This book is an initial attempt at addressing some of these problems. In many ways, this book can be considered as a response to Eggins and Macdonald's (2003) call for a more systematic study of the impact of teacher development. In contrast to Kahn and Baumes' (2004) rather theoretical study, the focus here is on evidence-based research. Indeed, this book addresses some gaps in the literature which are detailed by others elsewhere, and thusly presents a comprehensive review on the state of research on the impact of teacher development programmes, and the persistent problems related to conducting research on this topic. The primary aim of this book is to encourage fruitful debate that can bring impact research to its next level.

In order to foster the development of theory, this book provides evidence and investigates factors that determine success in teacher-training. To reach this end, this book also includes theoretical studies that attempt to disentangle the relationship between independent variables and between the independent variables and programme success. This allows for the improvement of our understanding of the way in which different variables are linked, and on the scope conditions under which they operate. The theoretical papers included either present authors' aggregated findings from their own previous research (Stes and Van Petegem; Norton, Norton, and Shannon) or build a theoretical framework about the relationship between different institutional variables investigated in this book and elsewhere and the impact of teacher development programmes (Roxå and Mårtensson).

This book also expands geographically on the current research programme, by including studies from four countries that are not commonly included in discussions on instructional development. Firstly, in his study, Knapper discusses instructional development in Canada. Secondly, Chng and Soong take us to Singapore for an analysis of the National University of Singapore's programme. Finally, while Karm, Remmik, and Haamer bring this discussion to Estonia, in Central Europe, Renc-Roe and Yarkova discuss such programmes at the Central European University in Hungary, which is an international academic institution.

Some of the problems with impact research cannot be solved at the current level of development of instructional development programmes. With regard to these issues, we decided to structure this book to include a diversity of topics, in order to highlight these problems and possible approaches in responding to them. Our choice to maintain diversity and single-country case studies is also a product of our conviction that at the current stage of development of programmes, they are too diverse to be compared across countries. Indeed, programmes are too varying in their structure, target audience, level of institutionalization, and development, as well as in their policy environment, for their effects to be meaningfully compared.

This book makes four main contributions to the field of research on instructional development. First of all, this book problematizes the purpose and aims of teacher development, because it is essential to understand what is expected out of teacher-training in order to consider its effectiveness. As stated by Gibbs and Coffey (2004), the primary aim of the HE process is to influence student learning; however, it is argued here that this is only one of many of its objectives. Contributors to this book examine some other outcomes and intervening variables brought about by teacher-training, such as changes in teaching behaviour (Davies and Maguire; Nevgi; Renc-Roe and Yarkova), and such outcome variables as changes in job placement (Ishiyama et al.) and expectations towards teachers in and out of the classroom (Berndtson and Quinlan).

Next, this book presents a discussion of who should be included in teacher development, and on how to adjust the measurement of impact of a particular programme in relation to its particular target group. Accordingly, this book includes chapters discussing programmes for PhD candidates (Renc-Roe and Yarkova; Ishiyama et al.; Knapper), for newly hired faculty members (Chng and Soong), and for faculty members with any given length of teaching experience in HE (Davies and Maguire; Karm, Remmik, and Haamer). Ishiyama et al. attempt to understand the relationship between teacher-training for graduate students and their performance as teachers in HE once they secure such a position. At the same time, while Ishiyama and associates limit their analysis to tenure-track faculty members, Davies and Maguire, for example, analyse the impact of a programme "open to all those involved in learning and teaching support across the institution" (Davies and Maguire).

Thirdly, this book's contributors use diverse research methods to overcome the difficulty of researching programmes that are relatively new so that effects on student learning cannot yet be assumed. Aside from having appeared recently, some programmes also have relatively small numbers of graduates, of which only a few are willing to participate in research about programme effectiveness. Because of this, most study samples are convenience samples, including those subjects that are available and willing to participate. Thus, while Karm, Remmik, and Haamer interviewed twenty participants in their study, Chng and Soong targeted the whole population of trainees but ended up with a voluntary survey of fifteen professors. Davies and Maguire used much the same technique of data collection and analysis, whilst only targeting a subsection of the study population using an online survey.

Many of the authors included in this book attempt to overcome the limited amount of data available by collecting information from many sources. For example, while Murphy supplements interviews of programme directors with interviews with programme graduates, Nevgi combines interviews, classroom observations of teaching, learning diaries, personal study plans, and reports of teaching practice in her groundbreaking longitudinal study. Also, Renc-Roe and Yarkova rely on course evaluation questionnaires and on material submitted by trainees during the course, including, for example, course syllabi. In this way, the authors overcome the obstacle of following the students, who are all from different countries, once they complete the course by limiting analysis to immediate effects. Ishiyama et al. choose to analyse the effects of teacher-training on employability rather than on individual teachers and students. Finally, while most empirical papers included in this book use qualitative research methods, Ishiyama et al. apply statistical methods of analysis.

Lastly, this book also contributes to the debate on the levels of outcome of teacher development programmes. An analysis of contributors' reasoning and choices of outcome measures will be presented in order to contribute to the ongoing debate on outcomes of teacher development programmes.

BOOK STRUCTURE

In general there are two types of chapters in this book. The first type examines the development and influence of one specific teacher development programme (Nevgi; Norton, Norton, and Shannon; Murphy; Renc-Roe and Yarkova; Chng and Soong; Davies and Maguire; and Karm,

Remmik, and Haamer). These chapters have a uniform structure in that they all begin by discussing the given programme, and then move on to inquire into its effectiveness. Some chapters link institutional development to programme improvement (Davies and Maguire; Karm, Remmik, and Haamer; Chng and Soong) and are thus directly relevant for managers in HE. The remainder of the book offers a counterbalance to these practically oriented chapters by taking a more general approach to the topic, either by presenting theoretical arguments (Roxå and Mårtensson; Stes and Van Petegem) or by offering a wider perspective on the subject matter (Trigwell; Quinlan and Berndtson).

The book is organized into four sections. Part I shows that programmes may not solely exist for the purpose of improving student learning, as is often assumed in the literature. As such, this section problematizes the dependent variable of impact research. If the purpose of programmes varies, then the definition and measurement of impact needs to be re-evaluated so as not to simply be considered in terms of student learning. Also, this section focuses on programmes aimed at training graduate students to teach, and calls attention to the diversity of purposes for which they can be trained. By featuring programmes from different countries and thus existing within varying contexts of national policy, it also shows how the nature of governmental policies (i.e., permissive, absent of non-applicable) influences the design of teacher development programmes.

The second part of this book demonstrates the practical usefulness of assessing teacher development programmes by showing how impact measurement can be used as a policy tool at the micro level. It documents how inquiry into the more or less successful aspects of a programme can allow teaching centres to align their programmes to the professional needs of their trainees and also to their own local contexts.

Part III analyses the influence of institutional, national, and regional-level policies on teacher development. Studies in this section discuss how such policies can help or hinder efforts at assisting teachers to develop. Quinlan and Berndtson, as well as Murphy, discuss the regional context and how regional integration and national-level institutionalization of HE create new demands and challenges for the teaching process at the tertiary level. As part of this, Nevgi and Norton, Norton, and Shannon consider the influence of institutional policies on the development and implementation of teacher education at the tertiary level, and discuss the role of university-wide, departmental, and disciplinary culture in fostering the creation of successful instructional development courses.

Part IV builds off of the previous section in adopting a broad approach to considering teacher development, specifically focusing on impact measurement as a research project and as an academic enterprise. Roxå and Mårtensson, as well as Stes and Van Petegem, increase our theoretical knowledge of the subject by systematically reviewing the factors that are brought up in past research as having influenced the success of teacher development. Trigwell summarizes the current state of impact research in the hope of that future research will be directed towards filling gaps in the literature.

NOTES

1. Different terminology is used to describe activities that promote teaching and learning in higher education. *Teacher-training* is prevalent in the U.S., while *teacher/instructional development* is common in Europe and Australia, and recently, the term *enhancement* has come to replace *development* in the UK, following the adoption of the expression *quality enhancement* (Gosling 2009, 8–9). The literature presents no consensus on best terms to use, and so different developers use different terms. In this book, all terms are used interchangeably. Another widely used expression is *staff and educational development*, which denotes "systematic and scholarly support for improving both educational processes and the practices and capabilities of educators" (Stefani 2003).
2. The Teaching Community Approach describes a situation where a group of university teachers meet on a regular basis to discuss student learning and good teaching with the aim of developing a reflective practice.

BIBLIOGRAPHY

Bauer, Marianne, Berit Askling, Susan Gerard Marton, and Ference Marton. 1999. *Transforming Universities. Changing Patterns of Governance, Structure and Learning in Swedish Higher Education.* London: Jessica Kingsley Publishers.

Baume, David. 2003. "Monitoring and Evaluating Staff and Educational Development." In *A Guide to Staff and Educational Development*, edited by Peter Kahn and David Baume, 76–95. London: Kogan Page.

Berk, Ronald A. 2005. "Survey of Twelve Strategies to Measure Teaching Effectiveness." *International Journal of Teaching and Learning in Higher Education* 17 (1): 48–62.

Blackwell, Richard, and Paul Blackmore. 2003. *Towards Strategic Staff Development in Higher Education.* Buckingham, UK: SRHE.

Boice, Robert. 1992. *The New Faculty Member: Supporting and Fostering Professional Development.* San Francisco: Jossey-Bass.

Boote, David N., and Penny Beile. 2005. "On the Centrality of the Dissertation Literature Review in Research Preparation." *Educational Researcher* 34 (6): 3–15.

Coffey, Martin, and Graham Gibbs. 2000. "Can Academics Benefit from Training? Some Preliminary Evidence." *Teaching in Higher Education* 5 (1): 385–389.

Donnelly, Roisin. 2006. "Exploring Lecturers' Self-perception of Change in Teaching Practice." *Teaching in Higher Education* 11 (2): 203–217.

Eggins, Heather, and Ranald Macdonald. 2003. *The Scholarship of Academic Development.* Buckingham, UK: Society for Research into Higher Education and Open University Press.

Evans, Linda, and Ian Abbott. 1999. *Teaching and Learning in Higher Education.* London and New York: Cassell.

Fitzpatrick, Donald. L. 1994. *Evaluating Training Programs: The Four Levels.* San Francisco: Berrett-Koehler Publishers.

Gibbs, Graham. 1989. *Induction and Initial Training of Teachers in Higher Education*. Birmingham, UK: SCED Publications.

Gibbs, Graham, and Martin Coffey. 2000. "What Is Training of University Teachers Attempting to Achieve, and How Could We Tell If It Makes Any Difference?" *International Consortium for Educational Development Conference*, University of Bielefeld.

———. 2004: "The Impact of Training of University Teachers on their Teaching Skills, Their Approach to Teaching and the Approach to Learning of Their Students." *Active Learning in Higher Education* 5(1): 87–100.

Gosling, David. 2001. "Educational Development Units in the UK—What Are They Doing Five Years On?" *International Journal for Academic Development* 6 (1): 74–90.

———. 2009. Educational Development in the UK: A Complex and Contradictory Reality. *International Journal for Academic Development* 14 (1): 5–18.

Groom, Barry, and Irmeli Maunonen-Eskelinen. 2006. "The Use of Portfolios to Develop Reflective Practice in Teacher Training: A Comparative and Collaborative Approach between Two Teacher Training Providers in the UK and Finland." *Teaching in Higher Education* 11 (3): 291–300.

Guskey, Thomas R. 2000. *Evaluating Professional Development*. Thousand Oaks, CA: Corwin Press.

Hannah, Sean T., and Paul B. Lester. 2009. "A Multilevel Approach to Building and Leading Learning Organisations." *The Leadership Quarterly* 20: 34–48.

Ho, Angela. 1998. "A Conceptual Change Staff Development Program: Effects as Perceived by the Participants." *The International Journal for Academic Development* 3 (1): 24–38.

———. 2000. "A Conceptual Change Approach to Staff Development: A Model for Programme Design." *The International Journal for Academic Development* 5 (1): 30–41.

Kahn, Peter, and David Baume. 2004. *Enhancing Staff and Educational Development*. London Routledge Falmer.

Knapper, Christopher. 2010. "Plus Ça Change . . . Educational Development Past and Future." *New Directions for Teaching and Learning* 122: 1–5.

Knight, Peter, Jo Tait, and Mantz Yorke. 2006. "The Professional Learning of Teachers in Higher Education." *Studies in Higher Education* 31 (3): 319–339.

Knopf, Jeffrey W. 2006. "Doing a Literature Review." *PS: Political Science and Politics* 39 (1): 127–132.

Kreber, Carolin, and Paula Brook. 2001. "Impact Evaluation of Educational Development Programmes." *International Journal for Academic Development* 6 (2): 96–108.

Levinson-Rose, Judith, and Robert J. Menges. 1981. "Improving College Teaching: A Critical Review of Research." *Review of Educational Research* 51 (3): 403–434.

MacDonald, Ian 2001. "The Teaching Community: Recreating University Teaching." *Teaching in Higher Education* 6 (2): 153–167.

Martin, Elaine, and Paul Ramsden. 1994. *Evaluation of the Performance of Courses in Teaching Methods for Recently Appointed Academic Staff*. Canberra: Australian Government Publishing Service.

McLean, Monica, and Joanna E. Bullard. 2000. "Becoming a University Teacher: Evidence from Teaching Portfolios (How Academics Learn to Teach)." *Teacher Development* 4: (1): 79–101.

Norton, Lin, John T. E. Richardson, James Hartley, Stephen Newstead, and Jenny Mayes. 2005. "Teachers' Beliefs and Intentions Concerning Teaching in Higher Education." *Higher Education* 50: 537–557.

Olsson, Thomas, and Torgny Roxå. 2008. "Evaluating Rewards for Excellent Teaching—a Cultural Approach." Engaging Communities Proceedings of the 31st HERDSA Annual Conference, Rotorua, NZ, 1–4 July, 261–272.

Postareff, Liisa, Sari Lindblom-Ylänne, and Anne Nevgi. 2007. "The Effect of Pedagogical Training on Teaching in Higher Education." *Teaching and Teacher Education* 23: 557–571.

Prosser, Michael, and Simon Barrie. 2003. "Using a Student-Focused Learning Perspective to Align Academic Development with Institutional Quality Assurance." In *Towards Strategic Staff Development in Higher Education*, edited by Richard Blackwell and Paul Blackmore, 191–202. Berkshire, UK: McGraw-Hill Education.

Prosser, Michael, and Keith Trigwell. 1999. *Understanding Learning and Teaching*. Buckingham, UK: SRHE/Open University Press.

Reichert, Sibylle, and Christian Tauch. 2005. *Trends IV: European Universities Implementing Bologna*. Brussels: European University Association.

Reinalda, Bob, and Ewa Kulesza. 2006. *The Bologna Process: Harmonizing Europe's Higher Education. Including the Essential Original Texts*, 2nd revised edition. Opladen, Germany, and Bloomfield Hills, MI: Barbara Budrich Publishers.

Shannon, David M., Darla J. Twale, and Matthew S. Moore, 1998. "TA Teaching Effectiveness: The Impact of Training and Teaching Experience." *The Journal of Higher Education* 69 (4): 440–466.

Smith, Holly. 2004. "The Impact of Staff Development Programmes and Activities." In *Enhancing Staff and Educational Development*, edited by Peter Kahn and David Baume, 96–116. London: Routledge Falmer.

Stefani, Lorraine. 2003. "What Is Staff and Educational Development?" In *A Guide to Staff and Educational Development*, edited by Peter Kahn and David Baume, 9–23. London: Kogan.

Stes, Ann, Mieke Clement, and Peter Van Petegem. 2007. "The Effectiveness of a Faculty Training Programme: Long-Term and Institutional Impact." *International Journal for Academic Development* 12 (2): 99–109.

Stes, Ann, Liesje Coertjens, and Peter Van Petegem. 2010. "Instructional Development for Teachers in Higher Education: Impact on Teaching Approach." *Higher Education* 60: 187–204.

Stes, Ann, Sven De Maeyer, David Gijbels, and Peter Van Petegem. 2011a. "Instructional Development for Teachers in Higher Education: Effects on Students' Learning Outcomes." *Teaching in Higher Education* 16: 1–14, iFirst Article.

———. 2011b. "Instructional Development for Teachers in Higher Education: Effects on Students' Perceptions of the Teaching–Learning Environment." *British Journal of Educational Psychology* 102: 1–22.

Stes, Ann, Mariska Min-Leliveld, David Gijbels, and Peter Van Petegem. 2010. "The Impact of Instructional Development in Higher Education: The State-of-the-Art of the Research." *Educational Research Review* 5: 25–49.

Part I

Training for What? Instructional Development for Graduate Students

2 Preparing Doctoral Students for a Teaching Career

The Case of an International University with a History of Regional Engagement

Joanna Renc-Roe and Tatiana Yarkova

INTRODUCTION

This chapter discusses the historical background, the institutionalization process and the effectiveness of a teacher development course for doctoral students offered by the Curriculum Resource Centre (CRC) at Central European University (CEU), located in Budapest, Hungary. CEU is an international graduate university offering programmes primarily in social sciences and humanities. The university, which has recently celebrated its twenty years' anniversary, prides itself on its unique character resulting from U.S. and Hungarian accreditation, a highly internationalized student body, academic excellence resulting from research-intensive profile, and a strong outreach agenda.

CRC is a faculty and curriculum development unit offering a range of programmes to external audiences, as a rule from the traditional CEU region of non-EU Eastern and Central Europe, former Soviet Union, and Mongolia. CRC trainers manage programmes for visiting professors from these countries, connect universities from the region with CEU, provide training for CEU's own doctoral students as future teachers, and support the university on matters of accreditation and quality assurance, in particular in areas related to teaching and learning.

This chapter showcases the development and current state of evaluation of the CRC training programme for CEU doctoral students "Teaching in Higher Education." The course targets current doctoral students who come from a variety of countries and academic backgrounds and, as a rule, have no or limited teaching experience. The course is designed not simply as a training programme in teaching, assessment, and course design techniques but as a foundation course that aims to develop the students' ability for innovative, reflexive, and scholarly teaching. The programme is thus aimed at producing a long-term impact—self-renewing teaching practitioners constantly engaged in inquiry about student learning and a critical review of their teaching practice.

In this chapter, however, we do not attempt to judge the long-term programme impact due to difficulties with obtaining relevant data. Instead, we focus on assessing the general effectiveness of the training programme—that is, to what extent it fulfils its stated goals or, put simply, its "fitness for purpose."

The approach in this chapter is based on studying samples of available student work as documentary evidence combined with three separate sources of student evaluation: regular end-of-course anonymous evaluation questionnaires, focus-group interviews organized after each course, and an online survey of all course alumni.

THE PROGRAMME: INSTITUTIONAL
CONTEXT AND HISTORY

CEU is a highly international university with students coming from 110 countries and faculty coming from more than thirty (CEU 2011). Located in Eastern Europe, it is anything but a typical Eastern European university. Founded in 1991 with the generous support of the philanthropist George Soros, it has had from the onset a clear-cut mission of "building open and democratic societies that respect human rights" (CEU 2011). This is combined with a focus on research-intensive, policy-relevant research, and a strong drive to provide a new quality of excellent graduate-level education. A strong outreach component has also been a part of this mission.

Initially, CEU has been oriented towards Eastern and Central Europe and the former Soviet Union, but lately the emphasis has been on becoming more global. CEU has both U.S. and Hungarian accreditations, and therefore it is able to function as both an American and a European university. It has no single defined national majority among faculty or students. Its hybrid character contributes to a specific institutional culture of openness and flexibility, which allows for considerable academic freedom in research and teaching.

CEU is a graduate-only institution[1] with a focus on social sciences and humanities. It aims to attract some of the best student applicants, and a considerable proportion of its graduates go on to pursue an academic and teaching career, while the majority work in the private sector, government, and international organisations.[2] Due to its graduate-only nature, there is a strong culture of student-faculty collegiality and an appreciation of small-group, seminar-based teaching. Moreover, due to its specific mission, there is a strong sense of common identity and a sense of purpose. This unique character of the university reflects the overall approach to our programme design and evaluation. As a small programme within a small but diverse institution, our interest is not so much in numbers and trends but in narratives and interpretations.

The courses "Teaching in Higher Education I and II" form a two-semester-long training programme which aims to help our doctoral students (and any visiting doctoral students) get thorough preparation for the job as future teachers in diverse and changing higher education contexts. The programme aims at developing the skills of CEU students as prospective academic teachers and starting the process of their professional development using a scholarly and reflective approach to university teaching in order to ensure effective and deep student learning. The philosophy of the programme is based on current trends in academic development, in particular in the Anglo-Saxon and Nordic countries (e.g., Eggins and Macdonald 2003; Roxå 2005), which moves beyond simple skills training of how to teach an effective seminar or a lecture, and so on, to the principle of reflective practice (Schön 1983), and the scholarly approach to teaching (e.g., Kreber 2002).

We encourage young academics to look at their own classrooms as areas for the development of pedagogical content knowledge or higher education pedagogies, innovation in course and teaching design, and an ongoing, self-initiated inquiry. We also believe in exploring the sociological, contextual, disciplinary, and departmental nature of teaching in higher education; as such, it is not uncommon for the programme to include sessions on higher education policy change, or to discuss comparative higher education systems as well as distinct teaching "genres." Individual students are encouraged to consider their institutional contexts and disciplinary "homes" as well as possibilities offered by the unique cross-disciplinary collaboration within the course in developing their own approaches to student learning.

The target group for the programme is CEU doctoral students, as a rule coming from Eastern and Central Europe and the former Soviet Union. In terms of future career destinations, students tend to target their own home university systems for future jobs, other universities in our region, or they may be preparing to function on the international academic market (which usually means an Anglo-Saxon, Northern European, or Western European university system).

In the past few years the university has increasingly recognized the needs of doctoral students in the broad area of career skills development, and in particular in terms of the necessity to gain teaching experience in addition to research preparation during the doctoral study. However, since the university does not have any undergraduate programmes where PhD students could teach, teaching practice is not easily provided. While some departments try to create opportunities for their students to be teaching assistants in their MA-level courses, these opportunities are not available to all and only expose the students to a graduate-level audience, which often calls for different approaches and techniques than an undergraduate one. The courses "Teaching in Higher Education I and II" often become the primary way in which students prepare for teaching during their doctoral study.

The training programme for CEU doctoral students was first piloted in the 2004–2005 academic year. In the pilot year, we focused mainly on intensive in-class training sessions and skill development, but the programme has since gained in complexity in both its design and expectations.

In contrast to the first workshop-intensive pilot year, we have added teaching simulations, optional classroom observation, student-led final workshops with presentations, faculty-led roundtable discussions on teaching and professional development, and a set of individual written assignments, leading to writing a teaching portfolio in the second part of the course.

To date, over 130 CEU students and alumni and around eighteen visiting participants took part in the programme (completing either one or both training courses). This means that about 30 percent of all doctoral students have taken the course at some point in their studies.

The first of the two currently available training courses is called "Teaching in Higher Education I: A Key Skills Training Course" and it forms the first level of the training programme. The students are asked to complete a series of small written assignments (pieces of reflexive writing, lesson plans, and a draft syllabus) as a starting point for their future teaching portfolio. In this course, we address areas of teaching such as basic course design, principles of student assessment, and key teaching methods and issues (lecturing, seminars, and lesson planning). The course also provides some space for micro-teaching or teaching simulations.

The second course is called "Teaching in Higher Education II: Contexts, Teaching Areas, and Professional Development." This second course adds a more pronounced focus on higher education research, scholarship of teaching and learning, higher education policy, student and faculty evaluation, further specific areas of teaching such as tutoring, supervision, teaching academic writing or critical thinking, various teaching methodologies such as problem-based and research-based learning, integrative learning, and so on. In the second-level course students produce their teaching portfolios which consist of teaching-philosophy statements, teaching-methods designs, reviews of literature, their own designs of syllabi, and other documents showing their own professional development in and reflection on teaching and learning.

Some of the success of institutionalizing the training programme can be attributed to doctoral students' own demands for increased attention given to their career development at the university. A survey of doctoral students' experience undertaken by the CEU administration in 2007 revealed a good level of satisfaction with the course, which was greater than with some other components of their doctoral experience. In the same university survey, students stressed the importance of teaching experience as an integral part of their studies. During a student-organized PhD orientation weekend in September 2009 aimed to air student voices in all areas of the CEU doctoral experience, the programme was discussed in a student position paper on positive improvements of doctoral study at CEU.

Ongoing informal communication with students and trends in course registration indicate that with each year the course becomes more institutionalized into university life. Based on unsolicited feedback, several course alumni have attributed success in job interviews and subsequent employment directly to skills gained and support received during the course, while some others have written to us to indicate that the course has helped them in adjusting to teaching roles in new contexts.

ANALYSING COURSE EFFECTIVENESS

In this study we resorted to a combination of already available and some specially designed research tools. The most basic tool for studying course effectiveness is regular anonymous final course questionnaires, which include qualitative and quantitative measures of student satisfaction related to each course goal. In terms of more direct data, the documents that students produce during the courses are the closest approximation of their learning process, as are our observations of their teaching in the final course workshop. At present, the latter are not recorded on a regular basis; however, the written student work is collected and can be studied. These materials consist of several formats of reflective writing, syllabi, lesson plans, teaching designs, and complete portfolios.

Analysis of Student Work

Based on samples of student course work we were able to provide some tentative answers to the questions concerning course effectiveness in relation to the development of critical, reflective, and scholarly teaching potential, and the scope of student teaching skills demonstrated through their design work. One specific qualitative analysis consisted of a random sample of reflective documents produced by participants in three years of the programme (five documents from each academic year were considered: fifteen documents in total from the years 2005, 2006, 2007). In another qualitative sample analysis we assessed how students reflect on their educational development in order to build their sense of academic identity (Renc-Roe 2008). To achieve this, we analysed a random sample of students' educational biographies.[3]

Analysis of Student Feedback

Another source of data is generated through two specially designed evaluation tools: focus-group interviews and an anonymous Web questionnaire. Two focus-group interviews that form the material for this research were carried out with groups of four to five course participants in the period between December 2008 and May 2009, in order to inquire into students' perceived learning outcomes not long after each course was completed. Each subsequent year we have continued to use the focus-group evaluation format at least once a year. Further to that, a Web questionnaire has been designed and sent to the course alumni in April 2009 (101 participants received the survey), resulting in thirty completed questionnaires. The survey was the closest tool we have which can help us in finding some data on the impact of the course on its alumni. The analysis below makes use of all of these sources of data in order to outline our analysis of the programme's effectiveness.

DEVELOPING PROFESSIONAL TEACHING APPROACHES

The most practical goal for the programme, and one that would be recognizable in other institutions, is the need to help young academics develop a set of basic teaching skills or an understanding of good practice in a range of genres in university teaching. The fulfilment of this programme goal should result in the participants' ability to design well "aligned" university courses (Biggs 2003), design various teaching activities for students, and appropriate student assessment tasks. The participants in the course learn by experimenting with these three design areas in order to produce their own plans, such as a syllabus, a lesson plan or lecture outline, and a design of student assessment format.

Analysis of Student Work

We have analysed thirteen course syllabi and fifteen lesson plans produced by the students in the fall 2008 course. Based on a sample of syllabi and lesson plans from the course, we were able to clearly see that student work ranged in quality from drafts to fully fledged documents. However, they all demonstrated at least partial adaptation of the principle of constructive alignment which underlies the good syllabus writing as a tool for the development of effective teaching. The students managed to address some of the expectations that CRC trainers would have of a well-written syllabus.[4] There is particularly strong evidence of students writing course goals and learning outcomes, mentioning their teaching and student assessment approaches, and dividing the content into meaningful sections.

Regarding the sample of lesson plans: these were all basically adequate, and had clearly defined goals for the teaching session. Most provide an overview of the structure of the teaching sessions where different activities are used to achieve specific goals. The lesson plans were also tried out in practice during the teaching simulations; the presenters received feedback from the course participants and trainers.

Analysis of Student Feedback

According to the Web survey (and the participants' self-analysis), the programme manages to achieve the goal of developing students' teaching skills to a high or considerable extent (eighteen respondents thought the course was helpful for their teaching skills development in many ways; eleven thought it was helpful in some ways—total responses to this question were twenty-nine).

In more specific terms, the students endorsed the following skills as either important or very important: learning to design a university course, learning to plan for a single class, discussing lecturing and seminar methods, discussing more complex teaching methods, learning about theories of student assessment and innovative assessment techniques, and discussing supervision and tutoring skills. The students also appreciated having their teaching observed and evaluated during the teaching simulations.

The qualitative responses to the survey also suggested that impact on this area of participants' skills was perceived and stressed by them as the most pronounced: out of twenty-one generated additional comments, seventeen considered this area of impact as significant. The actual comments ranged from pointing out definite impact on the teaching process and student learning (due to being able to design and implement one's own course or to rethink one's own teaching) to general understanding of appropriate techniques that were acquired. Where impact was not yet clearly felt was due to lack of available teaching experience, and even here the course was considered as a useful tool for future teaching, or for the job application process.

The focus-group participants (of the 2008–2009 cohorts) also clearly articulated the effects of the course for them as consisting of skill development leading to a professional approach to teaching in higher education. In the first-level course (fall 2008) focus-group interview, the learning of course design skills was particularly stressed as an outcome of the course. As one of the course participants said, "The syllabi part [course design and syllabus writing] was almost a discovery, how many elements there are and how useful a syllabus can be. That was the greatest change of perspective from student to teacher, because for students it boils down to 'should I take this course or not,' but for a teacher it is much more."

Similarly, in the focus-group carried out in May 2009 most of the answers generated in response to the question "What did you achieve by attending this class?" concerned the fulfilment of this programme goal: "Now when I look at a reader (syllabus) I look for the concept behind it to see what is the message and how it is organized, and I hope to be able to do the same" (focus-group participant).

We may conclude from these sources of evidence that this goal of the programme, which is perhaps the most basic and the most important for our participants, is being met, even if we cannot really measure the impact on students' skills directly. Of course, when we discuss the process of teaching these areas, there is still room for improvement in course delivery in order to fulfil these goals even better in the future.

DEVELOPING THE SKILL OF REFLECTIVE PRACTICE

Reflective practice is the second important skill area that our programme aims to develop. It follows best practice in faculty development approaches where training has generally moved from "tips and tricks" on teaching to the development of critical self-analysis of one's own teaching. We can understand reflective teaching as the voicing and questioning of personal experience, preconceptions, assumptions, and theories of teaching in order to enhance one's own understanding. This may be categorized as reflection on action and the building of theory of practice (Schön 1983). We need to find evidence that our course participants are questioning their pre-existing assumptions about teaching in order to stimulate further self-initiated improvement.

Analysis of Student Work

Here we consider what direct evidence is available to support the claim that the courses do stimulate reflective thinking on teaching and learning. If we look at the qualitative analysis of types of reflections generated in student writing undertaken in three subsequent years (in a random sample of fifteen documents), we can see that the total count of reflections present was forty-two. These included reflection on the student's own history in education, reflection on personal identity in the discipline, reflection on teaching practices and goals, reflection on teaching strategies, and reflection on student learning. Some of the reflections were well developed while others were only hinted at. Moreover, reflection on student learning was not as common as reflection on teaching practices or on participants' own identity development.

The second qualitative analysis, which was focused more specifically on the formation of teaching identity through reflective writing (in educational biographies), showed that students displayed a range of techniques in order to verbalize their growth as teachers, often combining autobiographical writing with familiar academic writing formats and genres (essay writing, critical response to reading) in order to construct meaningful narratives of their identities. Some of the resulting pieces of writing were only partial stories, while some were descriptive rather than strongly reflective. Altogether, though, sixteen reflective accounts were clearly identified, whereas four clearly displayed potential for more developed reflection (the total number of documents in this evaluation was twenty-one).

Analysis of Student Feedback

Both focus-group interviews provide some data that developing reflective practice was, in fact, an important goal of the course, and they provide some evidence that this process has in fact been stimulated: "The goal of the programme was to see teaching as a craft, something that can be learnt, not something that depends on personal character only, to see that if you know what you are supposed to do you can overcome your weaknesses and develop your strong points" (focus-group participant). Similarly, some of the comments generated through the survey claim that the participants developed as reflective practitioners. For example, one participant said,

"Excellence [in teaching for me] would mean the employment of appropriate and well thought through methods plus reflection on the achievement of student learning, reflection on each bit of your teaching so that you can draw conclusions for the future."

Overall, we may say that the ability to reflect on one's skills, concrete teaching experiences, and further development needs has indeed been well targeted in our courses. Our general approach, particularly the insistence on some reflective writing (such as educational biographies in the first-level course and statements of teaching philosophy in the second course), the focus on reflective and critical discussion on higher education policy and practice during training sessions, and the selection of readings employing various perspectives on the aspects studied, are all managing to produce a reflective practitioner attitude among our course participants.

The critical comment can be made that it is the quality of the reflection generated that matters more than its mere presence. In order to specify the levels of reflective thinking, a more in-depth qualitative approach would need to be employed in future research.

DEVELOPING THE POTENTIAL FOR INNOVATIVE OR EXCELLENT TEACHING

The goal of developing the potential for innovative and excellent teaching is a direct continuation of the work we do with students regarding the development of their teaching approaches; however, the aim here is to try to move beyond issues of mere effectiveness to lay the foundations for future excellence in teaching (e.g., Kreber 2002). In our case this means not only stimulating students' interest in understanding a range of discipline-derived "signature pedagogies" (Shulman 2005) when planning their current or future teaching activities, but also moving away from them when needed in order to innovate and change students' learning. Alternatively, this means developing a more informed individual understanding of the possibilities for making an intervention into student learning that is going somewhat beyond the capacity to use basic teaching techniques effectively, or to fulfil typical course goals adequately.

We start the process by outlining more complex teaching methods already in the first-level course, though the majority of work on this is carried out in the second-level course. Some of the comments generated by the 2008 focus group give voice to this area of skill development as beginning already at this stage, though much of our input is of a mainly inspirational nature and it is oriented towards future practice. A course participant said, "I think I gained the possibility to be innovative. I think so far I could only think in terms of what I experienced myself. We were shown so many methods of teaching, so it helped me to move out of this circle that may not be adequate but to try and do something different, like to try other approaches. I can't say that I am innovative or ready yet but it's a possibility."

To answer the question of whether a discipline-specific and innovative approach to teaching methodology can be achieved by the course participants, we have to look at the second-level course outcomes in which we provide training in selected more complex teaching methodologies and students apply these in their own teaching portfolios. The "teaching method application projects" of one cohort of students (winter 2009 course, six participants) presented at the final workshop of the course, and submitted as part of the teaching portfolio, were analysed as an output of the programme, which can signify the fulfilment of this goal.

Analysis of Student Work

In the winter 2009 course, all six students prepared either an application of a complex teaching method or of a student assessment method, and four were able to present them to their peers in the final workshop. All students were able to develop more sophisticated methodological planning related to a particular topic or unit of study in their selected field, or envisaged for integration into a whole course.

The student projects included the implementation of student portfolio in a criminal-justice course, choosing between different options of applying structured debate simulations in a human rights class, teaching critical thinking and academic writing through structured reiterated reflections on readings in gender studies, developing analytical skills in a history class through case studies of primary materials, further development and extension of fieldwork methods in undergraduate archaeology, and developing critical thinking skills in medieval studies through a "reading seminar" and student research portfolios. Even a preliminary look at these titles tells much about the range of creative and domain-based pedagogical thinking that is being developed by these students, much different from the generic seminar or lecture-type lesson plan that would normally be a product of an early professional skill development course.

Though some of the students developed separate complex student assessment tasks as part of their portfolio, most teaching methodology applications projects in fact merged student assessment techniques with their selected teaching methodology, providing for a more holistic vision of the principle of constructive alignment. These documents show that students do apply complex teaching and assessment methods in their teaching portfolios in an individual and discipline-specific way, thus indicating the development of the potential for excellent or innovative teaching.

Analysis of Student Feedback

The focus-group interviews of the same course cohort support the achievement of the goal of developing the potential for innovative and excellent teaching to some degree. The course participants were able to see this only as a potential that had been created to be realized in their future practice. As one of the participants stated, "We learnt different teaching techniques in depth—these are more advanced approaches to teaching which can be studied further and applied once we have a concrete course to design and to teach." Looking at the evidence from the anonymous survey, we may also see some support for the claim that we have implemented this goal. The respondents to the questionnaire (thirty) indicated that they did produce several pieces of work that aimed at developing their potential as innovative teachers: eight respondents designed a way to utilize a complex teaching method, twelve prepared a full teaching portfolio, twenty-one prepared a statement of teaching philosophy, and ten prepared a separate student assessment strategy.

Overall, fourteen out of twenty-seven respondents ranked the element of learning about specific complex teaching methods as "of great importance." As for learning about advanced student assessment techniques, twelve considered it of great importance. Of course, we may not be able to judge this goal as skill development in some absolute terms. The participants are still only experimenting and progressing in relation to their level of teaching experience, which ranges from nonexistent to significant (in a small minority of cases). As such, we are still talking more about early creative design attempts than about rigorous testing of theory in practice.

DEVELOPING THE POTENTIAL FOR SCHOLARLY TEACHING

The goal of developing the potential for scholarly teaching is the final and possibly the most advanced one that any training programme in higher education teaching can aim for, following current best practice in the field (e.g., Murray 2009). The difficulty with this goal hinges on what is understood under scholarly teaching, and what level/degree of scholarly teaching is being targeted in a professional development programme (Mårtensson, Roxå, and Olsson 2011). The general approach relates to Ernst Boyer's (1990) concept of "the scholarship of teaching," which has come to denote university teaching as an aspect of scholarly academic work (McCarthy 2009).

Existing conceptualizations of this area of research in the field of academic development allow for both a narrow categorization that amounts to a faculty's member's inclination to carry out systematic research into the learning process of their students (Adams 2009; Gale 2009), and a broader conceptualization of a scholarly approach to teaching denoting a potential for an inquiry based on reading, understanding of pedagogical knowledge (general and discipline specific), and systematic reflection (e.g., Huber and Hutchings 2005; Kreber 2007).

In this training programme we aim to create the potential for scholarly teaching, rather than actual products of scholarship of teaching, as we are working with very young academics, often before they have any chance to teach their own courses. Therefore, at this stage, the participants cannot investigate student learning, but they can become aware of the best practice in such investigations (and in pedagogical practices) through reading appropriate literature, responding to it, and thinking about ways of documenting their future students' learning. The course participants also develop the skills of documenting their own professional progress; for example, by writing educational autobiographies (first-level course), statements of educational philosophy, and teaching portfolios which include reflections on relevant experiences, teaching designs, and responses to readings (second-level course).

Analysis of Student Work

The evidence of a more scholarly approach to teaching is best gathered by looking at student writing. This is usually done by producing argumentative responses to educational literature, by integrating relevant literature in the process of designing a teaching method application, or as a separate element of a teaching portfolio. Looking at the student work in the first-level course, nearly all reflections on the course integrated relevant and student selected literature into their reflection. The texts referred to a range from educational development literature (on teaching methods, student assessment, course design) to broader educational writing and educational research and more specific disciplinary examples investigating a method or a critical issue in teaching and learning. Regarding the portfolios submitted as part of the winter 2009 course, two of the methods-application projects integrate relevant literature to a high degree and one portfolio includes a separate critical review of readings.

Analysis of Student Feedback

Developing as a scholarly teacher is endorsed by our participants as a goal of the course that is largely being achieved. For example, in the alumni survey, learning how to document and develop one's teaching was considered as important (nine—of great importance, ten—of some importance, two—of little importance). But it was clearly not as decisive for the respondents as the impact on their teaching skills discussed above.

However, when we look at the responses to the last question during the focus-group interview, which was meant to elicit current theories of practice that students developed as a result of participating in the programme (the explicit question was: "What are your associations with the term teaching in higher education?"), almost all responses hinted at aspects of practice that are integral or very much related to the notion of scholarly teaching.

For example, six comments (out of twelve comments made) concern aspects of scholarly approaches to teaching, starting with a professional responsibility for student learning (and gathering evidence for it); several participants discussed aspects of integration of teaching and research and their challenges and opportunities as the most salient aspect of teaching in higher education, and one asserted in explicit terms that teaching needs to be understood as an activity as serious as research: "And [teaching is] more serious. It's the whole responsibility. I can't just say I am saying some things to people and if they understand, OK, if not, then it's their own fault. So it's not that easy anymore. Lecturers should be responsible for the success of their students . . . it was somehow [my thinking] before, but now I know much more what that means, how to realize this seriousness or how to make students perform better."

Taking this into consideration, we may say that the programme manages to instil in the students the capacity for scholarly thinking about teaching and learning in their discipline, and their work shows this to some extent. But there is certainly scope for further thinking about how this important element of the course can be better achieved and evaluated. Creating more opportunities for the development of scholarly thinking might include more work with those students who do have a chance to teach a course and to implement, and then evaluate, a specific aspect of teaching and learning. This would require some additional resources or a new programmatic tool to help students put into practice and research their innovations.

CONCLUSION

In summary, the "Teaching in Higher Education" programme at CEU has become a well-institutionalized and appreciated programme for preparing future faculty. The popularity of the course with the PhD students grows with every year. Overall, as far as our ongoing assessment suggests, the training programme manages to develop basic teaching and course design skills and to begin the formation of a more confident, self-reflexive teaching persona. Evidence found in student works and acquired from student feedback suggests that they develop an appreciation of and capacity for scholarly teaching and a strong potential for becoming self-renewing, innovative teaching professionals.

However, as with any training programme, it has its limitations. For one thing, due to limited staff resources that can be dedicated to it, it is not very flexible in terms of timing and scheduling to allow even more students to benefit from it. As the three CRC trainers run a number of programmes simultaneously, the time we can spend on delivering the course is limited, and we presently cannot expand it or offer any follow-up opportunities.

Perhaps more importantly, the current schedule does not guarantee that all students who really need the course can take it at the time when they most need it—for example, during their teaching assistantship or shortly before applying for academic jobs. The teaching practice component of the programme is very limited. Therefore, one area for improvement of the programme is finding some better ways to integrate the course in the students' actual teaching experience for the purpose of teaching portfolio development and to stimulate integrative learning. This means finding better ways to collaborate with CEU departments in integrating the course into students' doctoral experience.

In the future, it would be advisable to develop a follow-up programme, perhaps an inquiry-based teaching fellowship for the programme alumni, once they actually secure a teaching position. A whole range of more basic and more department-specific or domain-based programmes could complement this programme. This is becoming possible at CEU in the near future, as CRC is in the process of organisational restructuring and will eventually become integrated into an institutional Centre for Teaching and Learning at the university. This might open up a whole range of new opportunities in terms of what we can offer to both CEU doctoral students and junior teaching staff.

The future of the programme will require more intensive consultation with the programme stakeholders (students, programme alumni, doctoral programme directors, heads of departments, career services staff). It may include further modularization, alternative timing of the courses, specific new content, integration of teaching practice and teaching observation, seeking international accreditation for the programme, and other developments.

So far, this course represents a significant institutional innovation in terms of the standard-level practice of academic development in the geographical area of Central and Eastern Europe. The programme contributed to the CEU's recognition as an institutional leader in the Scholarship of Teaching and Learning (in graduate education) by the Carnegie Foundation for the Advancement of Teaching, as the only continental European institution to receive this recognition. With adequate institutional support, resources, and academic leadership it may well become a significant feature of CEU's doctoral education in the future.

NOTES

1. With an exception of CEU Business School.
2. Thirty-five percent of all CEU graduates pursue a career in education and research institutions, according to an alumni survey conducted by CEU's Alumni Relations and Career Services in 2008.
3. Educational biography is a short piece of reflective writing, dealing with the institutional and disciplinary development of the doctoral candidate as it is understood by them in autobiographical terms. That is, it asks the students to reflect on what the formative moments, experiences, institutions, locations, or personalities were that have "formed" them as teachers/researchers at this stage in their development.
4. A CRC syllabus template includes areas such as goals and learning outcomes, course description including the course's "vision," location in the discipline

and the curriculum, week-by-week topics with readings listed, a description of teaching, and assessment and grading principles.

BIBLIOGRAPHY

Adams, Pamela. 2009. "The Role of Scholarship of Teaching in Faculty Development: Exploring an Inquiry-based Model." *International Journal of Scholarship of Teaching and Learning* 3 (1): 1–22.

Biggs, John. 2003. *Teaching for Quality Learning at University: What the Student Does.* Buckingham, UK: Open University Press/SRHE.

Boyer, Ernest L. 1990. *Scholarship Reconsidered: Priorities of the Professoriate.* Lawrenceville, NJ: Princeton University Press.

Central European University (CEU). 2011. "Welcome from the President and Rector." Central European University Web site, http://www.ceu.hu/about/president-rector-welcome, accessed 16/09/2011.

Eggins, Heather, and Ranald Macdonald, eds. 2003. *The Scholarship of Academic Development.* Buckingham: Open University Press.

Gale, Richard. 2009. "Asking Questions that Matter . . . Asking Questions of Value." *International Journal for the Scholarship of Teaching and Learning* 3 (2): 1–9.

Huber, Mary Taylor, and Pat Hutchings. 2005. *The Advancement of Learning: Building the Teaching Commons.* San Francisco: Jossey-Bass.

Kreber, Carolin. 2002. "Teaching Excellence, Teaching Expertise, and the Scholarship of Teaching." *Innovative Higher Education* 27 (1): 5–23.

———. 2007. "What's It Really All About? The Scholarship of Teaching and Learning as an Authentic Practice." *International Journal of Scholarship of Teaching and Learning* 1 (1): 1–4.

Mårtensson, Katarina, Torgny Roxå, and Thomas Olsson. 2011. "Developing a Quality Culture through the Scholarship of Teaching and Learning." *Higher Education Research and Development* 30 (1): 51–62.

McCarthy, Marian. 2009. "The Scholarship of Teaching and Learning in Higher Education: An Overview." In *The Scholarship of Teaching and Learning in Higher* Education, edited by Rowena Murray, 6–15. Maidenhead, UK: SRHE/Open University Press/McGrawHill.

Murray, Rowena, ed. 2009. *The Scholarship of Teaching and Learning in Higher Education.* Maidenhead, UK: SRHE/Open University Press/McGrawHill.

Renc-Roe, Joanna. 2008. "Writing for the Formation of Scholarly and Reflective Teachers out of Graduate Research Students at an International University." In *The NAITRL/CASTL Graduate Education Symposium Proceedings*, edited by A. Hyland, National Academy for the Integration of Learning, Teaching and Research, 27–44. Cork, Ireland: University College Cork.

Roxå, Torgny. 2005. "Pedagogical courses as a way to support communities of practice focusing on teaching and learning." In *Higher Education in a Changing World, Proceedings of the 28th HERDSA Annual Conference*, Sydney, 3–6 July, 440–448.

Schön, Donald. 1983. *The Reflective Practitioner: How Professionals Think in Action.* New York: Basic Books.

Shulman, Lee S. 2005. "Signature Pedagogies in the Professions." *Daedalus* 134 (3): 52–59.

3 Graduate Student Teacher-Training Courses, Job Placement, and Teaching Awards in the United States

John Ishiyama, Alexandra Cole, Angela D. Nichols, Kerstin Hamann, and Kimberly Mealy

INTRODUCTION

How well have political science graduate programmes in the U.S. performed in preparing graduates for teaching in the field? In this chapter we find that research productivity is still the best predictor of faculty job placement at all institutions, be they primarily research or teaching institutions. Indeed, despite the existence of teaching-preparation courses at many universities, these had little effect on enhancing the placement of graduates, even at political science departments that emphasise teaching over research. Further, we find that award-winning teachers primarily completed their doctoral work at top-ranked research institutions in the country, particularly public institutions.

Many studies have indicated that in the social sciences, graduate programmes have failed to adequately prepare graduates of doctoral programme for careers at institutions that primarily emphasise undergraduate teaching. This is a particular problem given that most available faculty positions are located at institutions that primarily have a teaching focus—only 26 to 35 percent of faculty positions in political science are located at doctoral-granting departments.[1] Thus, only about one-third of doctoral graduates in political science in the U.S. can expect to become faculty members at research universities similar to their graduate institutions with a heavy emphasis on research and perhaps less emphasis on teaching. The remaining positions are located at institutions where teaching and service are of equal or greater importance than research and publication.

However, as Gaff et al. (2003) note in their study of doctoral programmes in political science, most generally do not adequately prepare graduate students for the realities of faculty life at the institutions where most will begin their careers. They contend that "better preparation for academic careers includes understanding the missions, faculty roles and rewards, and academic culture of the various institutions. Preparation should also allow students to experience the full range of roles faculty play in these institutions and to develop the skills that will allow them to compete for and succeed in faculty positions" (Gaff 2003 et al., 2). In particular they point to a lack of adequate preparation for careers as teachers. Indeed, although many graduate students have an opportunity to teach sometime during their experience as doctoral students, these are often not structured experiences that prepare them to deal with issues such as "assessment, different types of student learning, the pedagogy of the discipline, curricular innovations, the impact of technology on education, or the variety of teaching styles that may be helpful with students from different racial, ethnic, or cultural backgrounds" (Gaff 2003 et al., 3).

In political science, studies have indicated that less than half of PhD departments in the U.S. offer teacher-training (Rothgeb, Spadafore, and Burger 2007; Ishiyama, Miles, and Balarezo 2010). Pleschová and Simon (2009) find that a similar proportion of European institutions (49 percent) offer some form of teacher-training. Further, they find that research institutions are more likely to offer teacher-training than less-research-intensive universities. This finding is consistent with the findings of Ishiyama, Miles, and Balarezo (2010) regarding the U.S.

Further, an American Political Science Association (APSA) Task Force Report on Graduate Education (2004) points out that with the growing number of employment opportunities for graduates of political science PhD programmes at primarily undergraduate institutions (PUIs) and community colleges (two-year institutions), departments should not simply prepare students to be political scientists but also to be teachers of political science. Rothgeb, Spadafore, and Burger (2007), in their survey results from 1,197 department chairs in the U.S., found strong support for the idea that teaching experience and training play an important role in hiring decisions.

Other efforts to improve teacher-training and professional preparation for careers at primarily undergraduate institutions include the past Preparing Future Faculty (PFF) programmes (PFF 4 included the APSA and four PhD-granting institutions in political science—Indiana University, University of Colorado–Boulder, Howard University, and the University of Illinois–Chicago). Additionally, in 2004, APSA held the first annual Conference on Teaching and Learning in Political Science and, in 2007, conference organisers created a track on graduate education. This track focused on, among other things, teacher-preparation for graduate students. The APSA also provides online and print teaching resources and mentoring opportunities for graduate students and junior faculty on a variety of issues, including teaching and learning.

Many departments in the U.S. have also instituted graduate teacher-training courses as part of the graduate curriculum. Ishiyama, Miles, and Balarezo (2010) identified forty-one departments (out of approximately 122 PhD-granting political science programmes) that offered a graduate-level course on teaching political science. Of the forty-one departments that offered such a course, twenty-eight required the course be taken by at least some of their graduate students. In thirteen cases, the course was optional or listed as an elective. The large majority (thirty-eight of forty-one) were located at public universities as opposed to private ones.[2] Thus in this study we focus primarily on the seventy-three public PhD-granting political science departments in the U.S. as opposed to all institutions.

Some political science departments in the U.S. have already fashioned their programmes to explicitly prepare students for careers as teacher-scholars. The political science department of Miami University (Ohio),[3] for example, established a "College Professor Training Program" for its doctoral students, which includes a mentor programme to train students for independent teaching and course work on teaching political science to undergraduates. Similarly, Baylor University inaugurated a new PhD programme in political science in 2005 that has been designed specifically to train teacher-scholars (for a description, see Ishiyama, Miles, and Balarezo 2010). Indiana University offers a three-course graduate seminar series on teaching to help prepare graduate students to teach effectively.

What have been the effects of these efforts? In the following sections we offer two different ways to assess the impact of these efforts. First, does the institution of a teacher-training class enhance the "hireability" of graduates from such programmes? In other words, do such programmes increase the likelihood of placement of graduates at higher education institutions? Second, which programmes tend to produce "award-winning" instructors of political science? Are programmes that are more teaching oriented more likely to produce award-winning instructors?

ASSESSING DOCTORAL PROGRAMME PERFORMANCE ON GRADUATES' JOB PLACEMENT

The Data

To assess job placement performance, we construct a measure of placement rates based on two sources (for a similar measure, see Schmidt and Chingos 2007). The first consists of a database of current PhDs employed at academic institutions in the U.S. provided by the American Political Science Association. These data have been widely used to impute the performance of graduate departments in terms of graduate student placement and have also been used to calculate rankings for PhD granting departments (for a discussion, see Schmidt and Chingos 2007). The database records not only the institution at which the individual was employed, but also where the individual received the PhD degree, and in what year, as well as the gender of the individual.

We restrict our data to faculty who were awarded a PhD between 1999 and 2007[4] because 2007 is the last year for which data on the number of Ph.D.s awarded by a university are reported by the Integrated Postsecondary Data System (2011; IPEDS). Also, only faculty holding tenure-track professorial positions are included in the analysis. In other words, lecturers, adjunct professors, postdoctoral fellows, visitors, and those in other positions are not included in the analysis. Including non-tenure-track temporary appointments would include faculty who are often evaluated by their departments using different criteria than tenure-track faculty—thus we exclude them from the analysis. We focus only on faculty who received their PhD after 1999 (for a total of 1,716 faculty) because most teacher-training programmes have been adopted only fairly recently (generally in the 1990s) by graduate programmes. We also included information on the institution where students received their PhDs and on what type of institution they were employed (either a PhD-granting department or otherwise). We then derived a total of employed PhDs by PhD-granting department, which constitutes the numerator for the assessment measure.

To calculate the denominator (the number of PhDs the departments produced during the same time period, 1999–2007), data were derived IPEDS from the National Center for Education Statistics produced by the U.S. Federal Department of Education (IPEDS 2011). We collected the number of PhDs produced for each of our seventy-three cases (public universities) in political science and international relations (as long as the university did not also have a separate international relations department).[5] IPEDS reports that between 1999 and 2007, five thousand PhDs were granted by these public departments.

While there are potential problems with our measure of placement, we agree with Schmidt and Chingos (2007, 526). They contend that although "ideally information collected would track the school at which graduates are placed three to five years after they leave graduate school (any earlier would not give careers sufficient time to stabilise, but any later might allow faculty to drift from the career path they established in graduate school) but such data are not readily available." Further, we are also cognizant of other potential shortcomings of these data. For instance, the database does not report placement in non-academic jobs (such as in government, research think tanks, non-profit organisations, and the like). This, however, does not present a problem for our analysis since we are primarily interested only in finding out whether requiring a teaching course helps place PhDs in finding employment in higher education as university or college faculty. The APSA database is based upon a directory of all political science faculty members. The database was built from reports from departmental faculty rosters.

Nonetheless, we agree with Schmidt and Chingos' (2007) justification for the use of these data in that the database provides the advantage of accessibility and convenience; in addition, it is validated by the leading professional society in the field. Further it is the only database currently available to conduct such analyses. Although admittedly flawed, it nonetheless provides a useful starting point to calculate placement rates.

The Analysis

Our first dependent variable is the ratio of PhDs employed over PhDs produced for each of the seventy-three public graduate departments in our study.[6] Our second dependent variable is the number of PhDs produced in a department that is employed at teaching institutions (i.e., not PhD-granting departments) over the total number of PhDs produced by the PhD-granting department. We use this measure because it is possible that the presence of teacher-training/professional socialization courses provides advantages for PhDs seeking jobs at primarily teaching departments but perhaps less so for those seeking jobs at departments that focus primarily on research.

In addition, the analysis includes two control variables. These controls were selected because they act as alternative explanations for placement (research productivity) and the size and capacities of the programmes (which may also affect placement). For the first variable, research productivity of the PhD-granting department, we employ the international ranking of political science departments as reported by Simon Hix (2004). The Hix ranking of political science programmes assessed 1,255 programmes in the U.S. and elsewhere and ranked the 400 best programmes based on faculty productivity in the top-ranked sixty-three political science journals in the world. This index is the most comprehensive ranking based on research productivity in existence. We used the Hix index (for only U.S. institutions) as opposed to other commonly used rankings such as those that use peer evaluations, for example, the U.S. National Research Council and the *US News and World Report* (2007) because of the often cited problems with such rankings; furthermore, these rankings are often based on additional characteristics beyond research productivity.[7] Further, we use the Hix index rather than other rankings that are based on content analysis of leading political science journals (Welch and Hibbing 1983; Miller, Tien, and Peebler 1996; Ballard and Mitchell 1998; Garand and Graddy 1999; McCormick and Rice 2001). Most indices only include the top twenty to fifty institutions, relegating the "others" to a common lower ranking. Only the Hix index examined all political science programmes (including primarily undergraduate programmes) and used sixty-three international political science journals to measure research productivity. The second control variable measured the "size" of the programme, or the total number of full time equivalent (FTE) faculty reported by the department.[8]

To examine whether the existence of a required teacher-preparation course enhanced the employability of PhD graduates from institutions that offered, and in some cases required, such courses, we regressed the dependent variable, the overall placement rate, against the three independent variables, using the seventy-three public PhD programmes. Table 3.1 reports the results. As indicated, the best predictor of placement was the ranking on the Hix index. The more highly ranked a department in terms of research productivity, the larger the proportion of PhD graduates who were in faculty positions as reported by Schmidt and Chingos's 2007 article (rankings were listed as one being highest and higher numbers indicating lower rankings). Whether the graduate programme required some level of teacher-preparation for its students was slightly positively related (though not statistically significant) to the proportion of the programme's PhD graduates after 1999 who had obtained faculty positions. The size of the graduate department as measured by faculty FTE was generally unrelated to the placement rate. Finally, as indicated by the VIF scores, the independent variables were not collinear with one another.

Table 3.2 reports the results of an analysis of a subset of the data, those programmes that were not ranked in the top forty of the Hix index (i.e., we exclude the most highly ranked research productive departments in the U.S.). These are presumably departments that may seek to produce graduates who are prepared to teach at institutions focusing on teaching rather than emphasizing primarily research. The subset includes fifty-eight public PhD-granting departments. Table 3.2 shows the results of regressing the overall dependent variable against the three independent variables in our model using these fifty-eight cases.

Again as with the results reported in table 3.1, even when considering PhD programmes that are not in the top forty on the Hix index (i.e., the most highly research productive departments), the more highly ranked a department in terms of research productivity, the larger the proportion of PhD graduates who held tenured or tenure-track faculty positions. Thus it appears that even for less research-intensive graduate departments, the more

Table 3.1 Coefficient Estimates and Collinearity Statistics for Dependent Variable (PhDs Placed over Total Number of PhD Degrees Granted 1999–2007)

Variable	Coefficient (Standard Error)	Beta	VIF
Was course on teaching required for graduate students from which the faculty member received their degree?	.045 (.056)	.084	1.030
Ranking on Hix index	−.002**** (000)	.543	1.346
Size of Graduate Department in FTE	.003 (002)	.014	1.320

Adj R^2 = .266
* p < .10
** p < .05
*** p < .01
**** p < .001

Table 3.2   Coefficient Estimates and Collinearity Statistics for Dependent Variable (PhDs Placed over Total Number of PhD Degrees Granted 1999–2007) for PhD Programs Not in Top Forty on Hix Index

Variable	Coefficient (Standard Error)	Beta	VIF
Was course on teaching required for graduate students from which the faculty member received their degree?	.069 (.066)	.124	1.028
Ranking on Hix index	−.002**** (000)	−.498	1.095
Size of Graduate Department in FTE	.003 (003)	.102	1.073

Adj R^2 = .228
* p < .10
** p < .05
*** p < .01
**** p < .001

research intensive is the department the greater the likelihood that the department places its graduates in faculty positions, even when controlling for the size of the department in terms of faculty members. As with the results for the entire sample, whether the graduate programme required some level of teacher preparation for its students was not related to placement rates.

Table 3.3 uses a slightly different measure of placement rates—the number of PhD graduates placed at non-PhD granting departments over the total number of PhDs produced. Indeed, it may be the case that requiring a teacher-preparation course enhances the ability of less research-intensive

Table 3.3   Coefficient Estimates and Collinearity Statistics for Dependent Variable (PhDs Placed at Non-PhD-granting Departments over Total Number of PhD Degrees Granted 1990–2007) for PhD Programs Not in Top Forty on Hix Index

Variable	Coefficient (Standard Error)	Beta	VIF
Was course on teaching required for graduate students from which the faculty member received their degree?	.047* (.035)	.175	1.028
Ranking on Hix index	−.001** (000)	−.261	1.095
Size of Graduate Department in FTE	.001 (002)	.111	1.073

Adj R^2 = .059
* p < .10
** p < .05
*** p < .01
**** p < .001

departments to place their graduates at primarily undergraduate teaching institutions that might be less interested in the research background of their new hires and more interested in their teaching preparedness.

The results presented in Table 3.3 indicate that the more research intensive is the department, the greater the likelihood that the department places its graduates in faculty positions *at teaching institutions*. Further, a PhD-granting, less research-intensive department's requirement that the students take a teacher-preparation course does not significantly increase the placement rate of the department's graduates at teaching institutions. Thus, when combining these findings with the results from Table 3.2, although requiring a teacher-preparation course raises the likelihood of employment for PhDs produced by a department generally, it does not increase the likelihood that the PhDs from that department find employment at primarily teaching institutions.

The above results are suggestive. In general, the existence of teacher-training courses had a marginally positive effect on placement rates. However, the existence of such courses did not necessarily enhance the placement rates of PhDs from lesser-ranked research departments at primarily teaching institutions, contrary to the justification for the existence of such training courses at less research-intensive graduate departments. What does seem to affect placement is the extent of the research productivity of the graduate department. This may be because such departments afford their graduate students the opportunity to engage in research themselves (and more importantly to get published, which enhances the graduate student's marketability) or that even primarily teaching institutions base their hiring decisions on the research reputation of the faculty candidate's department or the research record of that candidate. In other words, a department's research productivity still remains the best predictor of job placement for its PhD students.

However, one should be cautious as to interpreting the results. For instance, it should be noted that college teacher-training can be incorporated into the graduate curriculum beyond or instead of simply offering a course. Thus, the PhD programmes at Baylor University's and Miami University's (Ohio) past programmes offer alternative cost-effective ways to achieve such integration, although using very different models—one is based on the apprentice system; the other one uses resources to supplement their programme often found at the faculty development or teaching and learning centres at most universities (for a discussion of such programmes, see Ishiyama, Miles, and Balarezo 2010). Neither offers an explicit graduate teacher-training course, but instead both use innovative techniques to provide better teacher-training opportunities for their graduate students. Further research must take such alternative measures into account when examining the impact of graduate teacher-training on placement rates.

In addition, although requiring a teacher-training course may not enhance "hireability," it should be remembered that taking a course on teaching is not the same as having teaching experience. Indeed, teaching experience is a much better indicator of preparedness for teaching than is one's course work, and is likely to impact more on a hiring decision than what appears on a transcript (for this point, see also Rothgeb, Spadafore, and Burger 2007). In part this is because, as Ishiyama, Miles, and Balarezo (2010) point out in their analysis of the content of such courses, most courses focus more on the mechanics of course design (such as syllabus construction and design of assignments, etc.) as opposed to teaching technique. However, our data cannot currently capture whether or not a department offers teaching experience as part of its graduate training.

Although placement is certainly an important aspect of preparation, another way to gauge the extent to which programmes prepare teachers is to examine which departments produce "great teachers" in the field.

WHICH DEPARTMENTS PRODUCE THE GREAT TEACHERS?

A second indicator of graduate programme preparation for teaching relates to whether a programme produces highly effective teachers. In order to ascertain which political science PhD programmes are most effective at producing outstanding teachers, an original data set compiled by Alexandra Cole and John Ishiyama (2008) was used. The dataset is based on the teaching awards reported in each issue of *PS: Political Science & Politics*. *PS* data were collected by using back issues available through JSTOR (short for "Journal Storage") for the years 1968–2003. The "News and Notes" (1968 through Summer 1981) and "People in Political Science" (Autumn 1981 through 2003) sections include announcements of teaching awards (which included departmental and university awards), which constitutes our basic data source. Although it might be argued the reported teaching awards do not constitute an exhaustive list of teaching awards given to political science faculty, there are two advantages of using this measure as our primary data source. First, if a department considers the award important, it is often reported in *PS* in order to showcase a major achievement. Second, *PS* represents the only systematic source of data for teaching awards across the discipline.

Award recipients were included based upon the description of the awards. Awards had to be primarily based on teaching—awards granted based on a combination of teaching, research, and service were not included because it cannot be determined whether teaching was the predominant criterion used in the granting of the award. The award recipient's name, awarding institution, and year of the award were entered into a database. We then searched the "Dissertation Abstracts" database by name to determine the recipient's degree-granting institution. For award recipients whose degree-granting institutions could not be ascertained through the "Dissertation Abstracts" database, we conducted a Google search of the award recipient's name and award-granting institution to locate the individual on a department Web site. For many, this provided information on the degree-granting institution and year of degree awarded. In the cases in which we were able to find only the degree-granting institution but not the year of the degree, a second search using the "Dissertation Abstracts" was undertaken, this time using the degree-granting institution as an additional field.

The data set includes 384 observations. For twenty-one cases, the degree-granting institution could not be identified. In the tables below, we report the overall rankings of the top twenty-six political science graduate programmes in terms of the number of award-winning teachers produced by the department. Table 3.4 shows the overall ranking based on all teaching awards for the top twenty graduate programmes with the number of teach-

Table 3.4   Awards at all Universities

PhD-Granting Department	N	% of total
University of Chicago	16	4.2
Indiana University	15	3.9
Yale University	15	3.9
University of Wisconsin–Madison	14	3.6
Harvard University	13	3.4
University of California–Berkeley	13	3.4
Columbia University	12	3.1
Ohio State University	12	3.1
University of Michigan	10	2.6
University of Minnesota	10	2.6
University of North Carolina–Chapel Hill	10	2.6
Syracuse University	9	2.3
University of California–Los Angeles	9	2.3
Washington University	9	2.3
University of South Carolina	8	2.1
Georgetown University	7	1.8
Princeton University	7	1.8
University of Iowa	7	1.8
Cornell University	6	1.6
Johns Hopkins University	6	1.6
New York University	6	1.6
Rutgers The State University of New Jersey–New Brunswick	6	1.6
University of Maryland College Park	6	1.6

ing awards presented to graduates from that programme and the percent of total teaching awards won by PhDs from that programme.

The top teaching-award-producing graduate departments are the University of Chicago, Indiana University, Yale, University of Wisconsin–Madison, and Harvard, which are also some of the top research institutions in the country. However, it may be the case that such institutions better prepare their graduates for faculty roles at similar institutions, such as other research-intensive/extensive institutions—but what of teaching at primarily undergraduate institutions?

Table 3.5 reports the rankings for only those teaching awards that were given at non-Research 1 (using the Carnegie Classification System) institutions. Although only teaching awards were examined in this analysis, given

Table 3.5   Awards at Non-Research 1 Universities

PhD-Granting Department	N	% of total
1. Indiana University	7	3.9
2. Ohio State University	6	3.3
2. Syracuse University	6	3.3
2. University of California–Berkeley	6	3.3
5. University of Chicago	5	2.8
5. University of North Carolina–Chapel Hill	5	2.8
7. Columbia University	4	2.2
7. Cornell University	4	2.2
7. Georgetown University	4	2.2
7. Rutgers The State University of New Jersey–New Brunswick	4	2.2
7. University of Georgia	4	2.2
7. University of Iowa	4	2.2
7. University of South Carolina	4	2.2
7. University of Virginia	4	2.2
7. University of Wisconsin–Madison	4	2.2
7. Washington University	4	2.2
18. Harvard University	3	1.7
18. Johns Hopkins University	3	1.7
18. Michigan State University	3	1.7
18. New York University	3	1.7
18. University of Tennessee	3	1.7
18. Yale University	3	1.7

the generally greater weight and emphasis placed on teaching at non-research-intensive/extensive institutions, it is useful to examine the extent to which programmes prepare their graduates at primarily teaching institutions.

In Table 3.5, Indiana, Ohio State University, the University of Chicago, and the University of California–Berkeley remain in the top five, joined by Syracuse University. Harvard and Yale drop to eighteenth place, perhaps because PhDs from these departments are less likely to find employment at institutions primarily focused on teaching. Nonetheless, in absolute terms there is little to differentiate the list of departments in Table 3.5 from those in Table 3.4.

How do the teaching-award rankings compare with other departmental rankings based on reputation, research productivity, and number of citations of PhDs produced? Table 3.6 displays the two rankings listed above in Tables 3.4 and 3.5, along with the *US News and World Report* rankings (2007) and Hix (2003) rankings, for U.S. universities only. Again, we used the Hix rankings rather than other rankings because it was based on citations appearing in sixty-three international political science journals as opposed to a small set of U.S. political science journals, which is common in many other rankings. In addition we report the Masuoka, Grofman, and Feld (2007) rankings based on citations, the production of PhDs who are listed in the "Political Science 400" (PS400), the 400 most-cited U.S. political scientists, and the production of PhDs in the PS400 as a proportion of the total number of PhDs produced.

In Table 3.7, we report the two teaching rankings, and in the third column an overall ranking of political science departments by combining the rankings for the reputational *US News and World Report*, the Hix index, and the Masuoka, Grofman, and Feld (2007) ranking of PhDs produced who are in the PS400 by the total number of PhDs produced. Table 3.7 lists the top fifteen institutions.

In Table 3.8 we summarise the results from Table 3.7. Interestingly, a number of programmes appear in all three rankings: teaching awards in all universities, teaching awards at non-Research 1 schools, and the ranking based upon scholarship. These include the University of California–Berkeley, the University of Chicago, Indiana University, the University of North Carolina–Chapel Hill, Ohio State University, and the University of Wisconsin–Madison. Programmes that produced award-winning faculty at only Research 1 schools (but not at primarily teaching institutions) and were top research institutions as well included Columbia University, Harvard, the University of Michigan, the University of Minnesota, UCLA, and Yale University. Graduate programmes that seemingly specialised in teaching included Syracuse, the University of South Carolina, the University of Virginia, the University of Georgia, Cornell University, Georgetown University, and Rutgers University.

Several observations can be derived from these results. First, it appears that although some departments are apparently somewhat better at

Table 3.6 Comparing Teaching-Award Rankings and Other Rankings Based on Reputation, Citations, and PhD Production

Cole and Ishiyama (2007) Ranking Based on All Teaching Awards	Cole and Ishiyama (2007) Ranking Based on Teaching Awards Received at Non-Research 1 Schools	US News and World Report (2007)	Hix (2003)	Matsuoka et al. (2007) Rank Based on Citations	Matsuoka et al. (2007) Rank Based on Number of PhDs Produced in PS 400	Matsuoka et al. (2007) Rank Based on Number of PhDs Produced in PS400 as Proportion of Total PhDs Produced
1. University of Chicago	1. Indiana University	1. Harvard	1 Columbia University	1. Harvard	1. Harvard	1 CalTech
2. Indiana University	2. Ohio State University	2. Stanford	2 Harvard University USA	2. Stanford	2. Yale	2 Yale
2. Yale University	2. Syracuse University	3. University of Michigan	3 Stanford University	3. Yale	3. UC Berkeley	3 Harvard
4. University of Wisconsin Madison	2. University of California–Berkeley	4. Princeton	4 Ohio State University	4. Michigan	4. Michigan	4 Rochester
5. Harvard University	5. University of Chicago	5. University of California–Berkeley	5 University of California–San Diego	5. Columbia	5. Chicago	5 Washington
5. University of California–Berkeley	5. University of North Carolina–Chapel Hill	5. Yale University	6 University of California–Irvine	6. UCLA	6. Princeton	6 Stanford
7. Columbia University	7. Columbia University	7. University of California–San Diego	7 Indiana University–Bloomington	7. UC Berkeley	7. Columbia	7 Michigan
7. Ohio State University	7. Cornell University	8. Duke	8 Princeton University	8. UC San Diego	8. Stanford	8 UC Berkeley
9. University of Michigan	7. Georgetown University	8. University of Chicago	9 Yale University	9. Princeton	9. UNC Chapel Hill	9 Princeton
9. University of Minnesota	7. Rutgers The State University of New Jersey–New Brunswick	10. Columbia	10 University of California–Berkeley	10. Duke	10. Wisconsin	10 Chicago
9. University of North Carolina–Chapel Hill	7. University of Georgia	10. MIT	11 Michigan State University	11. Cornell	11. MIT	11 U of Iowa

12 UNC Chapel Hill
13 Northwestern
14 U of Delaware
15 Wisconsin
16 Minnesota
16 Duke
18 MIT
19 U of Illinois Urbana-Champaign
19 Wisconsin-Milwaukee

12 Northwestern
12 Rochester 1
14 Minnesota
15 Cornell
15 UCLA
15 Duke
15 U of Iowa
15 Washington Univ.
15 CalTech
21 U of Illinois Urbana-Champaign

12 Indiana
13 Ohio State
14 Univ. of Maryland
15 NYU
16 UNC Chapel Hill
17 UC Irvine
18 Northwestern
19 Univ. of Washington
20 Wisconsin

12 University of Chicago
13 University of California–Los Angeles
14 Georgetown University
15 Massachusetts Institute of Technology
16 State University of New York–Binghamton
17 Florida State University
18 University of Michigan,
19 Johns Hopkins University
20 Texas A&M University

12. Syracuse University
12. University of California–Los Angeles
12. Washington University
15. University of South Carolina
16. Georgetown University
16. Princeton University
16. University of Iowa
17. Cornell University
17. Johns Hopkins University
17. New York University
17. Rutgers The State University of New Jersey–New Brunswick
17. University of Maryland–College Park

7. University of Iowa
7. University of South Carolina
7. University of Virginia
7. University of Wisconsin–Madison
7. Washington University
18. Harvard University
18. Johns Hopkins University
18. Michigan State University
18. New York University
18. University of Tennessee
18. Yale University

10. UCLA
13. Ohio State University
13. UNC Chapel Hill
13. Rochester
16. University of Wisconsin–Madison
16. Washington University
18. Cornell
18. NYU
18. University of Minnesota
21. Northwestern

Table 3.7   Teaching-Awards Rankings Compared to Overall Rankings of
Graduate Departments

Cole and Ishiyama (2007) Ranking Based on all Teaching Awards (Top 15)	Cole and Ishiyama (2007) Ranking Based on Teaching Awards Received at Non-Research 1 Institutions (Top 15)	Overall Rankings Based on Scholarship (Top 15)
1. University of Chicago	Indiana University	Harvard University
2. Indiana University	Ohio State University	Yale University
2. Yale University	Syracuse University	Princeton University
4. University of Wisconsin–Madison	University of California–Berkeley	University of California–Berkeley
5. Harvard University	University of Chicago	University of Michigan
5. University of California–Berkeley	University of North Carolina–Chapel Hill	University of Chicago
7. Columbia University	Columbia University	Columbia University
7. Ohio State University	Cornell University	Ohio State University
9. University of Michigan	Georgetown University	Washington University
9. University of Minnesota	Rutgers The State University of New Jersey–New Brunswick	University of California–Los Angeles
9. University of North Carolina–Chapel Hill	University of Georgia	University of North Carolina–Chapel Hill
12. Syracuse University	University of Iowa	Indiana University
12. University of California–Los Angeles	University of South Carolina	University of Wisconsin–Madison
12. Washington University	University of Virginia	University of Iowa
15. University of South Carolina	University of Wisconsin Madison	University of Minnesota

producing PhD graduates that subsequently turn into teaching-award-winning faculty, they do not monopolise the production of such faculty. Clearly, award -winning faculty members have been produced by a large number of different political science departments. In some ways it is reminiscent of a saying from the Disney film *Ratatouille*—although not everyone can become a great political science teacher, a great political science teacher can come from anywhere.

Second, the top schools producing award-winning faculty also tend to be from some of the top research institutions in the country (University of California–Berkeley, University of Chicago, Indiana University–Bloomington, University of North Carolina–Chapel Hill, Ohio State University, University of Wisconsin–Madison). Without further investigation into the

Table 3.8   Summary of Different Graduate Programs

Graduate Programs in Top 15 in Teaching in All Schools and Research	University of California–Berkeley, University of Chicago, Indiana University–Bloomington, University of North Carolina–Chapel Hill, Ohio State University, University of Wisconsin–Madison
Graduate Programs in Top 15 in Research and Teaching at Research 1 Schools	Columbia University, Harvard, Michigan, Minnesota, UCLA, Yale
Graduate Programs in Top 15 in Research and Teaching at Non-Research 1 Schools	University of Iowa
Graduate Program in Top 15 in Research Only	Princeton
Graduate Program in Top 15 in Teaching at Research 1 Schools Only	Syracuse, South Carolina
Graduate Programs in Top 15 in Teaching at Non-Research 1 Schools Only	Virginia, Georgia, Cornell, Georgetown, Rutgers

teacher-preparation programmes at each of these institutions over time and given the time frame of the analysis, it is difficult to ascertain why these programmes are successful in producing teaching-award-winning faculty. However, there is one interesting observation regarding at least two of these five programmes. Both Ohio State University and Indiana University–Bloomington have had a long connection with the Preparing Future Faculty Program (sponsored by the Council of Graduate Schools and the Association of American Colleges and Universities), which is a programme designed to prepare graduate students for faculty careers at primarily teaching institutions. As mentioned already, Indiana University in particular was selected along with Howard University, University of Colorado–Boulder, and the University of Illinois–Chicago as the designated political science PFF programme in 1999. So it is little wonder that along with being a highly ranked research programme, the Indiana University programme would produce a number of award-winning political science teachers as well.

CONCLUSION

This chapter has demonstrated that overall, research productivity is still the best predictor of faculty job placement at all institutions, be they primarily research or teaching institutions. Indeed, requiring teaching-preparation courses had little effect on enhancing the placement of graduates, even at political science departments that emphasised teaching over research. Although surprising, when viewed in combination with the analysis of where award-winning teachers received their PhDs, this finding becomes less surprising. Award-winning teachers primarily completed their doctoral work at top-ranked research institutions in the country, particularly public institutions.

A possible explanation for this finding has been alluded to above. The provision of a course designed to train political science graduate students on teaching is likely not as effective as providing the opportunity to teach. Large research-extensive universities in the U.S. often provide many opportunities to teach courses independently, as well as participate in observations of teaching (either good or bad) as a teaching assistant. Thus it is little wonder that some of the best teachers are also produced (perhaps unintentionally) by some of the top research institutions in the country. However, the top performers, departments like Indiana University and Ohio State University, have also intentionally helped prepare teachers via programmes like PFF.

What is it about a graduate school experience in some of the top graduate departments in the country that helps develop a good teacher of political science? This question is beyond the scope of this chapter, and the answer will have to await further research. However, there is something that happens at some of the top research departments in the country that also promotes the development of good teachers and, perhaps also, ideal teacher-scholars. It may be the case, as is the case at our current institution, that larger research institutions provide opportunities to teach independent courses (such as via "Teaching Fellowships"). Or perhaps it is because some of the top research universities in the country are also located in urban areas, where teaching opportunities at other colleges and universities are more available. Whatever the case, this will have to wait unit further research is conducted.

NOTES

1. The lower figure is presented by Nerad and Cerny (2003), who report positions at Research 1 institutions of the Carnegie Classification System; Lopez (2003) reports a figure of 35 percent in doctoral-granting departments, which may include departments in schools that are not classified as Research 1 institutions. According to the APSA, currently about 34 percent (as of 2011) are located at doctoral-granting institutions. This figure represents the U.S. academic job market only and refers to the percentage of all faculty positions in political science located at doctoral-granting institutions in the U.S. and is based upon APSA e-jobs data.
2. In our previous study we coded the department as a public institution if it was state supported in some way, or an exclusively private institution. This included institutions such as the University of Pittsburgh, as well as Miami University, which, although independently funded and in many ways much

like a private institution, is supported in part by state funding and hence is classified in this study as a public institution.
3. Unfortunately, the PhD programme at Miami University has since ceased operations.
4. Schmidt and Chingos (2007) limited their study to 2004 to avoid "statistical noise."
5. The exceptions were University of Southern California, Claremont Graduate School, and University of Denver, where the departments there generally produce PhDs who find employment in political science departments.
6. We deliberately refrain from naming individual institutions in this chapter, so as to not unduly embarrass departments that have been less successful in placing their PhD graduates. All results are thus reported in the aggregate.
7. There have, of course, been several noteworthy problems with this approach. In particular, such assessments are largely subjective. The biases of this approach have been investigated and it has been argued that because the sample of academic judges has only very limited information about the output of departments, they are forced to base their judgments on other reputation, which favors already established programmes at the expense of up-and-coming ones (Katz and Eagles 1996). Further, the reputation of the department may be confounded by the reputation of the institution as a whole, which some researchers have referred to as the "halo effect" (Lowry and Silver 1996; Jackman and Siverson 1996). Second, the peer assessments are quite costly to conduct and hence are only updated infrequently.
8. If this was not explicitly reported, we counted the number of full, associate, and assistant professors in a department (we excluded any faculty that were listed as "visiting" or "adjunct" or "temporary" or "lecturer" from the count).

BIBLIOGRAPHY

APSA Task Force on Graduate Education. 2004. "Report to the Council." *PS: Political Science & Politics* 38 (2): 129–135.
Ballard, Michael J., and Neil J. Mitchell. 1998. "The Good, the Better, and the Best in Political Science." *PS: Political Science & Politics* 31 (4): 826–828.
Cole, Alexandra, and John Ishiyama. 2008. "Who Produces the Great Teachers? Ranking Graduate Political Science Programs via Teaching Awards." Annual Meeting of the Teaching and Learning Conference, American Political Science Association, San José, California, February.
Gaff, Jerry G., Anne S. Pruitt-Logan, Leslie B. Sims, and Daniel D. Denecke. 2003. *Preparing Future Faculty in the Social Sciences and Humanities.* Washington, DC: Council of Graduate Schools and Association of American Colleges and Universities.
Garand, James C., and Kristy L. Graddy. 1999. "Ranking Political Science Departments: Do Publications Matter?" *PS: Political Science & Politics* 32 (1): 113–116.
Hix, Simon. 2004. "A Global Ranking of Political Science Departments." *Political Studies Review* 2 (2): 293–213.
Integrated Postsecondary Data System (IPEDS). 2011. Washington, DC: Federal Department of Education, http://nces.ed.gov/ipeds/, accessed 07/07/2010.
Ishiyama, John, Thomas Miles, and Christine Balarezo. 2010. "Training the Next Generation of Teaching Professors: A Comparative Study of Ph.D. Programs in Political Science." *PS: Political Science & Politics* 43: 515–522.

Jackman, Robert W., and Randolph Siverson. 1996. "Rating the Rating: An Analysis of the National Research Council's Appraisal of Political Science Ph.D. Programs." *PS: Political Science & Politics* 29 (2): 155–160.

Katz, Richard, and Munroe Eagles. 1996. "Ranking Political Science Departments: A View from the Lower Half." *PS: Political Science & Politics* 29 (2): 149–154.

Lopez, Linda. 2003. "Placement Report: Political Science Ph.D.s and ABDs on the Job Market in 2001–2002." *PS: Political Science and Politics* 36 (4): 384–389.

Lowry, Robert C., and Brian D. Silver. 1996. "A Rising Tide Lifts All Boats: Political Science Department Reputation and Reputation of the University." *PS: Political Science & Politics* 29 (2): 161–167.

Masuoka, Natalie, Bernard Grofman, and Scott Feld. 2007. "Ranking Departments: A Comparison of Alternative Approaches." *PS: Political Science & Politics* 40 (3): 361–366.

McCormick, James M., and Tom W. Rice. 2001. "Graduate Training and Research Productivity in the 1990s: A Look at Who Publishes." *PS: Political Science & Politics* 34 (3): 675–680.

Miller, Arthur H., Charles Tien, and Andrew A. Peebler. 1996. "Department Rankings: An Alternative Approach." *PS: Political Science & Politics* 29 (4): 704–717.

Nerad, Maresi, and Joseph Cerny. 2003. *Career Outcomes of Political Science Ph.D. Recipients: Results from the Ph.D.s Ten Years Later Study*. Seattle, WA: Center for Research & Innovation in Graduate Education.

Pleschová, Gabriela, and Eszter Simon. 2009. "Teacher Training for Political Science Ph.D. Students in Europe Determinants of a Tool for Enhanced Teaching in Higher Education." *Journal of Political Science Education* 5 (4): 233–249.

Rothgeb, John, Annemarie Spadafore, and Betsy Burger. 2007. "Faculty Training in Political Science: Results from a Survey of Department Chairs." *PS: Political Science & Politics* 40 (4): 759–763.

Schmidt, Benjamin, and Matthew Chingos. 2007. "Ranking Doctoral Programs by Placement: A New Method." *PS: Political Science & Politics* 40 (3): 523–529.

US News and World Report. 2007. *America's Best Graduate Schools 2007 Online Edition*, http://www.usnews.com/usnews/edu/grad/rankings/phdhum/brief/polrank_brief.php, accessed 01/12/2009.

Welch, Susan, and John R. Hibbing. 1983. "What Do the New Ratings of Political Science Departments Measure?" *PS: Political Science & Politics* 16 (3): 532–540.

4 The Impact of Training on Teacher Effectiveness
Canadian Practices and Policies

Christopher Knapper

INTRODUCTION

Until about forty years ago, most academics worldwide received no organised preparation for their teaching role. But in the 1970s universities in many Western nations started to offer programmes that would help improve teaching, either for new or potential faculty members, or for those in mid-career. Although almost all Western-influenced universities now provide some type of teaching-related development for their staff, the targets and approaches vary considerably from one country to another. Many academics, especially in North America, lack any preparation or training in teaching methods. Furthermore, there is little empirical evidence for the effects for such training on teacher effectiveness or student learning.

This chapter describes the situation in Canada, which, although part of North America, has an education system that continues to be influenced to some extent by European traditions and practices. In the following pages I describe the evolution of educational development in Canadian universities, with a particular emphasis on the preparation of academics for their teaching role, and explore reasons why such initiatives have had less impact than programmes in Britain, the Nordic countries, and Australasia.

CANADIAN HIGHER EDUCATION: A VERY BRIEF BACKGROUND

In multinational monographs like this, chapters about things Canadian are something of a rarity. The U.S. is so large, rich, influential, and so all-pervasive that our much smaller nation to the north (smaller in population, not of course in geographical area) is often overlooked, or it is assumed that North America is one large homogeneous culture. That is a pity, because Canada does have its own distinctive history, politics, and values, which are in part reflected in our higher education institutions, drawing from traditions in Europe and Britain as well as the U.S.

The first Canadian universities were established in the mid-nineteenth century, and were largely modelled on examples from Britain and France. They were small, elite, usually with close ties to the church. The teaching methods they used would look quite familiar to anyone who had attended Oxford or the Sorbonne—lectures, extensive reading assignments, tutorials, and assessment largely based on general retrospective examinations at the end of several (usually three) years (see Ross 1896; Wallace 1948).

After World War II, however, teaching programmes and methods increasingly reflected practices in the U.S: discrete "courses" (modules) that typically lasted a term or semester rather than a whole year, continuous assessment based on assignments and tests (often multiple-choice) to earn course credits that were accumulated until requirements for a degree had been met (Neatby 1953). Compared to European institutions, there was considerable choice of courses for most degree programmes, and usually reliance on a single prescribed course text rather a comprehensive reading list. Teaching was largely through lectures, supplemented by laboratories or seminars in some cases. Different approaches were sometimes used in professional programmes such as medicine where there was a major emphasis on clinical practice in real-life settings. In the humanities and sciences some honours programmes continued the British tradition of requiring an undergraduate thesis (something that still survives at many older Canadian universities), though not the practice of using external examiners to provide a check on internal assessment of student performance.

These changes were partly due to the large number of academic staff who had received their postgraduate training in the U.S. By the 1960s, decision making about academic matters had been largely devolved from the university administration to the faculty, who served on committees to plan programmes and curricula, decided on degree requirements, and made teaching assignments. Faculty set and implemented academic policies and procedures, for example, dealing with such matters as student discipline, grading student work, and the career reward system for academic staff (tenure, promotion, etc.). By 1970 almost all department chairs were short-term elected positions (typically for three years), and most administrative posts were held by faculty from within the institution for fixed terms, after which they returned to their normal teaching and research responsibilities. This was also a time of great expansion in higher education throughout the Western world. Canada saw the creation of numerous new universities, existing institutions rapidly expanded, and many private universities dropped their religious affiliations in order to take advantage of government funding.

Today, Canada has about fifty major universities,[1] plus a number of smaller denominational colleges that are for the most part affiliated with larger public institutions. In contrast to the situation in the U.S., all the major Canadian universities are public and under government auspices, even though each one is nominally independent and self-governing. Unlike most European nations, in Canada education is a provincial responsibility,[2] which means that at the federal (national) level there is no ministry of education or higher education—though the federal government does fund the national research agencies which provide most of the financing for university research in the sciences, medicine, social sciences, and humanities. The nature and responsibility for funding and oversight has implications for teaching, learning, and educational development, as we will see later. For example, not only are salaries and terms of employment unique to each institution, but there can be no national coordination of curriculum or quality audit, as is common in countries like Australia,[3] Hong Kong, and many European institutions.

Despite considerable institutional autonomy and variation in size, compared with many other higher education systems Canadian institutions are remarkably homogeneous in terms of teaching methods and curricula—possibly because there is a good deal of informal contact between administrators and faculty from different universities. For example, the system is small enough for all the university presidents to meet regularly to discuss common issues and problems.

THE BEGINNINGS OF EDUCATIONAL DEVELOPMENT

The rapid expansion of the university system in the 1960s and 1970s brought an influx of new students, many of whom came from non-traditional backgrounds. This in turn required considerable growth in academic staff, many recruited from abroad. It was a time of student protests in Europe and North America—activism that was directed partly at national and international political events, but also concerned with internal issues of university governance and the quality of teaching. Students sought power and influence, for example, membership of key university committees, and more accountability through such measures as student evaluations of courses and teachers, the results of which were published as "anti-calendars."[4] It was this context that gave rise to a number of educational development initiatives, including the establishment of teaching and learning centres to help improve the quality of instruction.

The Canadian Association of University Teachers (CAUT) is a professional organisation to which almost all Canadian faculty members belong, and in 1970 CAUT created a Professional Orientation Committee to consider how faculty are prepared for their roles as academics and make recommendations for future practice. The terms of reference of the committee began by commenting that "No requirements for the specific function of teaching are set for those entering the profession, nor with very few exceptions are there systematic procedures for assisting new members of the profession in undertaking their teaching responsibilities." Then followed a set of questions for the committee's attention, beginning with: "Should training for university teaching be attempted in graduate schools as part of the programmes which prepare scholars for university positions?" Thus, the document raised an issue that has still not been resolved in the Canadian context.

In fact the new committee became waylaid by concerns about evaluation of teaching that diverted its attention from issues of preparation and training. Its first initiative was the development of a policy on student evaluations (see Knapper 1972), and this was followed by a position paper about how teaching was dealt with in annual performance reviews of academic staff (Knapper 1974). Later the committee developed the teaching dossier[5] approach to documenting teaching—an idea that is now familiar in universities all over the world (Shore 1975; Shore et al. 1980).

There is some argument about which was the first educational development centre in Canada, but certainly McGill's Teaching and Learning Services, founded in the late 1960s, was one of the earliest and most influential, with a continuous history to the present.[6] The number of centres grew rapidly, especially among the larger Ontario universities, and now almost all Canadian universities have such units. Their programmes typically include workshops and short courses, newsletters, and other publications on teaching issues, a library of books and periodicals, linked to a Web-based resource collection, special programmes for graduate student teaching assistants, individual consultations with faculty seeking advice on new teaching methods or instructional problems, and in many cases a small grants programme to support small-scale teaching research and innovation. In addition, most centres provide advice at the policy level on issues related to teaching and learning, such as programme review, curriculum development, evaluation of teaching, academic performance appraisal, and academic dishonesty.

In 1985 a group of educational developers from southern Ontario founded the Society for Teaching and Learning in Higher Education (STLHE), which now has over 700 members across Canada and abroad. STLHE organises a well-regarded annual conference, publishes a series of short guides on teaching and learning methods, sponsors an electronic journal on the scholarship of teaching and learning,[7] and for the past twenty years has run the prestigious 3M Teaching Fellowships programme, which each year honours ten university faculty members for their excellence in teaching as well as work with colleagues to enhance teaching quality. STLHE maintains ties with its sister organisations in Britain, Australia, and the U.S. However, the Canadian organisation differs in having a majority of its members who are rank-and-file faculty rather than educational developers. The latter comprise a special division of STLHE known as the Educational Developers Caucus, which runs a number of independent activities including an annual conference that attracts up 200 delegates.

STLHE was one of the founding members of the International Consortium for Educational Development (ICED), and one of the three editors of

ICED's journal (*The International Journal for Academic Development*) has been a Canadian since that publication's inception. Although membership in STLHE is drawn from all Canadian provinces, the society operates mainly in English, and representation from francophone Québec is limited. Many of the leading francophone educational developers are affiliated with Association Internationale de Pédagogie Universitaire (AIPU), a network for French-speaking university teachers in Europe, North America, and Africa.

THE PREPARATION OF CANADIAN UNIVERSITY TEACHERS

In Britain a very early and widespread activity of educational development centres was the provision of induction courses for new faculty. Initially such courses were intensive one- or two-week affairs, typically offered just before the start of the academic year, and covering such topics as effective lecturing, fostering student interaction and discussion, assessing and grading student work. The British/European training model was generally much less common in North America, where there has traditionally been a reluctance to be overly prescriptive. Hence a more usual Canadian and U.S. approach has involved offering a wide range of stand-alone workshops, from which faculty members could select according to their self-perceived needs or interests, supplemented by individual consultations for those faculty having teaching problems or wishing to try a new instructional method. Generally such consultation was offered by centre staff, though a number of universities, for example, the University of Alberta, developed peer consultation systems involving teaching observation and advice by trained colleagues.

One limitation of the workshop-plus-consultation approach is that only a minority of teachers participate in such programmes, and it seems likely that many poor teachers ignore such opportunities. Furthermore, having teachers select workshops according to their interests runs the risk that they may overlook areas of weakness or ignorance, even if the workshop programme is comprehensive—which in many universities is not the case.

PROGRAMMES FOR GRADUATE STUDENT TEACHING ASSISTANTS

A great deal of teaching in North American universities is carried out by graduate students, and almost all Canadian educational development centres offer some special programmes for this group. Teaching assistants (TAs) typically run seminars and "tutorials,"[8] supervise laboratories, and mark tests and exams. In principle all these duties are performed under the guidance of a faculty member, although the diligence of this supervision varies considerably. Because first- and second-year classes in Canadian universities are often very large (500 students or more is not uncommon), the TA is perhaps the only member of the teaching staff that students come to know well and can contact easily for advice and help. TAs also act as an important liaison between students and the teacher in charge of the course. Hence the competence of teaching assistants is a major concern.

Many Canadian universities run orientation programmes for TAs (see Chapnick 2004). In a few cases these are organised by the relevant academic departments, which has the advantage of communicating a departmental commitment to effective teaching, and allows for training in issues that are peculiar to the discipline concerned. But much more common are large general or generic programmes offered to TAs at the start of the academic year. Typically such programmes are provided by the educational development centre, and last one or two days, with attendance being in practice voluntary (in the sense that there are no penalties for non-attendance).

Topics include effective presentation and communication methods, principles of assessment and grading, dealing with difficult students, responding to students from different cultural backgrounds, coping with academic dishonesty, and so on. Many programmes offer a wide range of sessions from which participants may choose, and few involve any hands-on experience to practise the different teaching approaches being discussed. In most cases there is no follow-up to the initial programme, and the work of TAs is rarely evaluated, although sometimes there is a question about laboratories and seminars on the generic course evaluation form administered at the end of term.

PROGRAMMES FOR NEW AND POTENTIAL FACULTY MEMBERS

Publicity for TA-training sessions often stresses their value to students who intend to become teachers, but in practice few of the many thousands of Canadian graduate students who are employed as teaching assistants will ever become academics. In the case of doctoral students, almost half will not have completed their degrees within ten years, and of those who do only a little over a third typically become university teachers (Auriol 2007; *Economist* 2010).

Some Canadian universities do offer more comprehensive programmes for doctoral students who plan to pursue academic careers and are more serious about acquiring teaching skills. For example, at Queen's University the author helped plan and then taught a term-long credit course on university teaching and learning, which has now been offered for over ten years ("credit" in the sense that having taken the course it will appear on the student's transcript). The course is highly task-oriented and students are encouraged to try out ideas and techniques discussed in class in their own teaching—either as a teaching assistant or, in the case of some senior students, in an undergraduate course that they may be teaching under supervision of a faculty member. Tasks involve preparing a segment of teaching that is videotaped and then critiqued by classmates, observing an experienced academic teach and then carrying out a follow-up discussion, designing a new curriculum for a course they are teaching or would like to teach, and maintaining a teaching portfolio in which experiences throughout the teaching term are documented and reflected upon.

The Queen's course, which is typical of programmes offered at a number of Canadian universities, has been evaluated very positively by participants, many of whom have in fact gone on to successful academic careers. However, the numbers who take such courses are small, they are restricted to potential future faculty rather than working academic staff, and there is no evidence for their effectiveness beyond the favourable opinion of participants.

In contrast to the situation in countries like Australia, the United Kingdom, and the Nordic nations, there are relatively few programmes in English-speaking Canada that cater exclusively to new faculty. Those that exist are almost always offered to both senior graduate students (usually doctoral students in the final stages of their programmes) and faculty at any level, both new and more experienced. It appears that the former greatly outnumber the latter, which entails the dilemma that such in-house programmes, which are mostly cost-free to those enrolled, are largely benefitting students who will shortly move elsewhere—a minority to take teaching positions at other universities and most to become professionals in business or government (Auriol 2007).

Nonetheless, courses on teaching continue to thrive. Simmons (2007) reported sixteen Canadian university courses on teaching and learning in higher education,[9] some offered at the institutional level, some at the level of a department or school. The great majority were offered for senior graduate students, awarded some sort of academic credit for completion, were "stand-alone" courses (i.e., not part of a more comprehensive certificate programme), and were only rarely a prerequisite for a teaching appointment. More recently, Knorr, McCurdy, and Vajoczki (2010, 3) reported that "Many teaching and learning development programs aimed at graduate students are in existence in Canada, but there are few structured and accredited faculty programs." They were able to identify seven programmes open to faculty members (compared to seventeen in Australia and New Zealand, for example), with the average annual number of participants being twenty-three, and the average number of courses in such programmes being five. In no case was completion of the programme a requirement for tenure.

The oldest such programme designed for faculty is the Faculty Certificate Program on Teaching and Learning at the University of British Columbia (UBC), which began in 1998 (see Hubball and Burt 2006). This is an eight-month programme that can accommodate up to twenty-four participants each year. Although there are regular face-to-face meetings of the whole group to help establish a "community of practice," collaboration, and peer feedback, each participant follows an individual learning plan intended to combine "theory, practice, and critical reflection pertaining to a wide range of integrated learning experiences" (Hubball and Burt 2006, 335) that include action research, discussion forums, and preparation of a teaching portfolio. Hubball and his colleagues have conducted a number of evaluations to assess the impact of the programme on faculty attitudes and behaviour (e.g., Hubball and Burt 2006; Hubball, Collins, and Pratt 2005).

Perhaps the most ambitious Canadian training programme is the one initiated in 2009 at the University of Windsor for doctoral students and early-career faculty with the aim of facilitating "critically informed and reflective teachers able to maximize student learning" and the "development of a community of scholarly educational leaders able to work autonomously when necessary, but also able and willing to collaborate and cooperate to foster positive educational change" (Potter 2009, 5–6). The programme is unique in North America in having accreditation from the UK-based Staff and Educational Development Association (SEDA). It offers graduate certificates at three levels, each one normally taking a year to complete. The first level is entitled "Fundamentals of University Teaching," the second level is called "Theory and Practice of Scholarly Teaching," and the final level is called "Leadership in University Teaching."

The first-level certificate entails two graded courses, one on learner-centred teaching and the second on course design, plus an additional half course on either leading discussions, effective lecturing, or online education (Potter 2009). At the second level, students must complete a teaching practicum, take a course on the theory and philosophy of university teaching, another half course on authentic assessment, and select another of the half courses mentioned above. The third-level certificate comprises a required course on educational leadership plus two additional half courses on self-directed learning and mentoring and supervision. All three levels require participants to maintain a teaching portfolio documenting their progress and reflections, and the portfolios are an important component of the assessment evidence for the award of a certificate.

The programme was taught first in September 2009, so it is premature to assess its popularity and effectiveness, though there are plans for ongoing evaluation. Enrolment to date has been relatively modest, with seventeen students spread over three "cohorts," of which about one-third hold faculty positions (Kustra et al. 2010).

FACULTY PARTICIPATION AND RESISTANCE

While the UBC and Windsor programmes are impressive, there are relatively few comprehensive programmes in Canadian universities that prepare faculty for a career in teaching and it remains the case, despite the recommendations of CAUT over forty years ago, that most Canadian faculty receive no preparation for their role as teachers. In the course of designing the proposal for the Windsor certificate programmes, Potter (2009) contacted a wide range of Canadian educational development centres to inquire about similar initiatives. He concluded that

> Many programs at other universities consist of just one course, learning community membership, or a series of workshops, more still involve little to no assessment or evaluation (frequently attendance and participation is all that is required). Although several Canadian programs offer a "certificate," it is often merely a certificate of completion or letter, not formally recognized by the host university, the province, nor any other body. (Potter 2009, 40)

He might have added that most participants are graduate students rather than full-time faculty members, as indicated by the results of Simmons' (2007) survey, cited above. In other words, with few exceptions the programmes that exist are often piecemeal, largely unassessed, and often comprise a single course or an assembly of workshops that teachers select according to their interests, supplemented in some cases by completion of a teaching portfolio. This falls far short of programme requirements specified by SEDA or the demands of well-established courses at a number of British, European, and Australian universities, all of which require completion of several substantial courses over a one- or two-year period, linked to documentation of, and reflection about, teaching and assessment strategies used in the faculty member's own classes. In this respect, Canadian practice more closely reflects the situation in the U.S., where formal preparation for teaching is limited.[10] Given this situation, it is worth asking why so few faculty members engage in teacher-training, and why there is not more pressure to enhance the scope and depth of programmes to prepare new faculty for their teaching roles.

Faculty Attitudes and Conceptions of Teaching

Since most faculty members never avail themselves of the training opportunities that do exist, it seems plausible to conclude that a majority of Canadian academics fail to recognise a need for such preparation. While there are few empirical studies on attitudes to initial training, anecdotal evidence suggests that many faculty believe that good teachers are "born, not made," that teaching is an art that cannot easily be imparted through courses, and that teaching is something best learned on the job through a process of trial and error (see Hattie 2009). Models for university teaching hence come from faculty members' own university teachers, which perhaps explains why teaching methods have remained largely unchanged for so long (see Knapper 2010).

At many universities there are still relatively few conversations about teaching (although, because of the growth of educational development centres, many more than in the past), and faculty are rarely exposed to alternative pedagogical approaches. Indeed, there is an almost complete ignorance on the part of most Canadian academics of the considerable empirical literature on university teaching and learning that could (and should) guide good practice. Teachers can argue that the present system seems to work well enough: student evaluations of teaching and exit polls are quite positive, and graduates continue to get jobs and earn substantially more than those without degrees. There is in fact little public debate in Canada about the quality of university education, so what is the impetus for change?

Linked to these faculty beliefs are concerns about greatly increased workload and student numbers over the past decade, and the (largely correct) perception that career advancement for academics is based mainly on research and publications rather than teaching effectiveness—especially effectiveness as indicated by student evaluations, which are often regarded as flawed.

Efficacy of Training

A more challenging issue that many educational developers fail to confront is the deep-seated scepticism on the part of many colleagues about the effectiveness of teacher-training, based in part on perceptions of the school system. While the value of initial training would be readily accepted in the case of, say, physicians, airline pilots, or structural engineers, in the case of schoolteachers opinion is more divided.

There is in fact some research evidence to support such doubts. Hattie (2009, 111), in a recent massive synthesis of over 800 international meta-analyses of factors affecting student learning achievement in primary and secondary schools, concluded that "the effect size of teacher education on subsequent student outcomes is negligible." Summarising the empirical literature on the effectiveness of teacher-training programmes (for the most part initial training offered at colleges and universities), Hattie (2009, 110) writes that

> Spending three to four years in training seems to lead to teachers who are reproducers, teachers who teach like the teacher they liked most when they were at school, and teachers who too often see little value in other than practice-based learning on the job.

On the matter of professional development more generally, Hattie (2009) found that it is more likely to change teacher learning than it is to affect teacher behaviour and student learning. More positively, he comments that "critical effects on student learning were very much a function of professional development that challenged the teachers' prevailing discourse and conceptions about learning" (Hattie 2009, 121). Also important were establishment of a professional community of practice and supportive school leadership. While it might be argued that the teaching at university level is in some ways different from primary and secondary teaching, it remains true that underlying principles of learning, and many pedagogical strategies, have universal applicability (see Knapper and Cropley 2000; Knapper 2004). In view of the paucity of data on effects of training university teachers, Hattie's comprehensive survey is hard to ignore.

THE IMPACT OF TRAINING FOR UNIVERSITY TEACHING

In the case of education and development at the postsecondary level, there are far fewer relevant empirical studies. However, there is some Canadian evidence that faculty involvement in educational development improves teaching. For example, Murray (2005) used data from student evaluations over several years to show that ratings of effective teaching have steadily improved since the onset of educational development programmes in Canadian universities. This trend by itself could be attributed to a number of possible causes, but more telling is Murray's finding that ratings have increased significantly more for those faculty members who sought professional consultation with an educational developer about their teaching. Complementing Murray's findings is the work of Piccinin (1999), who found that faculty who consulted the educational development office at the University of Ottawa for help with a teaching issue or problem were subsequently evaluated more positively by students compared with a control group of faculty who did not engage in a teaching consultation. Moreover, this effect persisted over time.

There are no comparable Canadian studies of the effectiveness of programmes to prepare new faculty, and indeed very few worldwide. The most ambitious attempt to study the effects of taking a course on university teaching was done by Angela Ho at Hong Kong Polytechnic University (Ho, Watkins, and Kelly 2001), which demonstrated that a faculty training programme designed to change conceptions of teaching and learning produced changes in teaching conceptions and practices for two-thirds of participants. Even more significant was the fact that for half those who changed there were positive changes in learning approaches on the part of their students.

Most of the studies on programme effectiveness have measured participant satisfaction and reported changes in teaching approaches. For example, Cilliers and Herman (2010) studied effects of participation in a four-module training programme at Stellenbosch University; and although they claim positive impacts on both teachers and students, their data are based solely on participant perceptions. A much-cited study by Gibbs and Coffey (2004) attempted to examine the effectiveness of teacher-training at twenty-two universities in eight countries, and—unusually—had a control group of faculty who had received no such training. Dependent measures included changes in student ratings of teacher effectiveness, teacher conceptions of their teaching approach, and changes in approaches to learning on the part of the participants' students.

Not surprisingly in view of the logistical complexity of the research, the study has major methodological flaws, and hence the reported findings of positive impact have to be viewed with considerable caution. Even then, the authors conclude that "We are still not in a position to demonstrate that it was the training itself that resulted in the positive changes, merely that those institutions that had training also had teachers who improved" (Gibbs and Coffey 2004, 99). Moreover, the authors were unable to pinpoint particular characteristics of programmes that might have caused such improvement. More recently a series of empirical investigations of training programmes at the University of Antwerp by Stes (2008) found that participation did have an effect on conceptions of teaching, but not on educational practice or student learning outcomes.

This type of study is difficult and costly to undertake, and no comparable research has been done in Canada. Indeed, it would be logistically very hard to do so because, in contrast to the situation in Hong Kong and Europe, most Canadian students do not belong to a "cohort" that takes similar courses from the same group of instructors, and hence monitoring changes in students' learning approaches and attributing these to the influence of particular teacher or group of teachers would in most cases not be possible. Nonetheless, in a series of studies on the UBC Faculty Certificate Program (described above), Hubball and his colleagues have demonstrated positive impacts of participation on conceptions of teaching and reported teaching practices (Hubball, Collins, and Pratt 2005; Hubball and Burt 2006). Similarly, Chugh (2010) reported positive changes in teaching-related attitudes by faculty who had taken part in the University of Calgary's Teaching Enhancement Program.

TEACHER-TRAINING AND HIGHER EDUCATION POLICY

Two decades ago, a commission of inquiry into Canadian higher education sponsored by the Association of Universities and Colleges of Canada recommended that teacher-training be made mandatory for all new full-time faculty (Smith 1991). But this idea was never taken up by universities, and twenty years later the situation is unchanged.[11] No Canadian (or U.S.) university to my knowledge has a senate policy requiring new appointees to undertake pedagogical training, nor does any faculty union collective agreement contain such a provision. Given the burgeoning growth of educational development centres and programmes in Canada since the 1960s, why is it still true in 2011 that so few Canadian academics receive any formal training in teaching—for example, compared to Britain, Australia, the Netherlands, and Scandinavia?

First, it is not at all clear that most Canadian academics, including new appointees, perceive a need for formal training in teaching, which is seen as one of those skills that most faculty members have acquired by simple observation and their lengthy experience as students (rather as if being a frequent theatregoer imbued the skills of acting). This view may in part be based on a general Canadian scepticism about the value of teacher-training in the school sector, mentioned briefly above. This relates to the issue, discussed at some length above, concerning the general lack of evidence that involvement in training programmes improves the performance of teachers and the learning effectiveness of their students. Although I personally believe, based on my experience as a teacher and educational developer for over fifty years, that educational development initiatives have indeed changed Canadian higher education for the better, I am forced to admit that the empirical evidence for such change is modest.

A second explanation relates to the ethos surrounding research and publications, which is thought to be the distinguishing characteristic of the Canadian university compared to, say, schools or colleges. This is reflected in the academic reward system, which is perceived by most faculty members as placing much greater emphasis on research and publications than on teaching accomplishments. There is a paradox here in that many faculty members complain that teaching is undervalued, most Canadian university policies with respect to career advancement (awarding tenure and promotion) assign equal weight to teaching and research, and decisions about such matters are largely in the hands of faculty committees rather than university management. Canadian academics tend to identify themselves primarily in terms of their discipline: asked what they do for a living, the most likely response is "a chemist" or "an historian," rather than "I teach history" or even "I'm a history professor."

Of course these attitudes about the role of an academic and the efficacy of teacher-training exist in many other parts of the world, but they are particularly problematic in Canada and the U.S., where there is no national oversight of higher education. Here there is almost no government pressure to require or collect evidence for the effectiveness of different programmes and teaching approaches, and few public demands that academics be better prepared for their most important role.

CONCLUSION

I have tried to present the case that although educational development initiatives are common in Canadian universities, and many training programmes exist, they are attended mostly by graduate students and only a small number of new faculty members. Of course it is possible that some new teachers will have undergone some course on teaching as graduate students, but for the most part these will have been the short sessions organised for TAs, since we know (e.g., from Simmons' 2007 survey) that enrolments in more comprehensive programmes are relatively small. Participant response to such programmes is largely positive, though evidence for an impact of teaching practice and student learning is quite limited. Does this mean the current situation will continue indefinitely—implying dominance of rather conservative teaching approaches with only a minority of faculty becoming engaged in educational development, teaching innovation, and change? I think there are a number of reasons to think otherwise.

Firstly, although government oversight and audit of university teaching is currently almost nonexistent in Canada (compared to the UK, Australia, or Hong Kong, where there are regular national public reviews of institutional teaching effectiveness), that situation is likely to change as the costs of higher education continue to rise and governments demand more accountability for their investment in the postsecondary sector. For example, the government of Ontario recently established a Higher Educational Quality Council to undertake research and provide advice on institutional effectiveness, including teaching effectiveness. While to date the role of the council has been advisory, it is easy to see how that may change—for example, to undertake or oversee quality audits. The same government has also encouraged universities to participate in the annual National Survey of Student Engagement, which gathers data from students on perceptions of their educational experience at university. Since Ontario has by far the largest postsecondary sector, its initiatives are closely monitored by other provincial administrations.

Secondly, while Canadian universities have traditionally competed with each other (e.g., for students) quite politely, if at all, in an increasingly market-driven environment where institutions seek to develop their own particular "brand," it seems inevitable that one or more universities will wish to emphasise teaching quality as their distinguishing characteristic, and it is then a small step to advertising that all new faculty have teaching qualifications. This could set a precedent that encourages more universities to require completion of a certificate in teaching and learning (of the type offered at UBC, Windsor, and some other institutions) as a prerequisite for granting tenure.

Thirdly, it is untenable over the longer term for institutions that exist in large part to provide training for most of the key professions not to require similar training and accreditation for their own staff. It seems plausible that professional bodies in such fields as medicine, engineering, law, and business will increasingly raise questions about the qualifications, preparation, and continuing professional education of the faculty who in effect act as gatekeepers and quality-control agents for everyone but themselves.

NOTES

1. In addition to universities, each Canadian province supports a college system which provides vocational training and usually some non-credit programmes for the general public. The discussion in this chapter relates only to the major degree-granting institutions.
2. Like the U.S. and Australia, Canada has a federal system of government. There are ten provinces and three more sparsely populated northern "territories." There are universities in each province, with most of them located in Ontario.
3. Although, like Canada, Australia has a federal system of government, responsibility for Australian education is at the national level.
4. Called anti-calendars because the information was intended to contrast with official course descriptions contained in the official university calendar.
5. Outside Canada, the more usual term is teaching portfolio.
6. The original name of the unit was the Centre for Learning and Development.
7. *The Canadian Journal for the Scholarship of Teaching and Learning*; see http://www.stlhe.ca/resources/journals/cjsotl/, access: 27/08/2011.
8. In Canada a tutorial does not normally imply a one-to-one session with a teacher, as exists at Oxford and Cambridge. Rather, it entails a meeting with twenty or more students to offer further explanations of materials presented in lectures, or guide students through problem sets.
9. Simmons suggests, however, that there are other programmes at institutions that did not respond to her survey.
10. As long ago as 1932 the idea of a doctor of arts (DA) degree was proposed in the U.S. as an alternative to the research-based PhD. Several universities introduced DA programmes, but the degree failed to win acceptance, and now only a handful of such programmes remain in existence.
11. The one example I have been able to find of a mandatory programme is the Instructor Support Program of Mount Royal College in Calgary, which has been a requirement for every full-time faculty member since 1999 and has continued since the institution became Mount Royal University in 2009.

BIBLIOGRAPHY

Auriol, Laudeline. 2007. *Labour Market Characteristics and International Mobility of Doctorate Holders: Results for Seven Countries*. Paris: OECD.

Chapnick, Adam. 2004. "Training Teaching Assistants Helps Everyone." *University Affairs* 45 (3): 40.

Chugh, Urmil. 2010. *Evaluation of the Teaching Enhancement Programs*. Calgary, Alberta: University of Calgary Teaching and Learning Centre.

Cilliers, Francois J., and Nicoline Herman. 2010. "Impact of an Educational Development Programme on Teaching Practice of Academics at a Research-Intensive University." *International Journal for Academic Development* 15 (3): 253–267.

Economist. 2010. "The Disposable Academic." *The Economist*, December 18, 157.

Gibbs, Graham, and Martin Coffey. 2004. "The Impact of Training of University Teachers on their Teaching Skills, Their Approach to Teaching and the Approach to Learning of Their Students." *Active Learning in Higher Education* 5 (1): 87–100.

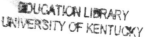

Hattie, John. 2009. *Visible Learning: A Synthesis of Over 800 Meta-Analyses Relating to Achievement*. London: Routledge.

Ho, Angela, David Watkins, and Mavis Kelly. 2001. "The Conceptual Change Approach to Improving Teaching and Learning: An Evaluation of a Hong Kong Staff Development Programme." *Higher Education* 42 (2): 143–169.

Hubball, Harry T., and Helen Burt. 2006. "The Scholarship of Teaching and Learning Theory: Theory-Practice Integration in a Faculty Certificate Program." *Innovative Higher Education* 30 (5): 327–344.

Hubball, Harry T., John Collins, and Daniel Pratt. 2005. "Enhancing Reflective Teaching Practices: Implications for Faculty Development Programs." *Canadian Journal of Higher Education* 35 (3): 57–81.

Knapper, Christopher K. 1972. "Student Evaluation: An Aspect of Teaching Effectiveness." *CAUT Bulletin* 21 (2): 26–34.

———. 1974. "A Question of Merit." *CAUT Bulletin* 22 (4): 13–18.

———. 2004. "Research in College Teaching and Learning: Applying What We Know." Commissioned paper for the Teaching Professor Conference, Philadelphia, 21–23 May.

———. 2010. "Changing Teaching Practice: Barriers and Strategies." In *Taking Stock: Research on Teaching and Learning in Higher Education*, edited by Julia C. Hughes and Joy Mighty, 229–242. Montreal and Kingston: McGill-Queen's University Press.

Knapper, Christopher K., and Arthur J. Cropley. 2000. *Lifelong Learning in Higher Education*, 3rd ed. London: Kogan Page.

Knorr, Kris, Terry McCurdy, and Susan Vajoczki. 2010. *Developing Development: A Systematic Methodology for a Formalized Faculty Development Program*. Hamilton, Ontario: McMaster University Centre for Leadership in Learning.

Kustra, Erika, Michael K. Potter, Pierre Boulos, and Alan Wright. 2010. *Provoking Change through Intentional Design: An Internationally Accredited Certificate Program*. Windsor, Ontario: University of Windsor, Centre for Teaching and Learning.

Murray, Harry G. 2005. "Student Evaluation of Teaching: Has It Made a Difference?" Paper presented at the annual conference of the Society for Teaching and Learning in Higher Education, Charlottetown, Prince Edward Island, 10 June.

Neatby, Hilda. 1953. *So Little for the Mind*. Toronto: Clarke, Irwin.

Piccinin, Sergio. 1999. "How Individual Consultation Affects Teaching." In *Using Consultants to Improve Teaching*, edited by Christopher K. Knapper and Sergio Piccinin, 71–83. San Francisco: Jossey-Bass.

Potter, Michael. 2009. *Proposal for a Graduate Certificate Program in University Teaching*. Windsor, Ontario: University of Windsor Centre for Teaching and Learning.

Ross, George W. 1896. *The Universities of Canada, Their History and Organisation*. Toronto: Warwick Brothers and Rutter.

Shore, Bruce M. 1975. "Moving Beyond the Course Evaluation Questionnaire in Evaluating University Teaching." *CAUT Bulletin* 23 (4): 7–10.

Shore, Bruce, Steven Foster, Christopher K. Knapper, Gilles G. Nadeau, Neil Neill, and Victor Sim. 1980. *Guide to the Teaching Dossier: Its Preparation and Use*. Ottawa: Canadian Association of University Teachers.

Simmons, Nicola. 2007. "What's Different Under the Gown: New Professors' Development as University Teachers." PhD dissertation, Brock University, St. Catherines, Ontario.

Smith, Stuart L. 1991. *Report of the Commission of Inquiry on Canadian University Education*. Ottawa: Association of Universities and Colleges of Canada.

Stes, Ann. 2008. "The Impact of Instructional Development in Higher Education: Effects on Teachers and Students." PhD. dissertation, University of Antwerp.

Wallace, W. Stewart, ed. 1948. *The Encyclopedia of Canada, Vol. IV*. Toronto: University Associates of Canada.

Part II

Using Programme Assessments to Improve Programme Design

5 Mentorship in Teacher-Training

A Preliminary Review of a Professional Development Programme for Tertiary Teachers in Singapore

Huang Hoon Chng and
Alan Soong Swee Kit[1]

[The programme] has broadened my mind. I no longer think only about the quality and the accuracy of the information I am "dispensing." I give thought to how the students will be able to use it best. Whether or not it is working, remains to be seen. . . . I think it is a great idea to get the popular and well-recognized teachers to come in to share their thoughts and experiences. I've learnt the hard way that there is no manual of teaching . . . no right way to do it. So seeing how others go about it helps. (A participant of our instructional development programme)

. . . but I am not a natural teacher, I am a teacher by default, so for me to have a very "teacher-process-oriented course" supported with a rationale of how I can change, has been very useful. (Rust 2000)

INTRODUCTION

As part of our own regular reflection of our careers as a university teacher, it has always struck many of our colleagues as highly ironical that we are accepted as qualified to teach in an institution of higher learning when the same acceptance would not have been automatic if we had applied for a teaching position in a non-tertiary institution. In fact, we would have been told, in most situations, that we would have to first undergo a certification course for teachers before we present ourselves to the non-tertiary student audience. The reason underlying this paradox is simple: what we academics have are PhDs, not a teaching certificate. Many of us who have PhDs, not just in Singapore but also elsewhere (e.g., Ramsden 1992; Donnelly 2008), share this somewhat strange experience—that we are *assumed* to be able and *expected* to teach well just because we have successfully completed our graduate education. Few if any of us have been given any training in teaching during our graduate school education, or in the post-PhD years. In short, we are what Rust's (2000) informant has aptly called "a teacher by default."

Today, as universities around the world, especially research-intensive universities, refocus their energy on delivering good education experience, there is increasingly overt recognition that staff development programmes for faculty members are essential. This belated admission that teaching is a skill that requires continuous development and the need to ensure quality education make it imperative to provide training for faculty.

In August 2008, one of the authors was appointed the director of the Centre for Development of Teaching and Learning (CDTL) at the National University of Singapore. As a new director inheriting at that time a twenty-three-year-old teaching/learning unit, an immediate task that she embarked on was a review of the centre's existing initiatives to determine their continued usefulness and relevance and to determine if they are in need of revision. A major programme that became the focus of review is the in-house staff development programme, called the Professional Development Programme-Teaching (or PDP-T).

The PDP-T is a university-mandated staff training programme that is conducted for all new staff appointments, and it is designed for academic colleagues who have less than three years of teaching experience in a tertiary institution prior to their arrival to our university. As a major programme run by CDTL since 2000, the time was right to undertake a review of its effectiveness and continued relevance. This paper documents a preliminary study that was carried out to evaluate the usefulness of the PDP-T and its impact on faculty members' reflection on their teaching.

The purpose of this study is to embark on a systematic study of the impact of the PDP-T on faculty members' reflection on their teaching, and this first-phase evaluation focuses on four cohorts of programme participants from January 2009 to August 2010. This constitutes the first of a two-phase evaluative exercise for the programme—to talk directly to the immediate stakeholders of the programme, i.e. the colleagues/participants themselves, about how the programme has helped them in their teaching, and later to undertake a more comprehensive study to evaluate the programme in terms of the measurable outcomes that may be said to result from a programme like the PDP-T. The study aims to answer two research questions, one general and one specific. The general question is: how have faculty members been impacted by the staff development programme as a whole; and more specifically, we wish to know if two particular elements in our programme—the mentorship and teaching practicum—have made any positive (or negative) impressions on them.

A survey was designed and administered to a group of faculty members who attended the PDP-T. In addition, e-mail follow-ups were done with a few faculty members for further clarification after the survey was carried out. The findings indicate that the programme has helped to enhance faculty members' reflection of their teaching and has generally proven useful to guide new colleagues in teaching at the university. In addition, both the mentorship and teaching practicum have received positive evaluations.

There is preliminary evidence from faculty members' reflection that the PDP-T has positively impacted their teaching and this gives us good reasons to continue to develop such a staff development programme in spite of various institutional challenges.

In the following sections, we situate the issue of quality assurance in general and staff teaching development in particular, in the wider Singapore tertiary education context, and describe the PDP-T programme structure. Subsequent sections provide details of the preliminary study and a discussion of the findings, as well as the conclusions and lessons we draw from this study.

QUALITY ASSURANCE IN EDUCATION AND STAFF TEACHING DEVELOPMENT PROGRAMMES IN SINGAPORE

In Singapore, education commands a prominent place in the national agenda in that a high priority is assigned by the government to the need to cultivate, maintain, and constantly nurture an educated population. In fact, next to defence and healthcare, education is among one of the key concerns that claims a substantial slice of the national budget each year. Quality assurance in all sectors in general and quality assurance in education in particular are therefore taken very seriously in this small tropical island state of just over five million people. But though discussions about improvements and regular reviews of the state of mathematics and science education, the standard of English, and how best to teach schoolchildren second languages like Mandarin, Malay, and Tamil take place at regular frequency, the more general question of the state and direction of teacher education has not, to date, been as adequately addressed.

At the national level, the Ministry of Education (MOE) directly oversees matters relating to school curriculum at the non-tertiary levels: primary, secondary, and postsecondary. Though it conducts a regular five-year quality assurance review of the tertiary institutions, the MOE leaves the management of the universities to its own governing body. There is a teacher-training unit, called the National Institute of Education (NIE), that is sited within one of the universities, the Nanyang Technological University (NTU), but this teacher-training unit, which evolved from decades of teacher-training history, confines its mandate to the development of school-teachers at the non-tertiary levels (Nanyang Technological University 2010a, 2010b). Teaching development within the universities is therefore a matter that each of the four universities in Singapore—namely the two comprehensive universities, the National University of Singapore (NUS) and Nanyang Technological University; the private university, Singapore Management University (The Centre for Teaching Excellence 2010—SMU), and the university that is devoted to adult education, Singapore Institute of Management University (The Teaching and Learning Centre 2010—UniSIM)—currently undertake on their own initiative.

As mentioned above, the Ministry of Education engages a high-level panel to review the universities once every five years, and it is through this review platform that each university accounts for how it is maintaining standards in various aspects of education. This includes ensuring the quality of their teaching staff through specific professional staff development programmes. NTU, for example, has a Centre for Excellence in Learning and Teaching (CELT), formerly known as Centre for Educational Development, that was established since the early 1980s. The centre runs various teacher development programmes, including annual teaching and learning seminars and a certificate programme in teaching for higher education, which ensure that NTU teachers keep up with current modes of teaching and learning. Over at SMU, the Centre for Teaching Excellence runs programmes with various focus of intensity, ranging from two-day Faculty Teaching Forums which orientate new faculty to SMU's teaching philosophy and best practices, to regular workshops and seminar series on topics that would help faculty build up their capacities in teaching.

UniSIM, formally established in 2005, evolved from an open-university-styled institution that has been existence in Singapore since the 1990s. Its teacher development unit had just been newly established with the appointment of a director of teaching and learning, and being an institution that hires large numbers of part-time staff, it devotes close attention to the formal training of their adjunct teaching staff. NUS, with its longer and more established history, has a twenty-five-year-old unit, Centre for the Development of Teaching and Learning (CDTL), that is devoted to professional staff development, and through its long history, CDTL, like NTU's CELT, has built up an established range of staff (and student) development programmes.

CDTL had a modest start back in 1984, when it was still called Centre for Educational Technology (CET), as a small audiovisual support unit for teaching staff at NUS. As the university has expanded from a mere 14,000 students back in the 1980s to the current 37,000-strong student population, CDTL as it currently stands has undergone at least three transformations. In 1996, CET's "technology" side was split from its "pedagogy" side and was renamed CDTL, a pedagogy unit. In 1999 and 2008, more resources were allocated to CDTL to enable it to expand its mission. In each of these changes, the primary motivation had been to enhance the capacity and mission of CDTL to serve the NUS teaching and learning community better. The latest restructuring just over three years ago in 2008 saw, for example, the dedication of three full-time positions that allow CDTL to expand its output and influence in the university community.

But even before the 2008 restructuring, many teacher development programmes have already been put in place, such as the Professional Development Programme-Teaching (PDP-T) for assistant professors; the Teaching Assistant Programme for graduate students who serve as teaching assistants in the departments; the Continuing Professional Development Programme

(CPDP) for all academic staff, to encourage lifelong learning and regular reflection of teaching practices; and also, on a smaller scale, a student workshop series to help students become better learners. Starting in 2008, with a new leadership in place, many of these programmes and practices came under critical review to evaluate them for their continued relevance and to find ways to increase their impact. One such programme that became the focus of critical review is the main programme in CDTL's offering, the Professional Development Programme-Teaching or PDP-T.

The PDP-T was devised in 2000, the purpose being to provide faculty colleagues with a staff development programme. This programme consists of three segments—a three-day in-house training programme that covers core issues like small- and large-group teaching, and issues in active and lifelong learning. In the second segment, comprising a sixteen-hour elective course (which translates into eight two-hour elective courses), colleagues are given options from a range of pedagogy workshops (involving both IT skills and relevant teaching issues) offered throughout the year. The third segment is a teaching experiment or practicum, involving a pedagogy-related proposal to be tried out in the classroom, and this proposal gets discussed with relevant colleagues acting as mentors/facilitators, then implemented and, finally, a final report is generated to document this practicum experience.

PDP-T participation for new faculty members, especially newly appointed assistant professors, usually begins with an invitation from the Provost's Office, calling for heads of departments to identify their new colleagues for the programme. CDTL then follows up when the name list is received and invites relevant individuals to come to the PDP-T, at the first available session (either in January or August of each academic year). Based on these declarations, CDTL obtains the list of participants for the programme and follows through accordingly, starting with the three-day in-house training sessions, to the electives, and ending with the practicum. Admittedly, there will be colleagues who should have come through the programme but did not, because they were not brought to CDTL's attention. In addition, there may be a small number of colleagues who did not attend the programme due to schedule conflicts. What CDTL does is to follow through conscientiously with every colleague who should be invited to attend the programme—the rest is left to individuals to make the "right decision" to go through the training so as to prepare them for teaching in the university.

There had been occasional discussions about colleagues who, for whatever reason, may not have fulfilled all their PDP-T requirements; and the question is, should lack of completion be a ground for withholding a contract renewal, for example? This can be a complex issue, given that there are colleagues who are naturally gifted teachers, and who arguably may not necessarily need the support of a professional development programme. The key issue to us is that academic leaders and colleagues in the university must agree and follow through before any rule about such a measure can be exercised. While it is desirable for all new colleagues to undergo the PDP-T, beyond a certain limit of persuasion, colleagues ultimately make their own decisions about their degree of involvement in such training programmes.

Having said all the above, the good news is that in the past two years there have been changes within the institution that underscore the importance of professional development and teaching itself. For example, in the past year alone, CDTL has been approached to help specific colleagues to improve on their teaching. In addition, more and more new colleagues are persuaded of the usefulness of staff development programmes. These assure those of us who put our time and energy into teaching development work that the leadership is serious in repositioning teaching in a way that is on par (or close to being on par) with research. But as with most "new" messages, it will take time for "the ground" to get the message, especially in a climate where research is emphasized.

METHOD AND DATA COLLECTION

Since the year 2000, the PDP-T has been offered twice a year, usually at the start of each academic term before teaching begins at the university, in early January and August. Previously, a group of colleagues have attempted a study of the PDP-T, with a focus on its impact on teaching styles (Pan et al., n.d.). The current study departs from this earlier study in that it is a preliminary evaluation exercise of the PDP-T after it had undergone some programme revisions in January 2009. The present study therefore focuses on the impact the programme may have on faculty members and how two specific elements—the mentorship and teaching practicum—may have been received by them.

Four cohorts of participants from five faculties who embarked on the programme in January 2009, August 2009, January 2010, and August 2010 were invited to participate in this preliminary evaluation. After a close look at the existing programme structure, two changes to the PDP-T will be explored— one involving the introduction of an informal mentorship element into the teaching practicum (from January 2009); and at a later time, a second change involving restructuring the elective workshops offered on the PDP-T platform. In this study, we wish to focus on the mentorship element, and on the teaching practicum itself, though the survey questionnaire we devised covered the entire PDP-T process. For a start, we invited participants from just five faculties (arts, dentistry, engineering, English communication and medicine, including nursing) so as to get some domain-specific viewpoints about the programme.

A nine-question qualitative questionnaire survey was designed and, after rounds of feedback from fellow centre's colleagues, was tweaked before it was implemented for this study. In total, seventy-five PDP-T participants were contacted via e-mail for this pilot evaluation. The e-mailed questionnaire method was used because it was the quickest way to reach a fairly large number of participants within a short time frame. The investigators first e-mailed all seventy-five potential participants for this study, and after they agreed to participate in our study, they received the questionnaire.

Of the seventy-five colleagues originally targeted, 21.3 percent or sixteen colleagues responded that they would participate. Of the sixteen who initially said they would participate in this pilot study, fifteen colleagues submitted their responses to the e-mailed questionnaire about the programme: five of these participated in the January 2009 training, four in the August 2009 training, three in the January 2010 training, and three in the August 2010 training.

Of these fifteen, six are from medicine (includes nursing); three from engineering; three from arts; two from dentistry; and one from English communication. Although the return rate was relatively low (fifteen out of seventy-five in the target base), it is noted that the representation profile in terms of faculty and cohort was quite even, with representations from all five faculties and all four cohorts.

Once the questionnaire was returned, the findings were tabulated and each participant was coded, and relevant follow-ups were done where further clarification was needed. We contacted three of these participants for further clarifications and gave them the option of a face-to-face chat or an e-mail chat and in all three cases, the e-mail platform was chosen due to faculty members' busy schedules.

SURVEY FINDINGS

Two significant and positive findings regarding the PDP-T as a whole have emerged from this survey: that there is a positive shift in mind-set in the way some colleagues think about their teaching and their professional development as teachers; and that the programme promoted a sense of community and camaraderie among colleagues from different disciplinary domains. For example, one informant said that "The programme has caused me to reflect about my teaching and my students' learning"; and another informant noted that where he used to be more self-focused in terms of the quality and accuracy of the information he delivered in class, he was now more student-centric in that he thought more about how his students might use the information he provided. These changes in the way colleagues view the teaching endeavour testify to the need for such professional development programmes because these programmes overtly provide opportunities for all of us to actively reflect on what we do daily as a matter of course in our classrooms from semester to semester.

Perhaps even more significant is the second finding that community bonding through the PDP-T has been affected as many informants indicated that they valued the camaraderie promoted on the PDP-T platform. In our work in the teaching and learning centre, we see it as among our central mission to bring colleagues together on a common platform, particularly because ours is such a large university of 37,000 students and 2,000 teaching staff. Occasions like the PDP-T training programme may be viewed as opportunities to gather people at one location and allow for collegial interaction and mutual sharing of experiences. What one of our informants said to us is representative of what we are used to hearing from the majority of the PDP-T participants that we have hosted through the years: "I really enjoy meeting teachers from other faculties. There is much to learn from one another and it makes one keener to share their life experiences." And just as they have benefited from this kind of platform for sharing teaching strategies and experiences, some have indicated they would consider facilitating future workshops to pass on their own expertise of teaching to other (newer) colleagues.

As mentioned earlier, the first segment of the PDP-T comprised a three-day in-house training programme that all new colleagues are invited to participate in. The key outcomes to be achieved in this three-day programme include the general orientation of new colleagues to university practices, exposing these new colleagues to effective methods of teaching that experienced colleagues in the university have developed, and infusing a positive mind-set in all colleagues towards education and teaching. The survey findings showed that these intended outcomes have largely been achieved through this programme segment as many colleagues surveyed commented positively on the exposure provided for effective classroom management and the inspiration that more senior colleagues have given them throughout the three-day formal and informal interactions.

The second segment—the sixteen-hour elective requirement—consists of a range of workshops, each usually two to three hours long, that are offered throughout the year, to be accessed at colleagues' convenience. Some of these are pedagogy workshops, dealing with important issues such as writing learning outcomes or creating assessment tasks; and some are technology-enhancement skills workshops to help our colleagues deploy IT tools within their classrooms. Some positive outcomes include the direct benefits that colleagues said they gained from learning and interacting with other colleagues who facilitated these workshops and they appreciated greatly that they need not "reinvent the wheel" through trial-and-error experimentation given that they now have opportunities to learn directly from the best practices developed by other colleagues.

There are, however, sobering lessons too. For example, the sentiment expressed by one informant is not an isolated one: "I attended [these elective workshops] simply because of the requirement that I must attend a certain number. I personally disagree with the formal requirements on attendance, as there is no benefit to attending unless a topic is of interest." We are more than aware that we do have colleagues who literally presented themselves at our centre not because they wished to but because they "had to." This has caused some negative feelings among some colleagues who have very different ideas about what they need in a training programme and a few felt they do not need any training at all.

The challenge to us running centres for professional development is to admit such realities and importantly, on the other hand, to persevere in creating that positive buy-in among as many colleagues as possible. We do so by constantly finding ways to accommodate colleagues' schedules and to create meaningful/useful workshops for them, as well as to exercise our own quality-control measures to ensure that our programmes meet quality standards. In the next section, we discuss the findings for the third and last component of the programme—the teaching practicum itself.

THE VALUE OF THE TEACHING PRACTICUM AND THE IMPORTANCE OF MENTORSHIP

This small pilot study has brought up two elements in the PDP-T as most salient and meaningful for our colleagues, and these are the teaching practicum requirement of the programme and the mentorship element that pervades the programme in general and the teaching practicum in particular. This section will discuss these two elements in some detail.

The teaching practicum is the segment of the programme that requires colleagues to reflect on their classroom practice and to propose, and later implement, an idea that they wish to try in their own classrooms for the benefit of their students' learning. This seems to be the most welcomed and valued part of the programme, perhaps because it is the most practice-based component. We have identified four salient points from speaking to colleagues regarding the value of the practicum (Table 5.1). Below we discuss each point in more detail.

Table 5.1   The Value of the Teaching Practicum

1. It forces teachers to more consciously and systematically document, reflect, and evaluate their own teaching practices.
2. It encourages teachers to think out of the box.
3. It encourages teachers to adopt the familiar "research mode" to their teaching practice.
4. It constitutes a first step for colleagues to make their teaching practice visible.

The Practicum "Forces" People to More Consciously and Systematically Document, Reflect, and Evaluate Their Own Teaching Practices

Many of us, with or without a programme like the PDP-T, delve in some form of informal reflection and constant innovations (even if they are just a form of "trial-and-error" mode of operation) when we teach our students. The value of a practicum platform in the PDP-T is, for one informant, to make what has so far been an informal effort evolve into a more formal, and, in the process, more rigorous process of articulating the rationale and the method, and analysing the effects of our classroom strategies on our students' learning. This implies that the practicum seems to help in encouraging faculty members to be more reflective about their teaching experience. Leinhardt and Greeno (1986) claims that reflection on teaching has led to the development of more complex conceptual structures (as cited in Kreber and Castleden, 2009). This in turn, according to Kreber and Castleden (2009), could enhance instructors' teaching practice and eventually improve student learning. This, in our view, is by far the most valuable outcome of requiring a practicum component in the staff development programme.

The Practicum Encourages People to Think out of the Box

We have few rules about the practicum component but we encourage colleagues to try out "something novel" in their classes that they have not thought of doing before. This simple instruction has, it seems, gotten some colleagues to "think [of] something novel and out of the box," a sentiment explicitly expressed by one informant. The willingness to experiment with new approaches is an important element in enriching one's teaching, and we are therefore more than gratified to know that the practicum carries this value for some of our colleagues.

The Practicum Encourages Colleagues to Adopt the Familiar "Research Mode" to Their Teaching Practice

As our colleagues are all academics practicing in specific fields of study, already familiar and comfortable operating as researchers, it makes sense to "speak the language of research" when encouraging reflective teaching. The practicum offers a research-like platform for colleagues to inquire into their teaching—how to teach, what the outcomes are, and how to make things better when outcomes are less than ideal—and this has resonated well with some colleagues who are "naturally disposed" towards a research orientation. According to Zuber-Skerritt (1992), such an attempt towards active research would be "likely to have a more powerful effect on the improvement of learning, teaching and staff development than research (solely) produced by educational theorists." This has possibly made the practicum component a salient value-added element for our PDP-T colleagues and is a mentality that could, and should, usefully be spread to all colleagues.

The Practicum Constitutes a First Step for Colleagues to Make Their Teaching Practice Visible

The interest to share their findings in education journals is something that some colleagues have shared with us after they have completed their practicum. The series of conversations that were held through the practicum platform—with a mentor/senior colleague and with peers—has generated interest and motivated some colleagues to feel the desire to share their teaching experiences further afield. To the extent that such an interest and passion for sharing may be seeded by the practicum process means that the practicum component has added value in our colleagues' professional development. In fact, the possibility of publishing such teaching experiments in education journals has been realized by at least one informant who participated in this survey and the experience has greatly added to her motivation to continue to reflect on her teaching and to experiment with new methods in her classroom.

We will now take a closer look at the mentorship element within the practicum process and in the PDP-T as a whole. Prior to 2008, facilitators were identified to provide feedback for practicum projects that were undertaken by PDP-T colleagues. From 2009, we introduced an informal mentorship system, consisting of three steps:

1. We contact PDP-T colleagues who are ready to discuss their practicum proposals and facilitate a preferred time slot for two to four colleagues to meet up with a senior colleague (preferably from the same faculty, if not from the same department) who will act as a mentor for this group;
2. At the proposal discussion with the mentor, the mentor offers constructive feedback on how best to go about the practicum project. Once the proposal discussion is done, the PDP-T colleagues then commence on their classroom experimentation. When these colleagues are ready to make their presentation of findings, we again try to get the same mentor to come back to listen to the presentation and offer more feedback;
3. After this presentation, a final report (or a brief article bound for our in-house publication platform) is done and the mentor gets to take one more look at the project and offers further written comments.

In the above three-step system, we hope to achieve a kind of consistent mentoring by one colleague from the PDP-T colleague's faculty or department for a project from start to finish, thus sustaining a conversation about pedagogy, and a bond, among colleagues. However, it is not always possible

Table 5.2   Importance of Mentorship in the Teaching Practicum

1. The mentorship element provides the role models for effecting good teaching and learning.

2. Mentors offer constructive feedback, give pointers and advice as well as support to junior colleagues.

3. Exchange of ideas between the mentor and the teacher stimulates the passion for teaching and learning.

4. Mentors can help to inspire new colleagues and initiate them into a positive teaching and learning culture.

for us to match colleagues from the same faculty with the programme participant due to schedule constraints and the availability of mentors. In such cases, we look for someone outside the faculty but we ensure that the mentor is always someone who is committed to the teaching enterprise and has years of experience in teaching in our institution.

In the view that many institutions struggled to obtain sufficient mentors (Angelique, Kyle, and Taylor 2002), this mentoring system has been designed to be short-term and project-based, with the hope to attract more senior/experienced colleagues to help as mentors. Also due to the shortage of good mentors, this mentoring system focuses solely on the practicum, unlike other mentoring models which cover issues faced by faculty members in higher education, such as social support, research, teaching, and work-life balance (Limbert 1995; West 2004; Darwin and Palmer 2009).

From this study, what emerged about the role of mentors and the usefulness of having a mentorship element woven into the programme are summarized in Table 5.2. The following section provides details on each point listed in Table 5.2.

The Mentorship Element Provides the Role Models for Effecting Good Teaching and Learning

One informant captures this need for role models well when he said that "I think it is a great idea to get the popular and well-recognized teachers to come in to share their thoughts and experiences. I've learnt the hard way that there is no manual of teaching . . . no right way to do it. So seeing how others go about it helps." Indeed, the effort we make is to cultivate a pool of enthusiastic facilitators among our colleagues who have a consistent record of excellent teaching, and have them come along to the programme to function as mentors, to discuss education issues and guide junior colleagues as the latter embark on their teaching career in the university. There is obvious value in getting colleagues who teach well to show other colleagues what has worked or not worked without subjecting our new colleagues to reinvent the wheel, as it were.

Mentors Offer Constructive Feedback, Give Pointers and Advice as Well as Support to Junior Colleagues

The question of fit is important in implementing a mentorship element. One informant, for example, indicated that one mentor assigned during one phase in her PDP-T was much more helpful than the other, with one providing "stimulating discussion" for her practicum and the other not quite being able to add value in terms of useful feedback. The assignment of mentors is based primarily on domain matching (e.g., we make effort to match a science colleague with an experienced colleague from science who will act as a mentor), but sometimes, people's schedules are such that we are not always able to honour this fit. In addition, there are always personality issues involved in a mentorship relationship. These factors can create the effect experienced by the informant who felt that one mentor worked well for her and the other left her wishing for better. Whatever the case may be, mentors in general are good sources of support for junior colleagues, due simply to their experience of having taught for several years in the institution.

Exchange of Ideas between the Mentor and the Teacher Stimulates the Passion for Teaching and Learning

This, in our view, is a crucial role of mentors in any mentorship programme—in this case, to provide our junior colleagues with someone who could serve as a sounding board for ideas about teaching and learning. Very often, we find ourselves not lacking in ideas per se, but as a new practitioner in the field of teaching and learning, it is a common experience to find ourselves at a loss over what may be the best way forward. Having someone to guide us, or just to listen to us and provide friendly critique for our ideas, can be a tremendous help.

Mentors Can Help to Inspire New Colleagues and Initiate Them into a Positive Teaching and Learning Culture

A point that we wish to underscore here is that the mentorship element has been considered as a crucial aide to teaching within higher education (Daloz 1986). In our view, the two most significant features of mentorship are the social and psychological support provided to colleagues and the inspiration that mentors can provide for them. Inspiration therefore lies at the heart of the mentorship element. In a research-driven university culture, no matter how much we readily acknowledge the importance of teaching/ education, the added push anyone needs to truly commit to teaching and learning amidst a heavily peppered schedule is to feel that spark of inspiration. This is often something that the right colleagues—those who can serve as mentors, those who themselves are inspired and inspiring teachers—can provide. No amount of training programmes will do if the inspiration and impetus for excellence in teaching are not made available.

CONCLUSION

Though this is a small preliminary study of how our own staff development programme has been received by our colleagues, the feedback we received from fifteen informants gave us much to go by in looking at our ten-year-old programme. In a context where no formal teacher-training is given to young academics, such a programme allows everyone the opportunity to learn from others who have more classroom experience. It does not surprise us that the idea of mentorship has been well received, especially when the matching between colleague and mentor is done well. The teaching demonstrations, advice, and inspiration that mentors provide to new colleagues are invaluable input that bodes well for the mentorship element within the programme.

It is also encouraging to know that getting people to learn through doing, through practice, and experiment on the practicum platform has shown good results. In fact, if we really wish to effect active reflection in teaching and learning, we must continue to develop the practicum in positive ways that are fruitful to all parties. While it has been an absolute pleasure to listen to colleagues' practicum ideas and share in their findings, what we have to continue to do in the future is to find ways to improve the quality of these projects. Very often, we find that most colleagues stop at thinking about and implementing a small teaching project that may enhance one small part of their teaching and their students' learning but fail to take the extra steps to develop their ideas into a holistic, rigorous, and longer term research project that may usefully add to their own longer term professional development. Like any good research endeavour that we hope will carry longer-lasting impact, we hope to find ways to help colleagues develop longer term goals in their teaching endeavours by building on these small bits that individual colleagues have already begun to undertake in their individual practicum projects within the programme framework. One way in which we have already begun to build up on the small bits is to gather and put them into a themed issue for one of our publication platforms, *CDTL Brief*. This serves to "consolidate" different project ideas within the same topic area in one place and to showcase as well as share the ideas of colleagues in various departments within the teaching community.

In the next phase of evaluating the programme, we will need to gather the views of more informants, particularly informants from other faculties not included in this preliminary evaluation. It would be interesting to examine more closely how colleagues from each professional domain perceive the programme and the kind of concrete impact the programme may have on their individual classroom practices. For the time being, we are happy to say that this first step will enable us to gather more data about the PDP-T's reception by colleagues and, later, to develop a full-blown analysis and evaluation of the programme.

NOTE

1. The authors would like to thank all informants who participated in the questionnaire survey conducted in October 2010.

BIBLIOGRAPHY

Angelique, Holly, Ken Kyle, and Ed Taylor. 2002. "Mentors and Muses : New Strategies for Academic Success." *Spring* 26 (3): 195–209.

Daloz, Laurent A. 1986. *Effective Teaching and Mentoring: Realizing the Transformational Power of Adult Learning Experiences*. San Francisco: Jossey-Bass.

Darwin, Ann, and Edward Palmer. 2009. "Mentoring Circles in Higher Education." *Higher Education Research & Development* 28 (2): 125–136.

Donnelly, Roisin. 2008. "Lecturers' Self-Perception of Change in Their Teaching Approaches: Reflections on a Qualitative Study." *Educational Research* 50 (3): 207–222.

Kreber, Carolin, and Heather Castleden. 2009. "Reflection on Teaching and Epistemological Structure: Reflective and Critically Reflective Processes in 'Pure/Soft' and 'Pure/Hard' Fields." *Higher Education* 57 (4): 509–531.

Leinhardt, Gaea, and Greeno, James G. 1986. "The cognitive skill of teaching." *Journal of Educational Psychology* 78 (2): 75–95.

Limbert, Claudia A. 1995. "A Peer Mentoring Group for Faculty and Staff Women." *National Women's Studies Association Journal* 7 (2): 86–99.

Nanyang Technological University. 2010a. "The Centre for Excellence in Teaching and Learning." Nanyang Technological University Web site, www.ntu.edu.sg/CELT, accessed 24/06/2010.

———. 2010b. "National Institute of Education." Nanyang Technological University Web site, www.nie.edu.sg, accessed 24/06/2010.

Pan, Daphne, Emil Cheong, Lisa-Angelique Lim, Kiruthika Ragupathi, Krishna Booluck, and Yuen Kwong Ip. n.d. "Effects of a Professional Development Programme on the Development of Teaching Styles." Unpublished manuscript.

Ramsden, Paul. 1992. *Learning to Teach in Higher Education*. London: Routledge.

Rust, Chris. 2000. "Do Initial Training Courses Have an Impact on University Teaching? The Evidence from Two Evaluative Studies of One Course." *Innovations in Education & Training International* 37 (3): 254–262.

The Teaching and Learning Centre. 2010. Singapore Institute of Management Web site, www.unisim.edu.sg, accessed 24/06/2010.

The Centre for Teaching Excellence. 2010. Singapore Management University Web site, www.smu.edu.sg/centres/cte, accessed 24/06/2010.

West, Damian. 2004. "Group Mentoring: Benefits and Tensions." *Training and Development in Australia* 31 (2): 22–24.

Zuber-Skerritt, Ortrun. 1992. *Action Research in Higher Education: Examples and Reflections*. London: Routledge.

6 Combining International Experience with the Local Context

Designing and Improving Instructional Development in a Post-Soviet Setting

*Mari Karm, Marvi Remmik,
and Anu Haamer*

INTRODUCTION

The quality of teaching in higher education (HE) has become a global issue in recent years, and the need to improve both teaching skills and pedagogical thinking is now acknowledged to be essential (Postareff, Lindblom-Ylänne, and Nevgi 2008). Although research recognizes that excellent teaching, based on scholarship and skills, maximizes deep learning, as Scott (2003) points out, the global attainment of teaching excellence will require a cultural change in higher education institutions (HEIs). This requirement is a particular problem in Central and Eastern Europe. For Estonia this is an outcome of the combination of regional (the collapse of the Soviet Union) and global factors (economic crises), which have caused a dire need for change in the national approach to teaching in HEIs. The process of change in Estonia was complicated by the social-political-economic transition process of the 1990s, restoration of independence in 1991, and membership in the European Union in 2004.

The tasks required to raise the quality of teaching in Estonian HEIs were, therefore, threefold: (i) a teaching skills development programme (TSDP) needed to be developed, which conformed to the particular cultural setting and addressed the most vital teaching-related problems in HEIs. This training programme was required to utilize the accumulated knowledge and experience from both the national and international scholarly communities of teacher development. (ii) At the same time as formulating the development programme, Estonia's HE infrastructure required changes in order to be able to sustain the TSDP in the long term. (iii) Finally, it was vital to assess, through impact research, how successfully courses within the TSDP could be adapted to meet local needs and most effectively carry out the intended changes concerning teaching in HEIs. Impact research on the efficacy of the TSDP has also provided feedback for further developing the programme to ensure it meets the requirement of being an ongoing process searching for the best system for training HE teachers in the context of their particular HEIs.

We show in this chapter how scholarly knowledge about pedagogical training in HEIs in other contexts and academic disciplines, as well as the application of impact research, is vital for formulating the goals, content, and structure of TSDPs. We first review the political and ideological backgrounds of Estonia's HE system, before explaining the theoretical and methodological outlines that form the foundations of the teaching skills development programme. Finally we introduce the results of the impact research of the pedagogical courses and the resulting changes in TSDP. We use the example of the University of Tartu to make our case.

THE CONTEXT: ESTONIAN HIGHER EDUCATION IN TIME OF TRANSITION

After the Soviet Union's 1940 occupation of Estonia, the Soviet education system, regarded in the twenty-first century as the antithesis of good teaching and effective learning, replaced the extant Estonian education system. During the Soviet occupation periods of 1940 and 1944–1991 there were very limited possibilities for developing any independent education policy. Higher education was subject to the necessities of the planned economy, not only politically, administratively, and financially, but also in regard to quality control. The defining aspects of the Soviet Union were the pervasive all-powerful control and supervision systems, which impacted on the education system, and were reflected in the curricula that in the Soviet Union were known as "study plans." A study plan was an official document that was intrinsically stiff, inflexible, and dictatorial in detail concerning the content, number of classes, and methods of conducting classes and assessments from which the lecturers did not have much freedom to plan their teaching independently (Raudsepp 2006). The Soviet system favoured content-centred teaching and the lecturer's main role was to be the imparter of the information, while the students were left with the role of passive listeners.

Political renaissance started with perestroika at the end of 1980s and reached fulfilment with the restoration of independence in 1991, which heralded a period of major changes at all levels in society. Estonia spent the initial years after independence bringing in new legislation to underpin the reorganisation of economic activities and society. Although Soviet HE was efficient in certain respects, it was also responsible for some of the problems Estonian HE faced in post-Soviet times. The most acute aspects were: the ideology and paradigms of education; the structure of education; the relationship between different levels of education; the quality of education; legislation and administration of education; the relative proportions of public and private initiatives and the supply of personnel and finances (Must, Kõrgesaar, and Kala 1995, 307). The Estonian Law of Education, adopted in 1992, declares that the goals of education should include: promoting the development of personality, the family, and the Estonian nation, as well as of national minorities, of Estonian economic, political, and cultural life, and of nature preservation in the global economic and cultural context; to educate loyal citizens; and to set up the prerequisites of continuing education for everyone (Vaht, Udam, and Kütt 2000).

Since 1991, Estonia has undertaken several extensive reforms in the field of HE, including signing the Bologna Declaration in 1999. These reforms took into account the aim of integrating into the structures of the European Union. At the same time, teaching in HE faced multiple external pressures, many of which were closely linked to the process of political and economic transition and the changes in society. As education became more democratic and more accessible, HE experienced rapid expansion in both HEIs and student numbers. There were six HEIs in 1990 with 25,899 enrolled students, but by 2009 there were thirty-four HEIs with 68,986 enrolled students (Estonian Statistical Database 2010). Concomitant to the increases in student numbers was a greater diversity of students (for example, adult learners) and a significant increase in average class size. However, it quickly became apparent that traditional teaching methods and course designs were ill-suited to coping with this expansion.

Consequent to the transition reforms and changes in education, the workloads of academic staff had significantly increased. Yet the education system retained serious flaws, some held over from the Soviet period, in the almost nonexistent support by government and institutions, and academic staff's salaries were among the lowest among intellectual professions. The latter being a prime reason for absence of any competition for teaching positions.

A key flaw in Estonia's HE system is that insufficient attention has been paid to developing university teachers' pedagogical skills. Consequently there exists no government guiding strategy. The initial reaction to providing pedagogical training was fragmented. Every HEI was providing pedagogical training independently, according to their individual needs and resources. As HEIs did not have a common policy of enhancing teaching, some HEIs did not do anything in regard to teaching skill development.

Since the end of the 1990s, e-learning began developing rapidly. The Estonia government had in 1998 allocated funds for Tiigrihüpe (Tiger's Leap), a project aimed at investing in the development and expansion of a nationwide information and communication technology (ICT) network with an emphasis on education. Subsequent to the success of Tiigrihüpe, substantial resources at both governmental and institutional levels were put into developing the infrastructure for an e-learning environment, the success of which tempted many HEIs to transfer a lot of their teaching into e-learning environments.

An important moment for Estonia's TSDP was the accession to the European Union in 2004. Accession gave Estonia the opportunity to apply for funding from the European Regional Development Fund and from the European Social Fund for developing nationally substantial areas. Resources for developing both the overarching quality of HE and academics' teaching skills were given priority status in the field of education for which respective programmes with thorough plans of action were developed.

The receipt of EU funding has meant increased cooperation among HEIs and enabled academic developers to approach upgrading the teaching skills of university teachers in a more systematic and consistent manner. In 2008 EU funding has allowed the establishment of two academic development centres, at the University of Tartu and the University of Tallinn. These centres ascertain university teachers' personal development requirements for university teachers and exchange information about existing pedagogical courses, which are provided by academic developers in faculties. In 2010, they developed a competence model for university teachers, which included teaching among the necessary competencies. Supplementary to the TSDP, a system for the evaluation of university teachers has been developed and is being used in several HEIs and a conference was held in January 2011 that focused for the first time in Estonia on learning and teaching at HEIs. We may reasonably conclude that the HEIs have recognised the TSDP as an important element of the HE system.

DEVELOPING UNIVERSITY TEACHERS' PEDAGOGICAL COURSES AT THE UNIVERSITY OF TARTU

Two key sources supplied the data used in the design, creation, and development of TSDPs in independent Estonia. The primary source was the experience of foreign countries available through research literature, guest lecturers, and collaboration with academic development centres. The secondary source was the context of the HE system in Estonia, the HEIs, and their university teachers. Based on these sources, we have created our own teaching skills development programmes and developed own team of academic developers at the University of Tartu.

Impact Research and Setting the Theoretical Foundations of Our Teaching Skills Course

The scholarly literature indicates that a training course may not necessarily improve teaching quality, and indeed Norton et al. (2005) could find little evidence that training would have an effect on the teaching practices of university teachers. However, several other studies do affirm that pedagogical courses bring about an expanded awareness of teaching and assessment methods and teaching in general, while longer pedagogical courses trigger changes in perception (Gibbs and Coffey 2004; Postareff, Lindblom-Ylänne, and Nevgi 2007; Remmik and Karm 2009).

Gibbs and Coffey (2004) found that university teachers became less teacher-centred and more student-centred by the end of courses lasting four to eighteen months. So, while changes in attitudes (e.g., to a more learning-centred approach) can occur in the course of longer courses, shorter courses seem to have the opposite effect of making university teachers more uncertain about their teaching abilities (Postareff, Lindblom-Ylänne, and Nevgi 2007). Research indicates that training courses can encourage a shift towards the student-focused approach, but this is a slow process (Gibbs and Coffey 2004; Postareff Lindblom-Ylänne, and Nevgi 2007); and without the support of training, university teachers may move in the opposite direction and reduce the extent to which they adopt the student-focused approach (Gibbs and Coffey 2004).

Research into the impact of courses shows that the impact is factor dependent: the length and the quality of the course, the coherence between the course and post-course activities, such as monitoring the classes and consultations (Halliday and Soden 1998; Postareff, Lindblom-Ylänne, and Nevgi, 2007; Remmik and Karm 2009), values dominating in the faculty (Gibbs and Coffey 2004), and HE students' opinions, attitudes, and the actual learning environment (Stes, Clement, and Van Petegem 2007). The training courses' influence on the concepts and practices of academics also devolves on the activities and tasks practiced in the training courses and on the way they are interpreted. The training activities depend strongly on the courses' goals and theoretical conception. Academic developers use different training techniques or strategies because they are trying to achieve different outcomes and different strategic goals (Coffey and Gibbs 2001, 253).

Therefore, our first practical task in developing the programme was to establish its aims. On the basis of the historical and cultural specificities of Estonia's HE system, we considered the familiarization of academic staff with the concept of a learning-centred teaching approach: reflecting on their personal teaching practices and developing and applying the new ideas into their teaching practices as the most urgent and principal goals of our programme. Knowing from the research of Adams and Rytmeister (2000), Kreber (2000), and Åkerlind (2005) that academic life is globally a solitary experience and that supporting networks are crucial in ensuring the long-term effects of training, we added a fourth goal to our agenda, the creation of communities of teaching.

First, we deemed it crucial to make our course participants consciously aware of what they believe about teaching and learning, because this influences how they plan, conduct, and evaluate educational activities. Research findings show that university teachers' personal conceptions of teaching are related to their approaches to teaching, teaching practices, and also to the learning approaches of their students (Trigwell and Prosser 1996; Kember 1997). Kember and Kwan (2000) identify the characteristics of two broad approaches, content-centred and learning-centred approaches, and explain how these approaches relate to the teaching and learning concepts of university teachers.

Once university teachers become more aware of their teaching concepts and their effect on the learning process, they need to understand that learning is best nurtured by learning-centred approaches. Therefore, the aim of explaining the concepts of teaching and learning is to enable teachers to see the value of doing more learning-centred teaching, that is, making a change in their methods toward such a teaching style. This is, however, not an easy task because changing concepts is time-consuming; but, above all, it requires university teachers to develop critical self-reflection.

In the context of university teachers' development, reflection could be defined as a process of thinking about their professional identity, personal teaching theory, and teaching practice that may cause the changes in currently used actions and future strategies. Reflection can help university teachers in making informed decisions, observing and interpreting their activities in the context and planning of teaching. McAlpine and Weston (2000) suggest that reflective practitioners teach more efficiently for three reasons: (i) their reflection focuses on learning from their experience of teaching; (ii) undertaking reflection involves cognitive engagement; (iii) reflection involves a willingness and ability to take risks in their actions.

Consequently, in order to improve professional practice, conscious systematic reflection is required (Boud, Keogh, and Walker 1985; Daudelin 1996). The pressures of academic work often encourage a focus on obtaining a rapid solution for a practical problem—rather than shedding light on the underlying issues (Korthagen and Vasalos 2005). Deeper reflection processes are enhanced by circumstances such as time and place, supporters, a critical friend or colleague, an emotionally supportive environment, the necessary knowledge base, and metacognitive skills (Boud, Keogh, and Walker 1985; Handal and Lauvås 1987; Day 1993; Moon 1999, 2004). In their daily work, university teachers rarely experience all of the necessary conditions for conscious and deep reflection, which is why it is important to make time for, and stress the importance of, doing this on a daily basis during the pedagogical courses.

However, even when teachers learn new concepts and they are enthusiastic about them, the transfer from one context (pedagogical training) to another (teaching) does not happen automatically. The transfer needs metacognitive and reflection skills and strategies to help learners transfer knowledge or skills from one situation to another. Argyris and Schön (1974) contend people have difficulty learning and adopting new theories of action because the theory acted upon is different from the espoused theory and that they may not be aware of the incompatibility of the two theories. Therefore, as it is vital that university teachers make this leap from theory to practice, we developed the curriculum of our programme so as to encourage university teachers to put the new ideas, such as new teaching methods, into practice.

Finally, we aimed at establishing a teaching community of practice, that is, a group of "people who share a concern, a set of problems, or a passion about a topic, and who deepen their knowledge and expertise in this area by interacting on an ongoing basis" (Wenger, McDermott, and Snyder 2002, 4). Our goal in establishing such a community from the course participants of a TSDP was that once participants had finished their coursework, they would have an existing support network to rely on. The community of practice would offset the often experienced professional isolation of university teachers, which is a common experience of both those academics early in their careers and those with more experience (Bolander-Laksov, Mann, and Dahlgren 2008; Barrett et al. 2009).

Ironically, despite the strong preference for individual work in many disciplines, especially in the context of teaching, university teachers conceptualise their knowledge about the discipline and their knowledge about teaching not in isolation or independently but within a community (Kreber 2000). Communities of practice help academics to break out of their isolation by fostering communication and collaboration across HEIs (Kreber 2000).

Thus, a community of practice built around teaching practice can play a vital role in fostering and deepening knowledge. On the one hand, university teachers will evaluate their teaching and invent new ways of organizing teaching and learning, but will also reflect on their practice and share their ideas of new ways to support learning (Bolander-Laksov, Mann, and Dahlgren 2008). Such collective reflection helps university teachers to "step outside" of themselves in order to notice patterns and trends in their work (Kitchen, Parker, and Gallagher 2008). Finally, a teaching community formed during, and supported after a TSDP course is one way to foster the effective application of knowledge learnt at the course.

Using Foreign Expertise in Course Design

We relied on already accumulated knowledge before turning to the scholarly literature on academic development in HE. While we always found it important to take into consideration the local context, we believed we could learn a lot from colleagues in countries that had a tradition of academic development, so we developed contacts with them. Initially the university teacher-targeted TSDP courses were conducted mostly as short-term summer schools and were taught by guest professors.

Since 2004, we have developed TSDP in Estonia and particularly at the University of Tartu. The availability of funding and a systematic approach enabled us to broaden and think about international cooperation strategically. Instead of just inviting guest professors, we now visit professional development centres in other universities and participate in the conferences on higher education teaching and learning.

Our international contacts helped us in the short term by establishing a more vigorous TSDP. For example, the conceptual background of the basic course was designed in cooperation with colleagues from foreign universities such as Gunnar Handal and Kirsten Lycke (University of Oslo,

Norway), Sari Lindblom-Ylänne (University of Helsinki, Finland), and Sam Mathews (University of West Florida, U.S.). They all played an important role in creating the concept and philosophical background of the course. Our international contacts have also helped us in the long term to understand better the specifics of TSDP courses, the role of academic developers and the opportunities for supporting university teachers' learning processes, and ultimately our goal of our own academic development unit.

Pedagogical Courses at the University of Tartu

One of our essential principles has been to offer different TSDP options for university teachers in developing their teaching skills and also to give them the opportunity to select the most appropriate courses for their professional development. As academic developers, we have evaluated the variety of choices, which could give university teachers the freedom to plan their professional development according to their developmental needs. As clear policy guidelines about the importance of TSDPs do not fundamentally exist, we deemed it is best to allow university teachers to decide which of the choice of available courses they would attend, and therefore attendance at our TSDP is voluntary. This "voluntary" aspect gives each teacher a lot of freedom and responsibility to create and direct their own professional development.

We have established various forms of pedagogical courses: a long basic pedagogical course (six ECTS) as well as other short courses (one to three ECTS), which focus on one specific topic (for example, curriculum development, assessment, problem-based learning, teaching strategies, communication skills). There are also summer and winter academies taking place, which started in 2006 and focus on special issues such as active learning, supervision, or students' motivation. These academies are mostly conducted by guest professors.

Since 2004, the University of Tartu provides a long-term professional development programme in pedagogy, "Learning and Teaching in Higher Education" (six ECTS). Although the course is designed as a basic course, experienced university teachers have participated because they did not have any opportunities to attend pedagogical courses at the start of their careers. The TSDP "Learning and Teaching in Higher Education" consists of eight contact days and a combination of peer observation sessions and Web-based support. While course enrolment is voluntary, attendance of participants at all course workshops is mandatory.

Besides the more general principles that we have elaborated previously, we established more direct course objectives. There are two main purposes to each workshop: (i) to introduce and discuss essential pedagogical themes and (ii) to experience and analyse different teaching methods. Within the parameters of our purposes, we established our post-course objectives (outcomes for course participants), and then began to design our course around the key topics and the learning and teaching strategies (see Table 6.1).

Table 6.1   Outcomes and Contents of Basic Teaching Skills Course in the Context of Higher Education Environments

Post-course Outcomes	Key Topics	Learning and Teaching Strategies
Able to understand key theories of learning and teaching	Theories of learning	Interactive lecture
	The roles and dilemmas of teachers	Jigsaw
Know how to plan a learning-centred teaching-learning process in accordance with:	Students as learners	Group discussion
	Course design in accordance with:	Free writing
		Metaphor
(a) learning outcomes	(a) learning outcomes	Academic controversy
(b) assessment methods	(b) assessment	Case study
(c) learning strategies	(c) learning strategies	Circulating review
Acquired skills for implementing in practice methods of:	(d) teaching strategies	Graphic organiser
	Possibilities for	Role play
(a) learning	(a) group work	Debate
(b) teaching	(b) students' motivation	Teaching case
(c) assessment	(c) supervision	Think-pair-share
Able to understand the process of supervision	(d) ethical issues	Peer Observation
Have experienced reflection strategies to develop their teaching		

It is an important principle for us to use different learning-teaching methods in the training courses so that the participants themselves could experience how the different teaching-learning methods work and so they could apply them later in their own teaching practice. Between the course's classes, participants submit individual assignments in the virtual e-learning environment "Moodle." All course participants add examples of their amended learning outcomes and assessment criteria and also summaries of scientific articles, discussions, and so on. The main aim of using Moodle is to learn about the possibilities of using virtual e-environments in the teaching-learning process and to encourage communication among course participants.

A substantial element of the basic TSDP is the peer observation of teaching practice in small groups of four course participants and a mentor. The role of the mentor is to organise the setup of the visits and to coordinate the process of feedback among the members. The practice of conducting peer observations is not commonly practised among Estonian university teachers, which creates quite a challenge for academic developers in fostering a collegial and supportive atmosphere.

In the process of enhancing the basic course, we have also added an individual observational visit by the mentor, which means that each course participant's class is visited twice, first by the mentor alone and second by the group. The benefit of two observations is that the course participants might feel more relaxed with just the mentor, as opposed to the whole group, observing.

The course participants also have to create their portfolios during the course. The first part of the portfolio contains the reflective materials created during the course, for example, reflection exercises, analysis from peer observations, and the final essay. The second part includes an improved syllabus of one course taught by the course participants consisting of learning outcomes, teaching methods, and assessment criteria and methods.

IMPROVING OUR PROGRAMME: THE IMPACT OF UNIVERSITY TEACHERS' TRAINING

Since the number of TSDP courses and their graduates showed a constant increase, we were keen to find out if the training courses have any actual impact on the course participants' teaching practices. Therefore we carried out an impact research study on the courses. We needed to ascertain whether our principles and their interpretations into course structure and content were effective in the academic culture of the University of Tartu. In the course of our impact research, we established four domains that we paid particular attention to: (i) knowledge gained from the training course; (ii) application of the new knowledge and skills into practice; (iii) the formation of the communities of practice on teaching; and (iv) changes in the feedback of course participants' students.

The last of these was included as we recognised that we can only refer to improvement in teaching if it benefits students. Furthermore, student feedback is a key aspect of professional practice for university teachers in enabling them to improve their teaching (Nicholls 2002; Ramsden 2003).

Methodology

We used twenty semi-structured interviews with university teachers, conducted between December 2007 and May 2008, as the research method for examining the impact of the pedagogical courses. All twenty university teachers had taken part in the training courses for at least six ECTS (i.e., they had attended one long course or a mix of short courses). The teachers had come from four academic disciplines: humanities (five), medicine (two), social sciences (three), exact and natural sciences (seven). The interviews focused on the university teachers' teaching concepts and approaches but each was also asked why they had attended the pedagogical courses and what they had learned and then applied into the practice. All the interviews were transcribed and analysed with the help of thematic coding (Flick 2006).

RESULTS

The overall evaluation of our training courses was positive. The interviewees pointed out that they had learned several teaching aspects during the course. They gained more comprehensive knowledge of teaching and acquired a clearer vision of the teaching-learning process (including establishing the learning goals, feedback planning, and its significance in the success of the whole teaching-learning process). One outcome was that opportunities for enhancing the learning-teaching methods are appreciated. The interviewees positively mentioned the following aspects of the courses: (i) becoming acquainted with new learning-teaching methods, (ii) experiencing these new methods during the course, and (iii) analysing previously used methods in depth.

It also appears that our courses helped participants in improving their teaching through reflection:

> I started doing things more consciously. I have used a number of methods sub-consciously. Probably I have gone half-way but now I could give the method a name and meaning and I learned to see how to go full way to get maximum benefit out of it. (Tiina)

After the pedagogical courses, the interviewees had also noticed positive changes in their students' feedback, in that they have welcomed the use of more diverse teaching-learning methods. Also the more systematically structured teaching-learning process and methods of assessment have received positive feedback from the students.

Moreover, several interviewees said that as a result of attending the courses they had started to use a more student-centred approach in the teaching-learning process. They had tried to use more student involvement and also learned to look at teaching processes from the students' perspectives and started to value communication more than their own lecturing in the teaching-learning process. In addition, they had also reached the understanding that learning requires time and time is something that HE students need to be given.

On a more personal level, the interviewees acknowledged that taking part in the course had helped them to find a balance in their teaching and confirmation that they are on the right track. The courses had also helped the interviewees to understand that problems in teaching are just a natural part of the process and are not signs of their own inabilities.

While the knowledge and experiences gained from the course received mostly positive feedback, the application of this knowledge into their teaching practice proved to be a stumbling-block for a number of the interviewees. As one interviewee, Mirjam, explains, new methods did not automatically work:

> I couldn't efficiently apply some things that I practiced *myself* at the course. This means that it needs some more training on how to do

things the way that there would be some essential result as well or something. (Mirjam)

She also added:

> When I tried out some of these methods on my students, I got the feeling that they don't work. They were somehow childish, hollow or . . . I think that deeper digging or contemplation is needed in order to figure out why I'm messing around with those coloured labels. So that it wouldn't turn into kindergarten folding and pasting lesson, so that it would have some more substantial justification other than it's cooler or funnier.

Failure to apply new methods could occur for several reasons: the theoretical background of new teaching-learning methods was not clear enough; the university teachers had not yet started to believe in them (i.e., a change in their teaching concepts had not yet taken place); and their hesitations were visible or they did not know how to connect the method with the specifics of their subject.

Problems might also have occurred if they had not informed their students about the changes in teaching methods. Changes in teaching methods may receive a negative reaction from students, if neither the university teacher nor their students know how to react to the challenges created by the new teaching situation. Using collaborative teaching methods requires group leadership skills, which, if the university teacher does not possess, need to be acquired.

Our initial reasoning about the importance of communities of practice has been confirmed. However, it is a challenging concept in Estonian academic culture because most of the interviewees indicated that it is not common practice in Estonian HEIs to share teaching problems amongst colleagues. However, all the interviewees did admit that at the beginning of their careers, the aspect they missed the most was the opportunity to consult with a peer university teacher. On many occasions, they were simply too shy to ask for help. One of the interviewees articulated this as:

> It's not popular to speak about teaching in our workplace, it's probably not popular anywhere. Everybody thinks he or she is a professional. I was even weird to talk about teaching—if you are already holding a position or have been elected, then you should know how to do things. How could you say or ask how things should be done . . . It is viewed as exposure of your weakness, exposure of your shortcomings. (Tiina)

We also achieved our aim of helping to establish communities of practice during the courses. The interviewees noted that they had started to discuss teaching with their colleagues more frequently and even described the notion of regular discussions between colleagues, if several of them from the same HEI had taken part in the course. Also, communication between colleagues from different disciplines has increased, which has helped to understand the specifics of teaching other disciplines and to come to the realization that many of the teaching problems are similar, irrespective the discipline.

> I really liked to get together with the lecturers from other faculties, especially because we do not meet otherwise. And for example it was very interesting to hear that in some other faculty group work was done on daily basis while it is never done in our faculty. Before talking to these people I didn't know that things work differently in other faculties. I just have not thought about the fact that learning in the faculty of physics or philosophy could be this different. (Erkki)

Yet a lot of challenges remain, especially when it comes to changing teaching methods in practice. We have presented examples of how, despite the course participants' best intentions, new methods learnt at the course do not work in practice. We also had to realize that many of our course participants faced additional barriers to changing their methods; specifically, a lack of motivation and the teacher-centred teaching traditions in their disciplines. Gibbs and Coffey's (2004, 98) findings support our result that if the values and attitudes in the course participant's faculty differ from those learnt at the course, the training course will not have an effect on teaching performance. Furthermore, pressure for teacher-centred teaching may play a role as well as peer pressure in the form of criticism for moving away from traditional methods (Gibbs and Coffey 2004, 98).

In our particular context, a medical teacher admitted to having doubts as to whether the teaching traditions of medicine were the most supportive for the students to learn. At the same time, she said that despite attending the course her teaching method had not really changed. This outcome was mostly due to a lack of confidence and motivation but also because she viewed teaching as an annoying obligation to her medical practice.

The impact of the courses depends on the course participant's motivation to be open for changes and to have the willingness to teach even better in the future. Several interviewees suggested that, had they attended several courses, they still would not have changed their teaching practice. The explanations are varied: the teachers were self-satisfied with their performance, and did not consequently have any doubts about their teaching methods and did not let the course have an impact. Also, the more positive feedback from the students supported this opinion and did not give reasons to the teacher to believe that introducing changes to their teaching was necessary. One of the interviewees acknowledged that although their teaching had not changed much after the course, they had started to contemplate their teaching more frequently.

Our research also confirmed that it takes time for the changes to develop and might not happen during a short course (Postareff, Lindblom-Ylänne, and Nevgi 2007, 2008). For example, one interviewee pointed out that the short training course (over two consecutive days) did not give the opportunity for analysing topics in depth. For that reason, the discussion of an important topic remained superficial and therefore the interviewee deemed it unsuitable for his/her teaching practice.

Programme Change: Establishing a Follow-Up Activity

As a result of the impact research study, we realised that university teachers need support when they start to implement new strategies in their teaching practice; and therefore we, as academic developers, had a new challenge in devising a method to encourage university teachers to implement new ideas.

In order to motivate and support teachers in applying their learning-centred methods into practice, and to create opportunities for the notion of a supportive community and self-analysis, we designed an experimental follow-up course, based on the concept of community of practice—"Colleague to Colleague." This course consisted of five sessions with peer observations within one semester. The prerequisite for attending "Colleague to Colleague" was to have attended and completed the "Teaching and Learning in Higher Education" course.

The formal post-course objectives are primarily that course participants have applied at least one new method or idea into their teaching practice and have analysed the results of applying the new idea as well as drawing conclusions for the future. A secondary set of objectives is that the course participants have been consciously developing their professional skills and have received feedback via peer observations.

The format of the "Colleague to Colleague" course enables course participants to experiment with new alternative methods and to analyse their teaching via the sharing of their experiences, reflecting on them and receiving the support and feedback from the group of course participants. At the beginning of the course we deal with course participants' self-analysis and self-conceptions with the aim of making concrete or experimental teaching plans. We also ask course participants to express their needs, so that we can select which topics to focus on during the activities of community of practice. In every successive session we focus on one teaching theme and on the analysis of the experience of implementing of new ideas in teaching practice.

For the purpose of evaluating the results of the "Colleague to Colleague" programme, the semi-structured interviews were carried out with all participants of the course after the programme. The "Colleague to Colleague" courses have revealed several aspects that academic developers should pay attention to in order to ensure that a course based on this type of collaboration and cooperation is successful. One of those aspects is the low level of interest towards classroom observations. Integral to the "Colleague to Colleague" course is the agreement amongst the course participants to observe each other's teaching. But as we have explained earlier, there is no tradition in Estonian HEIs of conducting peer observations, so participating in one as a university teacher is a high-stress situation for which there is little enthusiasm. Nevertheless, one of course participants did acknowledge that the peer observation was an eye-opening experience:

> This classroom observation is quite a good thing indeed. It helps more than just a sterile discussion. I myself would not have noticed all the aspects that we all jointly paid attention to during the classroom observation. All the things that have an impact on the teaching/learning process. (Jaan)

Another aspect that needs more attention is the emphasis of systematic and deep reflection. Reflection taking place in the "Colleague to Colleague" sessions was mostly surface, meta-level talk and viewed in the context of problem solving (Seligman 2008; Noordewier, Korthagen, and Zwart 2009). Because university teachers are not accustomed to reflect on their teaching, they need guidance and support to find the focus for the analysis of their practice. Therefore, the communities of practice must ensure that all course participants feels they are members of a discreet, friendly, and supportive group, which will support any member willing to risk applying new methods to their teaching practices, as well helping them with reflective self-analysis. In summary, we conclude that a follow-up activity like the "Colleague to Colleague" course is a suitable format for helping university teachers in applying new methods into their teaching practices and should be considered as a natural element any TSDP.

CONCLUSION

Our personal experience as academic developers and research results have shown that the TSDP courses for university teachers are essential for both the course participants and the quality of all HE's learning-teaching processes and should be a more visible element of each HEI's quality system.

Similar to the results of research into raising the quality of teaching in HE, our study affirms that not every course triggers a change in teaching practice. Changes only take place as a result of longer courses and several ensuring activities such as classroom observations, follow-up courses, and consultations (Halliday and Soden 1998; Gibbs and Coffey, 2004; Postareff, Lindblom-Ylänne, and Nevgi, 2007). Our experience has shown that the implementation of new ideas and strategies needs more support, which means that the entire pedagogical development plan and the structure of the courses must support the implementation of knowledge gained from courses into real-life teaching practice. This outcome requires constant reflection on both: the experiences during the course and the development of practice.

The development of teaching skills needs to be supported by broadening the variety of course activities: follow-up activities, mentoring, communities of practice, conferences, networking, and so on. We deem it vital that university teachers should not rely on TSDP courses to develop their teaching skills, but that they should examine and analyse their teaching experiences. Self-analysis of teaching experiences is vital for developing the scholarship of teaching, for which reason we are designing courses on pedagogical research (research methodology, action research, etc.) for university teachers of all academic disciplines.

The context of the professional development of university teachers is changing constantly and the ever-changing system requires changes in development activities as well. Researchers such as Diseth (2007), Postareff, Lindblom-Ylänne, and Nevgi (2007, 2008), and Cilliers and Herman (2010) indicate that it is essential to analyse the efficacy of pedagogical courses and other development activities and their influence on the education quality of HEIs. Based on the analysis so far, research needs to develop an unobtrusive monitoring system that would provide university teachers with a reliable flow of pertinent data concerning the teachers' skills development activities and requirements.

By developing our TSDP courses we are following the same principles as described by Lindblom-Ylänne and Hämäläinen (2004) to enhance research-based educational development. It is vital that educational development is not based on feelings or intuitions but on research results. This is the only way it is possible to develop the best and the most functional teaching and learning methods for each discipline and each learning context (Lindblom-Ylänne and Hämäläinen 2004). We have realised that next step in the impact research of university teachers' training needs to incorporate classroom observations.

International collaboration has played a substantial role in forming Estonia's TSDP and establishing the academic developers. For the future development of the TSDP, this collaboration must continue towards the goal of collaboration in the field of research of teaching as well. The University of Tartu has managed to create the team of academic developers, who are committed to develop and carry out high-quality courses. As the next step, we aim at advancing our research into the effects of our programme to keep up with international standards.

If we wish to achieve the systematic and sustainable development of the pedagogical courses, policymakers need to be aware that onetime projects are no longer sufficient and that pedagogical training courses are an inseparable element in the quality of education at HEIs and would also provide the necessary means for HE to function and develop.

BIBLIOGRAPHY

Åkerlind, Gerlese. 2005. "Postdoctoral Researchers' Roles, Functions and Career Prospects." *Higher Education Research & Development* 24 (1): 21–40.
Adams, Maya, and Catherine Rytmeister. 2000. "Beginning the Academic Career: How Can It Best Be Supported in the Changing University Climate?" Conference proceedings of the Australian Society for Education Technology and Higher Education Research and Development Society of Australasia, University of Southern Queensland, 2–5 July, http://www.ascilite.org.au/aset-archives/confs/aset-herdsa2000/procs/adams.html, accessed 12/02/2010.
Argyris, Chris, and Donald A. Schön. 1974. *Theory into Practice*. San Francisco: Jossey-Bass.
Barrett, Margaret S., Julie Ballantyne, Scott Harrison, and Nita Temmerman. 2009. "On Building a Community of Practice: Reflective Narratives of Academic Learning and Growth." *Reflective Practice* 10 (4): 403–416.
Bolander-Laksov, Klara, Sarah Mann, and Lars Owe Dahlgren. 2008. "Developing a Community of Practice around Teaching: A Case Study." *Higher Education Research & Development* 27(2): 121–132.
Boud, David, Rosemary Keogh, and David Walker. 1985. "Promoting Reflection in Learning: A Model." In *Reflection: Turning Experience into Learning*, edited by David Boud, Rosemary Keogh, and David Walker, 18–40. London: Kogan Page.
Cilliers, Francois J., and Nicoline Herman. 2010. "Impact of an Educational Development Programme on Teaching Practice of Academics at a Research-Intensive University." *International Journal for Academic Development* 15(3): 253–267.
Coffey, Martin, and Graham Gibbs. 2001. "The Strategic Goals of Training of University Teachers." In *Improving Student Learning: Proceedings of the 8th International Symposium*, edited by Chris Rust, 253–261. Oxford: The Oxford Centre for Staff and Learning Development.
Daudelin, Marilyn Wood. 1996. "Learning from Experience through Reflection." *Organisational Dynamics* 24(3): 36–48.
Day, Christopher. 1993. "Reflection: A Necessary but Not Sufficient Condition for Professional Development." *British Educational Research Journal* 19 (1): 83–93.
Diseth, Åge. 2007. "Students' Evaluation of Teaching, Approaches to Learning, and Academic Achievement." *Scandinavian Journal for Educational Research* 51(2): 185–204.
Estonian Statistical Database. 2010, http://pub.stat.ee/pxweb.2001/Database/Sotsi aalelu/05Haridus/10Kergharidus/10Kergharidus.as, accessed 13/04/2010.
Flick, Uwe. 2006. *An Introduction to Qualitative Research*. London, Thousand Oaks, New Dehli: Sage Publications.
Gibbs, Graham, and Martin Coffey. 2004. "The Impact of Training of University Teachers on Their Teaching Skills, Their Approach to Teaching and the Approach to Learning of Their Students." *Active Learning in Higher Education* 5: 87–100.
Halliday, John, and Rebecca Soden. 1998. "Facilitating Changes in Lecturers' Understanding of Learning." *Teaching in Higher Education* 3 (1): 21–36.
Handal, Gunnar, and P. Per Lauvås. 1987. *Promoting Reflective Teaching: Supervision in Action*. Milton Keynes, UK: SRHE and Open University Press.
Kember, David. 1997. "A Reconceptualization of the Research into University Academics' Conceptions of Teaching." *Learning and Instruction* 7: 255–275.

Kember, David, and Kam-Por Kwan. 2000. "Lecturers' Approaches to Teaching and Their Relationship to Conceptions of Good Teaching." *Instructional Science* 28: 469–490.

Kitchen, Julien, Darlene Ciuffett Parker, and Tiffany Gallagher. 2008. "Authentic Conversation as Faculty Development: Establishing a Self-Study Group in a Faculty of Education." *Studying Teacher Education* 4 (2): 157–171.

Korthagen, Fred, and Angelo Vasalos. 2005. "Levels in Reflection: Core Reflection as a Means to Enhance Professional Growth." *Teachers and Teaching: Theory and practice* 11 (1): 47–71.

Kreber, Carolin. 2000. "How University Teaching Award Winners Conceptualise Academic Work: Some Further Thoughts on the Meaning of Scholarship." *Teaching in Higher Education* 5 (1): 61–78.

Lindblom-Ylänne, Sari, and Kauko Hämäläinen. 2004. "The Bologna Declaration as a Tool to Enhance Learning and Instruction at the University of Helsinki." *International Journal for Academic Development* 9 (2): 153–165.

McAlpine, Lynn, and Cynthia Weston. 2000. "Reflection: Issues Related to Improving Professors' Teaching and Students' Learning." *Instructional Science* 28: 363–385.

Moon, Jennifer A. 1999. *Reflection in Learning and Professional Development: Theory and Practice.* London: Routledge/Kogan Page.

———. 2004. *A Handbook of Reflective and Experiential Learning: Theory and Practice.* London, New York: Routledge Falmer.

Must, Olev, Jaan Kõrgesaar, and Ulve Kala. 1995. "Estonia." In *International Encyclopedia of National Systems of Education*, edited by Neville T. Postlethwaite. Oxford: Pergamon.

Nicholls, Gill. 2002. *Developing Teaching and Learning in Higher Education.* London: Routledge Falmer.

Noordewier, Saskia, Fred Korthagen, and Rosanne Zwart. 2009. "Promoting Quality from within: Towards a New Perspective on Professional Development and Changes in School Culture." Paper presented at the EARLI Conference, Amsterdam, 25–29 August.

Norton, Lin, John T. E. Richardson, James Hartley, Stephen Newstead, and Jenny Mayes. 2005. "Teachers' Beliefs and Intentions Concerning Teaching in Higher Education." *Higher Education* 50: 537–571.

Postareff, Liisa, Sari Lindblom-Ylänne, and Anne Nevgi. 2007. "The Effect of Pedagogical Training on Teaching in Higher Education. *Teaching and Teacher Education* 23 (5): 557–571.

———. 2008. "A Follow-Up Study of the Effect of Pedagogical Training on Teaching in Higher Education." *Higher Education* 56: 29–43.

Ramsden, Paul. 2003. *Learning to Teach in Higher Education.* London: Routledge.

Raudsepp, Margit. 2006. "Õppekavaarendusest Eesti kõrgkoolides aastatel 1980–2002." *Õppekavaarendus kõrgkoolis*, edited by Siret Rutiku and Tõnu Lehtsaar: Tartu: Tartu Ülikooli Kirjastus.

Remmik, Marvi, and Mari Karm. 2009. "Koolituse mõju õppejõudude õpetamisoskustele–väljakutsed ja võimalused." *Haridus* 11–12: 20–26.

Scott, Peter. 2003. "Challenges to Academic Values and the Organisation of Academic Work in a Time of Globalization." *Higher Education in Europe* 28 (3): 295–307.

Seligman, Martin E. P. 2008. *Ehe õnn.* Tallinn: Pilgrim.

Stes, Ann, Miekke Clement, and Peter Van Petegem. 2007. "The Effectiveness of a Faculty Training Programme: Long-Term and Institutional Impact." *International Journal for Academic Development* 12 (2): 99–109.

Trigwell, Keith, and Michael T. Prosser. 1996. "Changing Approaches to Teaching: A Relational Perspective." *Studies in Higher Education* 21: 275–284.

Vaht, Gunnar, Maiki Udam, and Kadri Kütt. 2000. "A Brief History of Higher Education." In *Higher Education in Estonia*. Tallinn: Tallinna Raamatutrükikoda.

Wenger, Etienne, Richard A. McDermott, and William Snyder. 2002. *Cultivating Communities of Practice. A Guide to Managing Knowledge*. Boston: Harvard Business School Press.

7 Institutional Factors in Re-Designing an Accredited Continuing Professional Development Course in Northern Ireland

Vicky Davies and Sarah Maguire

Traditionally the design and development of an accredited professional development course for higher education teaching and learning takes as its baseline and its impetus the generic needs of the individual. A sector-wide understanding of the extent of these has been established within the UK over the last fifteen years, which has culminated in a proliferation of postgraduate certificates in higher education teaching practice alongside which have been developed the UK Professional Standards Framework for teaching and supporting learning in higher education (Higher Education Academy 2006).

Whilst useful as general reference points, it has become increasing clear that this approach lacks institutional contextualisation and specificity. This chapter switches the direction of causation between institutional factors and professional development courses. It shows that institutional factors have a crucial role in the design of professional development courses, and describes the impact of institutional factors on course design within the context of the University of Ulster.

LITERATURE REVIEW

The traditional role of a university has long been viewed as one which embodies academic freedom and autonomy: academic staff are recognised as discipline experts and there has been no requirement for them to undertake a formal teaching qualification (Blackmore et al. 2010, 106). However, the last twenty years or so has seen a shift in the perception of what constitutes the role of a higher education institution (HEI), and the question of professionalism in the sector has come under closer scrutiny on a number of levels (Higher Education Academy and Genetics Education Networking for Innovation and Excellence Centre for Excellence in Teaching and Learning [GENIE CETL] 2009a, 23).

From a national perspective there is evidence that professionalism in UK higher education has been identified as an important issue since 1987, when the Committee of Vice-Chancellors and Principals (CVCP) called for lecturers "to maintain and enhance professional standards in teaching" (1987, 5). Ten years later, the Dearing report (1997) recognised that the future of higher education in the UK was dependent on the professionalism and commitment of its staff, and recommended that "institutions of higher education begin immediately to develop or seek access to programmes for teacher training of their staff, if they do not have them, and that all institutions seek national accreditation of such programmes" (Dearing 1997, Recommendation 13). In 2003, the government white paper *The Future of Higher Education* (Department for Education and Skills [DfES] 2003)—in anticipation of the professional standards to be agreed on—expected "all new teaching staff to obtain a teaching qualification which meets the standards from 2006" and the development of institutional "policies and systems to ensure that all staff are engaged in continuing professional development to maintain, develop and update their skills" (DfES 2003, 50).

The advent of the Higher Education Academy's UK Professional Standards Framework (Higher Education Academy 2006), developed in consultation with the sector, allows institutions to align their professional development programmes to a series of descriptors to ensure that teaching and learning standards are being met. The UK Professional Standards Framework (UK PSF) currently provides descriptors at three levels, against which institutions may determine their own criteria, thus affording them a contextual perspective and interpretation (Higher Education Academy 2006, 4). Table 7.1 shows the descriptors for Levels One and Two, together with indicative staff groups and the areas of activity to be covered, which provides the framework for the postgraduate certificate developed at the University of Ulster.

More recently, the *Independent Review of Higher Education Funding and Student Finance* (Browne 2010, 8) has called for improvement of "provision across the whole sector, within a framework that guarantees minimum standards," and the new chief executive of the Higher Education Academy, Professor Craig Mahoney, is reportedly in favour of new academics undertaking a formal teaching qualification (Attwood 2010).

Whilst maintaining its role as a place of academic learning, the very nature of the university has changed in recent times in response to external drivers and what may be deemed market forces. Universities in the UK are currently "coping with very volatile internal and external pressures" (Laycock 2010, 27): those associated with the notion of accountability and value for money are particularly prevalent given the recent proposal regarding university fees (Browne 2010). Reported increases in student complaints (Shepherd and Williams 2010) have prompted many to fear the rise of managerialism at the expense of academic autonomy (Barnett 2003; Archer 2008, 267; Winter 2009, 122). Some, however, would argue that

Table 7.1   UK PSF Standard Descriptors One and Two

Standard Descriptor	Example of Staff Group	Areas of Activity
Demonstrates an understanding of the student learning experience through engagement with at least 2 of the 6 areas of activity, appropriate core knowledge and professional values; the ability to engage in practices related to those areas of activity; the ability to incorporate research, scholarship, and/or professional practice into those activities	Postgraduate teaching assistants, staff new to higher education teaching with no prior qualification or experience, staff whose professional role includes a small range of teaching and learning support activity	1. Design and planning of learning activities and/or programmes of study 2. Teaching and/or supporting student learning 3. Assessment and giving feedback to learners 4. Developing effective environments and student support and guidance 5. Integration of scholarship, research, and professional activities with teaching and supporting learning 6. Evaluation of practice and continuing professional development
Demonstrates an understanding of the student learning experience through engagement with all areas of activity, core knowledge and professional values; the ability to engage in practices related to all areas of activity; the ability to incorporate research, scholarship, and/or professional practice into those activities	Staff who have a substantive role in learning and teaching to enhance the student experience	

Source: Higher Education Academy 2006, 3–4.

the operational aspects of universities no longer differ greatly from those of any large corporation (Bargh et al. 2000): increased competition, entrepreneurial necessity, and global economies mean that higher education is now subject to more rigorous checks and balances to ensure quality provision and customer satisfaction.

This emphasis on commercial and performative viability means that comparisons between universities and other commercial enterprises are easily drawn. There are, however, significant differences between the two types of organisation, not least of which involves the staff profile. In the commercial sector staff are predominantly employed for the specific professional qualities and/or qualifications they possess, which are commensurate with the position and role they have within the company.

A key difference, however, between the academic staff profile and that of its counterpart in the commercial sector is the apparent duality of roles: on the one hand academics are discipline specialists and on the other teachers (Rodaway 2007, 1; Kreber 2010, 172). In terms of their discipline specialism, academic staff have been allowed a considerable degree of freedom, and it is often the case that an individual's research may be somewhat removed from the curriculum content of the undergraduate programmes they teach. This notion of academic freedom may sit uneasily with the need to conform with an increasing number of checks and balances regarding teaching and learning which may influence the commercial viability of the institution in which they work.

The potential dichotomy of the academic role—discipline specialist and teacher—can be difficult to manage. The challenge to maintain currency on both fronts is not easy, and one which may be under additional strain if, as Olssen and Peters (2005, 313) claim, "The traditional culture of open intellectual enquiry and debate has been replaced with an institutional stress on performativity." In order to ensure a standard quality of teaching and learning across institutional provision, the traditional response of universities in the UK has been to instigate a Postgraduate Certificate in Higher Education teaching, and indeed this has been the widespread response of HEIs in the UK. According to research carried out by Gosling (2010, 1) on a sample of eighty-two UK HEIs, 80.5 percent required staff to complete all or part of the postgraduate certificate on offer, with the remaining 13.4 percent requiring staff to at least engage with this provision. Opinions vary on the efficacy of such approach, particularly since, as Gosling (2010, 3) points out, "institutions have little formal power" to enforce completion: such programmes need therefore to be characterised by development and professional engagement (Skelton 2005) so as to avoid becoming a mere exercise in compliance (Harvey and Knight 1996, 163; Land 2001, 4; Peters 2010, 45). Despite these opposing attitudes, Gosling (2010, 3) concedes that many of those who have been exposed to such programmes "have become enthusiastic advocates of the importance of a professional approach to teaching and assessment in higher education."

Given, therefore, the inextricable link between performance and funding (Bamber 2002, 11) at institutional level, and its attendant implications for academic staff, the need for "academic employability" (Rothwell and Rothwell 2010, 13) underpins the shift towards professional development, and has brought about significant changes in institutional priorities, not least of which is the "emergence of institutional CPD frameworks and the requirement by academic staff to undergo formalised teacher training" (Lynch 2006, 2).

Peters (2010, 45) counsels against the rush to instigate a Continuing Professional Development (CPD) framework without first conducting a review of institutional needs in order that the framework itself may be appropriately contextualised. Indeed, the notion of professional development as a "process that depends very much on the individual's own self-awareness" (Harvey and Knight 1996, 163; Blackmore et al. 2010, 108) would seem to run counter to a system based on institutional imperatives, but the two aspects are inextricably linked (Brew 2006, 107; Gosling 2009, 6; Mårtensson and Roxå 2009, 213). The contextualisation of the CPD framework at institutional level is therefore key (Gosling 2010, 4; Peters 2010, 50), and should take into account a broader reflection of academic practice (Light and Cox 2001, 38) situated within the wider institutional processes and systems. Peter's (2010, 50) Staff Professional Development (SPD) Framework diagram (reproduced below in Figure 7.1) illustrates the institutional factors that are brought to bear on a CPD framework.

It should be noted from the above that reward, recognition, and promotion feature prominently, and should form an integral part of any CPD framework (Kynaston and Maynard 2010, 159) but crucially these should be in the form of rewards that are understood by academics (Ramsden 1995, 14). Although Hall (2010, 40) claims that for the academics she interviewed "money was not the issue . . . nor really promotion," it is evident from other studies (Ramsden et al. 1995; Parker 2008; Higher Education

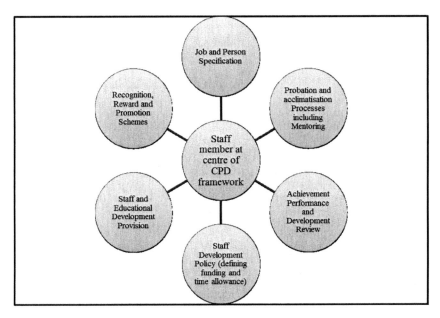

Figure 7.1   Relationships of an SPD Framework to other university systems and processes. Source: Peters 2010, 50.

Academy and Genetics Education Networking for Innovation and Excellence Centre for Excellence in Teaching and Learning [GENIE CETL] 2009a, 2009b) that academics value the importance of teaching, and that formalised institutional recognition should be a key consideration, particularly given the perceived favour afforded research within higher education. Although national recognition schemes are already in place, it has been suggested that at this level they have limited impact on the improved status of teaching (Higher Education Academy and GENIE CETL 2009a, 53). It is institutional recognition that "can play an important role in changing and embedding the culture" (Higher Education Academy and GENIE CETL 2009b, 2), and institutional policies are key to this paradigm shift in perception. The report goes further, and echoes calls (Ramsden et al.1995; DfES 2003) for the acquisition of a formal teaching qualification in higher education to be mandatory for all.

It should further be recognised that if academic professionalism in higher education is to be promoted and developed, there is a need to widen its scope from that of simply teaching and learning since it occurs "within a complex array of competing challenges and perspectives" (Crawford 2008, 143). In today's university it is not only the academic member of staff who provides teaching and learning support for students, and the range of professional practice is therefore much wider (Rowland et al. 1998, 133; Blackmore and Blackwell 2003, 20; Brand 2007, 9). At the University of Ulster, for example, staff from a wide range of non-academic departments—library, careers development, staff development, student support services as well as a range of technical staff and postgraduate demonstrators—are involved in supporting or delivering undergraduate teaching and learning. The roles of the respective staff are therefore evolving to meet these changing responsibilities.

In response to this diversification of roles and responsibilities, Clegg (2003, 46–47) makes three key observations regarding the scope of CPD, which she suggests should promote:

- Activities which are not limited to teaching and learning but which seek to reflect more wide-ranging professional practice in higher education;
- Inclusivity of provision and opportunity for all higher education personnel;
- Development which occurs in both formal and informal settings.

Complementary to the suggestions above is the ISIS model proposed by Blackmore et al. (2010, 111), whose broad principles can beneficially be applied to academic development in higher education:

- *Inclusive*—to acknowledge the contribution of all staff contributing to learning and teaching support;

- *Strategic*—to be positioned within the wider context of UK HE and facilitate both individual and organisational priorities;
- *Integrated*—to encompass a holistic approach to academic and related activities;
- *Scholarly*—to be grounded in quality research.

In developing the new Postgraduate Certificate in Higher Education Practice, the course team at Ulster sought to adopt these suggestions within the wider context of prevailing institutional factors and the impetus for increased professionalism.

ULSTER CONTEXT

The University of Ulster is situated in Northern Ireland. It comprises four campuses dispersed throughout the country, recruits approximately twenty-five thousand students (University of Ulster 2010, 2), and employs over three thousand staff. The university, through its Corporate Plan, Teaching and Learning Strategy and Research Strategy (University of Ulster 2006, 2008a, 2009a), aspires to be the leading provider of professional education for professional life on the island of Ireland, and also to undertake excellent research in selected areas of activity.

In terms of its entry level, the university welcomes a wide range of students who have diverse educational backgrounds. Although the majority of students come to the institution directly from school, having completed academic qualifications such as A levels,[1] there are many whose experience is different: examples of this diversity include vocational qualifications, pre-undergraduate foundation courses, industrial experience as well as qualifications from other countries, most notably given the geographical location from the Republic of Ireland. It should also be noted that the number of full-time undergraduate students from lower socioeconomic backgrounds is 16 percent higher than the UK national average.

CONTINUING PROFESSIONAL DEVELOPMENT

In 2007/08 the university demonstrated its commitment and approach to professional development through a dual approach.

Establishing a CPD Policy

Firstly, the approval of a continuing professional development policy and associated codes of practice for staff (University of Ulster 2009b) are tailored to meet institutional needs (Gosling 2010; Peters 2010). The extract from the policy below encapsulates this:

The University is committed to supporting and developing its staff to enable the achievement of institutional objectives and realisation of its staff's potential not only in the early stages of their career but throughout their employment. This is articulated in both the University value "provide quality learning and development for students and staff" and the Corporate Plan (2006–2010/11) key supporting objectives "to encourage all academic staff to undertake scholarly activity to support learning, teaching and enhancement in their subject" and "to ensure that staff engage on an on-going basis in appropriate career development and Continuing Professional Development (CPD) activities" based on a broad definition of CPD as being "any process or activity, planned or otherwise, that contributes to an increase in, or maintenance of knowledge, skills and personal qualities related to the person's role." (University of Ulster 2009b)

Centre for Higher Education Practice

Secondly, to further support professional development, the university established in 2008–09 a Centre for Higher Education Practice (University of Ulster 2008b) which functions as a facilitating and enabling arm of the Teaching and Learning portfolio, with the primary role of progressing the implementation of aspects of the Teaching and Learning Strategy (2008/09–2012/13), in collaboration with other key players within the institution. This is to be achieved through:

- Leadership (new ideas, approaches, and direction), drawing on national and international models, and providing a platform, with appropriate scholarly underpinning, to carry pedagogic initiatives forward;
- Support (advice, guidance, project funding) for academic and learning support staff to pursue enthusiasms and engage in practice that will enrich the learning experience for students;
- Opportunity (to participate in conversations and activities that address strategic priorities);
- Challenge (in addressing changing paradigms in higher education).

This dual institutional perspective was therefore a key driver for the reconfiguration of the existing programme.

POSTGRADUATE CERTIFICATE IN HIGHER EDUCATION PRACTICE

Historical Context

In 1991, the University of Ulster was one of the first UK universities to introduce an accredited Postgraduate Certificate in University Teaching

(PgCUT). This course was undertaken both by new staff and, through a version tailored to meet their particular needs, experienced lecturers at the university. While feedback on the value of the PgCUT, subsequently PgCHET (Postgraduate Certificate in Higher Education Teaching), was very positive from most staff, there were some issues raised, both by participants and their line managers. These indicated a need to reconsider the course in the context of an overall review of initial and continuing professional development opportunities for academic and other teaching staff.

Some of the emerging limitations were: the exclusive (*albeit* deliberate, given the origins of the course) focus on teaching and learning, the lack of choice within the course, the lack of flexibility in delivery approaches, and the time commitment and workload required of individual staff members.

In addition, an extensive survey of all categories of part-time teaching staff in 2000 included questions relating to the existing development opportunities for part-time teachers in the university, and sought to gauge the level of interest in an accredited learning and teaching module. It was clear from the findings of this research that a high proportion of our part-time teaching staff were extremely keen to obtain accreditation for their development as teachers. Many contract research staff, too, had expressed a desire to support their career development through accreditation of the training programmes they undertook.

These views guided the work of the then Continuing Professional Development Working Group. As a result, a CPD framework was developed and approved by senate, and came into effect for new staff with a teaching role in July 2004. The PgCHEP, validated in 2005, constituted a key component of this framework. In addition to specifying for which staff the PgCHEP is a requirement, the framework indicated where staff were required to undertake a module or modules from the certificate, depending on their job role and the nature of their contract. The Postgraduate Certificate in Higher Education Practice, or its equivalent from another institution, is a requirement for all new permanent full-time lecturers and teaching fellows. Those on fixed-term contracts are required to undertake at least one module, and are encouraged to work towards completion of the certificate.

Taking Stock

In the spring of 2009 the Course Team were required to prepare the course for the university's revalidation process and additionally to seek re-accreditation from the Higher Education Academy and the Staff and Educational Development Association (SEDA). At this juncture it proved timely to reflect on the changing landscape of higher education both within and outside the university, and to reassess both the Continuing Professional Development Framework and the Higher Education Practice provision. In addition, recent staffing changes had led to the course being housed within Staff Development, and Staff Development advisers became responsible for the delivery and assessment of all activities within the university's CPD framework (including the PgCHEP). Furthermore, members of the Staff Development team have key responsibilities in the management and delivery of the Centre for Higher Education Practice projects and professional enhancement activities. The complementary nature of all these activities provides a sound basis for their central co-location and their strategic alignment with each other and university priorities.

At this stage it was decided that, whereas the Course Team did not want to lose elements of the course that had worked, it also did not wish to be constrained by existing structures and curricula. It was important to preserve the freedom to be creative and to carefully design a course that would meet the needs of not only our participants but also the institution. As Staff Development advisers, the Course Team members interact with new staff, line managers, and senior staff and, as a result, are well positioned to have cognisance of internal drivers, priorities, and potential issues at multiple levels. In the re-design of this course it was recognised that we had a strategic opportunity to influence and change practice within the institution (Blackmore and Blackwell 2003).

To start this process, the Course Team undertook a pragmatic review of the available internal and external priorities and evidence that would inform decisions. More recently it has become clear that the processes undertaken were largely in concordance with subsequent research (Blackmore et al. 2010, 111; Peters 2010, 50): as such we have constructed our own model (Figure 7.2) to encompass the dual perspectives that informed our curriculum design and philosophy.

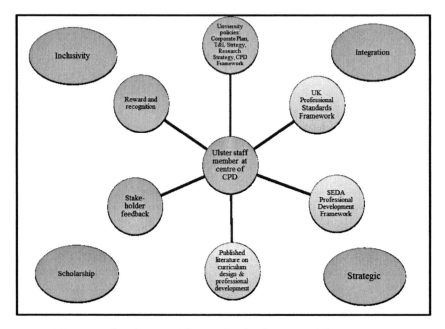

Figure 7.2　Internal and external factors for development of the new PgCHEP.

The external factors identified are common to many courses of this type and therefore will not be dwelt upon. However, it is important to highlight and address the key internal factors identified by the team, all of which distil wider national objectives and priorities within an institutional perspective.

University Policies

It was essential that the course be underpinned by relevant strategies and initiatives of the University of Ulster (2006, 2008a, 2008b, 2009a, 2009b). Whereas previously the course was informed almost exclusively by relevant teaching and learning strategies, particularly in the compulsory elements thereof, in keeping with received research (Clegg 2003, 2008; Kreber 2010), and in a move to engage more fully with the wider remit of academic practice, it was deemed necessary to encompass researcher development as well as other professional practice in higher education. It was felt that this move would meet with support and favour from course participants, line managers, and senior staff responsible for delivering against policy targets. Although taking cognisance of a range of institutional policies and strategies, it should be noted that the main driver remained the Teaching and Learning Strategy (University of Ulster 2008a), which had already refocused its aims and objectives within a broader, more inclusive framework, as encapsulated below in Figure 7.3.

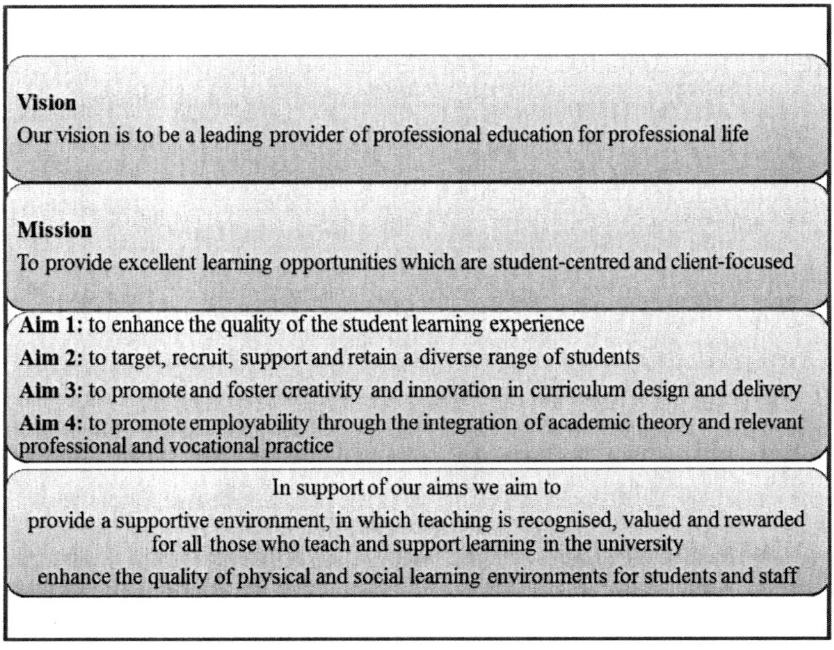

Vision
Our vision is to be a leading provider of professional education for professional life

Mission
To provide excellent learning opportunities which are student-centred and client-focused

Aim 1: to enhance the quality of the student learning experience
Aim 2: to target, recruit, support and retain a diverse range of students
Aim 3: to promote and foster creativity and innovation in curriculum design and delivery
Aim 4: to promote employability through the integration of academic theory and relevant professional and vocational practice

In support of our aims we aim to
provide a supportive environment, in which teaching is recognised, valued and rewarded for all those who teach and support learning in the university
enhance the quality of physical and social learning environments for students and staff

Figure 7.3 University of Ulster teaching and learning strategy: aims and objectives. Source: University of Ulster 2008a.

Reward and Recognition

As previously mentioned, reward and recognition are key to the promotion and embedding of teaching in higher education as a valued academic activity; at the University of Ulster promotion routes have been rewritten to include excellence in teaching and learning as one of the key criteria to be met. Internal reward mechanisms, mirroring national schemes, such as the Distinguished Teaching and Learning Support Awards, which are open to both academic and non-academic staff, do much to raise the awareness, and hence the status, of teaching and learning support throughout the institution. The very fact that the PgCHEP is open to all those involved in learning and teaching support across the institution does much to indicate the esteem with which these and related activities are held. The multiple accreditation afforded by individual modules, as well as the qualification as a whole, reinforces both the institutional and national recognition it engenders.

Institutional recognition is further underpinned by the mandate of the Centre for Higher Education Practice: early engagement with activities of the centre is promoted through the PgCHEP, with a view to promoting continued involvement with its rolling programme of events and initiatives, including small-scale funded project development. As a requirement of probation for new staff, there prevails a groundswell of opinion which recommends successful completion of the PgCHEP—or proof of UK PSF Level Two—as a prerequisite for all teaching-related promotion applications. It is hoped that this growing attitude will ensure that teaching and learning are clearly embedded within the academic and academic-support role, and hence serve to minimise the perceived dichotomy between discipline-based research and teaching.

Stakeholder Feedback

The evaluation cycle for all courses at the University of Ulster occurs every five years, with initial preparation for the revalidation beginning approximately twelve months prior to the event itself. With a revalidation date set for October 2009, the Course Team took approximately eight months to evaluate and redesign the course, with the remainder of the time spent in preparing all the relevant documentation. In preparation for revalidation, an online survey was conducted with current and recent course participants. Of the two hundred and forty former participants it was sent to, there were sixty-nine responses (29 percent response rate). These could be broken down into 60.3 percent female, 39.7 percent male, 84 percent academic staff, and 16 percent staff in other roles. Of these respondents, 20.6 percent indicated that they had undertaken the course due to it being a requirement of the CPD framework, 25 percent out of choice, and the majority (54.4 percent) for a combination of these reasons.

When asked, over 88 percent of respondents agreed that the course had been very useful or useful to their development as a teacher/provider of learning support, and 90 percent agreed strongly that it was a worthwhile undertaking. Responses highlighted the success of the course in supporting and encouraging participants to discuss their teaching and learning with both peers on the course (79 percent agreement) and colleagues in their disciplines (72 percent agreement). Where this version of the course was less successful was in developing participant knowledge of institutional priorities (68 percent agreement), and sector-wide teaching and learning priorities (54 percent agreement).

In addition, respondents were asked to provide qualitative responses highlighting the impact, if any, the course had had on their practice. The following provide an illustration of these:

- "I am part of a team that generated an idea through PgCHEP to collaborate with colleagues using art to teach anatomy . . . Complete transformation;"
- "The learning from the Teaching and Learning module supported me to think objectively about the modules I teach . . . students are clearer about what it is that is needed to succeed in a module and are given more space to articulate their learning in class;"
- "I am more aware of the varied needs of students and have introduced a wider range of teaching styles, activities and opportunities. . . . Students are more engaged, the pace changes throughout with more activities. I do more small group work which has improved group dynamics and improved communication ensures that students understand what they are doing and why I have set certain tasks;"
- "I use WebCT quite a bit in my teaching. . . . Students have evaluated highly the accessibility of my materials and the benefits of engaging with other students and learning in small groups."

Although feedback was predominantly positive, it was clear that a number of issues with the current course design were evident:

- Support to engage: "Having no support from the school (time off), it is very stressful to study whilst teaching." This is a key issue and one which is exacerbated by resource reductions and constraints facing many academic managers;
- Relevance for those with prior experience: "T&L module no real benefit gained as had developed teaching skills in clinical role for more than fifteen years prior to this job;"
- Institutional and external higher education priorities: responses highlighted that the current programme was not enabling participants to become familiar with or understand the benefits of engaging with the wider higher education agenda. Participants appeared to be reluctant

to move beyond their disciplinary base (Becher and Trowler 2001). "As I teach fine art practice, some of the approaches and the language need to be amended for the specific field."

As a result of these deliberations it was clear that the following principles needed to be encompassed in the curriculum design of the course (Figure 7.2). The course needed to:

- Be inclusive and flexible;
- Support integrated professional development;
- Introduce staff to continuing professional development opportunities that are strategic and scholarly;
- Strategically develop staff as future agents for change.

These are dealt with in turn in the following section together with examples of how they have been achieved in practice.

Inclusivity and Flexibility

The course developed seeks to provide a broad range of appropriate and relevant development opportunities to a wide body of participants, including full-time and part-time lecturers, associate lecturers and teaching fellows (for whom elements of the course are a requirement of probation), and those staff whose main professional priority is student support or research, for example, librarians, technicians, careers staff, contract research staff (Clegg 2003; Brand 2007). The need for flexibility is met by the provision of modules at a range of campus locations and by delivery times and modes which best meet the needs of staff, including online delivery. These are generally publicised online, at least six months in advance of delivery so as to enable participants and their line managers to plan accordingly.

The course comprises two part-time routes for completion depending on the participants' employment status. Figure 7.4 illustrates the normal progression route for a newly appointed member of academic staff who is required to meet the conditions set out in the university's CPD Framework (Route A); Figure 7.5 illustrates that of a member of staff who has opted to take the PgCHEP to meet their continuing professional development needs (Route B).

Successful completion of the full certificate enables participants to demonstrate that they have reached Level Two of the UK Professional Standards Framework for teaching and supporting learning in higher education, and to avail of national accreditation as Fellows of the Higher Education Academy. There are also two modules which offer accreditation as an Associate of the Academy (and Level One of the UK PSF) to those who opt to undertake them as a stand-alone option. This choice of accredited routes to Associate of the Higher Education Academy is another distinctive feature of the course, reflecting the commitment of the course team to inclusivity

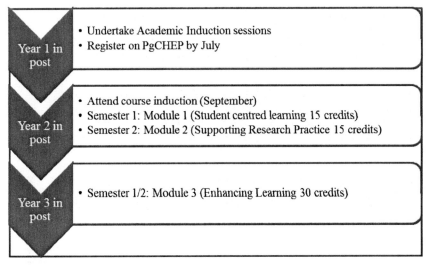

Figure 7.4 Illustration of normal progression for a newly appointed member of academic staff—Route A.

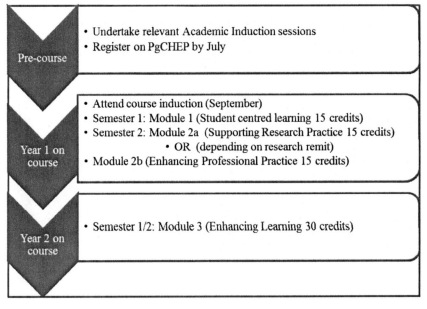

Figure 7.5 Illustration of normal progression for a member of staff taking course for CPD purposes—Route B.

and equality of opportunity. These modules also carry external recognition by SEDA leading to awards under their Professional Development (PDF) framework, namely: Supporting Learning, Enhancing Academic Practice in Disciplines, and Supporting Learning with Technologies Awards.

Supporting Integrated Professional Development

In re-shaping the course, consideration has been given to ensuring that it encompasses the breadth of professional development needed by staff as they settle in to a new role, or as their role changes. This accommodation of diverse roles, responsibilities, and professional development priorities is reflected in the use of the term "Higher Education *Practice*" rather than the more prescriptive "Higher Education *Teaching*," and there is extensive opportunity within the modules for contextualisation linked to participants' roles, disciplinary backgrounds, and institutional needs (Clegg 2003, 46–47).

The course aims to support the development of participants' roles through exposing them to recent scholarly evidence and effective approaches in modules covering teaching and learning, research practice, and professional practice. Particular examples of how this has been achieved are illustrated below; firstly in the inclusion of a module aimed at supporting staff who have a research remit to meet the aims of the university's research strategy by securing high-status research funding, and secondly by providing a module for professional staff whose roles require them to be aware of and adaptive to the changing needs of the sector.

Supporting Research Practice

This module has been designed to support participants' understanding and development of research practices necessary to engage fully with their research remit in a higher education context. It recognises that academics are both teachers and researchers. The latter role involves developing original knowledge and disseminating it to a range of audiences including fellow academics, the general public, policymakers, and industry.

World-leading and internationally excellent research in all disciplines, including pedagogy, requires external funding in order to recover essential costs such as supporting national/international collaborations, employing staff and postgraduates, as well as fieldwork and laboratory expenses. Hence, academics are facing increased pressure to write successful proposals, particularly to funders (e.g., research councils), who pay full economic costs.

This can be very difficult, however, as proposal writing is not a skill that is generally developed during the course of a research degree. Additionally, acquiring such funds is becoming ever more competitive with, for example, success rates of applications to prestigious funders currently on the order of 15–20 percent. The aim of this module is to provide professional training in acquiring research funding as, in general, this crucial skill is not developed through postgraduate research. As this module may also be relevant to staff not enrolled on the PgCHEP, it is also available as a stand-alone module for CPD purposes.

Enhancing Professional Practice

As the landscape of higher education is continually changing, this impacts upon the roles of professional staff within it, and their responsibilities in adapting to meet new challenges. Building on the student-centred learning module, this module has been developed to provide an opportunity for participants to explore and critique the established and evolving scholarly and professional evidence base in higher education practice relevant to their area of work, and use this to inform and shape their evolving practice.

Introduction to Continuing Professional Development Opportunities

Throughout the course, and particularly in the final module, Enhancing Learning, it is intended to provide participants with the tools and techniques to enhance the teaching and learning experience of the students in the evolving higher education context. It recognises that the role of those involved in teaching and learning support has changed, and continues to evolve in response to institutional and/or external drivers, including emerging technologies, changing student profiles, and the need for a more creative outlook within a discipline-specific and cross-disciplinary context. The new order of academe, and its inherent requirement to engage with the pedagogy and scholarship of teaching and learning (SoTL), may cause apprehension for those who are new to concepts of teaching and learning in higher education, be it through a refocusing of their traditional—discipline expert—role or through an extension of their support role.

Such a re-evaluation of one's fundamental role and practices may prove challenging (Brew 2006, 111), and implies a community of learning that transcends discipline boundaries and which may engender a new sense of self (Kreber 2010, 172; MacKenzie et al. 2010). The opportunity to engage with a cross-discipline community of practice of course participants ensures that this sometimes bumpy ride can be undertaken in a "safe" environment. The course also provides for early and ongoing engagement with the University's Centre for Higher Education Practice, highlighting the potential for continuing professional development both internally and within the wider higher education community, for example, the Higher Education Academy.

DEVELOPING AGENTS FOR CHANGE

If the Postgraduate Certificate is to have longitudinal impact on both the participants and the university, it is crucial that it empowers participants to consider their ongoing role as change agents. To achieve this, the course integrates understanding leadership styles, influencing skills, and implementing change within the modules. The course team have purposefully included leadership within the curriculum with participants being introduced to theory on supporting and implementing change at induction.

These ideas are further developed within the first module—student-centred learning—where participants are expected to reflect on their engagement with students and explore opportunities for enhancement and change that are well supported by evidence, as illustrated by the assignments below taken from the course documentation.

- Coursework 1: produce a report entitled "My students" which critically analyses the nature of your student cohort, and reflects upon the implications of this for your professional practice;
- Coursework 2: design/re-design part of a module to take into account the needs of your identified cohort. Utilise Biggs's (2003) theory of constructive alignment to underpin your development of a teaching learning and assessment strategy including: revision of the module outline, assessment tasks, assessment criteria, and feedback methods. You should provide a theoretically based rationale to justify your choices—ensure that you explain your decisions rather than simply describe them.

The module is only in its first iteration, but already unsolicited feedback indicates that participants are finding it has impacted upon their thinking and practice: "The focus of this module has been transformative—I think about my teaching in a totally different way."

CONCLUSION

The revised course was designed to build on the strengths of the previous Postgraduate Certificate in Higher Education Practice, by providing a fit-for-purpose course to develop and accredit the initial professional development of new academic staff in both teaching and research, and the continuing professional development of other staff that enhances the student learning experience. Taking into account recent research regarding higher educational trends and developments at a national level, the course team has crucially sought to interpret these within the context of the institutional framework and its related policies, thus providing staff with the opportunity to maximise the potential for learning at and through work, via the integration of theory and practice in their own organisational context within higher education.

NOTES

1. The traditional UK qualification taken at approximately eighteen years of age.

BIBLIOGRAPHY

Archer, Louise. 2008. "The New Neoliberal Subjects? Young/er Academics' Constructions of Professional Identity." *Journal of Educational Policy* 23 (3): 265–285.

Attwood, Rebecca. 2010. "Must Do Better: HEA Chief Calls for Teaching 'Licence' to End Inconsistencies." *Times Higher Education*, November 11, 2010, http://www.timeshighereducation.co.uk/story.asp?storycode=414179, accessed 20/11/2010.

Bamber, Veronica. 2002. "To What Extent Has the Dearing Policy Recommendation on Training New Lecturers Met Acceptance? Where Dearing Went that Robbins Didn't Dare." *Teacher Development* 6 (3): 433–459.

Bargh, Catherine, Jean Bocock, Peter Scott, and David Smith. 2000. *University Leadership: The Role of the Chief Executive.* Buckingham, UK: SRHE/Open University Press.

Barnett, Ron. 2003. *Beyond All Reason: Living with Ideology in the University.* Buckingham, UK: SHRE/Open University Press.

Becher, Tony, and Paul Trowler. 2001. *Academic Tribes and Territories,* 2nd ed. Buckingham, UK: SRHE/Open University Press.

Biggs, John. 2003. *Teaching for Quality Learning at University.* Buckingham, UK: SHRE/Open University Press.

Blackmore, Paul, and Richard Blackwell. 2003. "Academic Roles and Relationships." In *Towards Strategic Staff Development in Higher Education,* edited by Richard Blackwell and Paul Blackmore, 16–28. Buckingham, UK: SRHE/Open University Press.

Blackmore, Paul, José Chambers, Lesley Huxley, and Bob Thackwray. 2010. "Tribalism and Territoriality in the Staff and Educational Development World." *Journal of Further and Higher Education* 34 (1):105–117.

Brand, Anthony. 2007. "The Long and Winding Road: Professional Development in Further and Higher Education." *Journal of Further and Higher Education* 31 (1): 7–16.

Brew, Angela. 2006. *Research and Teaching: Beyond the Divide.* Basingstoke, UK: Palgrave Macmillan.

Browne, Lord John. 2010. *Securing a Sustainable Future for Higher Education: An Independent Review of Higher Education Funding and Student Finance.* Norwich, UK: HMSO, http://hereview.independent.gov.uk/hereview/report/, accessed 20/11/2010.

Clegg, Sue. 2003. "Problematizing Ourselves: Continuing Professional Development in Higher Education." *International Journal for Academic Development* 12 (2): 69–72.

Clegg, Sue. 2008. "Academic identities under threat?" *British Educational Research* 34 (3): 329–345.

Committee of Vice-Chancellors and Principals (CVCP). 1987. *Academic Staff Training: Code of Practice.* London: CVCP.

Crawford, Karin. 2008. "Continuing Professional Development in Higher Education: The Academic Perspective." *International Journal for Academic Development* 13 (2): 141–146.

Dearing, Sir Ronald. 1997. *Higher Education in the Learning Society.* Norwich, UK: HMSO, http://www.leeds.ac.uk/educol/ncihe/, accessed 20/11/2010.

Department for Education and Skills (DfES). 2003. *The Future of Higher Education.* Norwich, UK: HMSO, http://www.bis.gov.uk/assets/biscore/corporate/migratedd/publications/f/future_of_he.pdf, accessed 20/11/2010.

Gosling, David. 2009. "Educational Development in the UK: A Complex and Contradictory Reality." *International Journal for Academic Development* 14 (1): 5–18.

————. 2010. "Professional Development for New Staff: How Mandatory Is Your Post Graduate Certificate?" *Educational Developments* 11 (2): 1–4.

Hall, Julie. 2010. "Time to Develop My Career? That's a Fantasy! UK Professional Standards Framework and Ethical Staff and Educational Development." In *Embedding CPD in Higher Education*, edited by Mike Laycock and Liz Shrives, 37–44. London: SEDA.

Harvey, Lee, and Peter Knight. 1996. *Transforming Higher Education*. Buckingham, UK: SRHE/Open University Press.

Higher Education Academy. 2006. *The UK Professional Standards Framework for Teaching and Supporting Learning in Higher Education*. York, UK: Higher Education Academy, http://www.heacademy.ac.uk/assets/York/documents/ourwork/rewardandrecog/ProfessionalStandardsFramework.pdf, accessed 20/11/2010.

Higher Education Academy and Genetics Education Networking for Innovation and Excellence Centre for Excellence in Teaching and Learning (GENIE CETL). 2009a. *Reward and Recognition of Teaching in Higher Education: A Collaborative Investigation. Interim Report*. York, UK: Higher Education Academy, http://www.heacademy.ac.uk/assets/York/documents/resources/publications/Reward_and_Recognition_Interim.pdf , accessed 20/11/2010.

————. 2009b. *Reward and Recognition in Higher Education: Institutional Policies and Their Implementation*. York, UK: Higher Education Academy, http://www.heacademy.ac.uk/resources/detail/ourwork/evidencenet/Summaries/hea_genie_cetl_reward_and_recognition_in_he, accessed 20/11/2010.

Kreber, Carolin. 2010. "Academics' Teacher Identities, Authenticity and Pedagogy." *Studies in Higher Education* 35 (2): 171–194.

Kynaston, Rachel, and Carol Maynard. 2010. " 'There Just Seemed so Much to Do . . . ' Using Institutional Processes to Support the Development of Professional Standards at Liverpool John Moores University (LJMU)." In *Embedding CPD in Higher Education*, edited by Mike Laycock and Liz Shrives, 53–62. London: SEDA.

Land, Ray. 2001. "Agency, Context and Change in Academic Development." *International Journal for Academic Development* 6: 4–20.

Laycock, Mike. 2010. "CPD and Critical Learning Communities: You Can't Have One without the Other." In *Embedding CPD in Higher Education*, edited by Mike Laycock and Liz Shrives, 27–34. London: SEDA.

Light, Greg, and Roy Cox. 2001. *Learning and Teaching in Higher Education: The Reflective Professional*. London: Sage.

Lynch, Kathleen. 2006. "Neo-Liberalism and Marketisation: The Implications for Higher Education." *European Educational Research Journal* 5 (1): 1–17.

MacKenzie, Jane, Sheena Bell, Jason Bohan, Andrea Brown, Joanne Burke, Barbara Cogdell, Susan Jamieson, Julie McAdam, Robert McKerlie, Lorna Morrow, Beth Paschke, Paul Rea, and Anne Tierney. 2010. "From Anxiety to Empowerment: A Learning Community of University Teachers." *Teaching in Higher Education* 15 (3): 273–284.

Mårtensson, Katarina, and Torgny Roxå. 2009. "Leading Academic Teaching—a Contextual Approach." In *Improving Student Learning for the 21st Century Learner, Proceedings of the 17th International Symposium*, edited by Chris Rust, 212–219. Oxford: Oxford Brookes University.

Olssen, Mark, and Michael Peters. 2005. "Neoliberalism, Higher Education and the Knowledge Economy: From the Free Market to Knowledge Capitalism." *Journal of Education Policy* 20 (3): 313–345.

Parker, Jon. 2008. "Comparing Research and Teaching in University Promotion Criteria." *Higher Education Quarterly* 62 (3): 237–251.

Peters, John. 2010. "What Is the Purpose of a University CPD Framework?" In *Embedding CPD in Higher Education*, edited by Mike Laycock and Liz Shrives, 45–40. London: SEDA.
Ramsden, Paul. 1995. "Achieving Excellence in University Education: Recognising and Rewarding Good Teaching." Keynote address, 9th Annual Conference of the Educational Research Association (Singapore).
Ramsden, Paul, Don Margetson, Elaine Martin, and Sally Clarke. 1995. *Recognising and Rewarding Good Teaching in Australian Higher Education*. Canberra: Australian Government Publishing Service.
Rodaway, Paul. 2007. "Changing Perspectives on Teaching." *Journal of Further and Higher Education* 31 (1): 1–6.
Rothwell, Andrew, and Frances Rothwell. 2010. "Embedding CPD: Policy Implementation or Research Agenda?" In *Embedding CPD in Higher Education*, edited by Mike Laycock and Liz Shrives, 13–19. London: SEDA.
Rowland, Stephen, Catherine Byron, Frank Furedi, Nicky Padfield, and Terry Smyth. 1998. "Turning Academics into Teachers?" *Teaching in Higher Education* 3 (2): 133–141.
SEDA Professional Development Framework (SEDA-PDF). http://seda.ac.uk/pdf.html, accessed 20/11/2010.
Shepherd, Jessica, and Rachel Williams. 2010. "Student Complaints about Universities Rise Steeply." *The Guardian*, June 15, 2010, http://www.guardian.co.uk/education/2010/jun/15/students-complaints-universities, accessed 20/11/2010.
Skelton, Alan. 2005. *Understanding Teaching Excellence in Higher Education*. London: Routledge.
University of Ulster. 2006. "Corporate Plan 2006/07–2010/11," http://www.ulster.ac.uk/corporateplan/corporate-plan.pdf, accessed 20/11/2010.
———. 2008a. "Teaching and Learning Strategy 2008/09–2012/13," http://www.ulster.ac.uk/teachingandlearning/, accessed 20/11/2010.
———. 2008b. "Centre for Higher Education Practice," http://www.ulster.ac.uk/centrehep/, accessed 20/11/2010.
———. 2009a. "Research Strategy for 2009–2014," http://research.ulster.ac.uk/uuonly/policy/Research%20Strategy%202009_14%20Final.pdf, accessed 20/11/2010.
———. 2009b. "CPD Policy," http://staffdev.ulster.ac.uk/index.php?page=continuing-professional-development-cpd, accessed 20/11/2010.
———. 2010. "Institutional Briefing Document for QAA Institutional Audit Visit March 2010," http://www.ulster.ac.uk/quality/qmau/uuonly/ibd.pdf, accessed 20/11/2010.
Winter, Richard. 2009. "Academic Manager or Managed Academic? Academic Identity Schisms in Higher Education." *Journal of Higher Education Policy and Management* 31 (2): 121–131.

Part III

Top-Down Determinants of Success in Instructional Development Programmes

8 The Emerging European Higher Education Area
Implications for Instructional Development

Kathleen M. Quinlan and Erkki Berndtson

INTRODUCTION

This chapter presents a case study of the implications of broad policy contexts on instructional development in higher education. We discuss the challenges posed by the recent policy of European countries to create a unified European Higher Education Area (EHEA) and its implications for university teachers and, in turn, instructional development.

We have sought to explain the complex policy developments in a nutshell for readers outside Europe. We present the challenges this policy context poses for teaching practices in order to identify instructional development needs in this new context. We then analyse key strengths, weaknesses, and lessons from instructional development mainly in the global Anglo-American context (particularly in UK, U.S., and Australia).

Finally, we speculate on how instructional development in Europe might evolve to both address those opportunities within the field of educational development, as well as the needs of European higher education. These insights from abroad on educational development may be particularly useful in Eastern and Southern Europe where there is little or no established tradition of educational development, as there is in Scandinavia and the low countries of Northern Europe.

THE BOLOGNA PROCESS, THE LISBON STRATEGY, AND THE EUROPEAN COMMISSION

In Europe, as elsewhere, education was long considered a national—rather than regional—policy issue. The so-called Bologna Process (The Process), though, has changed the contours of the European Higher Education Area rapidly during the last decade (Reinalda and Kulesza 2006).

The Foundations of the Bologna Process

What began as a French (and German) initiative to change their own systems of higher education, bypassing the opposition in their countries and adopting an international strategy, soon captured the interest of other European governments. The Process started in 1998 when the British, German, French, and Italian ministers of education signed the Sorbonne Declaration on "harmonization of the architecture of the European higher education system" (Bologna Process Declarations 2011). The declaration launched "an endeavour to create a European area of higher education (EHEA)" and called on "other Member States of the Union and other European countries to join . . . in this objective."

A year later, twenty-nine European governments sent their ministers of education to meet in Bologna, leading to a short declaration with six specific objectives considered "of primary relevance in order to establish the European area of higher education" (Bologna Declaration [1999]—Bologna Process Declarations 2011):

1. *Adoption of a system of easily readable and comparable degrees* in order to promote employability and the international competitiveness of the EHEA;
2. *Adoption of a system based on two main cycles,* undergraduate and graduate;
3. *Establishment of a system of credits* such as in the European Credit Transfer and Accumulation system (ECTS)[1] as a means of promoting student mobility;
4. *Promotion of mobility* among students, teachers, researchers, and administrative staff;
5. *Promotion of European cooperation in quality assurance;*
6. *Promotion of European dimensions* in higher education, particularly with regards to curricular development, interinstitutional cooperation, mobility schemes, and integrated programmes of study, training, and research.

The Evolving Structure and Agenda over the First Decade

The Bologna Process is a transnational project, which has grown from the original twenty-nine countries to forty-seven (2011). In 2001, the Process became more organized, with a permanent Bologna Follow-up Group (BFUG), consisting of representatives of all signatory countries and the European Commission. In addition, there are eight consultative members: European University Association (EUA), European Students' Union (ESU), European Association of Institutions in Higher Education (EURASHE), European Association for Quality Assurance in Higher Education (ENQA), Council of Europe, UNESCO's European Centre for

Higher Education, Education International Pan-European Structure, and BUSINESSEUROPE.

The BFUG, jointly chaired by the country holding the presidency of the European Union (EU) and one non-EU country, oversees the process between the biennial ministerial conferences (Prague 2001, Berlin 2003, Bergen 2005, London 2007, Leuven/Louvain-la-Neuve 2009[2]—Bologna Process Declarations 2011), with oversight from the board and support from a Bologna secretariat staffed by the country hosting the next ministerial conference. Several working groups progress the key action lines of the process. In addition, to disseminate the Bologna reforms, participating countries and organisations regularly arrange seminars and conferences.

Thus, the Bologna Process is complex and bureaucratic. National governments, European Commission, and the consultative members all have their own agendas. For example, EUA has influenced the process from the beginning, helping to create the ideological terrain of the Bologna objectives with its important background reports (EUA Trends Reports 2011).

Students have become more visible since 2001, when it was announced that they "should influence the organisation and content of education," and that they were "full partners" in the process. The 2007 London Communiqué declared that higher education must become "student-centred" and move "away from teacher driven provision" (Bologna Process Declarations 2011). As to the EURASHE, when it became a consultative member in Prague, the communiqué duly noted the importance of "other higher education institutions" in the process (Bologna Process Declarations 2011).

The process has continued to evolve piecemeal with new objectives having been added in ministerial conferences. New objectives (or action lines, as they are now called) that have been set are: the principle of lifelong learning (Prague 2001), involvement of higher education institutions and students (Prague 2001), promoting the attractiveness of the EHEA worldwide (Prague 2001), promoting closer links between the EHEA and the European Research Area (ERA) (Berlin 2003, where doctoral studies were made the third cycle of studies). Although it seems that after Berlin there have been no new action lines, it is evident that the importance of the social dimension, that is, that the student body should reflect the diversity of Europe's population (Bergen 2005) and the employability of graduates (London 2007) have, in fact, become new action lines.

However, the process is not as uniform as it might appear from the unity of goals. The forty-seven countries have their own agendas and often interpret the action lines in different ways. Thus national policies, policies of the European Union, and those of "other relevant actors" constantly interact with each other, leading to negotiations between actors (Keeling 2004) and continuous reinterpretation of different objectives, action lines, and priorities. Many of these policies are, however, in line with the goals of the European Commission.

The Underpinning Social and Economic Agendas and the Role of the European Commission

Although Bologna is a transnational project, the European Commission has become a central player in the process. The commission helped to fund the 1999 Bologna Conference and many of its thematic interests have been included in the process (e.g., lifelong learning) (Balzer and Martens 2004, 14–15); most of the original six principles of the Bologna Declaration were already on the commission's agenda in the 1980s (especially a common system of credits and the promotion of mobility).

Spurred by the global ideology promoted by international organisations such as the OECD and the World Bank, the commission has also been active in introducing quality assurance for European higher education. The commission funded the European Pilot Project for Evaluating Quality in Higher Education (1994–1995), which started the cooperation in the field of quality assurance.

The role of the European Commission has been further strengthened by the adoption of the Lisbon Strategy in 2000 and its reformulation in 2005, intended to make the European Union "the most competitive and dynamic knowledge-based economy in the world."[3] The commission set the goals of EU cooperation in higher education in its 2006 "Modernisation Agenda for Universities: Education, Research and Innovation" (European Commission 2006), which emphasises curricular, governance, and funding reforms.

Curricular reform is addressed by the Bologna Process, while the Lisbon Strategy's complementary emphasis is on governance and funding reforms. Governance reform consists of making universities more autonomous (severing their ties with the state), forming strategic partnerships (especially with enterprises), and incorporating quality assurance mechanisms (reinforcing the Bologna Process). Funding reform requires that higher education institutions rely on diversified sources of income linked to their performance, including the possible role of tuition fees in countries where higher education has been free.

The close links between the Bologna Process, the Lisbon Strategy, and the overall policy of the European Commission can be seen, for instance, in a 2008 commission working paper, in which the three necessary reforms (curricular, governance, and funding) are grouped into nine measures:

1. Break down the barriers around universities in Europe;
2. Ensure real autonomy and accountability for universities;
3. Provide incentives for structured partnerships with the business community;
4. Provide the right mix of skills and competencies for the labour market;
5. Reduce the funding gap and make funding work more effectively in education and research;
6. Enhance interdisciplinarity and transdisciplinarity;

7. Activate knowledge through interaction with society;
8. Reward excellence at the highest level;
9. Make EHEA and ERA more visible and attractive in the world (European Commission 2008, 3).

There are several reasons for the commission's interest in education. First, the European economic agenda calls for a common labour market, with mobility of workers among member states. Second, education is seen as a way to create a European (rather than merely national) identity among the EU's population. Third, the commission fears that Europe cannot compete with U.S. and Asian universities in attracting the best researchers and students in an increasingly globalised education market. Finally, given the challenge of an ageing population, Europe must maximize the talents and capacities of all its citizens to maintain current standards of living.

All of these ambitions require that education be a lifelong process and that higher education institutions open their doors to social groups traditionally underrepresented in the student body. Everyone with the ability should take part in higher education. These social and economic agendas also underpin the current action lines of the Bologna Process itemised in the previous section.

The Bologna Process Today

The bureaucratic and shifting nature of the Bologna Process is evident in the communiqué of the 2009 Leuven/Louvain-la-Neuve Conference, as the "Ministers responsible for higher education" set priorities for the coming decade. The communiqué emphasised the role of European higher education in addressing the challenges of an ageing population in Europe, globalisation, accelerated technological developments, and the consequences of the global financial and economic crisis. Higher education was positioned as a vital contributor to a Europe of knowledge that is creative and innovative. Widening participation in higher education was seen to enable the talents and capacities of all European citizens to be fully engaged through lifelong learning (Bologna Process Declarations 2011).

These challenges can be seen in the ten priorities for the next decade. The current (Bologna Communiqué 2009, see Bologna Process Declarations 2011) priorities are:

1. *Social dimension: equitable access and completion,* intended to widen participation in higher education;
2. *Lifelong learning.* Qualifications should be obtained through flexible learning paths, including part-time studies or work-based routes approved through procedures for recognising prior learning. National qualifications frameworks are an important implementation step;
3. *Employability;*

4. *Student-centred learning and the teaching mission of higher education* (evolved from "Involvement of higher education institutions and students in the process," which was previously part of lifelong learning). Institutions should adopt new approaches to teaching and learning, support and guidance structures, and curricula focused more clearly on the learner, including individually tailored educational pathways. Particular attention is given to improving the teaching quality of study programmes through further implementation of the *European Standards and Guidelines for Quality Assurance* (ENQA 2005);

5. *Education, research, and innovation* (evolved from "Promoting the links between the EHEA and the European Research Area"). Education should be based on state-of-the-art research, including disciplinary, interdisciplinary, and intersectoral research;

6. *International openness* (evolved from "Promoting the attractiveness of the EHEA worldwide") through international recruitment and mobility and quality assurance mechanisms;

7. *Mobility* enhances teaching quality, research excellence, personal development, employability, respect for diversity, and cultural competence. Erasmus exchange is central, but joint degrees and study programmes (parts of the European dimensions earlier), flexible study paths, full recognition of study achievements abroad, and open international recruitment are also needed;

8. *Data collection* (with continuing stocktaking);

9. *Multidimensional transparency tools* (evolved from "Readable and comparable degrees" and from "a common system of credits"). Quality assurance has become the most important tool for transparency of European higher education;

10. *Funding.* Public funding remains the main priority for European higher education, but greater attention should be paid to seeking new and diversified funding sources and methods.

The priorities show how the original action lines have been reinterpreted and how these are more and more linked with each other. Of the original six objectives of the Bologna Process, only mobility has remained as a priority on its own. The other five objectives have advanced fairly well (the adoption of study cycles, the ECTS system) or been reinterpreted.

However, development is still uneven around Europe. The 2009 Bologna Process Stocktaking Report looked at the implementation of three policy areas (dividing them into ten sub-items): *the degree structure* (implementation of the first and second cycles, access to the next cycle, adoption of national qualifications networks), *quality assurance* (implementation of external quality assurance mechanisms, student participation, international participation), and *recognition of studies* (Diploma Supplement, implementation of the Lisbon Recognition Convention, adoption of the ECTS, recognition of prior learning). Of the forty-seven countries, only fifteen had implemented over half of these ten objectives fully (Rauhvargers, Deane, and Pauwels 2009, 122).

The Bologna Process seems to be most advanced in small Western European countries. Countries which had realised at least six of the ten policy fields were: Scotland (all ten objectives), Flemish Belgium (nine), Denmark (nine), Ireland (eight), the Netherlands (eight), Norway (eight), Sweden (eight), Finland (seven), Romania (seven), Austria (six), Iceland (six), Luxembourg (six), French Belgium (six), Portugal (six) and UK (England, Wales, and Northern Ireland [six]).

Interestingly, France and Germany, the main initiators of the process, had not restructured their higher education systems as successfully (France—three, Germany—three). The Central and Eastern European countries were also lagging behind (e.g., Poland—five, Slovenia—five, Czech Republic—four, Hungary—four).

Thus, the Bologna Process is still an evolving process, offering opportunities to participate in a discussion about the teaching practices in the European Higher Education Area. This is important, too, because existing instructional development programmes have usually been designed from the national perspective. The internationalisation and regionalisation of higher education policies therefore require a rethinking of instructional development. In the next section we will discuss the action lines related to social dimension, lifelong learning, employability, student-centred learning, and the promotion of mobility in greater detail because these issues have such strong effects on teaching, learning, and, thus, instructional development.

DIVERSITY OF STUDENTS AND CHANGING EDUCATIONAL GOALS

One consequence of the new European higher education policies is that the student body will be increasingly diversified through inclusion of students in different life situations (e.g., part-time students, older students, exchange students) and from traditionally underrepresented social and economic backgrounds. These "new" groups of students bring different life experiences, goals, motivations, and expectations.

In countries where attrition is high, universities will need to find ways to engage and retain these non-traditional students. Teaching methods that worked for traditional students may not be effective at engaging non-traditional students. In frustration, teachers can easily fall into the trap of "blaming the student" for failing to fit the traditional mould. Instead, teachers will need to learn about student learning in order to take a more "student-centred" perspective.

These problems are well illustrated by an increasing number of exchange students in European universities. Mobility of students has become an important part of European academic life after the Erasmus programme was launched by the European Commission in 1987. Student exchange has increased from a mere 3,244 in the first year of the programme (1987–88) to some 200,000 students annually now (see European Commission 2011). The commission still seeks to raise participation. However, there are four main challenges with increasing student mobility.

First, there are no minimum language requirements for exchanges; rather, students often study in another country precisely to develop their language skills, resulting in a vast heterogeneity of language abilities. The quality of classroom discussions conducted in a foreign language is often questionable (Bergström 2005; Van Cranenburgh 2005). In practice, when students do not know the host country language, they seek courses given in English. However, in many universities (outside the English-language countries) relatively few courses are offered in English, leading to a mélange of students from different disciplines in the available English-language courses.

Second, even when students take courses in their own disciplines, they bring different background knowledge of the subject because the contents of disciplines vary from country to country, particularly in the social sciences which are moulded by their political and social contexts. Thus problems of mobility are more complex than language barriers. Exchange agreements, which might substantially address language or curricular prerequisites, tend to be administrative, rather than substantive, though. Creating substantive agreements would require both understanding and taking into account the nature of different disciplines.

Third, as Oda Van Cranenburgh (2005) has noted, differences in cultural norms related to workload, grading, and teaching cultures affect both the quality of the student experience and the attitudes of teaching staff toward exchange. Course loads and reading and writing requirements for nominally equal courses (in ECTS credits) may vary from country to country. Grading systems are not uniform and grading can be culturally conditioned. Classroom "cultures" also diverge. In some countries, teaching is equated with lecturing; students have little or no contact with academics outside the lecture theatre. Elsewhere, students may have small classes that encourage discussion between students and with academics. Given the variety of cultural norms, exchange students are often confused by the different expectations of host countries.

Finally, many exchange students are interested mainly in broadening their life experience and meeting other students. This behaviour serves the political agenda of Europeanization, but can compromise educational agendas of learning high-level disciplinary skills and knowledge. Ultimately, universities must plan their teaching programmes so that they address their own requirements and needs, while accommodating students coming in and out. Thus, academics face curricular decisions, as well as teaching challenges. Changes in the student body also generate demands for flexible learning paths, which require more guidance, work which will likely fall to academic staff, increasing their workload.

Underlying the Bologna Process is the imperative to take better account of the needs of the labour market. Such an educational goal requires that higher education institutions reconsider their missions, as well as curriculum and instruction. Higher education in Western societies has historically embraced a variety of aims, including knowledge for knowledge's sake, the moral formation of students, and social reform. Meeting economic or employers' needs is only one possible aim of higher education.

Thus, these shifts in purpose are problematic. Academics, who traditionally value their disciplines, may see employability skills as outside their remit. Furthermore, many academics, particularly in pure fields of liberal art and sciences, may not have experience of working in the kinds of jobs into which their students will go. Thus, even if academics are willing to accept a new mission, they may be ill-prepared to adapt their teaching to meet employers' demands. Finally, the needs of the labour market are so varied it would be very difficult to base a systematic curriculum on them.

LESSONS FROM INSTRUCTIONAL DEVELOPMENT ELSEWHERE

One response to these new demands on the teaching process has been the design of instructional development courses for teachers in higher education. In this section, we review the key elements of educational development programmes in Anglophone countries.

Increased Student Diversity as the Impetus for Instructional Development

The earliest U.S. instructional development programmes emerged in the late 1960s and early 1970s, concurrent with a shift toward wider participation in higher education. As the student body became more diverse with returning adult learners and first-generation college students, faculty members found they needed new strategies to engage these non-traditional students (Cross 1971).

Since that time, other countries have also embraced agendas for wider access to higher education and, accompanying these widening participation policies, established instructional development programmes. In Australia, although the earliest instructional development centre dates back to the late 1960s, several of its pioneers argue that the field was stimulated by increasing numbers of students in higher education and increased numbers of first-generation university students (Lee et al. 2008).

In the UK, the number of such centres swelled with the conversion of polytechnics to universities in the early 1990s and again in the wake of the Dearing report (1997). More recently, Japan has experienced a massive increase in its participation rates in higher education and, following other developed countries, has established instructional development programmes to help academics cope with the new demands on their teaching presented by students with lower academic achievement (Sato 2010). In parallel, research on student learning in higher education has burgeoned in the countries with programmes for educating new tertiary teachers, forming the basis for instructional development programme curricula. The underpinning research, though, has been carried out almost exclusively in developed Western countries with domestic students.

The trend toward increasing diversity of the student body in Europe, as indicated above, means that Europe faces these same challenges of widening participation. The most academically able and intrinsically motivated students—the traditional participants in higher education—could manage even under conditions of relatively uninspiring and teacher-centric forms of education. Standards were high and universities failed students who did not meet them.

However, as less academically enthusiastic students with a variety of backgrounds, interests, and motivations enter higher education and national policy demands that they be served (not culled), academics with no prior study of education or learning and teaching must find a way to engage them and help them succeed. Instructional development has been the solution in other Western countries facing widening participation in higher education. However, most academics in Europe are not formally educated in learning and teaching.

Instructional development in many countries embraces student-centred views of learning. For example, Paul Ramsden's *Learning to Teach in Higher Education* (1992, 2003), a popular text in Australian and UK educational development programmes, focuses on changing teachers' conceptions of the learning-teaching process to embrace a view of education as "making learning possible" (Ramsden 2003, 110). In contrast, many lecturers in higher education who have not been through instructional development programmes and have themselves experienced didactic, teacher-centred, and lecture dominated modes of instruction adopt a view of education as "telling or transmitting knowledge" (Ramsden 2003, 108).

In the U.S., a different literature underpins instructional development programmes. Nonetheless, the emphasis is on student-centred approaches to teaching. For example, academics are urged to adopt active learning strategies, to interact with their students, to manage diversity, and to encourage peer-to-peer interactions (e.g., Chickering and Gamson 1987). Evidence suggests that well-designed instructional development programmes can help teachers become more student-centred (Gibbs and Coffey 2004).

Professional Standards Frameworks as Levers for Advancing Instructional Development

Educational development in higher education has increasingly been placed in the framework of quality assurance. In the UK, the recent Lord Browne review places teaching training squarely in the realm of quality assurance, recommending that universities report on the proportion of teaching-active staff with Higher Education Association qualifications by the subject (discipline) level. Sweden has recently developed its own compulsory national professional standards framework (Lindberg-Sand and Sonesson 2008), and similar initiatives have been undertaken in Belgium (Gilis et al. 2008) and the Netherlands (Tigelaar et al. 2004; Keulen and Ven 2006).

In the UK, the Browne Review explicitly mentions the desirability of instructional development. It recommended that it be "a condition of receipt of income . . . that institutions require all new academics with teaching responsibilities to undertake a teaching training qualification accredited by the HEA, and that the option to gain such a qualification is made available to all staff—including researchers and postgraduate students—with teaching responsibilities" (2010, 48).

Instructional development programmes are virtually universally available in the UK. The UK Professional Standards Framework, first launched in by the Higher Education Academy in 2006, has become so embedded in higher education in the UK that not only does almost every university offer a postgraduate degree related to learning and teaching in higher education that leads to fellowship status with the HEA, but almost all universities have made participation in some or all of those programmes mandatory for new academics. Universities that have not yet done so may well be required to under future legislation.

Based on the UK experience, de facto mandatory professional standards frameworks seem to be a key policy lever in advancing instructional development in higher education. These professional standards frameworks are arising at a national level, though, rather than a regional level. Creating a professional standards framework for the region would seem consistent with the European Commission's overall goal. A set of core knowledge, skills, and values would provide a common language for teaching and learning across the EU, facilitating discussion across Europe. It would likely lead to a greater convergence of norms across countries—addressing one of the key challenges of student mobility.

In the UK, the qualification earned through fulfilling the UK Professional Standards Framework assessment (Fellow of the Higher Education Academy [HEA]) has become a common, portable currency across UK institutions. HEA fellow status is increasingly being cited as a desirable qualification in academic job advertisements. Thus, a universally recognized teaching qualification across the forty-seven countries might also promote the staff mobility agenda.

The number of Erasmus staff exchanges has been slowly increasing (today it is just under 40,000 annually), but the exchange scheme has been unpopular, partly due to the lack of incentives to teach abroad (Berndtson 2005, 23). In practice, most teaching exchanges are very short, often as few as five days. Still, exchange staff must cope with differences in the way their disciplines are conceived and taught in their new host country and must understand the local cultural norms for learning, teaching, and grading. Europe-wide professional standards may help in overcoming the obstacles such teaching cultures may create, facilitating teaching exchanges.

European qualification standards have already been designed for the institutional level by ENQA (2005). These standards (and guidelines) were approved in the Bergen Bologna ministerial conference for the European Higher Education Area. In a sense, they underpin the whole Bologna Process, as many of the Bologna action lines (e.g., student-centred learning, employability of graduates, social dimension) are understood as measures of quality. Although not part of the European agenda, it seems possible that some of these standards could also form the basis for a properly monitored and accredited European teaching qualification to emphasise key aspects of the quality agenda, including attending to special needs of different student groups, designing student assessment procedures to measure the achievement of intended learning outcomes, and having clear published criteria for marking and student progress monitoring. These concepts are integral to the notions of quality embraced by established educational development programmes.

But, quality should not be considered solely on the basis of formal, quantitative criteria (e.g., participation in pedagogical training, evaluation by students), as is often the case. Too frequently, the result of quality assurance efforts is short-termism and narrowness of focus (Head 2011). In teaching, common mechanisms of quality assurance may discourage risk taking and innovation and threaten to trivialise this complex process. One-off classroom observations decontextualize the act of classroom teaching and overemphasise performance. Student evaluations of teaching, while important, too often are based on ill-conceived questions and inappropriate norm referencing. "Student-centred" can too easily become student consumerism, which threatens the educational relationship between teachers and students and risks educational standards. In the end, an overemphasis on quality assurance may actually lower the standards of teaching.

Furthermore, there is the risk of uniformity. Higher education systems are becoming more and more alike "thanks partly to accrediting organisations that apply national standards uniformly" (Clausen 2006, 35). While the Bologna Process seeks "harmonization" of systems, the diversity of educational institutions should reflect important local differences in culture and values which should be protected.

In that sense there are also significant downsides to the use of a common professional standards framework across the European countries. First, there is a serious risk of devaluing and losing important cultural differences between countries through the convergence of norms across countries. Diversity amongst the states and across universities may be inherently valuable. If so, policies, including professional standards, must enable and support this heterogeneity. Indeed, the UK professional standards framework simply articulates core areas of teaching, knowledge, and values and three levels of standards, deliberately leaving it to each university to create their own programmes that satisfy the criteria, while fitting their local contexts. Institutions value this flexibility and autonomy as it enables them to deal with the unique context of their institution.

Connecting professional standards frameworks tightly with quality assurance can also breed a deficit model. Insofar as the field of educational development in the UK is rooted in government mandates that imply that academics are not qualified to teach (Dearing 1997; Browne 2010), the literature on learning and teaching in higher education in the UK too often has a patronising undercurrent. In its early days in the U.S., the field struggled to shake off the perception that it existed for remediation of poor teaching. The recent literature on learning and teaching in higher education emphasising the scholarly dimensions of teaching, heavily influenced by Boyer (1990), takes a respectful, collegial view of teachers.

Finally, professional standards frameworks can lead too easily to mandating teaching development programmes. Mandating teaching "certification" threatens to create a minimalist, bureaucratic "tick-boxing" culture of teaching, rather than an engaged, scholarly culture, effectively undermining the guiding vision of the professional standards framework. This threat may be particularly true in academic cultures that recognise research more than teaching, giving few incentives for academics to focus on their teaching.

A Common Core in Educational Development

Most of the Western countries with established programmes also embrace certain key assumptions about learning and teaching and have common components in their provision. First, sustained programmes emphasise inquiry into one's own teaching and students' learning, including action research (Kemmis 1988), classroom assessment (Angelo and Cross 1993), and classroom research (Cross and Steadman 1996). The scholarship of teaching, first popularised by Boyer (1990), emphasised that teaching is a scholarly activity. Since that time, the term "scholarship of teaching" has been used to describe research that academics do on teaching in their own subject areas and its dissemination. A recent review of the scholarship of teaching in a variety of fields concludes that there remains a dearth of high quality literature on learning and teaching in specific disciplines (Huber and Morreales 2002).

One risk of emphasising the scholarship of teaching is that, rather than breaking down the research-teaching divide, it extends the expectations of a research culture (i.e., publishing and peer review) to teaching work. Some critics also contend that without sufficient training in educational theory and methodology, the results of academics' own inquiries are of low quality and utility and erode the reputation of educational research (Lynn McAlpine, pers. comm.). While the scholarship of teaching has high developmental value for individual academics, the challenge remains to link individual inquiry at the classroom level to more systemic or cumulative change. These movements indicate an emphasis on an inquiry-oriented approach to instructional development, clearly in line with inquiry-based and problem-based learning traditions.

Relatedly, there is a consistent emphasis on reflective practice (Schön 1983; Brookfield 1995; Brockbank and McGill 2007). One aim is to give academics tools to question their aims, methods, contexts, and effectiveness so that they can continually improve, long after a formal instructional development programme ends. Another aim of reflective practice is to help academics fundamentally reconceptualise the teaching process.

To the extent that instructional development strives for transformations in programme participants' conceptions of teaching (e.g., Ramsden 1992, 2003), it is vital that academics question their existing conceptions. Having experiences that contradict their existing conceptions (or confronting evidence that does so) and then re-examining their conceptions in light of this new evidence or experience are key parts of adult transformative learning (Mezirow and Taylor 2009).

Instructional developers often face a tension between taking a learning-centred approach that seeks to shift teachers' conceptions and participants' expectation of getting tips, techniques, or coping strategies. For participants who want a quick fix, scholarly programmes that focus on questioning may be dissatisfying.

To support and assess reflective practice, portfolios are, perhaps, the most common mode of assessment for instructional development programmes. Trevitt, Stocks, and Quinlan (2011) argue that portfolios used in degree-awarding programmes of academic development have the following defining features: (i) representations of practice; (ii) use of education; and (iii) sufficient breadth to include various teaching tasks, such as course design, teaching, assessment. While there are tensions created by balancing formative and summative assessment, these authors offer recommendations for their use, arguing that the strengths of the portfolio make its challenges worthwhile (Trevitt, Stocks, and Quinlan 2011).

Instructional development programmes and workshops are typically organised across disciplines, creating communities of practice (Wenger 1998). Academics typically discuss generic educational literature, with a focus on the teaching/learning process rather than on the content of courses or on pedagogical content knowledge—the specialised knowledge of how to teach particular content (Shulman 1987). Thus, in most instructional development programmes in higher education there is relatively little emphasis on discipline-specific aspects of teaching compared to secondary education, which often has separate courses or tracks for different subject matters. That said, same-subject mentors are often used to provide disciplinary perspectives on learning and teaching, but the value of those relationships is largely unexplored.

Academics generally enjoy the opportunity to interact with their colleagues in other disciplines, and comparing practices with people teaching in different contexts can help them problematize their teaching—providing experiences that allow participants to question their "taken-for granted" assumptions and conceptions of teaching. However, returning to Shulman's (1987) framework of teacher knowledge, the cross-disciplinary structure means that instructional development in higher education does a better job of enhancing general knowledge of teaching and learning than it does pedagogical content knowledge, despite the presence of inquiry-based models which could serve as a means of exploring and building that pedagogical content knowledge.

In a similar vein, just as university-based instructional development programmes in the UK and Australia tend to emphasise general processes of learning and teaching, they also tend to neglect matters of curriculum (Barnett and Coate 2005). While departmental conversations about teaching often centre on the content—what is taught—academics may have little opportunity to frame their discussions in terms of larger theories of the purpose of higher education and theories of curriculum. Educational development could fill that gap, but often does not, as the field of curriculum studies is less developed in higher education than it is in primary and secondary-level schooling.

Another limitation of typical courses is that although there is attention to individual, national, institutional, and departmental policy contexts, the courses tend heavily toward psychological orientations. Relatively little emphasis is placed on other disciplines that contribute to the field of education, such as the philosophy of education, anthropology, sociology, history, or economics. Most courses focus on learning and teaching as individual acts.

In part, this individual focus may be because existing instructional development programmes generally emphasise inducting new teachers. In the UK, requirements for completion of programmes are focused on probationary staff. In Australia, most programmes are focused on the "foundations" of learning and teaching in higher education (Hicks et al. 2010). While it is important to induct new teachers into their profession, a greater emphasis could be placed on educating more experienced staff for leadership roles in learning and teaching or engaging teams of staff in whole departments.

Sponsored by universities, the programmes, unsurprisingly, have a focus on the local context. Programmes are designed to meet institutional needs and interests so that teachers can succeed in the local context. Educational developers often feel torn between complying with university agendas—which may be rooted in a deficit model, managerialist assumptions, or a risk management mentality—and their own desire to stimulate change, continuous quality improvement, or achieve humanistic goals. More importantly, the local focus can make it difficult to work concertedly toward regional agendas.

While cultural orientation programmes are often provided to international graduate students who will be taking up teaching posts in the U.S. and Canada, programmes of cultural orientation for new international teachers are less common elsewhere.

Across programmes, there seems to be ambivalence about how to handle diversity. To the extent that education is an enculturating force, calls for bi-directionality of exchange and accommodation of difference along socially and politically sensitive lines are very radical ideas. Short of accepting radical reform to the concept of Western higher education, many studies of diversity and inclusivity conclude that what is good for the minority is usually good for (or at least does not do any harm to) the majority. Thus, although increased student diversity spawned instructional development, there remains an inherent, largely implicit tension associated with these issues.

While European countries just establishing instructional development will naturally look to peer countries for models, they must develop programmes that are sensitive to the larger policy agendas—national, regional, and international—that spawn them. They can also learn from the weaknesses of existing programmes elsewhere and invent different approaches that advance the field.

IMPLICATIONS FOR NEW INSTRUCTIONAL DEVELOPMENT PROGRAMMES IN EUROPE

The analysis of the European higher education context and the interpretation of common instructional development elements expressed above can serve as a starting point for designing new programmes. Here we present several ideas worth considering when establishing instructional development that could partly address the teaching challenges presented by current European Commission policies.

First, the mobility agenda suggests thinking beyond the local interest and context. Instructional development programmes elsewhere are typically funded by the institution and, thus, are designed to serve the institution's needs. The focus, then, is on preparing staff to teach in that particular university. The European agenda, though, is about integration and linkage across the member states, suggesting the need for a portable qualification that prepares academics to teach anywhere in Europe.

To support mobility, one alternative might be the creation of a central programme of instructional development for Europe, rather than devolving provision to universities. Another alternative is for instructional development staff to model and lead the way on staff exchanges, perhaps creating jointly run programmes across institutions or countries that would expose academics to multiple institutional contexts as part of their teaching development experience. While most programmes are intra-institutional, there are a few models for programmes that serve the entire country, including, in the U.S., the Carnegie Academy for the Scholarship of Teaching and Learning (CASTL) programme and, in the UK, programmes from HEA Subject Centres.

Alternatively, if local variation in educational cultures is important, then instructional development programmes would need to focus on cultural orientation for newcomers, even if those academics had received introductions to teaching elsewhere. It is possible that a combination of models could be constructed that includes both a substantial, portable, common core addressing a shared professional standards framework, combined with short cultural orientations at each institution serving visiting academics, such as the types used in graduate teaching assistant programmes in the U.S. Similar cultural orientations would also be useful for exchange students to ensure they can adjust to their new setting.

A region that is creating educational development anew has the opportunity to face these issues of internationalisation and diversity head on and explicitly. Doing so means facing curriculum, the aims of higher education, and the philosophical, social roles of higher education directly. By facilitating discussions among academics, educational developers can help them not only question core assumptions but clarify vital academic and cultural values and how those are taught. Thus, educational developers can also initiate and sustain critical responses to the larger policy context in which they find themselves.

For example, the policy agenda focuses on employability as the primary goal of higher education. Critical discussions might help refocus academics on how they can achieve those aims, while also addressing other aims of higher education, such as cultivating student character or moral development, contributing to social justice, or making better problem solvers in their disciplines. Educational development processes offer ways for academics to study and come to better understand the needs of employers and of students who are returning to university with workplace experiences. Inquiry and student-centred approaches to teaching are appropriate ways to make stronger links with employers and work-based learning.

One could imagine dedicated instructional development workshops that bring employers and academics together to design courses or co-teach particular units. Although community engagement efforts are common in universities in the U.S. and the UK, these agendas are not usually a direct part of the role of instructional development. Other offices are charged with that work. New programmes could be structured differently, however, to bring those two areas into closer alignment.

As described, there is a lack of emphasis on discipline-specific teaching. The European Commission agendas could be well served, however, by creating discipline-specific educational development institutes, perhaps centred around the development of joint degree programmes across universities. Such programmes could help address the problems of student mobility outlined above, contribute to richer cross-national collaboration within disciplines, provide natural homes for stimulating staff mobility, and assure curricular integrity and rigor, while facilitating student mobility between institutions within particular, specially designed and structured programmes. These efforts would be far more ambitious than the existing administrative agreements between departments. During the redesign process, there would be opportunities, too, for incorporating employers and work-based learning into the experience.

Alternatively, universities might choose to create an interdisciplinary component to their education, deliberately making use of students' tendencies to flock to English-language courses regardless of discipline. European universities might borrow from the American liberal-arts tradition, to create a semester or year-long interdisciplinary learning community that explores a key theme or two.

Imagine a group of second-year students from dozens of countries coming together to explore the challenge of Europeanization, environmental sustainability, orhuman virtue and goodness from a variety of disciplinary perspectives. Blackmore and Kandiko (2010) report on the experience of more than two dozen universities around the world that have engaged in interdisciplinary curricular reform. Typically such curricula are responses to broader societal or political contexts. They offer guidance on the factors that contribute to the success of such initiatives, which may be of interest to innovators in Europe.

A process of curricular re-design and innovation can have powerful impacts on the academics who are involved (Quinlan 2003) and serve as a vehicle for instructional development. Curricular re-design—particularly interdisciplinary programmes—promotes collaboration among academics who might not otherwise interact. Such teaching collaborations not only lead to changes in the way teachers work with students; it can help academics rethink their own disciplines, stimulating creativity in both teaching and research.

As instructional development takes root in other countries, we have to guard against colonialism and inappropriately applying literature, findings, and frameworks from other settings to quite different cultures. Particular caution is warranted in translating educational literature from one setting to another, as many of the models, taxonomies, and ideas are highly normative. Given that schooling has traditionally played an acculturating role, cultural values necessarily are a central part of educational discussions.

Studies carried out in Asia (Kember and Gow 1990; Kember 1996) challenged the applicability of the time-honoured deep versus surface approaches to learning Western framework (Marton and Säljö 1976; Marton and Booth 1997). This cross-cultural research enriched and extended the original theory, while sounding a cautionary note about assuming that research frameworks and findings can (or should) be applied to other cultures.

CONCLUSION

Through this chapter, we illustrate how instructional development could be used to serve interests far beyond the institution. In this case, it is interests of European governments, strongly supported by the European Commission, that have placed demands on European universities. These demands can be addressed, in part, through thoughtful instructional development programmes and initiatives. To the extent that instructional development is harnessed in service of these broad social and economic policies, the evaluation of its effectiveness will also need to be considered in the context of those policy agendas.

However, this chapter also suggests that educational development could create a context for richer policy debate by engaging academics at the coal face in critically evaluating the policy and its implications for students and the educational process. Instructional development can add to the knowledge of learning and teaching in higher education, both through teaching and research, which, in turn, can provide a base of evidence and expertise to create well-informed policy in the future.

NOTES

1. Full-time students are expected to take sixty credits per year. One credit equals twenty-four to thirty hours of workload, depending upon the country.
2. A special tenth anniversary conference was held in 2010 in Budapest and Vienna. The next regular conference will be held in Bucharest in 2012.
3. In 2010 the Lisbon Strategy was replaced by the EU2020-strategy. Its targets are the same as in the old strategy, but its emphases are slightly different.

BIBLIOGRAPHY

Angelo, Thomas, and Patricia Cross. 1993. *Classroom Assessment Techniques: A Handbook for College Teachers*, 2nd ed. San Francisco: Jossey-Bass.

Balzer, Carolin, and Kerstin Martens. 2004. "International Higher Education and the Bologna Process. What Part Does the European Commission Play?" Paper presented at the epsNet Plenary Conference, Prague, 18–19 June.

Barnett, Ronald, and Kelly Coate. 2005. *Engaging the Curriculum in Higher Education*. Buckingham, UK: SRHE/Open University Press.

Bergström, Tomas. 2005. "ERASMUS—The Swedish Experience: From Imbalance to Imbalance." In *Mobile Europe: Improving Faculty and Student Mobility Conditions in Europe*, edited by Erkki Berndtson, 43–46. epsNet Reports #9. Paris: European Political Science Network.

Berndtson, Erkki. 2005. "Student and Teacher Mobility in Europe: Opinions and Attitudes among European Political Scientists." In *Mobile Europe: Improving Faculty and Student Mobility Conditions in Europe*, edited by Erkki Berndtson, 19–24. epsNet Reports #9. Paris: European Political Science Network.

Blackmore, Paul, and Camille Kandiko. 2010. "Creating a 21st Century Curriculum: The Kings-Warwick Project Final Report," http://kingslearning.info/kwp/

attachments/134_KWP-Creating_a_21st_Century_Curriculum_Final_Report. pdf.pdf 23 May 2011, accessed 08/06/2011.

Bologna Process Declarations (Communiqués from 1998, 1999, 2001, 2003, 2005, 2007, 2009. 2010, 2011. 2011. The Official Bologna Process Web site, http:// www.ehea.info/article-details.aspx?ArticleId=3, accessed 27/05/2011.

Boyer, Ernest L. 1990. *Scholarship Reconsidered: Priorities of the Professoriate.* San Francisco: Carnegie Foundation for the Advancement of Teaching and Jossey-Bass.

Brockbank, Anne, and Ian McGill. 2007. *Facilitating Reflective Learning in Higher Education*, 2nd ed. Maidenhead, UK: SRHE/Open University Press.

Brookfield, Stephen. 1995. *Becoming a Critically Reflective Teacher.* San Francisco: Jossey-Bass.

Browne, Lord John. 2010. Securing a Sustainable Future for Higher Education: An Independent Review of Higher Education Funding and Finance. Norwich, UK: HMSO, http://www.bis.gov.uk/assets/biscore/corporate/docs/s/10-1208es-securing-sustainable-higher-education-browne-report-summary.pdf, accessed 12/10/2010.

Chickering, Arthur W., and Zelda F. Gamson. 1987. "Seven Principles of Good Practice in Undergraduate Education." *The American Association for Higher Education Bulletin* (March).

Clausen, Christopher. 2006. "The New Ivory Tower." *The Wilson Quarterly* (Autumn): 31–36.

Cross, K. Patricia. 1971. *Beyond the Open Door: New Students to Higher Education.* San Francisco: Jossey-Bass.

Cross, Patricia, and Mimi H. Steadman. 1996. *Classroom Research: Implementing the Scholarship of Teaching.* San Francisco: Jossey-Bass.

Dearing, Sir Ronald. 1997. *Higher Education in the Learning Society: The National Committee of Inquiry into Higher Education.* London: HMSO, http://www. leeds.ac.uk/educol/ncihe/, accessed 23/05/2011.

EUA Trends Reports. 2011. European University Association Web site, http:// www.eua.be/eua-work-and-policy-area/building-the-european-higher-educa-tion-area/trends-in-european-higher-education.aspx, accessed 27/05/2011.

European Association for Quality Assurance in Higher Education (ENQA). 2005. *Standards and Guidelines for Quality Assurance in the European Higher Education Area,* http://www.enqa.eu/files/ENQA%20Bergen%20Report.pdf, accessed 27/05/2011.

European Commission. 2006. "Delivering on the Modernisation Agenda for Universities: Education, Research and Innovation. Communication from the Commission to the Council and the European Parliament, COM (2006) 208 Final." Brussels, 10/5/2006, http://eur-lex.europa.eu/LexUriServ/LexUriServ.do?uri=C OM:2006:0208:FIN:EN:PDF, accessed 27/05/2011.

———. 2008. "Modernising Universities for Europe's Competitiveness in a Global Knowledge Economy. Commission Staff Working Paper. Accompanying Document to the Report from the Commission to the Council on the Council Resolution of 23 November 2007, COM (2008) 680 Final." Brussels, 30.10.2008, http://ec.europa.eu/education/higher-education/doc/com/sec2719_en.pdf, accessed 27/05/2011.

———. 2011. "Erasmus—Statistics," http://ec.europa.eu/education/erasmus/ doc920_en.htm, accessed 27/05/2011.

Gibbs, Graham, and Martin Coffey. 2004. "The Impact of Training of University Teachers on Their Teaching Skills, Their Approach to Teaching and the Approach to Learning of Their Students." *Active Learning in Higher Education* 5: 87–100.

Gilis, Annelies, Mieke Clement, Lies Laga, and Paul Pauwels. 2008. "Establishing a Competence Profile for the Role of Student-Centred Teachers in Higher Education in Belgium." *Research in Higher Education* 49 (6): 531–554.

Gosling, David. 2009. "Educational Development in the UK: A Complex and Contradictory Reality." *International Journal of Educational Development* 14 (1): 5–18.

Head, Simon. 2011. "The Grim Threat to British Universities." *The New York Review of Books* January 13.

Hicks, Margaret, Heather Smigiel, Gail Wilson, and Ann Luzeckyi. 2010. *Final Report on the ALTC Project: Preparing Academics to Teach in Higher Education*. Adelaide: University of South Australia, http://www.altc.edu.au/project-preparing-university-teachers-model-unisa-2007, accessed 23/05/2011.

Huber, Mary T., and Sherwyn Morreales, eds. 2002. *Disciplinary Styles in the Scholarship of Teaching: Exploring Common Ground*. Washington, DC: American Association for Higher Education and Menlo Park: Carnegie Foundation for the Advancement of Teaching.

Keeling, Ruth. 2004. "Locating Ourselves in the 'European Higher Education Area': Investigating the Bologna Process in Practice." Paper presented at the epsNet Plenary Conference, Prague, 18–19 June.

Kember, David. 1996. "The Intention to Both Memorise and Understand: Another Approach to Learning?" *Higher Education* 31 (3): 341–354,

Kember, David, and Lyn Gow. 1990. "Cultural Specificity of Approaches to Study." *British Journal of Educational Psychology* 60 (3): 356–363.

Kemmis, Stephen. 1988. "Action Research." In *Educational Research, Methodology and Measurement: An International Handbook*, edited by John P. Keeves. Oxford: Pergamon.

Keulen, Hanno van, and Martin van de Ven. 2006. "Basic Teaching Qualification in Dutch Universities." NETTLE Partner Meeting on Meta-Frameworks for European Standards for Teaching in Higher Education. Toledo, Spain: November 16–17.

Lee, Alison, Catherine E. Manathunga, and Peter Kandlbinder, eds. 2008. *Making a Place: On Oral History of Academic Development in Australia*. Milperra, NSW: Higher Education Research and Development of Society of Australasia.

Lindberg-Sand, Åsa, and Anders Sonesson. 2008. "Compulsory Higher Education Teacher Training in Sweden: Development of a National Standards Framework Based on the Scholarship of Teaching and Learning." *Tertiary Education and Management* 14 (2): 123–139.

Marton, Ference, and Shirley Booth. 1997. *Learning and Awareness*. Mahwah, NJ: Lawrence Erlbaum Associates.

Marton, Ference, and Roger Säljö. 1976. "On Qualitative Differences in Learning: I. Outcome and Process." *British Journal of Educational Psychology* 46 (1): 4–11.

Mezirow, Jack, Edward W. Taylor and Associates. 2009. *Transformative Learning in Practice: Insights from Community, Workplace, and Higher Education*. San Francisco: Jossey-Bass.

Quinlan, Kathleen M. 2003. "Effects of Problem-Based Learning Curricula on Faculty Learning: New Lenses, New Questions." *Advances in Health Sciences Education* 8 (3): 249–259.

Ramsden, Paul. 1992. *Learning to Teaching in Higher Education*. London: Routledge.

———. 2003. *Learning to Teaching in Higher Education*, 2nd ed. London: Routledge.

Rauhvargers, Andrejs, Cynthia Deane, and Wilfried Pauwels. 2009. *Bologna Process Stocktaking Report from Working Groups Appointed by the Bologna Follow-up Group to the Ministerial Conference in Leuven/Louvain-la-Neuve*, http://www.ond.vlaanderen.be/hogeronderwijs/bologna/conference/documents/Stocktaking_report_2009_FINAL.pdf, accessed 27/05/2011.

Reinalda, Bob, and Ewa Kulesza. 2006. *The Bologna Process—Harmonizing Europe's Higher Education*. Opladen, Germany, and Farmington Hills, MI: Barbara Budrich Publishers.

Sato, Hiroaki. 2010. "FD Map: A Conceptual Map on Faculty Development Programs." International Consortium of Educational Development. Barcelona, Spain, June 28–30.

Schön, Donald. 1983. *The Reflective Practitioner: How Professionals Think in Action*. London: Temple Smith.

Shulman, Lee S. 1987. "Knowledge and Teaching: Foundations of the New Reform." *Harvard Educational Review* (Spring): 1–22.

Tigelaar, Dineke E. H., Diana H. J. M. Dolmans, Ineke H. A. P. Wolfhagen, and Cees P. M. Van Der Vleuten. 2004. "The Development and Validation of a Framework for Teaching Competencies in Higher Education." *Higher Education* 48 (2): 253–268.

Trevitt, Chris, Claire Stocks, and Kathleen M. Quinlan. 2011. "Advancing Assessment Practice in Continuing Professional Learning: Toward a Richer Understanding of Teaching Portfolios for Learning *and* Assessment." *International Journal of Academic Development, iFirst*. doi: 10.1080/1360144X.2011.589004.

Van Cranenburgh, Oda. 2005. "The BA-MA Structure and Mobility of Students in European Political Science." In *Mobile Europe: Improving Faculty and Student Mobility Conditions in Europe*, edited by Erkki Berndtson, 55–61. epsNet Reports #9. Paris: European Political Science Network.

Wenger, Etienne. 1998. *Communities of Practice: Learning, Meaning, and Identity*. Cambridge: Cambridge University Press.

9 Teacher Development Programmes
National Policies Enabling Local Impact in Ireland

Jennifer Murphy[1]

INTRODUCTION

In the last decade, at least thirteen higher education institutions (HEIs) in Ireland have developed formal accredited programmes or modules in teaching and learning in higher education. This chapter outlines the factors that encouraged and enabled the development of these accredited programmes and provides an overview of commonalities and differences between them. In describing these programmes, reference is made to the trends in their structure, learning outcomes, and assessment. The methodology used to collect this information was through content analysis of various documents including programme handbooks, course Web sites, and module descriptors of available accredited programmes.

As many of the programmes in question are less than five years old, it would be somewhat premature to undertake a major evaluation of their impact. Hence, for the purposes of this chapter, just a short survey of the directors of accredited programmes in teaching and learning was disseminated in an attempt to investigate if any impact of these programmes is already evident. In addition to the survey, transcripts of interviews with a number of graduates from the masters programme of one institution are analysed.

BACKGROUND AND CONTEXT

Ireland is a small country with a total population of approximately 4.6 million (Central Statistics Office 2011). The public higher education sector in Ireland comprises seven universities, fourteen institutes of technology (IoTs), six colleges of education, and a number of smaller institutions. There are also a number of private institutions and research institutes. The funding and legislative authority for higher education and research in Ireland is the Higher Education Authority (HEA). Higher education in Ireland enjoys a high level of autonomy relative to the rest of the world. The sector is well perceived internationally with many positive features being highlighted in the report of the Economic and Financial Affairs Council (ECOFIN) of the European Union (St. Aubyn et al. 2009).

CHANGE CATALYSTS

In Ireland, a number of driving forces in the past decade have encouraged an interest in revitalising the status of teaching as a central aspect of the academic profession. In 1998 a colloquium focusing on university teaching and learning invited workgroups to compile recommendations on higher education issues. The workgroup concentrating on accreditation and development for third-level teachers had a number of recommendations. These included that policies be developed which give recognition of, incentives to, and rewards for good teaching, and that tenure and promotion policies and procedures take account of teaching in a systematic way (Irish University Training Network 1998). This challenge is further echoed in Skilbeck's (2001, 72) report on higher education in Ireland, which highlighted that "new and improved ways of teaching students is one of the challenges facing higher education staff." Additionally a report by the Organisation for Economic Co-operation and Development (OECD) calls for a more positive approach to staff development and a commitment of institutional resources to staff development programmes "in particular in the development and updating of teaching skills" (OECD 2004, 27).

Since the publication of these reports many forces have combined to drive change in the development of teaching and learning in contemporary Irish HEIs. The work that has been happening to develop initiatives and programmes to support teaching and learning in the UK have had a strong influence. In addition, the work of scholars in the U.S., in particular that of Lee Shulman, Pat Hutchings, Mary Huber, Howard Gardner, and others, have inspired a number of developments in Ireland (Hyland 2010).

These scholars informed the work of many Irish scholars not only through their research publications on teaching and learning but through their direct advice and assistance on teaching and learning initiatives which were developing in Ireland. These developments included efforts at advancing the scholarship of teaching and learning, catering for students' multiple intelligences, encouraging teaching for understanding, development of teaching portfolios, and integration of research, teaching, and learning (Lyons, Hyland, and Ryan 2002; Hyland 2004; O'Neill, Moore, and McMullin 2005; Murphy and Higgs 2009; Murphy, Griffin, and Higgs 2010).

The Bologna Process has been another catalyst for change with the literature widely reporting on the many transformations arising from the Sorbonne (1998) and Bologna (1999) Declarations and subsequent communiqués (Rauhvargers, Deane, and Pauwels 2009; Eurydice 2010; Gaston 2010). The commitments of the Bologna Process have significant implications for teaching methodologies and approaches. The learning outcomes approach to curriculum design, for example, and a shift in focus from teacher-centric to student-centred methodologies are strongly encouraged. Hyland (2010) acknowledges that the anticipated changes in course design and structure arising from the Bologna Process have training and up-skilling implications for teaching staff and that the provision of support through appropriate training and development initiatives is necessary to ensure alignment of learning outcomes, teaching approaches/pedagogies, and modes of assessment.

CHANGE ENABLERS

Over the last decade the funding agency for higher education in Ireland, the HEA, made funding available that enabled a "co-ordinated approach to supporting and enhancing teaching and learning" (Hyland 2010, 138). The refocusing of teaching and learning in many institutions can be traced back to the increasing emphasis on the link between research and teaching and learning in the HEAs Programme for Research in Third Level Institutions (PRTLI, Hyland 2007). Significant developments and innovations in teaching and learning were enabled by the Targeted Initiatives scheme and the Training of Trainers fund.

These schemes were a major impetus to teaching and learning, allowing individuals to apply for funding outside of their core budgets. In 2004, the Targeted Initiatives scheme was redefined and renamed Strategic Initiatives. This redefinition meant that proposals for funding in teaching and learning would have to tie into the university's overall strategy for improvement. Strategic Initiatives funded a number of proposals at the institutional level to develop teaching development centres, staff seminars on teaching and learning, and awards schemes for teaching excellence.

The groundswell of interest in developing resources, programmes, and initiatives to enhance teaching and learning in higher education led to the establishment of a number of national support networks including: Education Developers in Ireland Network (EDIN), All Ireland Society for Higher Education (AISHE), Irish Learning Technology Association (ILTA), National Digital Learning Resources (NDLR), Learning Innovation Network (LIN), and the National Academy for Integration of Research, Teaching and Learning (NAIRTL). These networks have the common objective of supporting teaching and learning in higher education. They enable a sharing of expertise and experience and provide resources and support for individual teachers as well as for institutional centres for teaching and learning.

The increased availability of funding and support from the HEA has enabled HEIs to provide formal opportunities for academic staff development in teaching and many have introduced certificate, diploma, and master's programmes in teaching and learning in higher education. Accredited programmes in teaching and learning in higher education were first introduced to Irish HEIs in 2001 by the Dublin Institute of Technology (DIT). Since then, these programmes have become an important element of developing the teaching and learning practices of higher education professionals.

At present, thirteen HEIs in Ireland offer programmes or modules in teaching and learning in higher education. These programmes and modules are administered, by and large, through institutional centres for teaching and learning, with six to eight individuals participating in the course delivery. The rapid adoption of such programmes over the last decade is evidence of the substantial demand for professional development in teaching and learning across the higher education sector.

METHODOLOGY

This study describes the available accredited programmes in teaching and learning in higher education in Ireland and reports on the similarities and differences between them. Data for the study were collected through a content analysis of relevant publically available documents. The sources of evidence used include programme handbooks, course Web sites, and module descriptors of available accredited programmes.

In addition, in April 2010, a survey was sent to thirteen directors of the various accredited programmes in teaching and learning. As the survey targeted particular individuals, it did not allow for anonymity and this is acknowledged as a limitation. The first page of the survey requested general information on what programmes in teaching and learning were available, that is, the course titles and modules of relevant certificate, diploma, master's, and doctorate programmes. As much of this general information was already found via the course handbooks and institutional Web sites, details of the course titles, modules, and contact details were prefilled into the survey before sending it to individual programme directors. They were then requested to check the prefilled information for accuracy and to complete the remaining eight questions. Two weeks was given to complete the survey, with a reminder being sent after one and a half weeks. Where a reply was not received by the deadline, programme directors were called by phone asking them to complete the survey. The response rate was 54 percent.

The eight questions included a mix of closed and open questions. The closed questions sought information on enrolment and completion numbers and asked whether or not specific challenges had been encountered during development of the programmes. The open questions invited programme directors to express, in their own opinions, what impact the accredited programmes in teaching and learning were having in their institution. The potential for bias here is fully acknowledged as it is probably in the programme directors' interest that such programmes would have a positive impact.

Survey respondents were also asked if graduates of their programmes had been recognized through any awards, grants, or promotions for their contribution to teaching and learning after completion of the programme.

It should be noted here that no attempt is made to infer a cause-and-effect relationship between programme completion and subsequent recognition. Relevant quotations are used from survey responses to the open-ended questions but the names of individual programme directors are not identified.

Finally, video recordings of interviews with three individuals who had completed the Masters in Teaching and Learning in Higher Education in one institution were examined. These interviews were carried out by one programme director, Dr. Marian McCarthy, University College Cork (UCC), as part of a collaborative project of the Irish National Academy for Integration of Research, Teaching and Learning (NAIRTL[2]), in which the author participated. This project concerned understandings of what it means to integrate research, teaching, and learning. Some clips from these recordings were deemed relevant to assessing the impact of the programmes in teaching and learning in higher education as respondents indicated that their academic practice had changed due to the knowledge that was gained through participation in the programme.

The interviewees were selected by the UCC programme director using convenience sampling based on individuals' availability and location. The clips were transcribed and relevant parts are quoted later in the chapter. The chosen quotations pertain to the impact of using a Scholarship of Teaching and Learning (SOTL) approach—an approach which was strongly advocated throughout the accredited certificate, diploma, and master's programmes in the institution in question. The quoted remarks only propose to indicate impact on the specific individual in question. A much larger and more representative sample would be required to make any general conclusions. Names of interviewees are not identified.

OVERVIEW OF AVAILABLE ACCREDITED PROGRAMMES

Four levels of accredited programmes in teaching and learning in higher education are available: certificate, diploma, master's, and doctorate. These programmes share the following objectives to a greater or lesser extent:

- To develop teaching for improved learning in Irish higher education;
- To act as a forum for reflection on teaching and learning methods;
- To provide an accredited structure that acknowledges professional development;
- To innovate on existing teaching and learning designs, curricula, and practice.

The next section will look at each of the programme types separately and will outline availability and trends in structure, learning outcomes, and assessment.

Table 9.1   Theory and Practical Modules Offered in Certificate Programmes

HEI Offering Certificate	Theory Modules	Practical Modules
NUI Galway	Introduction to Teaching and Learning in Higher Education	Course Design, Assessment, and Evaluation Reflective Practice and Professional Development
UCC	Theories of Teaching, Learning, and Assessment	Practice Approaches to Teaching, Learning, and Assessment

Postgraduate Certificate in Teaching and Learning in Higher Education

A graduate certificate programme in teaching and learning, targeted at academic staff, is offered by at least three HEIs in Ireland (although many HEIs that offer diplomas also award certificates for students who complete thirty ECTS [European Credit Transfer System]). The modules offered and their respective learning outcomes are strikingly similar across the institutions. To complete the certificate, students study theoretical approaches to teaching in higher education as well as putting these theories into practice through curriculum development, evaluation, and critical self-reflection.

The National University of Ireland, Galway (NUI Galway), and University College Cork (UCC) have structured their courses in a way that each of these objectives is embodied in at least one module (Table 9.1).

University College Dublin (UCD) has recently restructured its certificate programme in order to offer various pathways to achieving the necessary thirty ECTS. Although the UCD programme is structurally different from the others, the learning outcomes are largely similar, with elements of theoretical and practical development at the core of the course (Table 9.2).

All three accredited programmes share the same duration, running for one year over two semesters. Parallels can also be drawn in their delivery and assessment. NUI Galway, UCD, and UCC deliver the theory and practical modules through seminars or workshops and online discussions over two semesters. With regard to the assessment of these three programmes, in general participants are required to engage in short writing assignments, to participate in the workshops or seminars, and to produce a teaching portfolio or course review folder over the course of the year. The purpose of this portfolio or folder is to encourage reflective practice.

Table 9.2 UCD Structure of Accredited Programmes in Teaching and Learning

		↓ Pilot Scheme Sept – Dec 2010 ↓ (MGTA restricted entry) ↓				*Award*	*Award*	*Award*	*Award*
Essential Teaching Skills Modules	Any three of →	Becoming a Better Uni Teacher 5 Credits	Assessing & Teaching for Learning 5 Credits	Scholarship of Teaching 5 Credits	Mentoring Grad Teaching Ass. (MGTA) 5 Credits				
Scholarly-practice Modules	Any three of →	Evaluating Learning 5 Credits	Expert-Obs. of Teaching 5 Credits	Peer-Obs. of Teaching 5 Credits	School-based module 5 credits	**GCert** *in Teaching and Learning in Higher Education 30 Credits from any combination of these modules*	**GDip** *In Teaching and Learning in Higher Education 60 Credits from any combination of these modules*	**MA not yet validated** **MA** *(Teaching and Learning in Higher Education) 90 Credits (must include at least 2 research modules)*	Special purpose awards possible from single modules or combinations totalling less than 30 ECTS
		Reflective Teaching 5 credits	Scholarly Practice 5 Credits						
		Sept – Dec 2010 ↓ for new cohort							
CPD Modules		Designing and Developing Curricula in Higher Education 15 Credits		School-based module 5 Credits					
		Jan – May 2010 ↓							
Research Module		Literature Review (Research) 15 Credits		School-based module 5 Credits					
Research Module		Practitioner Research Project (Research) 15 Credits		Module activities can be School- or team-focussed					
Research Module		Writing for Publication 15 Credits							

Table 9.3   Academic Professional Development Modules for Postgraduate
              Students (Five ECTS)

HEI Offering Module to Postgraduate Students	Course Title	Learning Objectives
NUI Maynooth	Professional Certificate in Postgraduate Teaching and Learning	To begin the process of professionalising prospective academic staff through introduction to pedagogy and the scholarship of teaching and learning
UCC	Teaching and Learning for Graduate Studies	Engage with various sources of evidence and scholarship to evaluate and improve teaching practice
DIT	Certificate in Professional Development	Exploration of educational theories and development of a strong knowledge of learning styles and methodologies. Practical learning in the design and preparation of teaching and lesson plans

Certificate for Postgraduate Students Who Teach

A report of the Irish Universities Quality Board stated that all postgraduate students who teach should receive some support or training from their institution. In an effort to better prepare postgraduate students for their teaching responsibilities, at least three institutions have designed an elective accredited module for beginning teachers in higher education. National University of Ireland Maynooth (NUI Maynooth), DIT, and UCC offer one module (five ECTS) that blends the theories behind higher education teaching and learning with practical elements employed by the students (Table 9.3).

Postgraduate Diploma in Teaching and Learning in Higher Education

At least six Irish HEIs offer a diploma in teaching and learning in higher education. The similarities among diploma courses are evident in their learning outcomes and course structures. An accredited diploma programme comprises sixty ECTS (typically completed over two years of study). Students who complete a certificate in teaching and learning require only an additional thirty ECTS (typically completed over one year of study). HEIs that do not offer certificates in teaching and learning, but do offer diplomas, include in their two-year course those theoretical modules and practical modules that are a component part of the certificate programmes.

Table 9.4 Key Learning Objectives of Diploma Courses

Learning Objective Theme	NUI Galway	UCD	UCC	NUI Maynooth	UL	WIT
1. Develop Discipline Pedagogy	apply knowledge about various approaches to your own discipline	synthesise the results of pedagogical research with your own discipline	identify the key features of your discipline	examine a specific question/issue relating to your teaching	be competent in a teaching/research role within a specific discipline	develop your professional competence in specific subject areas
2. Self-Reflection	promote the concept of reflective practice	apply the reflective practitioner model	investigate how effective ... pedagogy is for disciplinary understanding and student learning	examine your own teaching in the classroom	acquire key skills for reflecting on your own practice	establish your own perspective on key issues relating to your practice
3. Diversity	appreciate a variety of ... approaches which may be undertaken within particular contexts	consider student and staff attributes that influence the teaching and learning process	identify the various intelligences and learning styles indicative of diversity	discuss curriculum design and related issues such as diversity	adjust competencies to different kinds of HE audiences	widen your repertoire of teaching methods
4. Information Technology/ Learning Technology	provide a theoretical and practical exposure to a range of technologies used in teaching and learning	review and evaluate aspects of current practice in online learning	participate in discussions (real and virtual) re teaching and learning	participate in online discussions	online interaction	consider the role of IT and emerging technologies
5. Context of Irish higher education (HE)	raise critical awareness of key issues in teaching, and learning ... in contemporary HE	critically evaluate the learning environment within which you work	examine some key theories of teaching, learning, and assessment in HE	explore the key practical issues associated with teaching and learning in HE	develop critical insights on current HE policy	broaden knowledge of the Irish further and HE systems

In addition to these theoretical and practical modules, the diploma programmes share some key themes within their learning objectives (Table 9.4). Among them is the development of participants' pedagogy for their discipline, the development of self-reflective practices and greater awareness, the development of participants' ability to teach diverse learning groups, the encouragement of greater consideration of the role of information and learning technologies, and to familiarise participants with the contexts of Irish higher education.

The delivery modes of these diploma courses share many similarities largely comprising lectures and workshops along with an online component, usually an interactive discussion board. This mode of delivery allows students to operate within a virtual learning environment (VLE) and to adapt the utility of a VLE to their own discipline. Like the certificate course, the diploma courses are also assessed by coursework and written assignments, and most HEIs also require a self-directed project. These projects take various forms, including sizable research papers, literature reviews, and extensive pedagogical critiques. All of the projects have the objective to develop a discipline-specific pedagogy that caters for diverse student groups and encourages greater self-reflection.

Beyond these traditional certification programmes, the Learning Innovation Network (LIN) in collaboration with the IoTs in Ireland is developing a flexible pathway to complete a postgraduate diploma or master's in learning and teaching. To be awarded the diploma, an individual must complete sixty ECTS credits from the available ten modules (nine elective and one mandatory). Seven ten-ECTS special purpose awards at level nine on the Irish national framework of qualifications are included among the elective modules being made available through various IoTs. Each module is led by a single institution but has been validated and piloted by various institutes. Each of the special-purpose modules available relate to a relevant aspect of teaching in higher education, for instance, mentoring, assessment and evaluation, technology-enhanced learning, enquiry-based learning, researching educational practice, and so on.

It is intended that this programme will cater for early career academics, academics with extensive teaching experience as well as academics seeking to combine subject discipline teaching with research interests. This modular framework facilitates different opportunities for IoT staff to develop a range of agreed generic core competences as part of a tailored personal professional development process.

Master's Programmes in Teaching and Learning in Higher Education

There are at least six master's programmes available in Ireland that relate specifically to teaching and learning in higher education. The programmes are largely similar with only modest deviation in learning outcomes and structure.

In UCC, participants must complete 120 ECTS to graduate with a master of arts (MA) in teaching and learning in higher education; in Waterford Institute of Technology (WIT), NUI Galway, and DIT, students complete ninety ECTS for the same qualification. These master's programmes provide module exemptions for those students who graduate with the sixty ECTS from a diploma programme, requiring them in most cases to take an additional thirty ECTS (sixty ECTS in UCC). University of Limerick (UL) offers a similarly structured course; however, it did not run in the 2009–2010 academic year and its continued operation is dependent upon student take-up.

The outcomes of these programmes (beyond the learning outcomes in the diploma programmes) include developing a research thesis, learning methodological approaches to writing about higher education, and dissemination of individual perspectives on the key issues facing teaching and learning in higher education. To achieve these goals, initially all programmes require students to take a module on research methods which is designed to familiarise students with existing literature in their chosen field of study and to identify appropriate research methodologies. Following this, students undergo individual study and research that will result in a dissertation. The dissertation is the primary mode of assessment for the programme.

One institution—DIT—offers two master's programmes related to teaching and learning in higher education with the second one being a master of science (MSc) designed for participants to focus more closely on the role that technology can play in education. The learning objectives of this two-year master's programme focus on development of student skills in Web-based communication tools like blogs, wikis, social networking sites, learning software, and VLEs. The course is delivered through a combination of both traditional seminar-style workshops and online sessions and comprises sixty ECTS, including a module on research methods and a research project on E-learning. So although the content of this course is much different from the MA programmes, the structure and assessment style is comparable.

It should be noted that a new master's programme designed for academics teaching in higher education was launched in Trinity College Dublin a short time after the survey was sent out and so details of this programme are not included here. There are also some relevant discipline-specific programmes available that are not dealt with in this chapter, most notably in health education; for example, NUI Galway has offered a diploma in clinical teaching since 2005, and a master's in clinical education since 2008. Additionally, the Royal College of Surgeons is offering a master's programme in leadership in education for health professionals since October 2010.

PhD in Academic Practice

Currently only one Irish HEI—NUI Galway—offers a PhD programme in academic practice. This programme offers participants further research opportunities in the field of teaching and learning in higher education. The PhD is assessed by completing a significant dissertation of original scholarship. Previous and current research projects include investigations into learning technologies, diversity in learning, reflective practice, civic engagement, and higher education policy.

THE IMPACT OF TEACHING AND LEARNING PROGRAMMES

Measuring the impact of individual programmes is a complex and even potentially controversial matter. It would need to consider intended impact and that which is realised unintentionally. Furthermore, limitations apply when attempting to measure the impact of programmes that are relatively new, where it may not even be realistic to expect significant measurable impact at such an early stage. This section does not provide an in-depth analysis of overall impact of the accredited programmes in teaching and learning but focuses instead on impact of the programmes as perceived by programme directors. In addition, it looks at what impact has been identified by three individual programme participants, where impact is identified as the change in their knowledge, academic practice, and recognition of their teaching. Finally, the wider impact on teaching quality and policy in the institution is considered.

Impact as Perceived by Programme Directors

Question six of the survey of programme directors asked: In your opinion what is the impact of the teaching and learning courses in your institution? Despite the fact that many of the teaching and learning courses are only in existence for a short number of years, five programme directors indicated that an impact is already evident. The impact at this early stage is largely focused on the programme participants. The impacts identified can be themed into three broad areas:

- Change in knowledge of participants;
- Change in practice of participants;
- Change in recognition of participants.

The change in knowledge of participants identified includes their "growing awareness of the literature on teaching and learning internationally." One respondent reported that one of the most significant impacts of these programmes was in "raising the profile of teaching and learning issues." Another referred to academic staff now beginning "to speak the language of student learning." The increased knowledge of teaching and learning issues and theories has, in some cases, led to a change in participants' practice.

The identified changes in participants' practice include their "facilitation of greater sharing of teaching and learning experiences," and greater professional collegiality. Among programme participants there is also more evidence of "networking," "building up collaborations," and "greater discussion of teaching and learning with colleagues." Participation in the accredited programmes has led to "increased confidence in trying new teaching and learning strategies" with some programme participants going so far as to change the design and delivery of their courses:

> The teaching and learning courses have had a huge impact on the delivery and improvement of individual courses/modules across all faculties ... colleagues provide substantial evidence of how they have redesigned courses and include student responses and feedback.

One respondent indicated that theoretical engagement produces the primary impact of the programmes where academic staff engage in scholarly activity in learning and teaching together with peer and self-reflection. Since all of the programmes in teaching and learning in higher education contain elements of theoretical education and reflective practice, it is likely that participation of increasing numbers of staff on teaching and learning programmes is leading to the redesign of many courses and modules across several disciplines.

Survey responses recognized that the programme participants have had the opportunity to disseminate their work and to network with others at teaching and learning conferences. It was indicated that this dissemination of their work has led to greater professional recognition for the individuals concerned.

The fifth question of the survey asked: Have any graduates of your course been recognized for their contribution to teaching and learning after taking a course (awards, grants, promotions)? All those that responded to this question said "yes." Many of them provided details of the recognition received by their programme participants. Recognition was identified in the form of requests to contribute to publications; receipt of research grants; receipt of institutional, national, and international teaching awards; and promotions.

Impact as Perceived by Programme Participants

The clips of interviews that were carried out with three individuals who had completed the master's in teaching and learning in higher education at one institution provide a useful account of impact as perceived by the programme participants. Once again the impacts identified can be themed into the same three broad areas:

- Change in knowledge of participants;
- Change in practice of participants;
- Change in recognition of participants.

One individual indicated that completion of the course contributed largely to an increase in his knowledge of pedagogical theory and practice:

> It has given me a language . . . in which I can explore my own teaching . . . a more systematic and rigorous way in which I can interrogate my own practice. It has given me a transformative lens with which I can look at what I am attempting to do in the classroom, with the students.

Application of this knowledge culminated in a change in the individual's academic practice. In fact, all interviewees indicated that they have become more scholarly in their teaching. One interviewee described how learning about teaching and learning issues in higher education helped her to more easily identify those aspects of the curriculum which students tend to find difficult. She also indicated that knowing this allowed her to work on improving the teaching of difficult concepts. All interviewees displayed a deep interest and enthusiasm for their teaching. The idea of enjoying teaching and taking risks in the classroom brought a "new excitement in the teaching and the students learning."

The interviewees echoed that the changes in their professional practice and dissemination of their work brought them greater recognition:

> It provided a wonderful opportunity for me as an academic to meaningfully link my research and teaching and to get far more public recognition for that type of work than I would ever have imagined when I started off on this journey; the process of researching into my teaching has been transformative . . . and has opened doors for me. I have had opportunities to get published in places I wouldn't have thought of before . . . the work I have been doing has been very well received, so much so that I have been invited to help other departments . . . for instance in Singapore.

It is also notable that all interviewees have received research grants to further their research since completing their accredited programmes on teaching and learning.

Institution-Wide Impact

The impact that accredited programmes have in focusing more people on the ways in which teaching and learning are conducted institutionally was referred to as a positive development in the survey responses. One of the most significant and enduring impacts of the implementation of accredited programmes in teaching and learning has been identified in the increased awareness of the centrality of teaching and learning practice in higher education. Details of completion numbers will be an important indicator of the extent of the impact that accredited programmes are having.

The survey showed that one institution is already graduating in excess of forty staff annually from the certificate programme, with more than 50 percent of these progressing to complete the diploma. Where courses are in their very early stages with low completion numbers the impact will be considerably less than in institutions where the completion rate is high.

Examination of documentary evidence in the form of institutional plans and policies strongly reflects the centrality of teaching and learning in higher education. Since 2001, the strategic plans of several of Ireland's leading HEIs have acknowledged the need for staff to be actively encouraged to engage in research-led teaching, to incorporate new technologies to aid learning and teaching, to reflect on their academic practice, and to support learning in innovative ways. In 2006 one institution, DIT, went so far as to require new academic staff, who do not have an equivalent qualification, to take the diploma in teaching and learning within two years of their start date.

Many HEIs, over the last decade, have begun to formally recognise excellence in teaching, with six institutions offering prestigious institutional teaching awards. In most cases the awards reflect excellence in those practices espoused by the teaching and learning programmes: reflective practice, curriculum design, innovative teaching, and learning effectiveness. Together with institutional awards, a number of high-profile regional and national awards for excellence in teaching have been established. These awards, in turn, create an environment in which the encouragement of excellence in teaching is publicly acknowledged and rewarded, representing a major cultural shift in institutional attitudes to teaching practice, the high profile of which can, arguably, be traced to the establishment of accredited programmes.

REMAINING CHALLENGES

The agents that have enabled the significant changes in the development of teaching and learning in higher education in Ireland have faced many complexities and challenges in their journey. Hyland (2010, 141) advises that such

> "change agents" must be eternally vigilant: to ensure that university strategic plans continue to be at the forefront of teaching and learning; and to ensure that teaching and learning remains a university priority when funding is being allocated within the university; to apply for new funding opportunities for teaching and learning at national and international levels; and to ensure that any new structures that are developed within the university to support and enhance teaching and learning are not eroded or destroyed by colleagues who would prefer the old status quo to be undisturbed.

While there are many positive impacts arising from the accredited programmes in teaching and learning in higher education, challenges still remain in their continued development and delivery. Some of the main challenges are highlighted by the survey respondents. Most programme directors underlined time constraints and the heavy workload of academic staff as obstacles to enrolment in teaching and learning programmes. This poses great problems for organising staff development opportunities. Some programme directors have tried to tackle this issue by holding classes during lunch hours and on Saturdays.

Another challenge cited by respondents was finding appropriate resources for their programmes. The onset of the economic recession brought with it a year-on-year reduction in expected state grant for HEIs. The imposed headcount reductions and recruitment freeze presented additional challenges to programme directors.

Finally, there is an emerging challenge facing the Irish HEIs on the issue of uniformity in programme accreditation. One survey respondent argued that programmes should "continue to be autonomously managed and accredited by individual institutions so that they can be closely matched to local context, strategic priorities, and disciplinary cultures." Such contextualisation is a key component of many such programmes. However, another respondent noted that this autonomous management makes it difficult for students to "carry credits from one programme to another in different institutes," and believes "more needs to be done to ease these institutional barriers."

CONCLUSION

Wieman, Perkins, and Gilbert (2010) maintain that although use of novel pedagogies has the potential to achieve far greater student learning, the didactic lecture remains the pervasive mode of teaching in universities. However, many changes to traditional academic practice are now evident in HEIs in Ireland. Until the late 1990s, there had been only limited provision of training and development courses in teaching in higher education. At this time, reports relating to higher education in Ireland began to focus on the importance of quality teaching and learning in higher education and the necessity for staff development initiatives. Developments in higher education in the UK and the U.S., together with the Bologna agreement (1999) and its successor agreements, were strong influencing factors on the Irish context.

The last decade has seen advancements in the quality of teaching in Ireland and the development of accredited programmes in teaching and learning have introduced the superiority of various other teaching methods to academic staff. These certificate, diploma, and master's programmes show great similarities in their design, delivery, and modes of assessment. In all cases participants are expected to develop reflective skills, knowledge of pedagogical theory, a contextual understanding of higher education in Ireland together with an array of teaching methodologies. Throughout these programmes participants are also exposed to new innovations in use of technology in teaching and learning and experience several different modes of course delivery.

Although many of the accredited programmes in teaching and learning are only in existence for a short time, already there is some evidence that they have positively impacted on participants, in their development of pedagogical knowledge and their ability to put that knowledge into practice. The collaborative networking, individual reflections, and advanced research that have emerged as a result of these programmes are significant. These programmes have facilitated greater knowledge in pedagogical matters and in many cases have led course participants to redesign their courses to enhance the student learning experience. Where programme participants are widely disseminating their work it has been found in some cases to bring them greater recognition in the form of opportunities to publish, promotion, and receipt of teaching awards. Teaching is now starting to receive greater recognition with institutional strategic plans and promotion guidelines increasingly showing evidence of parity of esteem for research and teaching.

With many countries only starting to embark on the establishment of accredited programmes in teaching and learning in higher education, it is hoped that this chapter will provide a useful guideline in determining the structure, design, delivery, and learning outcomes of new developing programmes. It is difficult to measure the impact of such programmes in their early stages; however, this study has identified that participants taking accredited programmes in teaching and learning in Ireland are potentially positively impacted through a change in their pedagogical knowledge, academic practice, and professional recognition. It is proposed that this is just the starting point. A much larger study would be required to determine to what extent participants' knowledge, practice and recognition actually change.

While challenges remain in the progression of accredited courses in teaching and learning, their influence to date on individual participants and institutions appears to be largely positive. The silent shift in teaching and learning experiences, attitudes, and ethos is becoming more evident as our higher education professionals, in increasing numbers, become students again in order to be better teachers.

NOTES

1. The author would like to thank the course directors who participated in the survey. Thanks are also due to Michael Cullinane for his assistance in compiling the data, to Professor Áine Hyland, Dr. Bettie Higgs and Dr. Carrie Griffin for reviewing the paper, and to Dr. Marian McCarthy for

providing the interview recordings. It is important to note that a number of the programmes outlined in this chapter are continuing to evolve and new programmes are developing in a number of HEI's; hence the programme information printed here only pertains to the state of play at the time of writing. For the most up to date information on available accredited programmes in the Republic of Ireland see http://www.nairtl.ie/accreditedprogrammes

2. The project in question resulted in a workshop at NAIRTL's third annual conference and it was published as a chapter in the conference proceedings (McCarthy, Murphy, and Cassidy 2010).

BIBLIOGRAPHY

Central Statistics Office. 2011. "Census of Population, 2011." http://www.cso.ie, accessed 21/05/2012.

Eurydice. 2010. *Focus on Higher Education in Europe 2010: The Impact of the Bologna Process.* Brussels: European Commission.

Gaston, Paul L. 2010. *The Challenge of Bologna: What United States Higher Education Has to Learn from Europe, and Why It Matters That We Learn It.* Sterling, Virginia: Stylus Publishing.

Hyland, Áine. 2004. *University College Cork as a Learning Organisation.* Cork: University College Cork.

———. 2007. *Good Practice in Quality Improvement in Teaching and Learning in Irish Universities, Interim Report, Consultation Draft.* Dublin: Irish University Quality Board.

———. 2010. "Competences, Learning Outcomes and Convergence: A Case Study—University College Cork." In *Higher Education for Modern Societies: Competences and Values,* edited by Sjur Bergan and Radu Damian, 135–143. Strasbourg: Council of Europe Publishing.

Irish University Training Network. 1998. "University Teaching and Learning: Policy and Practice Colloquium Proceedings." *Accreditation and Teaching Development,* http://odtl.dcu.ie/mirror/iutn/cutl-1998.html, accessed 10/03/2010.

Lyons, Nona, Áine Hyland, and Norma Ryan. 2002. *Advancing the Scholarship of Teaching and Learning through a Reflective Portfolio Process.* Cork: University College Cork.

McCarthy, Marian, Jennifer Murphy, and Stephen Cassidy. 2010. "Research-Teaching Linkages: Beyond Definitions." In *Research-Teaching Linkages: Practice and Policy, NAIRTL's Third Annual Conference Proceedings,* edited by Jennifer Murphy, Carrie Griffin, and Bettie Higgs, 63–71. Cork: NAIRTL.

Murphy, Jennifer, and Bettie Higgs, eds. 2009. *Teaching and Learning in Higher Education: Challenging Assumptions. NAIRTL's Second Annual Conference Proceedings.* Cork: NAIRTL.

Murphy, Jennifer, Carrie Griffin, and Bettie Higgs, eds. 2010. *Research-Teaching Linkages: Practice and Policy, NAIRTL's Third Annual Conference Proceedings.* Cork: NAIRTL.

OECD. 2004. *Review of National Policies for Education: Review of Higher Education in Ireland Examiners' Report.* Dublin: Higher Education Authority.

O'Neill, Geraldine, Sarah Moore, and Barry McMullin, eds. 2005. *Emerging Issues in the Practice of University Learning and Teaching.* Dublin: All Ireland Society for Higher Education.

Rauhvargers, Andrejs, Cynthia Deane, and Wilfried Pauwels. 2009. *Bologna Process Stocktaking Report.* Benelux: European Commission.

Skilbeck, Michael. 2001. *The University Challenged. A Review of International Trends and Issues with Particular Reference to Ireland.* Dublin: Higher Education Authority.

St. Aubyn, Miguel, Álvaro Pina, Filomena Garcia, and Joana Pais. 2009. *Study on the Efficiency and Effectiveness of Public Spending on Tertiary Education.* European Economy, Economics Papers 390, ECOFIN, European Commission.

Wieman, Carl, Katherine Perkins, and Sarah Gilbert. 2010. "Transforming Science Education at Large Research Universities: A Case Study in Progress." *Change* (March/April): 7–14.

10 The Influence of the Research Philosophy and Pedagogical Management Decisions of the University of Helsinki on University Teaching
A Longitudinal Study

Anne Nevgi

INTRODUCTION

In recent decades the quality of university teaching has aroused extensive interest in higher education (e.g., Trigwell and Prosser 1999; Brennan and Shah 2000; Skelton 2005; Biggs and Tang 2007). In order to improve the quality of teaching in higher education, instructional development courses and workshops have been offered to the faculty at universities. Many universities have developed diverse organisational structures in order to support teachers' pedagogical skills and improve the quality of university teaching.

Such structures have followed two models: the first model puts the emphasis on professional development of teaching and learning in higher education as a part of central administration, based on special funding. This approach is exemplified by the University of Oxford's Centre for Excellence in Preparing for Academic Practice, which was closed in September 2010. The second model emphasises research-based development of teaching and learning in higher education, and the educators are themselves also researchers of university teaching and learning and hold academic positions in the faculty or department.

This chapter will focus on the instructional development programme of the Centre for Research and Development in Higher Education at the University of Helsinki, which represents the later model based on research. While in both models research on teaching and learning in higher education is conducted, in the research-based model research is closely related to other research projects and interests of the educational sciences and psychology of the faculty, and the quality of teaching and learning is systematically developed based on research supported and resourced by the university.

This model originates from the Humboldtian educational philosophy of the University of Helsinki. As such, it offers a rare opportunity to explore the link between the development of courses and pedagogical support structures on the one hand and the university's values and ethos on the other. In addition, the teaching development programme of the University of Helsinki allows us to investigate the pedagogical development of academics and how this development process is related to the advance of pedagogical courses offered for them over time. Such studies are scarce, because following participants once they leave the training environment has often proved difficult and because many instructional development programmes are relatively new and so cannot offer longitudinal insights.

So, the aim of this chapter is twofold: first, it sets out to demonstrate how the instructional development programme has grown out of the educational ethos of a research-intensive university, exploring how research and teaching have been fostered by strategic decisions at the university. Second, it explores in what ways participation in the Programme of University Pedagogy during the first fifteen years the programme has been offered to the academics has influenced the pedagogical development of individual university teachers. Three cases based on a follow-up study are offered to shed light on the long-term effects of instructional development programmes.

THE PHILOSOPHICAL UNDERPINNING
OF THE UNIVERSITY OF HELSINKI

The University of Helsinki, founded in 1640, is Finland's oldest and biggest university. In 2011, the university had a student body of about 35,000 students, over five hundred professors, and 3,385 other research and teaching staff located in eleven faculties and twenty independent institutes (University of Helsinki Web site 2010). Since the 1990s, the changes both in the curriculum and in the organisation at the university have been encouraged by three factors: the challenges posed by globalisation, the Bologna Process, and the implementation of the new Universities Act (558/2009) in 2010[1] (University of Helsinki, Web site 2010).

Since the nineteenth century, the university has embraced Humboldt's ideas on science and culture and used them as guidelines for its teaching and research. The Humboldtian idea of the university was introduced in the mid-nineteenth century by Johan Vilhelm Snellman at the University of Helsinki, and it helped to redirect the university's research activities toward experimental, empirical, and analytical research and away from its earlier collection-centred approach (University of Helsinki Web site 2010). The basic ideas of a university presented by Wilhelm von Humboldt can be summed up in two sayings: unity of research and teaching ("Einheit von Forschung und Lehre"), and autonomy or solitude and freedom ("Einsamkeit und Freiheit") (Fehér 2001).

These two principles are based on the idea of *Bildung*, edification, self-formation (Fehér 2001). The idea of Bildung (education) stresses the importance of personality development through education; the education is regarded as something essentially individualistic, self-motivated, and non-utilitarian (Pritchard 2004). Bildung is interwoven with Forschung (research), an incessant and never-ending pursuit of knowledge (Fehér 2001). The Humboldtian values comprise two freedoms: teaching and learning. The unity of research and teaching involves that research and teaching are interwoven and the best teaching leads to lecturers learning as well as students (Pritchard 2004).

Such a philosophical underpinning of the university's activities is noteworthy because of its far-reaching implications. First, it has had a great impact on the Finnish national culture in terms of the high profile of research and learning. Second, it greatly affected the development of the educational system of Finland, which is well known for the high standards achieved in PISA tests (Programme for International Student Assessment of the Organisation for Economic Co-operation and Development [OECD]).

Thus, the Humboldtian ideas of the unity of research and teaching and the unity of teachers and learners played a crucial role in transforming the University of Helsinki into one of the leading research universities of Europe in many disciplines by the end of the twentieth century ("Strategic plan" 2010). The Humboldtian heritage lives on in that the university not only aims at producing high-quality research but also strives to integrate research and teaching. It is committed to the idea of research-based teaching. Consequently, all the teachers also do research and all the researchers teach (University of Helsinki Web site 2010). As international expert panels acknowledge, teaching provided by the University of Helsinki is of the highest level in Europe (Saari and Frimodig 2009).

THE DEVELOPMENT OF INSTRUCTIONAL DEVELOPMENT AT THE UNIVERSITY OF HELSINKI

From Ad Hoc Courses to the Programme of University Pedagogy

While the University of Helsinki has long valued high-quality scientific research and has embraced the Humboldtian values in integrating research and teaching, it has taken considerably longer to develop its instructional development programmes along these lines. Instructional development courses were first launched in the 1970s. While they did not set out to follow the Humboldtian ideas, the fact that they have always been based on scientific theories planted the first seeds in a move toward a more Humboldtian instructional development programme.

In the 1970s, most of the instructional development courses were based on behaviourist theories of learning. The emphasis was on teachers' interaction with students and students' activation in learning. Courses were offered to support individual teachers to develop their teaching skills, but no research was conducted to explore the impact. In many of them, teachers were encouraged to apply diverse group work methods in teaching and to focus on students' learning.

The 1980s saw several changes in instructional development which moved the courses towards the Humboldtian philosophy. The courses were research-informed and focused on new learning theories. Teachers were introduced to the pedagogical theories for designing a course, bringing a student-centred approach into the focus of teaching. The most influential model was that of Yrjö Engeström (1982), which emphasized students' own role in learning. Furthermore, courses began to be based on research done by the educators themselves, although real research-based courses did not appear until the early twenty first century. The Humboldtian idea of the university contributed to these first research-based attempts to analyse in what ways the instructional development courses influenced teaching and student learning (e.g., Gröhn et al. 1993).

In the 1990s two noteworthy developments took place. For the first time, instructional development courses were systematically offered to departments. In 1997, a number of courses were integrated and designed as a Programme of Basic Studies in University Pedagogy (twenty-five ECTS). The programme consisted of five modules and these were organised as one long course lasting for one and half academic years. Courses were based on socio-constructive ideas of learning. The participants' main task was to design a research-and-development project for their own teaching and to write a report on their project.

Thus the Humboldtian ideas of the unity of research and teaching became evident for the first time in pedagogical training as teachers learn to develop their courses and teaching based on small research activities. Reflective exercises started by introducing participants to research articles on teaching and learning. In addition, the advancement of instructional development courses was supported by the research focusing on the impact both on department-level changes and on individual teachers' and students' learning (e.g., Lonka 1997; Repo-Kaarento 2001).

During this decade, two faculties took on a pioneering role. The Faculty of Medicine changed in the problem-based learning approach in its curriculum for first two years of study and organised courses both on problem-based learning and basic courses of university pedagogy for staff. Topics of courses were based on the research results of the rapidly developing new research branch focusing on students' learning strategies and approaches to learning (e.g., Lonka 1997; Lindblom-Ylänne 1999; Slotte 1999).

The Faculty of Agriculture and Forestry organised several projects to develop teaching in order to change academic teaching and learning culture toward a more student-centred learning environment (Repo-Kaarento 2001, 2006). The pioneering projects' impacts were evaluated continuously (see Repo-Kaarento 2001), ensuring that the change was stimulated by providing new methods for teaching and learning, and by facilitating meaningful communication among staff and students. Based on the follow-up, the instructional development course was modified every year (Repo-Kaarento 2001, 2006). The hidden philosophical ethos of research-based teaching and learning at the university emerged in these attempts.

Developments in the Programme of University Pedagogy since 2000

Since 2000, the development of the Programme of Basic Studies in University Pedagogy has been based on systematic research into the impact of instructional development courses on teachers' pedagogical development (e.g., Löfström and Nevgi 2007, 2008; Postareff 2007; Postareff, Lindblom-Ylänne, and Nevgi 2007, 2008) and on the findings of the research on student learning (e.g., Kaartinen-Koutaniemi 2009; Hailikari 2010; Parpala 2010) or on the findings of students' conceptions of good teaching (e.g., Parpala, Lindblom-Ylänne, and Rytkönen 2011). The findings of these studies were implemented in the development of the programme.

In 2000, the structure of the Programme of Basic Studies in University Pedagogy (twenty-five ECTS) comprised two modules; a basic course for university pedagogy (ten ECTS) and an advanced course for university pedagogy (fifteen ECTS). The former focused on the theories of learning and teaching, designing, teaching methods, and assessment. The advanced course focused on the supervision, teaching and learning process, students' learning problems, and on the development of the participants' teaching practice. In both courses the working methods consisted of workshops, group work, and independent studies and both courses put emphasis on the participants' own activities to develop their own teaching in a research-based Humboldtian manner.

In the years 2003–2005, the subject studies in university pedagogy were organised for the first time, and since 2005, the University of Helsinki has offered for its staff the Programme of University Pedagogy for sixty ECTS including both basic studies and subject studies. Since 2009, the programme has also included the teacher qualification (teacher licence). The current curriculum of the Programme of University Pedagogy is described in detail in below.

The Programme of University Pedagogy Today

The structure of the curriculum for university pedagogy (sixty ECTS) is presented in Table 10.1. The first two study modules of the Basic Studies in University Pedagogy are mostly offered as an integrated course labelled the *University Pedagogy I* course. The aim of the first two modules is to give a teacher the basic skills to plan, instruct, and assess learning and teaching in their courses and to become capable of using learning-centred ways of teaching. The study modules include a short practicum during which participants observe classes and learn to give and get feedback on their teaching.

The University Pedagogy I course lasts from four to six months and the course is organised in three languages (Finnish, Swedish, and English).

After completing the University Pedagogy I course, the teachers can apply for the following three separate study modules of the Basic Studies in University Pedagogy: academic supervising (organised in Finnish, Swedish, and English), assessment of learning practices and quality of teaching (organised in Finnish only), and development of teaching and practical training (organised in Finnish only), five ECTS each. The three study modules focus on assessment, evaluation, and learning in higher education, supervision, and guidance in higher education, and on improving teaching skills and interaction with students.

Each study module is designed to be based on a different pedagogical model focusing on giving teachers an experience of being a student in problem-based learning, in blended learning, and in different inquiry-based teaching and learning methods. In line with the Humboldtian philosophy, the study modules encourage teachers to develop their teaching and courses based on inquiry into their own teaching methods and student learning.

Teachers can participate in the study modules according to their own preferences and complete them during one academic year or proceed more slowly. Thus a teacher can better plan how to integrate and balance their teaching responsibilities, research activities, and needs to develop themselves

Table 10.1 Curriculum for the Programme of University Pedagogy (Sixty ECTS) at the University of Helsinki

Basic Studies in University Pedagogy (25 ECTS)	
Offered as University Pedagogy I course	Teaching and learning in higher education (5 credits)
	Constructive alignment in course design (5 credits)
Offered as separate courses	Academic supervision (5 credits)
	Assessment of learning practices and quality of teaching (5 credits)
	Development of teaching and practical training (5 credits)
Subject Studies in University Pedagogy (35 ECTS)	
Subject studies (18 credits)	Didactics and discipline-specific approaches to teaching (4 credits)
	Curricular design and quality assurance in higher education (4 credits)
	Education and society (4 credits)
	Psychology of learning (3 credits)
	Learning in groups (3 credits)
Practical training (10 credits)	Practice in University Teaching (5 credits)
	Practice in School Education and in Adult Education (5 credits)
Research (7 credits)	Research in higher education (7 credits)

both as a teacher and a researcher. When all three separate study modules are completed, a teacher will be granted the Certificate of Basic Studies in University Pedagogy.

Upon completion of basic studies in university pedagogy, a teacher who aims to get a teacher qualification can apply for a programme of subject studies in university pedagogy, also known as a scholarship in higher education. It takes approximately two academic years for a teacher to complete the programme of subject studies. Besides the advanced courses in different topics like curriculum planning, learning psychology, education, and society, in subject studies there is a strong emphasis on practical training and how to support teachers to become reflective, pedagogically aware, competent teachers. Based on Humboldtian philosophy, teachers also learn to do pedagogical research and they investigate a research topic related to university pedagogy.

Creation of Support Structures for Instructional Development Courses

The university also established the capacity to conduct pedagogical activities that the instructional development programme requires. In the mid-1990s, the University of Helsinki founded a resource pool of fifteen pedagogical university lecturers[2] in order to offer extra resources for faculties in the research and development of teaching and learning. Accordingly, out of this pool faculties could apply for one or two university lecturers, who had a PhD and substantial experience both in research and development of teaching, for a five-year fixed-term project to develop quality of teaching (Hirsto, Lindblom-Ylänne, and Venna 2003).

In 1999, the pedagogical university lecturers created the Network of Pedagogical University Lecturers in order to share experiences, to support each other, and together to influence the improvement of teaching and learning in the university (Hirsto, Lindblom-Ylänne, and Venna, 2003). Also in 1999, the first pedagogical university lecturer was appointed in order to develop and organise the separate courses of university pedagogy in the Programme of University Pedagogy of sixty ECTS. The university lecturer was positioned in the Department of Education and worked in collaboration with the Network of Pedagogical University Lecturers. In order to support the programme the then Faculty of Educational Sciences established a professorship in university pedagogy in 2002, and in the same year the Centre for Research and Development in Higher Education (YTY) was also founded.

The network greatly influenced the development of instructional development courses and the programme of university pedagogy. Among the first collaboration efforts of the network was the publication of the first *Handbook for University Lecturers* published in Finnish (Lindblom-Ylänne and Nevgi 2002) which was followed with a new, revised edition seven years later (Lindblom-Ylänne and Nevgi 2009). These publications were widely used in instructional development courses. The pedagogical university lecturers also started a joint research project aiming to develop instructional development courses based on research and to improve teaching and learning in faculties (e.g., Ruohoniemi and Lindblom-Ylänne 2009; Virtanen and Lindblom-Ylänne 2010).

The activities and meetings of the network were initially coordinated by the Academic Affairs Unit. Since 2007, the Centre for Research and Development in Higher Education has assumed that task (Lindblom-Ylänne and Hämäläinen 2004; Lindblom-Ylänne 2006). Since 2005, pedagogical university lecturers have been tenured and are located on four different campuses. Today, each faculty and two independent institutes have at least one pedagogical university lecturer. The international evaluation panel for the Leadership and Management of Education in the University praised the

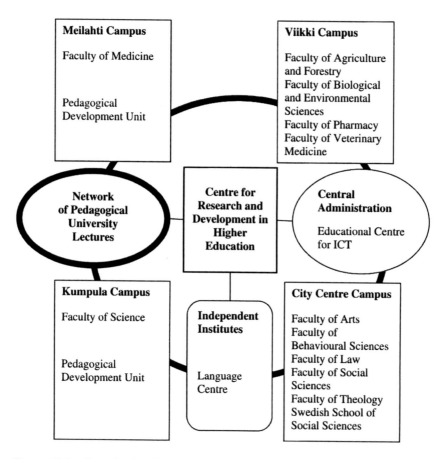

Figure 10.1 Organisational structure of support for pedagogical development in faculties at the University of Helsinki.

influence of the network in raising the awareness of student-centred teaching and in improving the quality of teaching in faculties (Saari and Frimodig 2009). Figure 10.1 presents the current support structure for the pedagogical development of university teaching at the University of Helsinki.

The majority of instructional development courses at the University of Helsinki are organised by the Centre for Research and Development of Higher Education (YTY), which is responsible for the design of all courses (Lindblom-Ylänne and Hämäläinen, 2004). Furthermore, in each of the eleven faculties, and in the Language Centre, in the Swedish School of Social Science, and in the Open University of the University of Helsinki, there is in each a pedagogical university lecturer who together with YTY is responsible for organising the University Pedagogy I course.

To further research-based teaching, the university also allocated funds for this purpose. In the 1970s and 1980s, the instructional development courses were funded separately by applications to the Ministry of Education, and the funding was not based on the university's own resources. However, in the mid-1990s, there was a significant change in the policy of the university, and the university began to support pedagogical training of faculty by reserving special funds (e.g., through the establishment of a pool of pedagogical university lecturers). Furthermore, the university's administration office directed additional resources towards the pedagogical training of teachers and researchers. ("Programme for the Development of Teaching" 2010).

In addition, changes in requirements for promotion helped to raise the profile of instructional development courses. Course attendance that was once voluntary is now compulsory for some academic positions (e.g., adjunct professor, university lecturer, clinical teacher) in the Faculty of Medicine. Furthermore, in the university's strategy 2006–2009, the quality of teaching skills and participation in courses of university pedagogy became highlighted as qualifications recommended for academics to be tenured. Following the guidelines of the university's strategy, faculties created the matrices for teaching competence and in these the participation in courses of University Pedagogy is recommended or required for teaching competence. However, in certain faculties (e.g., science) the pedagogical training is still not required for teaching competence.

Due to recommendations, participation in courses of university pedagogy rose expansively. As a result, since the mid-1990s, an estimated 970 (30 percent of the university staff) university teachers have participated in instructional development courses; however, most of them only in the first two modules of the Basic Studies in University Pedagogy. The number of participants is only indicative, because the complete statistics of all teachers who have participated in instructional development courses are not available. This number is based on the information gathered from the faculties and on the data recorded by the Centre for Research and Development of Higher Education.

Currently, approximately 140–160 teachers per year participate in the University Pedagogy I course and twenty to sixty teachers participate in the other study modules of Basic Studies in University Pedagogy. Approximately twenty teachers every alternate academic year begin their studies in the Subject Studies of University Pedagogy aiming for a teacher qualification. At the end of 2010, altogether eighteen teachers have completed the teacher qualification. Most of the participants in all instructional development courses are junior teachers or doctoral students (approximately 80 percent) with a temporary position in the university. Tenured participants are mostly university lecturers or researchers, and only few professors have taken part in the courses. For the development of the quality of teaching in the university, the great challenge is that only 10–20 percent of participants are tenured.

THE IMPACT OF THE PROGRAMME ON PROFESSIONAL DEVELOPMENT OF INDIVIDUAL TEACHERS

Due in large part to the fusion of Humboldtian ideas and pedagogical development, a number of studies have been conducted at the University of Helsinki. Some of them examined the change in teaching and learning at departmental or at the faculty level (Repo-Kaarento 2001, 2006) or what kind of disciplinary differences in approaches to teaching could be distinguished (Lindblom-Ylänne et al. 2006). Others focused on the change at the individual level (e.g., Löfström and Nevgi 2007, 2008; Postareff 2007; Postareff, Lindblom-Ylänne, and Nevgi 2007, 2008) or on teachers' professional identity and self-concept as a teacher (Nevgi and Toom 2009).

For schoolteachers, there is a long tradition of research on teacher development (e.g., Hubermann 1992; Beijaard, Verloop, and Vermunt 2000; Day and Gu 2007). However, longitudinal research on the professional development as a university teacher tends to be scarce, although some attempts have been made (e.g., Åkerlind 2003). In this study, the aim was to investigate the longitudinal process of nine university teachers' professional development to become a university teacher with a teacher qualification. By highlighting the professional development process of an individual university teacher, the aim was to gain a deeper understanding of the ways instructional development courses influence the development process and what kind of trajectories in professional development can be distinguished.

Those university teachers who, after completing the Basic Studies in University Pedagogy, finally aim to have a teacher qualification represent a very small minority (under 1 percent) of university's teaching and research staff. However, they also represent innovators and early adopters of pedagogical innovations in their departments and faculties (see Rogers 1995). Their experiences of instructional development courses and their choices to continue their pedagogical development as teachers highlight the impact of the programme in individual level.

Data and Research Method

The informants are nine (two males and seven females) university teachers who have completed their studies in the Programme of University Pedagogy and achieved the teacher qualification. All these teachers had a history of participating in pedagogical development courses for six to eight, and some even for thirteen, years. Two of the informants began their studies in pedagogical development course in the mid-1990s and five of them began their first pedagogical studies in 2003; two informants began their first pedagogical studies in 2005. The informants' teaching experience during their first instructional development course varied from one year to sixteen years. Teaching experience included typically practices, part-time teaching, and lecturing to undergraduate students but some also had experience of teaching outside university (e.g., in schools and training centres).

The data were gathered by means of interviews, classroom observations of teaching, learning diaries, personal study plans, and reports of teaching practice. This was done in three phases: in the first or second instructional development course, during the pedagogical training, and at the end of pedagogical training. The informants were interviewed at the beginning of their first or second instructional development course. During their pedagogical studies, the learning diaries and personal study plans were gathered. Finally, when the informants participated in the teaching practice for teacher qualification, they were observed in authentic teaching situations, and asked to reflect on their expectations and experiences of the practicum.

These nine university teachers came from diverse disciplinary backgrounds; five of them represented science and four of them represented humanities, social sciences, and arts (in order to assure the anonymity of informants, their disciplinary background is not revealed in their case descriptions). They all had the goal of improving their teaching and becoming a better teacher and they were all novices in pedagogy without any knowledge of learning theories and student learning.

At the beginning of the analysis, the interviews and documents of their pedagogical training were carefully read many times. Then the narrative of their teacher development was written up. The narratives were analysed in order to compare and contrast events in their teacher development. One strong theme which emerged was a teacher's constant struggle against the pressure to limit efforts for teaching and to focus only on research. Teachers also struggled against the negative attitudes of colleagues at departments and faculties and returned to pedagogical development courses with high motivation to strengthen their will to continue their development as teachers and to improve their courses. They reported that they needed to have a space to discuss teaching and learning with others interested in the topic.

Results: Three Trajectories of Teacher Development

The analyses yielded three different trajectories. They differ according to how the participation in pedagogical courses had influenced teachers' awareness of pedagogy and changes in their teaching. I have selected three cases to represent the typical trajectories of teacher development.

Angelina was a thirty-six-year-old university lecturer when she first time participated in the basic pedagogical development course (ten ECTS) in 2003. She had four years teaching experience comprising of lectures, tutorials, and part-time teaching. When interviewed at the end of the first instructional development course, she described how the course had changed her conception about herself as a teacher and how she no longer considered herself as a "good teacher." In her later reflections at the end of the last teaching practice, she describes the first course of university pedagogy as a catalyst for her pedagogical development.

She reported what a strong and eye-opening experience it was for her when she became aware of the importance of a student-centred approach in teaching. She also reflected that the most beneficial aspect for her development as a teacher was a sound theoretical background for teaching:

> Although back then, I felt that learning new teaching tools and methods was the most useful part of the studies. In retrospect I think that the theoretical discussion at the beginning had longer lasting and more profound effects. This is because it provided a framework with the help of which I could reflect upon my teaching practices, develop and implement new solutions appropriate to my subject, and organise different teaching tools and practices into a coherent whole. (Angelina)

After the first instructional development course, Angelina noticed that she got better feedback from her students, and this notion motivated her to continue her pedagogical studies three years later. She had accumulated more experience in teaching and she yearned to increase her pedagogical knowledge and understanding. The next course was for fifteen ECTS and included practice in teaching as a peer-assessed and pedagogical development task in her own teaching. During the course, she learned to focus on students and to reflect:

> Put simply, during the university pedagogy studies I have learned to shift the focus from my performance as a teacher to the students as learners. Consequently, I more and more plan my teaching reflecting on what students are doing in and out of class and on how my practices interact with and encourage their learning. I see myself much less as a "lecturer" and more as a learning facilitator. I have been devoting less time to lecturing and have been incorporating more student activities. (Angelina)

The observation data of her teaching practice during the final course before gaining the teacher qualification revealed that in her lecture Angelina systematically applied different modes of activating students' learning and understanding, as can be seen in the following quotation from the mentor teacher's observation diary:

> At the beginning of her lecture for thirty adult students, Angelina first asks students to discuss the topic in pairs, and then she collects the main points of discussion on a flap chart. Students are interested in and seem to be involved in learning. In the middle of her lecture, Angelina presents a problem to students and asks them to solve it independently. Then she shows the solution to the problem, and explains it in detail and encourages students to ask clarifying questions. (Mentor Teacher 1)

In the reflection afterwards, Angelina explained how she planned the lecture to enhance students' learning and understanding, and how she related the learning goals to the modes of teaching and learning activities. Just before gaining her teacher qualification, she again emphasised the role of reflection in her development as a teacher:

> In time my reflection has become more and more tuned to monitoring student cues and the interaction between my practices and students' behaviour. This regular reflection practice together with the feedback from university pedagogy lecturers has played an important role in the development of my pedagogical expertise. (Angelina)

For Angelina, her participation in the first pedagogical course has immediately profound effects; she reflects on herself as becoming a worse teacher and how her conceptions of teaching and learning have radically changed. The idea of learning to reflect as a teacher is repeatedly seen in her teacher development during the following years. She has also emphasised how important it is to gain theoretical understanding in order to enhance teaching. She has been trying out new teaching and assessment methods and returns to pedagogical courses in order to deepen her knowledge in theories of learning and teaching. Her trajectory to become a university teacher can be described as *a path for deepening understanding and reflection as a teacher.*

Diana was a thirty-seven-year-old assistant teacher when she first took part in the instructional development course in the mid-1990s. At that time she had gained teaching experience over fifteen years as a lecturer and an assistant for laboratory work. For her the first instructional development course in the mid-1990s had been helpful. She explained how she had learned to organise lectures and laboratory teaching settings and how she had got support for her own thoughts.

Four years later, she resumed her pedagogical studies and took part in the second instructional development course (fifteen ECTS) in order to gain the certificate for the Basic Studies of University Pedagogy (twenty-five ECTS). In the interview she described herself as a traditional lecturer who focuses on transmitting correct information to students. Diana explained how the participation in the second course had increased her feeling of competence as a teacher and how becoming familiar with teaching methods helped her to develop her teaching. Diana described how the pedagogical courses would be very useful for young doctoral students and those in the beginning of their academic career. She also explained how pedagogical courses are important because by participating in the courses one can meet teachers from other faculties:

> . . . then you meet other teachers from other faculties, and there is such a nice atmosphere, a strong solidarity and togetherness, the feeling that we all are in the same boat, and that we all have similar problems with students . . . (Diana)

Diana returned to pedagogical studies again after four years. She explained her motive to take part again was to refresh her teaching, which she felt had returned to old modes of lecturing. She also said that to get a certificate with sixty study credits of university pedagogy is highly valued in her faculty. Furthermore, she described that she had longed for the academic community as a place to discuss in depth the problems of teaching and learning. At the end of teaching practice, she reflected what she had learned:

> At the beginning, this teacher practice did not seem to me to be anything special, only observing teaching, preparing my own teaching, observing teaching, getting feedback on teaching . . . However, then my eyes opened, and I noticed I really need to reflect. . . . I discovered how by observing my colleagues teaching, and especially teaching in schools, I learned a new way of seeing teaching, and I decided to try new ways of interaction with students. (Diana)

Diana reported that the final teaching practice, during which she visited schools observing teaching and preparing her own teaching for adult learners in Open University of University of Helsinki, had helped her to understand how the teaching and learning cultures differ in different institutions, and how especially in schools, teachers really need to be professional. The observation of her teaching revealed that she applied mechanically student-centred teaching methods. In reflection with a mentor teacher she explained that she aimed to improve student learning. However, she pointed out that it is anyway up to a student if she aims to learn, thus revealing that she still held her previous concepts about teaching as delivering information to students.

Unlike Angelina, for Diana her first participation in an instructional development course only helps her to get some tips how to improve teaching. She continues her pedagogical studies but does not change her conceptions of student learning. Instead, she holds on to her ideals of a university teacher as subject expert. She regressed back to her old ways of teaching and returns to the instructional development course in order to meet colleagues and to refresh her teaching. She learns to apply student-centred teaching methods and to design and plan her courses. Finally, during her last teaching practice, for the first time she reflects on her actions as a teacher and even then her focus is on teaching skills and not on pedagogical theories and on student learning. Her trajectory path as a university teacher is therefore termed *a path of a subject expert improving her instructional skills.*

Fiona was a thirty-three-year-old assistant and doctoral student with a two-year stint as a teacher of science in university when she was first interviewed in 2003 at the end her first instructional development course. In her first interview, Fiona described how she had always been interested in teaching and that already, in her teenage years, she had been a teacher for younger ones, teaching them how to play a recorder. She had also been a part-time teacher in a school and in a vocational school. Fiona described herself as a novice teacher who had only had limited teaching experience in laboratory settings.

> I am only a novice teacher and my teaching experiences are quite various because the teaching situations in our department are mostly like the ones where we tutor the exercises. It is mostly like a group or like a face-to-face teaching, as I could describe it. And also, I don't have any great pedagogical [knowledge] in my educational background, so I'm just purporting to have something [pedagogical training] all the time. (Fiona)

Fiona also explained how her own experiences as a student, being lectured to and asked only to memorise, and her experiences as a part-time teacher had influenced her ideas about the ideal teaching she wished for her students in science. During the first course, Fiona was active and motivated. When asked about the importance of instructional development courses for university teachers, she felt strongly that the courses should be obligatory for all who wanted to become a teacher in a university.

> I have actually many times wondered; how it is possible that in a university you can be a teacher without any qualification and without any knowledge of pedagogy? . . . I think it is so important for teachers to learn about what is learning, about learning theories, students' learning strategies, how to support and facilitate student learning! (Fiona)

After her first instructional development course, she participated in the second instructional development course with fifteen ECTS and completed these studies in 2006. Next year, she continued on to the Subject Studies of University Pedagogy and finally in 2009 she participated in teaching practice in order to gain the teacher qualification. As for her teaching practice, she opted to practice as a tutor in a problem-based teaching course for university teachers. She justified her selection as being already familiar with teaching young students and children but not having any experience in teaching adults. During the practice, she also observed teaching in schools and in a polytechnic.

Her observations in schools made her reflect on how young students had changed compared to her own experiences as a schoolteacher in the late 1990s. The pupils were restless and a teacher had difficulties to keep the class in order. Observation in an upper secondary school and in a polytechnic strengthened her opinion about how teaching and learning culture is dependent on what kind of students are in a class and what is their ethnic and social background. These observations decreased her self-confidence to become a schoolteacher, so instead she explained how she now strongly identified herself as an university teacher and that she realized that she was not competent to be a schoolteacher.

In particular, her experiences as a member of a teachers' team and as a tutor in a problem-based course made her reflect that the best arrangement is to have a team of teachers for a course who design together and share teaching together. She described that to teach together with another teacher is beneficial because one can get immediate feedback on her teaching. She had no experiences in being a tutor in a problem-based course, so after her teaching practice she aimed to continue to develop her teaching skills in problem-based learning.

For Fiona, to become a teacher is a calling and she had reflected on teaching and learning even before her pedagogical studies. She is very motivated to develop herself as a teacher and her goal for pedagogical studies is to become a teacher, in particular a qualified teacher. She aims mainly to improve her teaching skills and she also tries new teaching methods in her teaching. Fiona is also very interested in how to improve the quality of teaching in her department and faculty. Pedagogical theories of learning and teaching are important for her if, by applying theoretical knowledge, it is possible to improve the quality of teaching. However, the final teaching practice reveals to her that she has no call to become a schoolteacher; instead, she realizes that first of all she is a teacher in a university. Her trajectory path as a university teacher is therefore termed *a path of the young scholar towards professional university teacher status*.

CONCLUSION

The idea of unity of research and teaching behind the Programme of University Pedagogy has come on a long way at the University of Helsinki.

Efforts to improve teaching started in the 1970s and it took decades to align it with the educational philosophy of the university. However, today, just as in other disciplines, instructional development in higher education follows the Humboldtian philosophy that propagates the fusion between teaching and research. Educational development programmes go hand in hand with research on their impact and success.

The model of research-based enhancement of instructional development courses has proved to be fertile and it has gained respect both in the University of Helsinki and internationally through increasing numbers of publications and by conspicuous appreciation in international evaluation (Saari and Frimodig 2009), but more than these, through the increasing number of university teachers attending the courses.

However, it should not be forgotten that change in the teaching and learning culture of the university has slowly emerged. It has taken more than twenty years at the University of Helsinki for the grade in "Excellence in Teaching" to be accepted as a self-evident part of academic expertise besides research expertise. Today, teaching expertise is required for many academics to advance their career. Nonetheless, the establishment of organisational support structure, especially the establishment of the Network of Pedagogical University Lectures and the Centre for Research and Development of Higher Education, changed the attitudes of academics in university to value teaching as important a duty for academics as research. This finding is in line with the ideas presented by D'Andrea and Gosling (2005) and Biggs (2003) that emphasise the whole institution of approach for improving the quality of teaching and learning at universities.

The three trajectories of teacher development highlight how the progress of instructional development courses towards a Programme of University Pedagogy (sixty ECTS) with teacher qualification has created a growing interest in teachers to constantly develop their teaching skills and to improve their courses and the quality of teaching in their departments and faculties. When Diana first took part in the instructional development course in the mid-1990s, the course focused on improving teaching skills and emphasised student-centred teaching. However, the idea of research-based development of teaching was just emerging and so Diana may not have gained such a start for her teacher development as Angelina and Fiona, who participated in their first courses when the research-based development of teaching and learning had gained an official status and was also mentioned for the first time in the university's strategy.

The three cases represent those many teachers who volunteer for instructional development courses for several years and have sometimes even a gap of three or four years between the courses. Particularly, Diana's case reveals the problems arising in teacher development with a long gap between course participation. There is a strong need to develop pedagogical development courses to include tools with which teachers can return to previously learned practices and examine for themselves their development as teachers. In the University of Helsinki, the first attempts have been made to develop the programme to include the elements which help teachers themselves to examine their own development as a teacher. As stated at the outset, the reformation is in line with the principles of research-based teaching and learning emerging from the Humboldtian heritage of the university.

To conclude, if a teacher development programme focuses only on pedagogical theories and teaching skills but is not based on research, it may lead to spurious results in the teachers' improvement and development. Even when such a programme comprises workshops and practices, it may not affect the teachers' approaches to teaching and pedagogical development. Instead, such a programme may strengthen the development as a subject expert without any development in pedagogical thinking. When academics themselves investigate their own teaching practices and learn to read critically pedagogical research literature, there is a chance that an in-depth change in their attitudes towards teaching and learning will take place. The research-based evidence is highly valued among academics and, for them, perhaps the only base they trust to change their attitudes, thinking, and approach to teaching and learning.

NOTES

1. In Finland the political decision of February 2009 led to the university reform as stated in the new Universities Act (558/2009). The aim of the reform was that the universities would become more independent and to develop "entrepreneurial culture" in universities instead of the previous tight control by the government.
2. In the Finnish academic rank, a university lecturer is below professor and in terms of responsibilities and recognition the position broadly corresponds to that of assistant professor in the U.S., to "docent" in Germany, or to the senior lecturer in the United Kingdom. The pedagogical university lecturer's main responsibility is to develop the quality of teaching and learning in the faculty and to promote research in these areas.

BIBLIOGRAPHY

Åkerlind, Gerlese. 2003. "Growing and Developing as a University Teacher—Variation in Meaning." *Studies in Higher Education* 28 (4): 375–390.
Beijaard, Douwe, Nico Verloop, and Jan D. Vermunt. 2000. "Teachers' Perceptions of Professional Identity: An Exploratory Study from a Personal Knowledge Perspective." *Teaching and Teacher Education* 16 (7): 749–764.
Biggs, John. 2003. *Teaching for Quality Learning at University*, 2nd ed. Buckingham, UK: SRHE/Open University Press.
Biggs, John, and Catherine Tang. 2007. *Teaching for Quality Learning at University*, 3rd ed. Buckingham, UK: SRHE/Open University Press.
Brennan, John, and Tarla Shah. 2000. *Managing Quality in Higher Education: An International Perspective on Institutional Assessment and Change*. Buckingham, UK: OECD/SRHE/Open University Press.

D'Andrea, Vaneeta, and David Gosling. 2005. *Improving Teaching and Learning in Higher Education: A Whole Institution Approach.* Buckingham, UK: SRHE/ Open University Press.

Day, Christopher, and Qing Gu. 2007. "Variations in the Conditions for Teachers' Professional Learning and Development: Sustaining Commitment and Effectiveness over a Career." *Oxford Review of Education* 33 (4): 423–444.

Engeström, Yrjö. 1982. *Perustietoa opetuksesta.* Helsinki: Valtionvarainministeriö, Valtion painatuskeskus.

Fehér, István M. 2001. "The Humboldtian Idea of a University: The Bond between Philosophy and the Humanities in the Making of the Modern University." *Neohelicon* 28 (2): 33–37.

Gröhn, Terttu, Antti Kauppi, Marjo Ranta, Joanna Jansson, and Soile Paananen. 1993. *Developing Teaching and Learning in Higher Education.* Helsinki: Helsinki University Press.

Hailikari, Telle. 2010. "Assessing University Students' Prior Knowledge: Implications for Theory and Practice." PhD diss., University of Helsinki.

Hirsto, Laura, Sari Lindblom-Ylänne, and Marja Venna, eds. 2003. *Kehityksen keihäänkärjet. Raportti konstorin opettajapoolista rahoitettujen yliopistopedagogisten asiantuntijoiden (tutkijalehtorien/yliopistonlehtorien) toiminnasta 1.8.1999-kevät 2003.* Helsinki: Helsingin Yliopisto: Kehittämisosasto, Opintoasioiden yksikkö.

Huberman, Michael. 1992. "Teacher Development and Instructional Mastery." In *Understanding Teacher Development*, edited by Andy Hargreaves and Michael G. Fullan, 122–142. London: Teacher College Press.

Kaartinen-Koutaniemi, Minna. 2009. "Tieteellinen ajattelu yliopisto-opinnoissa. Haastattelututkimus psykologian, teologian ja farmasian opiskelijoista." PhD diss., University of Helsinki.

Lindblom-Ylänne, Sari. 1999. "Studying in a Traditional Medical Curriculum— Study Success, Orientation to Studying and Problems That Arise." PhD diss., University of Helsinki.

———. 2006. "Enhancing the Quality of Teaching in Higher Education in Finland: The Case of the University of Helsinki." *New Directions for Higher Education* 2006 (133): 63–71.

Lindblom-Ylänne, Sari, and Kauko Hämäläinen. 2004. "The Bologna Declaration as a Tool for Enhanced Learning and Instruction at the University of Helsinki." *International Journal for Academic Development* 9 (2): 153–165.

Lindblom-Ylänne, Sari, and Anne Nevgi, eds. 2002. *Yliopisto- ja korkeakouluopettajan käsikirja.* Helsinki: WSOY.

———. 2009. *Yliopisto-opettajan käsikirja.* Helsinki: WSOY.

Lindblom-Ylänne, Sari, Keith Trigwell, Anne Nevgi, and Paul Ashwin. 2006. "How Approaches to Teaching Are Affected by Discipline and Teaching Context." *Studies in Higher Education* 31 (3): 285–298.

Lonka, Kirsti. 1997. "Explorations of Constructive Processes in Student Learning." PhD diss., University of Helsinki.

Löfström, Erika, and Anne Nevgi. 2007. "University Teaching Staff as Learners of the Pedagogical Use of ICT." *SeminarNet—International Journal of Media, Technology and Lifelong Learning* 3 (1), http://www.seminar.net/volume-3-issue-1-2007/university-teaching-staff-as-learners-of-the-pedagogical-use-of-ict, accessed 25/03/2008.

———. 2008. "University Teaching Staffs' Pedagogical Awareness Displayed Through ICT-Facilitated Teaching." *Interactive Learning Environments* 16 (2): 101–116.

Nevgi, Anne, and Auli Toom. 2009. "Yliopisto-opettajan opettajanidentiteett." In *Yliopisto-opettajan käsikirja*, edited by Sari Lindblom-Ylänne and Anne Nevgi, 412–426. Helsinki: WSOY.

Parpala, Anna. 2010. "Exploring the Experiences and Conceptions of Good Teaching in Higher Education: Development of a Questionnaire for Assessing Students' Approaches to Learning and Experiences of the Teaching-Learning Environment." PhD diss., University of Helsinki.

Parpala, Anna, Sari Lindblom-Ylänne, and Henna Rytkönen. 2011. "Students' Conceptions of Good Teaching in Three Different Disciplines." *Assessment & Evaluation in Higher Education* 36 (5): 549–563.

Postareff, Liisa. 2007. "Teaching in Higher Education: From Content-Focused to Learning-Focused Approaches to Teaching." PhD diss., University of Helsinki.

Postareff, Liisa, Sari Lindblom-Ylänne, and Anne Nevgi. 2007. "The Effect of Pedagogical Training on Teaching in Higher Education." *Teaching and Teacher Education* 23 (5): 557–571.

———. 2008. "A Follow-Up Study of the Effect of Pedagogical Training in Higher Education." *Higher Education* 56 (1): 29–43.

Pritchard, Rosalind. 2004. "Humboldtian Values in a Changing World: Staff and Students in German Universities." *Oxford Review of Education* 30 (4): 509–528.

"Programme for the Development of Teaching and Studies, 2010–2012." 2010. University of Helsinki Web site, http://www.helsinki.fi/strategia/pdf/Opetuksenjaopintojen_web.pdf, accessed 03/10/2010.

Repo-Kaarento, Saara. 2001. "Developing Learning and Teaching Culture in Higher Education: Cooperative Learning as a Tool." In *Te Rito o te Matauranga: Experiential Learning for the Third Millennium. Selected Papers from the Seventh Conference of the International Consortium for Experiential Learning, Vol. 2.*, edited by Nena Benton and Richard Benton. Auckland, New Zealand: James Henry Maori Research Centre, University of Auckland.

———. 2006. *Yliopisto-opetuksen yhteistoiminnallinen kehittäminen*. Licentiate thesis, University of Helsinki.

Rogers, Everett. M. 1995. *Diffusion of Innovations*, 4th ed. New York: Free Press.

Ruohoniemi, Mirja, and Sari Lindblom-Ylänne. 2009. "Students' Experiences Concerning Course Workload and Factors Enhancing and Impeding Their Learning: A Useful Resource for Quality Enhancement in Teaching and Curriculum Planning." *International Journal for Academic Development* 14 (1): 69–81.

Saari, Seppo, and Minna Frimodig, eds. 2009. *Leadership and Management of Education: Evaluation of Education at the University of Helsinki 2007–2008.* University of Helsinki: Administrative Publications 58. Evaluations, http://www.helsinki.fi/julkaisut/aineisto/hallinnon_julkaisuja_58_2009.pdf, accessed 28/10/2010.

Skelton, Alan. 2005. *Understanding Teaching Excellence in Higher Education.* London: Routledge.

Slotte, Virpi. 1999. "Spontaneous Study Strategies Promoting Knowledge Construction. Evidence from Admission Tests for Medical School and Health-Care Studies." PhD diss., University of Helsinki.

"Strategic Plan for the University of Helsinki, 2010–12." 2010. University of Helsinki Web site, http://www.helsinki.fi/strategia/pdf/STRATEGIA_web.pdf, accessed 03/10/2010.

Universities Act 558/2009. Finlex-säädöskäännökset-558/2009/englanti, http://www.finlex.fi/fi/laki/kaannokset/2009/en20090558.pdf, accessed 04/04/2010.

University of Helsinki Web site. 2010. http://www.helsinki.fi/university/index. html, accessed 04/04/2010.

Trigwell, Keith, and Michael Prosser. 1999. *Understanding Learning and Teaching: The Experience in Higher Education*. Buckingham, UK: SRHE/Open University Press.

Virtanen, Viivi, and Sari Lindblom-Ylänne. 2010. "University Students' and Teachers' Conceptions of Teaching and Learning in Biosciences." *Instructional Science* 38 (4): 355–370.

11 The Impact of UK University Teaching Programmes on Lecturers' Assessment Practice
A Case for Pedagogical Action Research

Lin S. Norton, Bill Norton, and Lee Shannon

INTRODUCTION

In this chapter we examine the issue of the long-term effects of UK university teaching programmes on participating lecturers' assessment practice, once they return to their everyday working lives. To do this, we will be drawing on the findings of three related empirical studies, which have explored lecturers' (both new and experienced) views on the pedagogy of assessment and on their own specific assessment practice. These studies were carried out under the auspices of the Write Now Centre of Excellence for Learning and Teaching (2011—CETL) over several years using a mixture of in-depth interviews and questionnaires.

Drawing on Fanghanel's (2007) framework of filters operating at the macro, meso, and micro level on the choices that academics make, we will focus specifically on what the findings have shown about institutional, departmental, disciplinary, and personal variables that might have overridden the effect of any pedagogically sound principles and practices of assessment learned on the programmes. Our argument is that while university teaching programmes do appear to have positive effects on introducing new lecturers to sound pedagogical assessment practice, and to changing their conceptual understandings of learning and teaching, the impact is lessened by contextual variables that are not easy to overcome. We have called these variables "constraints." We conclude by suggesting that one way of helping newly qualified lecturers to overcome such constraints is to encourage them to engage in pedagogical action research.

BACKGROUND

Since the face of higher education has changed from an elitist to a mass movement, there has been the increasing realisation that good university teaching does not just happen and that academics who teach should be

appropriately qualified. As a consequence, there has been an increasing proliferation of professional university teaching programmes across the world.
In this, the UK is not different; indeed, the inception of such programmes
can be traced back to Dearing's report (1997) and his recommendations
that university lecturers should be appropriately qualified to teach.

Since then, there has been much research to show the value of such programmes (see, e.g., Coffey and Gibbs 2000; Postareff, Lindblom-Ylänne,
and Nevgi 2007), but when looking at the concept of impact, it is crucial to analyse what happens to lecturers when they go back into their
own departments. Prosser et al. (2006) carried out a survey for the Higher
Education Academy (HEA) of thirty-two UK university institutions which
offered university teaching programmes. While pointing out the main benefits, such as helping participants become more student-focused and less
teacher-focused, the report concluded that there were also some problematic areas. Departments did not always see the value of such programmes
and there were issues around the relationship between generic and subject-
specific pedagogies and of university programmes.

In this chapter, we intend to explore some of the problematic areas highlighted by Prosser by looking specifically at the important issue of assessment.

ASSESSMENT: WHAT IS THE PROBLEM?

One of the main reasons why assessment in education has been seen as problematic at all levels and not just in higher education has been the dual purpose
that it is now expected to serve, which is both to certify achievement and to
facilitate learning. The certification purpose of assessment is, perhaps, the
one that there is most unease about, with calls for increasing transparency
and accountability from governments, parents, and students themselves as
major stakeholders. This requirement has impelled the drive for learning outcomes, currently being adopted widely across Europe, and the establishing of
and emphasis on assessment criteria (Norton 2011). The learning facilitation
purpose has been given great impetus by the work of Black and his colleagues
in the school context (Black and Wiliam 1998; Black et al. 2003) and is now
gaining credence throughout the university sector (see, e.g., MacLellan 2001;
Knight 2002; Taras 2002; Bryan and Clegg 2006).

Critically, these two broad purposes contradict each other, which is why
the assessment process, in attempting to do both, has become so difficult.
New lecturers need to understand these inherent conflicts and contradic-
tions and reflect on the effects on their own assessment, marking, and feedback as an integral part of the overall assessment/learning process.

Literature reviews of assessment and pedagogical assessment experts
confirm what has been known for many years, which is that assessment,
marking, and feedback practices tend to be the most criticised aspects of
the university experience (see, e.g., Rust 2002, 2007; Sadler 2009, in press;

Yorke 2009, 2011). In the UK, students, while being satisfied overall with their higher education experience, are less satisfied with assessment and feedback (National Student Survey years 2005–2010).

Not surprisingly, assessment is a particularly important feature of the university teaching programmes. In the UK, those programmes that wish to be accredited by the HEA must show evidence of how their programme maps onto the UK Professional Standards Framework. For a detailed account, please see the earlier chapter by Davies and Maguire (this volume), but briefly the framework consists of six areas of activity of which the relevant one here is "Assessment and giving feedback to learners," six statements of core knowledge, such as "How students learn both in the subject and generally," and five statements of professional values such as "Commitment to incorporating the process and outcomes of relevant research, scholarship, and/or professional practice."

Without specific formal academic development in assessment such as offered in university teaching programmes, it is interesting to ask what is likely to affect new lecturers when thinking about assessment. It might be their previous experience of being assessed themselves, or they might be more influenced by their departments and the institutions they work in. Another factor is likely to be the epistemological and pedagogical parameters of their discipline as suggested by Neumann, Parry, and Becher (2002).

A study carried out by Norton et al. (2010) was designed to explore some of these questions. Ten lecturers from an overall cohort of thirty taking part in the Postgraduate Certificate Learning and Teaching in Higher Education (PGCLTHE) programme at Liverpool Hope University agreed to take part and were interviewed about the programme and their views about how they thought it had shaped their beliefs about learning, teaching, and assessment. The interview questions included asking them about the programme's usefulness and weaknesses, whether or not it had changed their views on learning and teaching, whether or not they felt that the pedagogical theories they learned about on the programme were useful for their day-to-day teaching practice, and whether or not they felt they could easily apply what they had learned on the programme in their teaching practice.

The PGCLTHE programme at Liverpool Hope has subsequently been modified and revalidated but at the time of this research it was a two-year part-time programme based on core HEA principles and delivered in four interrelated modules: creating an effective learning environment; assessment and evaluation; curriculum design; managing the curriculum and professional practice.

Programme participants were expected to attend intensive two-day sessions for each module and then apply principles from the programme to their own developing understanding as practitioners with the help of a specially selected mentor in their subject discipline. Assessment of the modules involved reflection, a negotiated learning agreement, and a teaching/assessment portfolio.

In general, our findings showed that this small sample had valued the experience of taking such a programme, although they did mention the difficulties of balancing study within their workload and time was a major concern. Eight of the ten participants thought the theories introduced in the programme were relevant to their teaching practice, but only six of them felt able to apply what they had learned. Reasons for this difficulty included inherited patterns of assessment and teaching (it is not easy to change a course you have been given), as well as practical constraints such as the size of the class (some pedagogically sound methods of assessment are difficult to carry out with very large numbers).

When asked specifically about what they thought about assessment, six of the ten lecturers said they felt unable to easily change their assessment practices; the remaining four felt they could change practices but there were some difficulties. These included the institutional regulations required to make changes which often involved detailed paperwork and going through a series of committee approvals. This made it virtually impossible, for example, to change an assessment task in the middle of a course or module.

We concluded that while participants had found the PGCLTHE programme useful, there was evidence that they did not always feel able to put what they had learned into practice, and this was due to a number of interrelating institutional, departmental, and individual variables. These are described as filters by Fanghanel (2007), by which she means factors that influence academics to privilege or prioritise one set of activities over others.

These initial findings suggested that constraints may be operating to lessen the impact of what lecturers had learned on the programme, but since the study was a small one it led us to explore with a greater range of lecturers their views about assessment within the broader context of their philosophy of learning and teaching. Specifically, we intended to establish what lecturers thought were ideal conditions for student learning related to assessment practices, their views on marking and feedback, the emotional issues related to assessment practice, and the relationship between their past experiences and current practices. A concomitant aim was to seek lecturers' views of the value of formal training or continuing professional development in assessment and marking practice.

In this study (Norton et al. 2009; Shannon, Norton, and Norton 2009), we interviewed thirty lecturers who came from four universities in the United Kingdom and whose university teaching experience ranged from one to twenty-two years. Our research aim was to examine the relationship between their pedagogical philosophies and their actual assessment practice. In a wide-ranging and deep interview, the questions focused on the functions and purposes of assessment.

Using Braun and Clarke's (2006) guidelines on thematic analysis and interactive readings of the interview transcripts, together with repeated checking within the research team, six main themes were developed under the overarching framework of the relationship between pedagogical philosophy and assessment practice, using the shorthand device of an "ideal" and an "actual" dichotomy. By "ideal," we meant the pedagogical beliefs and values that our lecturers described in relation to learning, teaching, and assessment; and by "actual," we meant what went on in the lecturers' daily assessment practice in which we were looking for further evidence for the existence of constraints that we had identified in our earlier study.

The six themes were the relationship between lecturers' pedagogical philosophy and their assessment practice; purpose of assessment; marking beliefs and practices; feedback and its relationship to assessment; emotional issues related to assessment; and finally, development of assessment, marking, and feedback skills. Each of these themes will now be presented in detail.

Theme One: The Relationship between Lecturers' Pedagogical Philosophy and Their Assessment Practices

Our first main finding within the parameters of this theme was that lecturers were able to clearly articulate their pedagogical philosophies. Interestingly, we also found that many lecturers felt they had changed with experience. It was not clear from this specific study, however, how much of this experience included taking part in a university teaching programme. In general, our findings suggested that the lecturers had started teaching with a conception that the lecturer's role was about being a subject expert dispensing knowledge but they had moved in a fairly short time towards a role as a facilitator enabling students to learn:

> . . . where I felt that I changed is where I started to review how I was approaching second years, third years, postgraduates students where enthusiasm and comprehension weren't the primary concerns; it was guidance and elements of self-development, that sort of ownership and that sort of realisation that education was a sort of partnership rather than a case of superiors and subordinates . . .

This mirrors findings by Nyquist and Wulff (1996), who describe three stages in a new lecturer's development where there is a move from a self-survival stage that is concerned with being sufficiently knowledgeable to a concern with teaching skills and assessment methods, and only in the final stage do new lecturers actually begin to consider what and how their students are actually learning.

When we asked our lecturers whether they were able to translate such pedagogical beliefs into their assessment practice by making changes, it became clear that most of them did not appear to have the autonomy to actually change assessment tasks and practices. The reasons they gave included departmental ways of assessment, institutional processes, and requirements such as quality assurance procedures which made change difficult to do easily. This finding foregrounded the problematic issue of freedom versus autonomy, where the need to be accountable and transparent militates against individual pedagogical philosophies, no matter how educationally sound they may be.

Some lecturers mentioned the social pressure of being part of a large team when sometimes they felt theirs was but a small voice. Knight and Trowler (2000) found in their study of new academics that the power of the department could be considerable and could lead to quite stressful situations for newer colleagues who were trying to establish their place in the department. This is a factor that is likely to be acute for new academics but as this research shows still affects those even with many years of experience as a lecturer.

In this theme, then, we found evidence of certain constraints which might explain the limited impact of university programmes on assessment practice.

Theme Two: The Purpose of Assessment

When asked about the purpose of assessment, lecturers talked about how it should aid learning by expanding students' knowledge and understanding and by allowing them to progress. They also mentioned giving students targets to enable them to achieve and to focus their learning. Lecturers talked about how assessment tasks should be pedagogically appropriate, and they gave a rationale for different types of assessment such as essays, exams, and report writing (pedagogical rationale). They described how assessment tasks also need to be fit for purpose, by which they meant such tasks could be used as indicators of the level of students' learning as well as useful for institutional purposes and, in one case, relating to industry needs (certification rationale).

Another area that our lecturers were keen to talk about was the motivational aspect of assessment, which included targets that would drive the student to achieve, assessment used as an incentive for students to do well, and assessment tasks that would give them a focus for their learning. These pedagogically driven aims were thus conceptualised in our analysis as "ideal." Broadly speaking, there was a consensus that assessment should be *for* learning rather than *of* learning, which is a common principle propounded in UK university teaching programmes. However, achieving these ideals was frequently reported as difficult given the actual context where many lecturers mentioned that there is a prevailing focus on grades, which is the institutional and discipline requirement for the certification of learning, a consequence of the dual purpose of assessment that we mentioned earlier in this chapter.

It is not surprising that in such a culture of higher education, students become strategic and grade-orientated. This is a problem in the UK that is only going to get worse, given the fact that following the Browne (2010) review of higher education funding and student finance, students will face greatly increased tuition fees. Our lecturers talked about grade-chasing students who were only interested in their mark, those students who would ask, "What do I need to do to get a first?" Some of our lecturers talked about students losing their creativity as a result. Others mentioned students only learning what was needed to pass the assessment task and being "exam smart." They were also concerned about the range of students that they were currently expected to teach, in terms of their ability and motivation, such as different educational backgrounds, varying levels of literacy skills such as grammar and spelling skills, and their commitment such as unprepared students who are unwilling to read. This, together with large classes and students who come to university with differing expectations, made it hard to always use assessment in the way that our lecturers would have preferred.

Theme Three: Marking Constraints

Marking is an important theme because it is impossible to consider the pedagogical effects of assessment without considering how lecturers go about the practical process of marking work and assigning grades. When developing this theme from the interview transcripts, we discovered a difference in our lecturers' views about the role of marking/assessment criteria which could best be described as a continuum.

At one end was the "connoisseurship" approach, which many lecturers claimed was part of their identity as professionals and which was broadly taken to mean a holistic, judgment-based approach. At the other end of the continuum was the "highly regulated" approach, which typically involves marking on the basis of meeting various discrete criteria, often using marking grids.

The role of assessment criteria in making marking judgments has featured strongly in the literature (see, e.g., Elander and Hardman 2002; Newstead 2003). This might account for the perceptible shift that our interview data showed where few, if any, of our lecturers embraced the connoisseurship model without taking any account of the need for some sort of recognition of assessment criteria. This may be due to the pervading research literature, or, more likely, it was due to the code of practice for assessment laid down by the Quality Assurance Agency for Higher Education (2006—QAA), which is influential in the UK, since it is tied in with institutional review and audit. The code of practice is a

> statement of good practice that has been endorsed by the higher education community. As such it is useful in QAA's audit and review processes that consider the extent to which an institution, in developing and implementing its own policies, has taken account of the Code of practice and its precepts. (p. 2)

The QAA code of practice sets out definitions of assessment and fifteen principles together with examples. The principles that are related specifically to marking include that of having "transparent and fair mechanisms for marking and for moderating marks" where they advise the use of assessment criteria and marking schemes. This appears to have had some effect on lecturers where, in this study at least, many of them were prepared to encompass some of the more regulatory aspects of marking even when they personally favoured a more holistic expert judgment approach.

Perhaps more than any of the other themes that were developed out of this analysis, pedagogical philosophy appeared to be constrained here by the sheer practicalities of the marking process itself. Given the increase in student numbers over recent years without any subsequent increase in staffing in UK universities and the quick turnaround times that are required (again influenced by the QAA code of practice), lecturers often find themselves faced with a heavy marking load and not much time to do it in. This is in the context of a higher education system, where lecturers are expected to be research active and increasingly, in the UK, to be entrepreneurial and generate income for their university.

Our lecturers talked about how this leads to a strategy where they devote concentrated periods of time to marking, but others find it impossible to mark continuously for long periods of time. They commented that such lengthy periods can lead to confusion when marking (i.e., "What's being marked? Who wrote what? Have I already read this?"). Unfortunately, this can have the deleterious effect of lecturers developing avoidance strategies, which has consequences for students in terms of rapid and useful feedback but can also affect lecturers when they design assessment. Instead of designing assessment tasks that are pedagogically appropriate, they are sometimes forced to consider other methods of assessment simply to reduce the marking workload, such as setting examinations when they would prefer pedagogically to assess solely by coursework (Norton et al. 2006).

In summary, this theme showed that the practical requirements of marking appeared to collide with assessment philosophy. Our lecturers tended to adopt a stance that was somewhere between the opposite ends of the connoisseurship/regulated approach to marking, which perhaps indicates some sort of compromise to cope with what are often very diverse, one could almost say contradictory, demands.

Theme Four: Feedback as a Relationship

In this theme, lecturers saw ideal feedback as encouraging self-reflection in their students, being motivational and timely. In reflecting on the motivational aspects, they talked about how constructive feedback leads to motivation as the student is given positive comments on good aspects of their assessment but also practical advice of where, and how, to improve for their next piece of work, thus increasing their confidence.

They also said that good feedback allows students to reflect on their assignments, both in terms of their strengths and weaknesses, and leads students to a better understanding of the grades they have been given. Finally, our lecturers were keenly aware of the need to give feedback on assignments in time for students to act on it in order to improve their next assignments. Many lecturers also said that, ideally, feedback should be continual throughout the year.

This theme links closely with the previous theme of marking in highlighting constraints to sound assessment practice, because when it came to the actual situation that many of our lecturers faced there were a number of problematic areas which we have characterised as power relations, negative aspects for lecturers, the issue of unmotivated students, and the time factor.

By "power relations" we meant the way that our lecturers talked about how power can work in two ways. It can be seen as the lecturer having all the power, so students feel unable to enter into a frank and open dialogue about their work. It can also mean that students today are becoming increasingly litigious, are sometimes seen as the customer, and can use this power to question their marks and grades and even their lecturers' ability. This trend of student consumerism is increasing across the world, and not just in the UK (see, e.g., Naidoo and Jamieson 2005; Titus 2008). Giving honest feedback in this sort of situation can be very difficult:

> . . . instead of taking responsibility for their mark, what they actually end up doing is trying to basically say, "no, I think it's worth a B, you've given me a C, but I think it's worth a B and there's something wrong with the way that you've marked it."

Negative aspects for the lecturers encompassed several issues such as the student focus on grades, which was seen as unhelpful, and the fact that some students take negative feedback personally, even though there may be positive comments as well. As with marking, time was also a constraint where lecturers found mass feedback was problematic but providing individual feedback time on a one-to-one basis was not always successful because students did not always attend.

Time with students tended to be restricted even though many of our lecturers believed that more time would assist the learning process. Not having sufficient time to do all the things that a university lecturer is supposed to do added its own pressures.

> My feedback time is out of control and I know I have to rein that in for my sanity but also because of the other parameters that have been put on me but I feel I'm being squeezed all over the show.

Theme Five: Emotional Issues Related to Assessment

In this theme, our lecturers saw assessment as ideally a two-way process, involving both the lecturer and student, in which they have an understanding of the students' perspective in order to give feedback which is positive and encouraging. This, they felt, should be done through sustained dialogue.

The second issue they talked about, we have called "rewards for the lecturer," which captured their comments about needing a clear indication of students' progress, wanting to inspire and enthuse students, and the positive emotions when their students rise to challenges, particularly those who have not done so well in the first year. Seeing such students improve in confidence is rewarding:

> You like students to do well it gives you that positive feedback to yourself, if students excel in your area it makes you feel good, you feel a certain amount of responsibility for it . . .

The other issue was that of supportive colleagues. Here, our lecturers described how supportive colleagues enhanced the lecturing experience by sharing materials, and by being aware of the needs of the less experienced lecturers.

When it came to their actual practice, as opposed to their ideal situation, a different picture was painted with discussion again about the more negative aspects of power relations in which assessment practice often turned out to be one-way rather than two-way. These aspects were discussed in relation to feedback where the lecturers felt that sometimes they may be seen as service providers and their students as customers.

As well as finding it difficult to deal with students' negative emotions when given feedback, lecturers also talked about feeling stressed about marking, disheartened by students who did not appear to appreciate feedback or who could not comprehend the lecture material, or by students who were unprepared and handed in work of a poor standard. Such comments from our lecturers reflect a situation that is all too common in UK universities today, where some might blame the widening participation movement:

> We have some very academically able students . . . but we've also got a whole other group of students and actually I wouldn't say they're less academically able, I'd say they're less competent in a whole different variety of ways, they're less engaged with the learning process, they're less likely to come and seek help from you, they're more likely to put obstacles in the way almost like a form of ego protection, esteemed protection, and those students are a bit of a challenge . . .

Self-doubt was also expressed more by the newer, less experienced lecturers in our sample. They mentioned not having the self-confidence to implement innovative teaching styles and tended to leave decisions to more experienced lecturers until their confidence increases:

> I am not an academic, by experience and the vast majority of my working life, I am relatively new to academia and I will—I have views on things but I have to, I suppose if you like, defer to people who have been doing this for a lot longer until maybe I gain the confidence to actually argue more cogently, no I don't think this is working.

These less experienced lecturers were also concerned with their marking accuracy:

> My key worry in assessment, and I suspect that for most of us starting out, my key worry is about accuracy, am I marking accurately, am I giving the student a fair and just mark and, if I've done that, I think that's vital.

Such concerns show how important it is to take into account the emotional aspects of teaching and assessment, as some of our lecturers also said that it could be problematic when trying to introduce new ideas or innovative ways of teaching or assessing, if their subject colleagues were opposed (see, e.g., Knight and Trowler 2000).

In conclusion, our findings from the thematic analysis overall showed that lecturers in this study invested significant emotional capital in the assessment process and really cared about their students' learning. In an ideal world, supported by their colleagues, they saw themselves as engaged in a two-way, mutually positive pedagogical relationship with their students which would make them feel good about themselves. However, in the actual world, things were felt to be a little different. Power relations could constrain such two-way relationships with students and non-supportive colleagues could be frustrating, when trying to attain a match between their pedagogical philosophy and assessment practice.

Theme Six: Development of Assessment, Marking, and Feedback Skills

This final theme was developed from a specific answer to our probes about the value of continuing professional development, formal training in marking and assessment practice, and, by inference, their views about pedagogical research and the scholarship of teaching and learning. The consensus view from the lecturers we interviewed was that such formal training was *not* necessary; they preferred to learn their craft through experience, sometimes by informal training, which was usually at departmental level and done through observation, and by being mentored.

Despite recognition by our lecturers that assessment and marking can be problematic, there was still some resistance to formal training in the areas of assessment design, marking, and feedback. The following quote from one of the more experienced lecturers interviewed clearly describes how one can believe that one is a good marker/assessor, and think that while training might be useful for other colleagues, it is not necessary for oneself.

> I've been doing this for seventeen years now at various levels and I don't think I need training now, I think I know what I'm doing, I'm confident that I know what I'm doing and I have a great deal of experience in doing it and I'd be quite miffed if someone came along and said, "you've never had any training, go away and get some." On the other hand, and this might sound totally hypocritical, I think in principle it would be a good idea if people were given training and I'd be slightly wary of someone in my position saying what I've just said. I think I'm a bit confused and a bit ambivalent about that really. I'm confident that what I do, I do well and I do rationally and I do with the benefit of a great deal of experience having done it for many years and I'm also, like obviously I've read a lot of stuff since then, I've learnt a lot of stuff in practice and I've moderated a lot of other people's work so I'm not just working in isolation here. Quite how I got to know how to do it, I'm not sure.

In summary, the picture that emerged from these accounts was one in which many of the lecturers we interviewed had undergone some formal university teaching programme, and on the whole thought that such programmes were useful. At the same time, they did not appear to always put what they had learned into practice, preferring instead to rely on other colleagues, and learning by experience. There was no collective commitment to formal training. This adds some weight to Rust's (2007) argument for the need for staff development in assessment to be derived from a clearly articulated scholarship of assessment. His view is that an assessment scholarship should be built on the research literature and underpinned by social-constructivist theory, in which assessment is *for* rather than *of* learning.

In spite of Dearing's (1997) recommendation that all those who teach at university level should obtain a university teaching qualification, the input of the HEA, and the increasing burgeoning of pedagogical research, known sometimes as the scholarship of teaching and learning (Boyer 1990), there still appears to be a profound belief that teaching, assessment, and marking skills do not need to be formally acquired by lecturers; they will somehow pick it up from their practice. In effect, then, it appears from this study that they prefer to build on their own mental models of quality as argued by Wolf (1995), which are often derived from when they were students themselves, from observing how their colleagues work and from practising on their students.

Drawing the findings of this research together, it seems that there is some evidence here to explain why what is learned about assessment pedagogy in university teaching programmes cannot always be put into practice. There is a complex interrelationship of institutional, subject, and QAA drivers as well as perceived constraints such as student expectations and other pressures such as limited time and negative emotional experiences. Applying theory to practice is recognised as difficult in most academic subjects where there is a professional or vocational element, so it is not surprising that it is equally difficult in the context of a professional qualification teaching programme where lecturers are taught the theoretical pedagogical principles of assessment and how they relate to learning.

To explore this concept further, we designed a study specifically for analysing the views on assessment design of lecturers who were either currently taking or who had recently completed a professional university teaching programme. Our rationale for focusing on assessment design was that it most closely related to the pedagogical principles of assessment.

Five hundred and eighty-six lecturers from sixty-six institutions across the UK completed a questionnaire which we called the Assessment Design Inventory (ADI). Detailed findings of this research are reported elsewhere (Norton, Norton, and Shannon 2010, 2011), but the most relevant findings for this chapter are presented here. Firstly, we established that "new" lecturers did report a number of desirable assessment practices. We have defined "desirable" as pedagogically sound assessment design practice by drawing on the received wisdom in the assessment literature such as Nicol and Macfarlane-Dick's (2006) principles of good feedback practice. This is encouraging when thinking about the impact of university teaching programmes.

What was less encouraging, however, was our second main finding that there was also evidence of widespread agreement to several constraints to good practice, as identified on the ADI. These constraints included practical factors such as time, large numbers, little incentive to innovate, and student factors such as focusing on the grade. This questionnaire study confirmed our earlier interview study findings of the individual or personal influencing variables.

We also found evidence of disciplinary and institutional differences. For example, lecturers from hard disciplines (using Biglan's 1973 classification of hard-soft and pure-applied) and lecturers from traditional research-based universities (i.e., pre-1992 universities) tended to be more affected by constraints. Like our earlier study, this finding supports Fanghanel's (2007) concept of filters operating on individual academics at the macro and meso levels. Thus it would seem from this large-scale questionnaire study that there are some limitations to the effectiveness of the teaching programmes, when considering pedagogically appropriate assessment design practices.

The implications of our findings for those who teach such programmes would suggest that there is a real need to be sensitive to and aware of discipline differences and the sometimes major effect they have on lecturers' views of assessment, particularly when they return to their working lives.

OVERALL CONCLUSIONS FROM THE RESEARCH STUDIES

In this chapter, given the caveat that all our measures are self-reported (a common weakness in this type of research, as argued by Kane, Sandretto, and Heath 2002), we have drawn on the findings of three research studies with lecturers exploring aspects of assessment to establish as far as possible the impact or long-term effect that university programmes have when they return to their departments and disciplines.

What does seem to be robust is the general finding that despite evidence that their beliefs about learning, teaching, and assessment (their pedagogical philosophy) do appear to be changed, or at least enhanced, by taking university programmes, lecturers do not always find this easy to put into practice. More specifically, our studies were not able to show simple cause-and-effect explanations but suggested rather that there was a complex interaction of institutional, discipline, and individual differences that determined how well lecturers could enact pedagogically sound assessment principles learned on university teaching programmes.

We would suggest, in the case of assessment at least, that while the impact of such programmes can only be limited, the solution may not necessarily be formal staff development programmes. Our in-depth interview study showed that there was some resistance to this idea, and indeed work by the first author as an academic developer confirms that such formal training may be resisted (Norton 2003). Often what happens is a form of compliance rather than real interest and engagement.

Appealing to colleagues' intellectual curiosity as expounded in Breslow et al. (2004) could be one way of encouraging reflective practice and change. Breslow and her colleagues argued that educational developers need to take into account academics' beliefs about their role as university lecturers and their own personal beliefs about learning and teaching. If they do not, there is a risk that, although lecturers may comply by attending staff development events, there will be little or no impact on their actual learning, teaching, and assessment practices.

A CASE FOR PEDAGOGICAL ACTION RESEARCH TO EXTEND THE IMPACT OF UNIVERSITY TEACHING PROGRAMMES

When thinking about university teaching programmes for new lecturers, similar problems with reluctant compliance may well operate, so ways have to be found to engage academics' intellectual curiosity to realise an impact which will be ongoing throughout the individual's teaching career. Action research is one such approach, as it is carried out by lecturers themselves rather than by educational researchers. Pedagogical action research can be particularly powerful, as like all forms of action research it has a dual aim of contributing to new knowledge and improving lecturers' practice, which, in this case, can include their assessment practice.

The fundamental aim of pedagogical action research is for academics to identify a problematic issue either in their students' learning or in their own teaching and/or assessment practice. Having identified such an issue, the academic goes on to investigate it systematically by carrying out a research study which, depending on their own subject discipline, is likely to fall into one of three research paradigms with associated methodologies (O'Brien 1998).

The first of these is the positivist paradigm, which favours experimental design, quantitative data, and statistical testing, such as evaluating the effectiveness of an assessment intervention. The interpretevist paradigm attempts to understand what is going on within the person by taking a phenomenological approach, such as finding out what it is really like to be a student who has been given a challenging assignment. Thirdly, the praxis paradigm contextualises the research findings in an ongoing, reflective, often community-based account where the researcher may act in a number of roles such as planner, leader, catalyser, facilitator, teacher, designer, listener, observer, synthesiser, reporter. An example might be a department wishing to introduce portfolios into their assessment regime.

The rationale for this approach is that action research links to reflective practice, engagement with the scholarship of learning and teaching, and to continuing professional development in a way that is personally empowering rather than externally imposed (Norton 2009). It has also been shown to link to a learning-centred approach for staff on teaching programmes as advocated by Hubball and Poole (2004) and encourages more profound changes in teacher conceptions of learning (McLoughlin 2000). It is, however, not without certain risks.

As Brew (2006) argues, action research is likely to encourage "scholarly knowledge-building communities" that may well be critical of the context in which they operate. Critiquing educational practices can therefore be political and can lead to difficult questions about previously held assumptions and mores at the institutional, departmental, and discipline level. Pedagogical action research works particularly well when it is shared communally, as it establishes professional networks of support as well as of interest.

This communal aspect has been practised for several years at Liverpool Hope University. It was originally established in 2001 as a grassroots Pedagogical Action Research (PAR) group, and then was given institutional support. At Liverpool Hope, the way the PAR group has functioned has been as an interdisciplinary group in which members are encouraged to carry out research on their own learning, teaching, and assessment issues. By so doing, they engage with the relevant pedagogical literature, enhance their own reflective practice, and connect with the wider community of scholars. By meeting monthly, methodological problems as well as dealing with potential risks are shared and suggestions made for dealing with them. For example, one of the PAR members needed advice on how to present their research findings carried out on feedback practices in such a way as to encourage change at the departmental level. This is where an interdisciplinary approach can be helpful as it throws a fresh light on what may have previously been seen as unchangeable within the discipline.

Such a grassroots initiative is unlikely to survive or have much of an influence unless it is embedded within the institution. At Liverpool Hope, pedagogical action research has been deliberately related in two main ways to the revalidated university teaching programme, which offers a postgraduate certificate (PGCAP), diploma and master's (PGDipAP) in academic practice (MAAP).

Firstly, the concept of pedagogical action research is part of the PGCAP curriculum in which one of the assessment tasks is to design a small action research study on self/peer evaluations and student feedback. For those participants who wish to progress onto the MAAP, they take a whole course in action research in preparation for their dissertation course in which they are asked to carry out a substantial action research study in an area of learning and teaching in higher education.

The second way that the PAR model has been utilised to extend impact is by encouraging the PGCAP programme participants at Liverpool Hope University to attend the monthly PAR seminars (to which external pedagogical researchers are invited) and the annual PAR symposium day (in which colleagues present their own research studies). They are also encouraged to contribute their assessed pieces of work, or contribute articles to the in-house journal *Pedagogical Research in Maximising Education (PRIME)* (2011). To further extend their confidence and connect them with the wider community of researchers and practitioners, they are also invited to contribute papers to the biennial international Pedagogical Research in Higher Education (PRHE) conferences:

In this way, the intention has been to build on our new colleagues' interest in pedagogy which has been stimulated in the university teaching programme and continue to encourage a more long-lasting influence by enabling them to research learning and teaching issues which are of direct relevance to their own practitioner needs, set in the real context of their discipline and their department.

During the year 2009/2010 the PAR group had a membership of seventy university staff, of whom thirty-one came from sciences and social sciences, twenty-one from education, twelve from arts and humanities, and six from other university departments. In the 2008 annual PAR symposium event, colleagues from history, biology, computer sciences, music, and theology gave presentations related to their own research studies on assessment. Several of these have been developed into journal papers and led the individuals concerned into an ongoing active engagement with seeking to improve their assessment practice and their students' learning experience.

CONCLUSION

Ultimately, from the research, from the literature, and from the first author's practitioner experience of having taught on the PGCAP (and the previous PGCLTHE) programmes at Liverpool Hope University, there is a real case for arguing that the impact of university teaching programmes may be diluted by the realities of going back to carry out the duties of an academic lecturer within a given institutional, departmental, and disciplinary context.

Throughout this chapter, we have argued that there is no simple solution, such as making continuing professional development in pedagogy compulsory. Important though both initial (i.e., in university teaching programmes) and continuing professional development are, they may have only limited influence as illustrated in the research cited.

Encouraging colleagues to engage in pedagogical action research is not the only answer. However, it has the merit of enabling academics, if they are brave enough, to challenge the pedagogical status quo in their departments and disciplines and work towards improving learning, teaching, and assessment practice from an evidence-based perspective.

BIBLIOGRAPHY

Biglan, Anthony. 1973. "The Characteristics of Subject Matter in Different Academic Areas." *Journal of Applied Psychology* 58: 195–203.
Black, Paul J., Chris Harrison, Clare Lee, Bethan Marshall, and Dylan Wiliam. 2003. *Assessment for Learning. Putting It into Practice.* Maidenhead, UK: Open University Press.
Black, Paul J., and Dylan Wiliam. 1998. "Assessment and Classroom Learning." *Assessment in Education: Principles, Policy and Practice* 5 (1): 7–74.
Boyer, Ernest. 1990. *Scholarship Reconsidered.* Washington, DC: Carnegie Foundation.
Braun, Virginia, and Victoria Clarke. 2006. "Using Thematic Analysis in Psychology." *Qualitative Research in Psychology* 3: 77–101.
Breslow, Lori, Linda Drew, Mike Healey, Bob Matthew, and Lin Norton. 2004. "Intellectual Curiosity: A Catalyst for the Scholarships of Teaching and Learning and Educational Development." In *Exploring Academic Development in Higher Education: Issues of Engagement*, edited by Liz M. Elvidge, 83–96. Cambridge: Jill Rogers Associates.
Brew, Angela. 2006. *Research and Teaching: Beyond the Divide.* Basingstoke, UK: Palgrave Macmillan.
Browne, John. 2010. "Securing a Sustainable Future for Higher Education: An Independent Review of Higher Education Funding and Student Finance." *Department of Business Innovation and Skills*, http://www.bis.gov.uk/assets/

biscore/corporate/docs/s/10–1208-securing-sustainable-higher-education-browne-report.pdf, accessed 18/07/2011.

Bryan, Cordelia, and Karen Clegg, eds. 2006. *Innovative Assessment in Higher Education*. London: Routledge.

Coffey, Martin, and Graham Gibbs. 2000. "Can Academics Benefit from Training? Some Preliminary Evidence." *Teaching in Higher Education* 5: 385–389.

Dearing, Sir Ronald. 1997. *Higher Education in the Learning Society: The National Committee of Inquiry into Higher Education*. London: HMSO, http://www.leeds.ac.uk/educol/ncihe/, accessed 23/05/2011, accessed 18/07/2011.

Elander, James, and David Hardman. 2002. "An Application of Judgment Analysis to Examination Marking in Psychology." *British Journal of Psychology* 93: 303–328.

Fanghanel, Joelle. 2007. "Investigating University Lecturers' Pedagogical Constructs in the Working Context." *Higher Education Academy*, http://www.heacademy.ac.uk/assets/York/documents/ourwork/research/fanghanel.pdf, accessed 18/07/2011.

Hubball, Harry T., and Gary Poole. 2004. "Learning-Centred Education to Meet the Diverse Needs and Circumstances of University Faculty through an Eight-Month Programme on Teaching and Learning in Higher Education." *International Journal for Academic Development* 8 (2): 11–24.

Kane, Ruth, Susan Sandretto, and Chris Heath. 2002. "Telling Half the Story: A Critical Review of Research on the Teaching Beliefs and Practices of University Academics." *Review of Educational Research* 72 (2): 177–228.

Knight, Peter, ed. 2002. *Assessment for Learning in Higher Education*. Abingdon, UK: Routledge/Staff and Educational Development Association (SEDA).

Knight, Peter T., and Paul R. Trowler. 2000. "Department-Level Cultures and the Improvement of Learning and Teaching." *Studies in Higher Education* 25 (1): 69–83.

MacLellan, Effie. 2001. "Assessment for Learning: The Differing Perceptions of Tutors and Students." *Assessment and Evaluation in Higher Education* 26 (4): 307–318.

McLoughlin, Catherine. 2000. "Creating Partnerships for Generative Learning and Systemic Change: Redefining Academic Roles in Support of Learning." *International Journal of Academic Development* 5 (2): 116–128.

Naidoo, Rajani, and Ian Jamieson. 2005. "Empowering Participants or Corroding Learning? Towards a Research Agenda on the Impact of Student Consumerism in Higher Education." *Journal of Educational Policy* 20 (3): 267–281.

National Student Survey (NSS). 2005, 2006, 2007, 2008, 2009, 2010. *Higher Education Funding Council for England*, http://www.hefce.ac.uk/learning/nss/, accessed 18/07/2011.

Neumann, Ruth, Sharon Parry, and Tony Becher. 2002. "Teaching and Learning in Their Disciplinary Contexts: A Conceptual Analysis." *Studies in Higher Education* 27 (4): 405–417.

Newstead, Steve E. 2003. "Examining the Examiners: Why Are We so Bad at Assessing Students?" *Psychology Learning and Teaching* 2 (2): 70–75.

Nicol, David J., and Debra Macfarlane-Dick. 2006. "Formative Assessment and Self-Regulated Learning: A Model and Seven Principles of Good Feedback Practice." *Studies in Higher Education* 31 (2): 199–218.

Norton, Lin S. 2003. "Academic Development: Compliant Behaviours or Conceptual Change?" Trigger paper for Cambridge Conference on Engaging with Academic Development, University of Cambridge, 14–19 September, http://lin-norton.co.uk/wp-content/uploads/2011/04/Trigger-paper-revised-cambridge-conference-2003.pdf, accessed 18/07/2011.

———. 2009. *Action Research in Teaching and Learning: A Practical Guide to Conducting Pedagogical Research in Universities.* Abingdon, UK: Routledge.

———. 2011. "Learning Criteria, Learning Outcomes and Assessment Criteria." In *Encyclopedia of the Sciences of Learning*, edited by Norbert M. Seel, http://www.springer.com/psychology/book/978-1-4419-5503-6, accessed 18/07/2011.

Norton, Lin S., Ola Aiyegbayo, Katherine Harrington, James Elander, and Peter Reddy. 2010. "New Lecturers' Beliefs about Learning, Teaching and Assessment in Higher Education: The Role of the PGCLTHE Programme." *Innovations in Education and Teaching International* 47 (4): 345–356.

Norton, Lin S., Katherine Harrington, Bill Norton, and Lee Shannon. 2006. "Challenging Traditional Forms of Assessment: University Teachers' Views on Examinations." Paper presented at the Third Conference of the International Society for the Scholarship of Teaching and Learning (ISSOTL), Washington, DC, 9–12 November.

Norton, Lin S., Bill Norton, and Lee Shannon. 2010. "The Assessment Design Inventory: A Tool for Research and Faculty Development." Paper presented at the sixth international conference of the International Society for the Scholarship of Teaching and Learning (ISSOTL10), Arena and Convention Centre, Liverpool, UK, 19–22 October.

———. 2011. "The Assessment Design Inventory: A Tool for Research and Staff Development." In *Improving Student Learning: Proceedings of the 2010 ISSOTL/ISL Conference*, edited by Chris Rust. Oxford: Oxford Centre for Staff and Learning Development.

Norton, Lin S., Bill Norton, Lee Shannon, and Frances Phillips. 2009. "Assessment Design, Pedagogy and Practice: What Do New Lecturers Think?" Paper presented at the annual conference of the International Society for the Scholarship of Teaching and Learning (ISSOTL), Indiana University, Bloomington, Indiana, U.S., 22–25 October.

Nyquist, Jody D., and Donald H. Wulff. 1996. *Working Effectively with Graduate Assistants.* Thousand Oaks, CA: Sage.

O'Brien, Rory. 1998. "An Overview of the Methodological Approach of Action Research," http://www.web.net/~robrien/papers/arfinal.html, accessed 18/07/2011.

"Pedagogical Research in Higher Education (PRHE) Conferences." 2011. Liverpool Hope University Web site, http://www.hope.ac.uk/learningandteaching/lat.php?page=prhe andcurrent=prhe, accessed 01/02/2011.

Pedagogical Research in Maximising Education (PRIME). 2011. Liverpool Hope University Web site, http://www.hope.ac.uk/learningandteaching/lat.php?page=primeandcurrent=prime, accessed 01/02/2011.

Postareff, Liisa, Sari Lindblom-Ylänne, and Anne Nevgi. 2007. "The Effect of Pedagogical Training on Teaching in Higher Education." *Teaching and Teacher Education* 23 (5): 557–571.

Prosser, Mike, Mark Rickinson, Valerie Bence, Andria Hanbury, and Malgorzata Kulej. 2006. "Report for the Higher Education Academy: Formative Evaluation of Accredited Programmes." *Higher Education Academy*, http://www.heacademy.ac.uk/assets/York/documents/ourwork/research/formative_evaluation_of_accredited_ programmes_may_2006.pdf, accessed 18/07/2011.

Quality Assurance Agency for Higher Education (QAA). 2006. *Code of Practice for the Assurance of Academic Quality and Standards in Higher Education*, 2nd edition, Section 6: Assessment of Students, https://www.qaa.ac.uk/academicinfrastructure/codeOfPractice/section6/COP_AOS.pdf, accessed 18/07/2011.

Rust, Chris. 2002. "The Impact of Assessment on Student Learning: How Can the Research Literature Practically Help to Inform the Development of

Departmental Assessment Strategies and Learner-Centred Assessment Practices?" *Active Learning in Higher Education* 3 (2): 145–158.

———. 2007. "Towards a Scholarship of Assessment." *Assessment & Evaluation in Higher Education* 32 (2): 229–237.

Sadler, D. Royce. 2009. "Transforming Holistic Assessment and Grading into a Vehicle for Complex Learning." In *Assessment, Learning and Judgement in Higher Education,* edited by Gordon Joughin, 45–63. Dordrecht, Netherlands: Springer.

———. In press. "Assessment in Higher Education." In *International Encyclopedia of Education,* edited by Eva Baker, Barry McGaw, and Penelope Peterson. Oxford: Elsevier.

Shannon, Lee, Lin S. Norton, and Bill Norton. 2009. "University Lecturers' Assessment Beliefs: A Theoretical Model." Paper presented at the thirteenth biennial conference of the European Association for Learning and Instruction (EARLI), Fostering communities of learners, Amsterdam, Netherlands, 25–29 August.

Taras, Maddalena. 2002. "Using Assessment for Learning and Learning from Assessment." *Assessment & Evaluation in Higher Education* 27 (6): 501–510.

Titus, Jordan J. 2008. "Student Ratings in a Consumerist Academy: Leveraging Pedagogical Control and Authority." *Sociological Perspectives* 51 (3): 397–422.

Wolf, Alison. 1995. *Competence Based Assessment.* Buckingham, UK: Open University Press.

Write Now Centre of Excellence for Learning and Teaching (CETL). 2011. http://www.writenow.ac.uk/, accessed 01/02/2010.

Yorke, Mantz. 2009. "Grading Student Achievement in Higher Education: Measuring or Judging?" In *The Routledge International Handbook of Higher Education,* edited by Malcolm Tight, Ka Ho Mok, Jeroen Huisman, and Christopher Morphet, 211–223. New York and Abingdon, UK: Routledge.

———. 2011. "Summative Assessment: Dealing with the 'Measurement Fallacy.'" *Studies in Higher Education* 36 (3): 251–273.

Part IV

Theorizing about Instructional Development

12 How Effects from Teacher-Training of Academic Teachers Propagate into the Meso Level and Beyond

Torgny Roxå and Katarina Mårtensson[1]

INTRODUCTION

Teacher-training[2] has a positive effect on academic teachers' way of thinking about their practice and on the teaching practice itself. A number of studies establish a link between teacher-training and the development, among participants, of a learning-focused conception of teaching, in contrast to a teaching or content-focused conception (Prosser and Trigwell 1999). This link extends to students' approaches to learning (Ho, Watkins, and Kelly 2001; Gibbs and Coffey 2004; Ramsden 2005; Prosser et al. 2006; Postareff, Lindblom-Ylänne, and Nevgi 2007; Donnelly 2008; Ginns, Kitay, and Prosser 2010).

Other researchers (Giertz 1996) have interviewed departmental leaders and confirmed that these academic categories also acknowledge positive and visible effects from teacher-training among teachers. Similar visible changes in teaching practices have been self-reported by teachers (Stes, Clement, and Van Petegem 2007). A Swedish study surveyed 1,100 participants from six different higher education institutions regarding their experiences of a newly established national compulsory teacher-training programme. Again, the positive value of teacher-training was confirmed by the participants themselves (Gran 2006). If policymakers and practitioners wish to enhance academic teaching and student learning, it is clearly a good idea to organise teacher-training for academic teachers.

But there are issues to discuss. Participants report that what they have learnt during the training is often not valued within the local context (Gibbs and Coffey 2004; Gran 2006; Prosser et al. 2006; Stes, Clement, and Van Petegem 2007; Ginns, Kitay, and Prosser 2010). Such reports indicate that the causal link between training and development of teaching is not straightforward. Individual teachers benefit from training but might experience difficulties in their local context[3] in response to new ideas developed during training. These difficulties can manifest themselves as a lack of support and interest from colleagues or supervisors or as conservative attitudes on behalf of the students (Ginns, Kitay, and Prosser 2010). The main focus of this text is to explore this dissonance. So, training has documented positive effects on individuals, but these effects do not propagate naturally into the local context and beyond.

Related questions frequently discussed in relevant studies are whether training should be generic across disciplines or if it should be organised within the disciplines (Healey and Jenkins 2003; Trowler and Bamber 2005); if the departments should be the locus for training (Knight and Trowler 2000); or if training should be located within the everyday workgroup (Knight 2006a, 2006b). A recurrent argument maintains that it is within the discipline (or the department) that a teacher's professional identity is formed (Henkel 2005). Accordingly, this is where training and other kinds of professional development should take place. Taking individuals from their professional context, training them, and then expecting them to influence their peers once they return is hardly likely to happen, especially if the teachers trained are younger colleagues within a professional community.

Moreover, there is the matter of time. Stes, Clement, and Van Petegem (2007) and Postareff and Lindblom-Ylänne (2008) have documented effects related to time. The training has to have certain duration in time and the effects might not show until a period of daily practice has passed, which indicates that issues like professional identity and the acquisition of teaching skills relevant for new insights made during training need to develop over time. This very issue has also been discussed by Entwistle and Walker (2000).

Another theme concerns what objectives such training should have. One widespread objective is to support improved student learning, as measured, for instance, by students' approaches to learning, where a deep approach to learning (Marton and Booth 1997) among students is linked to teachers' conceptions of teaching (Prosser and Trigwell 1999). This outcome is well researched and supported (see above): training has positive effects on individual academic teachers' conceptions and subsequently on their students' learning. Other objectives, however, might also come into play, like the support of institutional goals as expressed in institutional policies (Clegg 2009; Macdonald 2009); how to contribute to the institution as a learning organisation (Senge 2006); how to support teachers as reflective practitioners (Schön 1983); or how to support an emerging academic culture based on the scholarship of teaching and learning (Lindberg-Sand and Sonesson 2008).

The aims and objectives of teacher-training are in fact numerous and sometimes also contradictory, turning the field of teacher-training into an institutional political arena where different managerial interests intervene and rearrange things (Harland and Staniforth 2008) often according to poorly considered ideologies (Trowler and Bamber 2005). Such contradictory aims and objectives, where the training of teachers appears to be the solution to many problems, such as the implementation of information and communication technology, widening participation, sustainable development, et cetera, highlight the fact that systemic effects from teacher-training in higher education is an area which is clearly underresearched.

SYSTEMIC EFFECTS FROM TRAINING

Below we suggest a perspective where the effects or lack of effects from teacher-training can be understood. We will focus on the issue of effects spreading from the individual into the local context—the meso level—and beyond. The purpose is to compose a systemic perspective and thereby contribute to a more comprehensive understanding of what a higher education institution can expect from organising training for its teachers, and perhaps what individual academics might expect from higher education contexts where such training is introduced.

We will discuss teacher-training in relation to the system in which it happens: the workgroup, the department, faculty/school, and the institution. Are there effects from teacher-training on these levels? How can we understand the system so that effects cannot only be measured but also explained and promoted further? This attempt relates to results presented by Ginns, Kitay, and Prosser (2010, 245), who, in a study about effects reported by participants in a Graduate Certificate in Higher Education programme, conclude: "Thus lack of support from academic managers and peers were identified as significant limiting factors in pursuing scholarly activities in teaching and learning."

Any attempt to detect effects from an intervention, like training of academic teachers, must include a perspective of what we are looking for, the intended outcomes of the training, and a clear view of the system in which we look. We would not know what to search for if we were unclear about the former, and we would not know where and when to search if we were unclear about the latter. Our emphasis will be on where to look for effects and how they propagate in the local context. Central to this perspective are the concepts of micro level, meso level, and macro level (Bauer et al. 1999; Hannah and Lester 2009).

Furthermore, the perspective used is a cultural one (Alvesson 2002; Trowler 2008; Ancona et al. 2009) where the kind of effects we are looking for are related to changes in how teaching and learning are understood as indicated during interaction among teachers while they try to make sense of the teaching and learning context in which they are active: choice of words during conversations, various actions related to teaching and student learning, the frequency of conversations, content in and the complexity of these conversations about teaching, the use of theory and the ambitions revealed during these conversations, how teacher-training is perceived, and so on. If these things change and can be related to teacher-training, they would constitute cultural effects. It is assumed that if teachers talk differently about teaching, think differently, and change their beliefs about teaching, the teaching practice will also change, and so will managers' opportunities to influence the system.

Culture, as it is used in this text, is not something an organisation has, but rather what it is. It refers to ways of doing, talking, and thinking about things, about patterns that make a group visible against the backdrop of other groups (Alvesson 2002). The habits and traditions of a group created during interaction over time gain structural property and thereby begin to influence individuals and their actions. These traditions and norms become something newcomers have to learn, either by participation or during formal induction processes. Newcomers also perceive the traditions more easily than older members of a culture, who tend to be blind to them. The relationships between individual agency and the structural properties of norms and traditions should be interpreted in line with Giddens's (2004) perspective on structuration, meaning that the individuals are influenced by the culture as they enact it. They can, as knowledgeable agents, of course, choose to deviate from what is normal and culturally expected from them and thereby influence the culture and perhaps even change it, and sometimes they do. But since this entails putting professional identity and individual status at stake, the individuals within a culture on the whole act according to norms and traditions rather than against them.

With a focus on culture we follow several recent studies which emphasise culture as the most important factor in processes of change and development in higher education (Kuh 1993; Bauer et al. 1999; Kezar 2007; Harvey and Stensaker 2008; Edvardsson-Stiwne 2009; Merton et al. 2009). This significance of culture is further emphasised by Stensaker (2006, 47), who summarises a study of change in Norwegian higher education: "Hence, in this organisation authority concerning the quality of teaching and learning would not follow the hierarchical but rather the informal structure, and through mechanisms such as socialisation and training."

Overall we use a perspective on organisational studies proposed by Ancona et al. (2009) in which they distinguish three lenses for the study of an organisation. The cultural lens has already been described. A second lens, the organisation as it is strategically designed, reveals how the organisation is consciously constructed and thereby intended to function: Who is reporting to whom and when? How can the flow of information be secured so that the managers can act strategically? What does the budget flow look like? How can resources be allocated so that long-term objectives are met? The aim is to construct an organisation that is aligned and pursues the organisational objectives as efficiently as possible (Ancona et al. 2009). However, in the literature that evaluates change initiatives in higher education, the designed (or line) organisation (rector/vice chancellor—dean—head of the department/chair) often fails to reach the intended outcomes (Bauer et al. 1999; Newton 2003; Hedin 2004; Osseo-Asare, Longbottom, and Murphy 2005).

The third lens presented by Ancona and associates (2009), the political lens, discerns the organisation with its stakeholders building alliances and struggling for power. In this text, as we mainly use the cultural lens, the organisation as strategic design and as a political system will not be in the foreground. But, as Ancona et al. stress, the three lenses are all necessary for reaching a comprehensive understanding of the organisation. Therefore, the organisation as strategically designed will appear in the text primarily during the discussion about the macro level while the political lens will appear as an undercurrent, constantly present but not in focus.

THE MESO LEVEL

Individual teachers constitute the micro level. As we have seen already, effects on this level have been detected and are well documented. Teacher-training no doubt has positive effects on individual teachers. The rest of this text will therefore discuss the meso level with the objective to clarify how effects from training propagate from the micro level; that is, where and how effects become visible beyond the individual teacher, or how we can understand the lack of effects in spite of sometimes large volumes of training. The last part of the text will discuss the macro level and in particular how effects, or the lack of effects, can be understood from the managers' point of view.

The meso level is sometimes referred to as the institution (Bauer et al. 1999), the department (Knight and Trowler 2000), the discipline (Kreber 2009), the workgroup (Trowler and Bamber 2005; Hannah and Lester 2009), or the significant networks (Roxå and Mårtensson 2009a, 2009b).

Because the meso level does not reveal itself naturally, it must be constructed analytically, and there are, as mentioned above, several candidates, of which we initially will consider the department and the discipline. The department is an organisational entity, which in, for instance, an older German academic tradition, based on the idea of the professorship, could equal the discipline. But this has changed over time. Nowadays, in many national contexts, several disciplines or subjects often constitute a department, turning it into more of a formal organisational unit within a faculty/school. Therefore we consider the department to be mainly a part of the formal and designed organisation (Ancona et al. 2009). Consequently, when using a cultural perspective, the department is considered to be of lesser interest as a locus for the meso level. As a part of the designed organisation, the department, as it has grown in complexity from equalling one discipline to an organisational host for several disciplines, has become questionable as a potent arena for change.

The discipline might be of greater significance since it has a more profound influence on the individual's professional identity than the department (Henkel 2005). After all, academics are socialised into their disciplines through a long period (undergraduate, graduate, and postgraduate studies) during which they are dependent on the approval from more senior members of the disciplinary community. Such induction processes normally leave considerable imprints on the individuals' professional identity (Van Maanen and Schein 1979).

Furthermore, disciplines have, gradually, constructed certain "ways of thinking and practicing" (Hounsell and Anderson 2009) which undergraduate and postgraduate students learn and internalise through a process of academic apprenticeship. By the time some of them advance further into the discipline as academic teachers, these ways are firmly internalised. Through such a perspective the disciplines come into view as culturally formed and sustained and therefore appear promising in our investigation.

Thus, if disciplines constitute the meso level, then effects of teacher-training should extend from the micro level and influence the ways of thinking and practicing signifying the disciplinary community. Since we are looking for systemic effects, this could be where we should look for them. But disciplines are not the stable constructions we sometimes think they are, nor do they have clear boundaries to other disciplines. New disciplines emerge and old disciplines expand into new areas. As expressed by Ronald Barnett: "[D]isciplines, insofar as they are taken up in the teaching situation, are always in-the-making. They are not fixed edifices, which the student simply has to surmount or knock against—or even fall from. They are rather fluid regions, with intermingling and conflicting currents" (Barnett 2009, xvi). This point of view displays disciplines as being in a constant flux, subjected to ongoing negotiation and contestation, a problematic elusiveness for anyone using them as a firmament for further scholarly exploitations.

Other scholars have criticised the essentialist perspective where each discipline has its specific way of teaching, or thinking of teaching (Trowler 2005, 2009). It has been convincingly argued that a discipline, as it presents itself, is dependent on social variation among the academics—"the tribe"— teaching it (Becher and Trowler 2001). Moreover, it has been shown that individual academics sometimes teach the same discipline differently while doing so in different collegial contexts (Lindblom-Ylänne et al. 2006). This becomes a problem for us when we look for the effects of teacher-training on the level beyond the micro level. Instead of appearing as a stable ground, governing teaching methods and perspectives, disciplines come forward as social arenas where the individuals in a given context govern just as many of the decisions made as does the discipline.

For our purposes, therefore, disciplines appear too complex and multifaceted; their in-the-making character, pointed out by Barnett, makes it hard to distinguish the effects of training from other natural fluctuations. Changes in ways of thinking and practicing (Hounsell and Anderson 2009) might be part of a natural variation as well as affected by training. In this text we suggest two other possibilities for the meso level; firstly the workgroup (Trowler 2008) and secondly the significant network (Roxå and Mårtensson 2009a). They are both explicitly related to higher education and supported by empirical data. In addition, they are discerned through a cultural perspective on higher education rather than from a perspective emphasising the designed organisation or epistemological essentialism.

Trowler (2008) suggests the workgroup as the meso level, claiming that this is where the work is done, and where development therefore starts. He further claims that a workgroup, being a group of individuals sharing a working context, can be described in cultural terms as a "teaching and learning regime" (TLR). TLR is the way in which the workgroup performs and talks about things in relation to teaching and learning. It includes assumptions about the students, about knowledge, the discipline, et cetera. It offers a workgroup its identity and distinguishes it from other groups. Often it can, during everyday conversations, be summarised with the words "This is how we do things around here" and thereby imply a notion of clear boundaries to other workgroups. But these boundaries should not be overstressed. A workgroup is hardly ever isolated; rather it is leaky in its relation to the surrounding world. Nor is it the result of a consensus. Trowler (2008) stresses the conflictual nature of TLRs. Power and contestation are always present, giving a workgroup an agentic relation to the world. The emphasis on power is of great importance for the perspective outlined below.

In the studies by Roxå and Mårtensson (2009a, 2009b), academic teachers were asked whom they genuinely discussed teaching and learning with. Answers revealed that all respondents had a few conversational partners with whom they had private, backstage (Goffman 2000), and trustful personal conversations about teaching and learning. Drawing from social psychology (Berger and Luckmann 1966), these partners, the significant others, constitute the individual teacher's significant network. Conversations within these networks are assumed to be of a greater importance for the individual than everyday talk with others. Therefore, the significant networks are the focal point where individual teachers construct and maintain their conceptions about teaching and learning. These conceptions may be played out in practice or remain hidden backstage for future use. Additionally, a significant network is not limited to working contexts or organisational boundaries, and the conversations within them can serve many purposes, for instance, to maintain or confirm a particular status quo or to explore and develop something related to teaching and learning. In contrast to the conflictual and power-loaded nature of the workgroups, the significant networks are characterised by trust, which render them more of a consensus nature.

It is timely here to clarify that both the workgroup and the significant network in this text are treated as ideal types. The description above is by nature oversimplified since both workgroups and significant networks in reality appear in many forms and variations and sometimes are more or less overlapping. If so, they would most likely show many characteristics of a community of practice (Wenger 1999), implying that the members of a workgroup also would be significant to each other.

However, if the effects of teacher-training would become visible at the workgroup level, they would most likely appear as changes in the practice performed by the group, in turn often, but not always, a result of new power relations within the groups. Changes are likely to come after a process of renegotiation within the group, a process that could run smoothly or with turmoil. Such a process would in many cases include displacements of professional identities, making it a delicate, unpredictable process.

With a focus on significant networks, the main effects would rather be on the conceptions of teaching, conceptions that are negotiated through backstage (Goffmann 2000) conversations with significant others. Thus, development could be measured through interviews or questionnaires to identify aspects of conceptual change. However, bearing in mind the backstage nature of much development, these changes might be invisible during daily practices. Effects can also become visible through small changes possible to enact in one's own teaching without colleagues' awareness. There could be several reasons for individuals to keep ideas hidden backstage instead of enacting them openly or for introducing new ways of teaching privately without collegial notice. An investigation into these reasons and a subsequent removal of barriers and structural obstacles could very well increase the visible effects of training, even though the training itself did not change.

Another matter of importance would be to determine the workgroups' or the networks' attitudes towards change versus stability. In the case of the significant networks, which are formed spontaneously, the individuals have in most cases freely chosen each other as significant others. Therefore these alliances are likely to have been formed through the influence of homophily, that is, "the principle that a contact between similar people occurs at a higher rate than among dissimilar people" (McPherson, Smith-Lovin, and Cook 2001, 416). In other words, McPherson, Smith-Lovin, and Cook (2001) investigate how people who are similar to each other also bond with each other, and dispute the alleged fact that all spontaneous social networks will be based on some kind of consensus. Individuals prefer to interact with others who confirm rather than challenge their own beliefs, a fact initially supporting the assumption that significant networks are likely to be conservative and that they promote stability.

However, both status quo and exploration can very well be considered as states of stability: either there is no development at all, that is, the present state of affairs is confirmed over and over again, or there is a steady enterprise of continuous development rendering a situation where the lack of advancement would be considered awkward. From this follows that even though the significant networks are consensus formations they are not necessarily hostile to change and development. As the workgroups are maintained through power relations they can also be either conservative or involved in continuous change and development (Trowler 2008).

In both cases and in relation to the propagation of effects, it is of the greatest importance for evaluators to know whether or not the workgroups or networks have a developmental enterprise. If the status quo were paramount, the effects from individual teacher-training would most certainly be absorbed within the social context and fade away. If the groups or the networks, on the other hand, were characterised by enterprises of development, teacher-training would fuel further development and accelerate the process. Hence, the effects of training can both be determined by the training itself and also by the social context in which the individual teachers are active.

An example of the phenomenon discussed above can be found in Ginns, Kinsay, and Prosser (2010), where two academic teachers, Anne and Belinda, illustrate different outcomes of an Australian Graduate Certificate in Higher Education programme—one leading to further development and the other to hesitation. Not because Anne and Belinda viewed the training itself differently but because they worked in entirely different social contexts in relation to teaching and learning. One context (Anne) supported participation with encouragement from both colleagues and management, while in the other case (Belinda), colleagues and management discouraged participation. "As a result, Belinda felt that 'it's kind of a disincentive to do it again'" (Ginns, Kinsay, and Prosser 2010, 240).

Prosser et al. (2006) report similar experiences, where again the outcome of teacher-training is perceived differently depending on the relation between the individual teacher and his or her collegial context (see also Gran 2006; Stes, Clement, and Van Petegem 2007). According to these studies, many academic teachers participating in training complain about collegial responses once they return from training, which suggests that the problems are encountered during interaction at the meso level. We argue that these negative responses indicate the presence of workgroups and/or significant networks that are orientated towards stability rather than change and development. Gran (2006) reported contrasting and positive exceptions, where teachers from one specific faculty within one of six surveyed institutions describe that the training they are participating in is positively valued in their collegial context. Here, the participants are "well aware of the fact that their active participation in [the faculty's] development strategy is highly valued" (Gran 2006, 9).

A conclusion to be made so far is that the first signs of propagation of effects from teacher-training would look different depending on which focus we use while studying the meso level. A simplified way to distinguish the two focuses would be: either we look for visible changes in teaching practices (focus on the workgroup), with possible measurable effects on student learning; or we look for changes in teachers' ways of thinking and talking about teaching and learning (focus on the significant network), even though we might not necessarily see any visible effects within the teaching practice.

These effects appear after passing thresholds of different kinds. In a workgroup, change occurs through the negotiation with others, often involving power issues and/or impacts on professional identity, while in a network the stakes are much lower. Here teachers can try out new ways of thinking and talking about teaching and learning, and do so among trusted colleagues at a low risk.

Therefore, viewed from a time perspective, changes in the significant networks would most likely surface prior to changes in the workgroups (unless of course the workgroup and the significant network are overlapping), placing the network focus closer to the micro level. Displacements in the significant networks would arguably be detectable before they became visible in the workgroups. On the other hand, widespread institutional change would not, other than under exceptional conditions, appear unless the workgroups are activated.

From a managerial perspective, changes in the workgroups might be the only ones of importance since teacher-training often is created to improve an institution's ability to support student learning or to promote institutional policy. On the other hand, based on the perspective suggested here, the workgroups will not change unless the individuals believe in the prospect of the change at hand, that is, unless they first explore their personal ideas about teaching and learning, explorations which take place within the significant networks (Roxå and Mårtensson 2009a).

For managers it is therefore worthwhile assessing whether policies and instructions require changes in teaching practices that deviate too much from the teachers' conceptions. If so, these teachers will have many opportunities to obstruct managerial plans. Such obstructions would certainly distort the intentions of any policy and thereby affect the outcome negatively. What is more, teachers might even, backstage and hidden from the managers, construct negative conceptions about the managers' leadership and thus disturb future managerial opportunities (Coates et al. 2010). Or, as articulated by an experienced academic manager expressing concern about the power possessed by key individuals in informal networks: "[Y]ou need to think through the relationships carefully because they have powerful networks that can be used to support or undermine your efforts" (Kezar and Lester 2009, 111).

So far we have offered the significant network as a possible first focus for the meso level. If we were to measure the initial effects of teacher-training on the meso level, this is where we would start looking. Do teachers discuss teaching more, or in new ways backstage, with their significant others or their critical friends (Handal 1999)? Do they use concepts and perspectives from training during interactions with colleagues? If these and other results would appear, it would indicate effects.

We have also argued that effects in the significant networks might remain hidden backstage for a long time, making it insufficient for managers and others who are looking for a cultural shift in terms of teaching and learning. To reach such an objective with the means of teacher-training, the effects most certainly have to advance even further into the workgroups. If this takes place, the culture will potentially be influenced and possibly transformed. But we have also provided arguments for why teacher-training on its own is insufficient to accomplish a cultural shift. Balancing forces (Senge

2006) can counteract early attempts to change teaching practices, and risks related to professional identity will discourage members of the organisation from leaving the backstage conversations within the significant networks and openly enter the front-stage arena. This issue is something we will return to later in the section where we discuss the macro level.

The introduction of this text touched upon whether teacher-training should be organised individually, in workgroups, within disciplines, or in departments. This can also be assessed through the perspective presented here, again related to the meso level. If the purpose of training is to promote effects beyond the micro level, the meso level should in some way be addressed also during training. Organising teacher-training for workgroups seems to be a good idea (Roxå 2005, 2007). That would allow the individuals to negotiate meaning and power relations continuously already during training.

A potential problem appears if the power relations within workgroups are too strong and too firmly established. If so, they can cause strategic behaviour or an edited style of conversation among the participants during training. In such a case the process of negotiation among participants would be hampered and the effects could, in the worst case, be negative. An example of the latter could be illustrated by strong power holders with a negative attitude towards training who actively try to devaluate training already during the experience and later even use the personal experience of training as evidence of its low value.

Inviting participants as significant networks, or promoting conversations with critical friends (Mårtensson, Roxå, and Olsson 2011), would most likely support an open style of discussion and a possibility for the network to identify and to work on a shared enterprise (Wenger 1999). On the other hand, these informal networks often run the risk of being governed by consensus (McPherson 2001), with the following risk that participants avoid critical debate and conflict. Again, this is a particularly important aspect for stakeholders who wish to promote a cultural shift.

THE MACRO LEVEL

A relevant question, at this stage is why anyone would want to influence the meso level in the first place. Universities have been teaching students and conducting research for a long time. Why would there be a need for change? One answer is that higher education now occupies politicians' and other stakeholders' interest simply because of the cost. In 2009 higher education reached the volume of 1.7 percent of Sweden's gross domestic product, making it the largest single part of state funding (Swedish National Agency for Higher Education [HSV] 2010).

The development is similar in the member states of the Organisation for Economic Co-operation and Development (OECD, see HSV 2010). The growing numbers of students represent another group of stakeholders as they invest time and money in their education. In Sweden, as in many other Western countries, students have had an important role in the growing demand for quality in university teaching; and so have academics themselves, using their reputation as an important argument while competing for the best students, best academics, and increased funding. All these changes place a growing demand on higher education institutions to develop better teaching practices, better, that is, in terms of improved student learning and, in the long run, in terms of improved research.

Above we have suggested the significant network or the workgroup as the locus for a meso level, and discussed possible effects or issues related to this level. We will now take one step further and suggest a perspective from above, or beyond, the meso level—that is, from the macro level. How can the meso level be conceived from a management level? How can a system of workgroups and/or significant networks be visualised and even influenced from the macro level? And what would the effects of teacher-training look like from the macro level, if there were any? By approximating the macro level with the institutional management, we deviate slightly from our previous emphasis on a cultural perspective in the direction of the designed organisation lens.

When we now reintroduce the designed organisation (Ancona et al. 2009) it is important to bear in mind that this does not diminish organisational members' agency, nor the agency of networks or workgroups. The relationships between a rector/vice chancellor, a dean, or a head of department/chair, and the academics in workgroups and networks are never a one-way communication. Instead, individuals, networks, and workgroups are active in their construction of what they consider to be valuable and not; they interpret aspects they encounter in relation to their own history, identity, and projected future. The result is a process of negotiation where members of the organisation interpret decisions and policies according to their own agendas and trajectories. (For an interesting phenomenographic account on the relation between loyalty and academic freedom, see Åkerlind and Kayrooz 2003).

Such agentic processes do not always appear rational or easy to understand or to predict for outside observers. A classic example in illustrating this (even though from a different domain) is Paul Willis's (1978) work on "the lads," a group of schoolboys in a working-class area of England during the 1970s. These boys are clearly significant to each other and together they construct a group identity which opposes the school and all its officially painted dreams of career and a prosperous future; instead, they actively construct a working-class identity which unintentionally makes them ready and able for the factory the very first day they graduate. The author's main point is that groups like "the lads" actively construct their identities and the trajectories that come with them, not because they are rational or well reflected in all aspects, but simply because these are the trajectories they feel comfortable constructing. The description is an ample example of what Giddens (2004) labels as "structuration."

For our purposes we suggest that networks or groups of academics, in their agentic relationship with the world, resemble "the lads." Undeniably, academic teachers live different lives and have different resources at their disposal than "the lads," but as human beings they too try to orient themselves in a complex world. An attempt to describe these processes in an academic context has been offered by Harvey and Stensaker (2008). Through a theoretical perspective the authors propose four different ideal types varying in terms of how active a workgroup is in relation to, for instance, an organisational context. For the continuation of this text, as we now try to overlook the meso level from a macro perspective, we should remember this agentic relationship with the world on the part of the academics within networks and workgroups. They construct and continuously maintain their understanding about the reality around them. This is undoubtedly one of the most important insights for managers in higher education to make. Academics are trained through their research careers to construct personal perspectives and to defend them (Latour 1987), making them particularly active in their construction of the world. As Åkerlind and Kayrooz (2003) have shown, it does not mean that they always oppose management initiatives even though they have a tendency to scrutinise them heavily.

For managers who want to promote learning and development in knowledge-intensive organisations, Hannah and Lester (2009) put forward a useful perspective. On the meso level, they depict a number of "semi-autonomous knowledge network clusters" (Figure 12.1). In relation to the perspective used in this text, the clusters can be both workgroups and significant networks. But in addition, Hannah and Lester also describe the sum of networks within an organisation as a system and thereby offer an intelligible macro-perspective.

Within this perspective, the individuals constitute the micro level and the semi-autonomous knowledge clusters the meso level. The macro level refers to the organisation as a whole. From the macro level the organisation becomes visible as a system of interrelated and overlapping clusters. Within clusters the individual members are connected to each other via links. Clusters are connected via "bridges" flowing from one member of a cluster to a member of another cluster. (The emerging picture confirms what has been found in other network studies [Granovetter 1973; Barabási 2003; Watts 2003].) A shortcoming, however, of the perspective suggested by Hannah and Lester (2009) is that it does not differentiate clusters as workgroups or significant networks as has been done in this text. Such a differentiation, as we have seen, can be crucial when observations about effects from teacher-training are to be interpreted and explained.

In their text, Hannah and Lester (2009) argue that the productive work in knowledge-intensive organisations appears mainly within the clusters. This is due to the complexity of the practice, making it impossible to accomplish

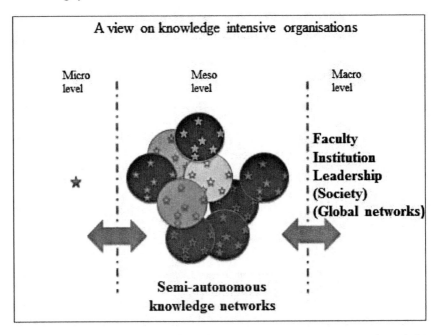

Figure 12.1 The micro, meso, and macro levels with semi-autonomous knowledge networks clearly visible at the meso level. Adapted from Hannah and Lester (2009).

detailed direction from the macro level. Innovation, adjustment, flexibility, or the pursuit of promising possibilities all ensue as a result of knowledge-able professionals working with the material at hand. The main problem for a manager, acting from the macro level, as described by Hannah and Lester, is to avoid stagnation because of excessive self-interest within the clusters (introversion), or a lack of identification with the organisation as a whole (detachment). As long as the clusters pursue their enterprises in relation to the interests of the organisation as a whole, all is well. As long as they interact with and challenge each other, further development will be fuelled. If not, the networks run the risk of falling prey to unproductive contentedness or to paralysing power struggles.

Hannah and Lester therefore recommend leaders of organisations to act on the basis that the clusters are the locus for development, but also to counteract the tendency towards introversion and detachment, by:

1. Demanding from each cluster a developmental enterprise;
2. Supporting individuals who display a developmental perspective on the part of their cluster and at the same time show an understanding for the organisation as a whole;
3. Encouraging clusters to put their results on display for critical review by other clusters by introducing suitable arenas;

4. Using a leadership which is both loose, by encouraging the clusters' self-chosen enterprises, and tight, by creating structures preventing the organisation to become partitioned;
5. Being explicit with an organisational vision, not only by the talk but also by the walk; and
6. Being patient.

We have discussed the development of teaching and learning from a network perspective elsewhere and problematized a phenomenon related to the second item in the list above, that is, a focus on individuals as change agents. It is not clear in academia to what extent leaders should focus on individuals while designing a strategy for change. "Rather we deem it likely that a multitude of inter-related initiatives over a long period of time distinguish any strategy successful in influencing academic teaching and learning cultures" (Roxå, Mårtensson, and Alveteg 2011, 109). As has been argued in this text, strategies for change in academia have often relied on the micro level, and produced small changes, at least very small in relation to the investments made. We argue that this is due to the meso level's ability to mitigate initiatives on the micro level.

For the purpose of this text, however, the six suggestions above outline a promising strategy for how to advance the effects of teacher-training from networks and clusters within the meso level out on the arena, which is the entire organisation. This further confirms how essential it is to influence the meso level in order to measure the systemic effects of teacher-training on the macro level. But the suggestions also imply that training alone will hardly produce a measurable impact on an institution as a whole. Other interrelated instruments have to be introduced. It means that a lack of measurable effects from training, viewed from a macro perspective, can be caused by bad teacher-training but also by a lack of enlightened determination among managers. It is also possible that some recurrent restructurings of academic development units (Gosling 2008, 2009; Harland and Staniforth 2008; Palmer, Holt, and Challis 2010) transpire not because these units are doing a bad job but because managers lack an effective understanding of how the entire organisation works or because they have an erroneous time perspective.

What emerges again and again is a pattern where effects from training propagate gradually. A personal engagement is in itself the very first sign of an effect. This engagement can appear backstage during collegial conversations within the significant network and/or in small changes in "private" teaching, possible to implement without collegial interference. If they pass this stage, the effects will appear as negotiations about teaching and learning within workgroups and these negotiations will often relate to professional identity issues and power. This is where management can choose to interfere from the macro level in the ways outlined by Hannah and Lester (2009), and thereby take the effects of teacher-training out into an even wider arena.

Different interests in an organisation typically balance each other out. Let us say that a number of clusters develop a new way of assessing students. If this starts to become known in the organisation as a whole and the notion is that it can spread further, it will trigger more conservative clusters to act by forming what Senge (2006) describes as "balancing forces." Furthermore, neutral clusters, if there is not much to gain from choosing sides, will withdraw without participating in the struggle between what we might call the radicals and the conservatives. Thus, the two active groups will struggle as long as they find it meaningful. However, neither side can win since there are no further supporters to gain from the neutrals. This might explain why resource-supported development projects, where individual teachers or groups of teachers receive funding for the pursuit of a particular teaching idea, very often fade away once the funding ends (Degerblad et al. 2005). External funding means that the organisation in fiscal terms is unaffected by the innovation. Once the funding ends, the organisation is affected, which is when the balancing forces start to act.

Again, the resolution to such a situation cannot be teacher-training alone. It must be a set of instruments implemented by open-minded, knowledgeable, determined, and patient leaders. If this is the case, the effects of teacher-training and other instruments in combination can become measurable beyond the meso level. If not, the effects of teacher-training will hardly reach beyond the borders of a limited number of workgroups and significant networks. The balancing forces mobilised by other workgroups and networks will counteract further spread.

CONCLUSION

In this text we have pursued a cultural perspective on how the effects of teacher-training may or may not propagate beyond individual academic teachers. While doing so we find it appropriate to acknowledge that a cultural perspective does not embrace the entire complexity of any organisation (Ancona et al. 2009). Despite this limitation we believe that the cultural perspective is the most rewarding if one seeks to understand how the effects may become visible in an academic context. Indeed, academics' tendency to form and defend personal perspectives in interaction with a few trusted colleagues very much supports this claim.

Effects cannot propagate without being negotiated in social contexts. We have suggested that this takes place on the meso level in significant networks and/or in workgroups. We have also argued that effects are most likely to become visible in the networks before they emerge in the workgroups. The key factor for effects to propagate on the meso level is determined by whether or not the networks and workgroups have established their own agenda for development.

This key factor appears as the most important one for managers to focus upon once they overlook an organisational landscape of networks and workgroups from the macro level. The effects of training are likely to propagate on the meso level and even beyond depending on whether or not the networks or workgroups have developmental agendas of their own. If they have, insights made by individuals or groups during training can fuel further advancement of those meso-level agendas.

In discussing the macro level we have pointed out several possible interventions that managers can use to enhance the effects of teacher-training. These measures are, however, not only tools for change; they are also analytical instruments that can be useful when evaluating teacher-training and its impact on the organisation as a whole. We strongly propose a combination of teacher-training and management interventions in order to render visible and measurable the effects of training on the macro level. Both variation in training and options for management interventions are discussed in the text.

Many institutions have struggled with the development of teaching and learning and most of these have done so by using a combination of measures, where teacher-training usually is one. The limited space here allows us to elaborate on less than a few of these examples but we would like to direct the readers to a small number of useful references (Barrie, Ginns, and Prosser 2005; Pilot and Keesen 2006; Kezar 2007; Brew and Ginns 2008; Roxå, Olsson, and Mårtensson 2008; Mårtensson, Roxå, and Olsson 2011). Even though this text is mostly theoretical, it thereby lands in a perspective that has references in academic reality.

NOTES

1. The authors wish to acknowledge the valuable comments and language sophistications contributed to this text by Sara Håkansson, senior lecturer, Lund University.
2. We use training even though we prefer pedagogical courses or even staff development.
3. Local context in this chapter refers to the collegial social setting where the actual teaching practice takes place. It might, for instance, be within a discipline, within a programme, and/or within a department.

BIBLIOGRAPHY

Åkerlind, Gerlese, and Carole Kayrooz. 2003. "Understanding Academic Freedom: The Views of Social Scientists." *Higher Education Research & Development* 22 (3): 327–344.
Alvesson, Mats. 2002. *Understanding Organisational Culture.* London: Sage.
Ancona, Deborah, Thomas Kochan, Maureen Scully, John Van Maanen, and Eleanor Westney. 2009. *Managing for the Future: Organisational Behaviour and Processes.* Mason, Ohio, U.S.: South Western/CENGAGE Learning.

Barabási, Albert-Laszló. 2003. *Linked: How Everything Is Connected to Everything Else and What It Means for Business, Science, and Everyday Life.* New York: Plume.

Barnett, Ronald. 2009. "Foreword." In *The University and Its Disciplines: Teaching and Learning within and beyond Disciplinary Boundaries*, edited by Carolin Kreber, xv–xvi. London: Routledge.

Barrie, Simon, Paul Ginns, and Michael Prosser. 2005. "Early Impact and Outcomes of an Institutionally Aligned, Student Focused Learning Perspective on Teaching Quality Assurance." *Assessment & Evaluation in Higher Education* 30 (6): 641–656.

Bauer, Marianne, Berit Askling, Susan Gerard Marton, and Ference Marton. 1999. *Transforming Universities: Changing Patterns of Governance, Structure and Learning in Swedish Higher Education.* London: Jessica Kingsley Publishers.

Becher, Tony, and Paul Trowler. 2001. *Academic Tribes and Territories.* Buckingham, UK: SHRE/Open University Press.

Berger, Peter L., and Thomas Luckmann. 1966. *The Social Construction of Reality: A Treatise in the Sociology of Knowledge.* New York: Penguin Books.

Brew, Angela, and Paul Ginns. 2008. "The Relationship between Engagement in the Scholarship of Teaching and Learning and Students' Course Experiences." *Assessment & Evaluation in Higher Education* 33 (5): 535–545.

Clegg, Sue. 2009. "Forms of Knowing and Academic Development Practice." *Studies in Higher Education* 34 (4): 403–416.

Coates, Hamish, Ian R. Dobson, Leo Goedegebuure, and Lynn Meek. 2010. "Across the Great Divide: What Do Australian Academics Think of University Leadership? Advice from the CAP Survey." *Journal of Higher Education Policy and Management* 32 (4): 379–387.

Degerblad, Jan-Eric, Lars Haikola, Sam Hägglund, Lars-Erik Jonsson, Lennart Köhler, and Roger Säljö. 2005. *Att utveckla den högre utbildning—testamente efter Rådet för högre utbildning.* Stockholm: Högskoleverket.

Donnelly, Roisin. 2008. "Lecturers' Self-Perception of Change in Their Teaching Approaches: Reflections on a Qualitative Study." *Educational Research* 50 (3): 207–222.

Edvardsson-Stiwne, Elinor. 2009. "The Ethos of a Study Program—a Barrier or a Springboard for Change." Paper presented at the Fifth International CDIO Conference, Singapore, 7–10 June.

Entwistle, Noel, and Paul Walker. 2000. "Strategic Alertness and Expanded Awareness within Sophisticated Conceptions Of Teaching." *Instructional Science* 28: 335–361.

Gibbs, Graham, and Martin Coffey. 2004. "The Impact of Training of University Teachers on Their Teaching Skills, Their Approach to Teaching and the Approach to Learning of Their Students." *Active Learning in Higher Education* 5 (1): 87–100.

Giddens, Anthony. 2004. *The Constitution of Society.* Cambridge: Polity Press.

Giertz, Birgitta. 1996. "Long-Term Effects of a Programme for Teacher Training." *The International Journal for Academic Development* 1 (2): 67–72.

Ginns, Paul, Jim Kitay, and Michael Prosser. 2010. "Transfer of Academic Staff Learning in a Research-Intensive University." *Teaching in Higher Education* 15(3): 235–246.

Goffman, Erwin. 2000. *Jaget och Maskerna.* Stockholm: Prisma.

Gosling, David. 2008. Educational Development in the United Kingdom. London: Heads of Educational Development Group.

———. 2009. *Report on the Survey of Directors of Academic Development in South African Universities.* Plymouth, UK: University of Plymouth.

Gran, Birgitta. 2006. *Pedagogisk utbildning för högskolans lärare—utvärdering av ett pilotprojekt.* Lund, Sweden: Lund University.
Granovetter, Mark. 1973. "The Strength of Weak Ties." *American Journal of Sociology* 78 (6): 1360–1380.
Handal, Gunnar. 1999. "Consultation Using Critical Friends." *New Directions for Teaching and Learning* (79): 59–70.
Hannah, Sean T., and Paul B. Lester. 2009. "A Multilevel Approach to Building and Leading Learning Organisations." *The Leadership Quarterly* 20: 34–48.
Harland, Tony, and David Staniforth. 2008. "A Family of Strangers: The Fragmented Nature of Academic Development." *Teaching in Higher Education* 13 (6): 669–678.
Harvey, Lee, and Bjørn Stensaker. 2008. "Quality Culture: Understandings, Boundaries and Linkages." *European Journal of Education* 43 (4): 427–442.
Healey, Mick, and Alan Jenkins. 2003. "Discipline-Based Educational Development." In *The Scholarship of Academic Development*, edited by Heather Eggins and Ranald Macdonald, 47–57. Buckingham, UK: SRHE/Open University Press.
Hedin, Anna. 2004. *Från ideal till praxis! Hur behandlas policyprogram på institutionsnivå? En granskning av hur det pedagogiska programmet vid Uppsala universitet har mottagits.* Uppsala: Uppsala University.
Henkel, Mary. 2005. "Academic Identity and Autonomy in a Changing Policy Environment." *Higher Education* (49): 155–176.
Ho, Angela, David Watkins, and Mavis Kelly. 2001. "The Conceptual Change Approach to Improving Teaching and Learning: An Evaluation of a Hong Kong Staff Development Programme." *Higher Education* 42: 143–169.
Hounsell, Dai, and Charles Anderson. 2009. "Ways of Thinking and Practicing in Biology and History." In *The University and Its Disciplines: Teaching and Learning within and beyond Disciplinary Boundaries*, edited by Carolin Kreber, 71–83. London: Routledge.
Kezar, Adrianna. 2007. "Creating and Sustaining a Campus Ethos Encouraging Student Engagement." *About Campus* 11 (6): 13–18.
Kezar, Adrianna, and Jaime Lester. 2009. *Organizing Higher Education for Collaboration: A Guide for Campus Leaders.* San Francisco: Jossey-Bass.
Knight, Peter. 2006a. *The Effects of Post-Graduate Certificates in Teaching and Learning in Higher Education—a Report to the Sponsor and Partners.* Buckingham, UK: Open University, Press.
———. 2006b. "Quality Enhancement and Educational Professional Development." *Quality in Higher Education* 12 (1): 29–40.
Knight, Peter, and Paul Trowler. 2000. "Department-Level Cultures and the Improvement of Learning and Teaching." *Studies in Higher Education* 25 (1): 69–83.
Kreber, Carolin, ed. 2009. *The University and Its Disciplines: Teaching and Learning within and beyond Disciplinary Boundaries.* London: Routledge.
Kuh, George D. 1993. "Ethos—Its Influence on Student Learning." *Liberal Education* 79 (4): 22–32.
Latour, Bruno. 1987. *Science in Action.* Cambridge, MA: Harvard University Press.
Lindberg-Sand, Åsa, and Anders Sonesson. 2008. "Compulsory Higher Education Teacher Training in Sweden: Development of a National Standards Framework Based on the Scholarship of Teaching and Learning." *Tertiary Education and Management* 14 (2): 123–139.
Lindblom-Ylänne, Sari, Keith Trigwell, Anne Nevgi, and Paul Ashwin. 2006. "How Approaches to Teaching Are Affected by Discipline and Teaching Context." *Studies in Higher Education* 31 (3): 285–295.

Macdonald, Ranald. 2009. "Academic Development." In *The Routledge International Handbook of Higher Education*, edited by Malcolm Tight, Ka Ho Mok, Jeroen Huisman, and Christopher Morphew, 427–439. New York: Routledge.

Mårtensson, Katarina, Torgny Roxå, and Thomas Olsson. 2011. "Developing a Quality Culture through the Scholarship of Teaching and Learning." *Higher Education Research & Development* 30 (1): 51–62.

Marton, Ference, and Shirley Booth. 1997. *Learning and Awareness*. Mahwah, NJ: Lawrence Erlbaum Associates.

McPherson, Miller, Lynn Smith-Lovin, and James M. Cook. 2001. "Birds of a Feather: Homophily in Social Networks." *Annual Review of Sociology* 27: 415–444.

Merton, Prudence, Jeffrey E. Froyd, M. Carolyn Clark, and Jim Richardson. 2009. "A Case Study of Relationships between Organisational Culture and Curricular Change in Engineering Education." *Innovative Higher Education* 34: 219–233.

Newton, Jethro. 2003. "Implementing an Institution-Wide Learning and Teaching Strategy: Lessons in Managing Change." *Studies in Higher Education* 28 (4): 427–441.

Osseo-Asare, Augustus E., David Longbottom, and William D. Murphy. 2005. "Leadership Best Practices for Sustaining Quality in UK Higher Education from the Perspective of EFQM Excellence Model." *Quality Assurance in Education* 13 (2): 148–170.

Palmer, Stuart, Dale Holt, and Di Challis. 2010. "Australian Teaching and Learning Centres through the Eyes of Their Directors: Characteristics, Capacities and Constraints." *Journal of Higher Education Policy and Management* 32 (2): 159–172.

Pilot, Albert, and Fried Keesen. 2006. "The Teacher as a Crucial Factor in Curriculum Innovation." Paper presented at the ICED 2006 Conference, Sheffield, UK.

Postareff, Liisa, and Sari Lindblom-Ylänne. 2008. "Variation in Teachers' Descriptions of Teaching: Broadening the Understanding of Teaching in Higher Education" *Learning and Instruction* 18: 109–120.

Postareff, Liisa, Sari Lindblom-Ylänne, and Anne Nevgi. 2007. "The Effect of Pedagogical Training on Teaching in Higher Education." *Teaching and Teacher Education* 23 (5): 557–571.

Prosser, Michael, Mark Rickinson, Valerie Bence, Andria Hanbury, and Malgorzata Kulej. 2006. *Formative Evaluation of Accredited Programmes*. York, UK: The Higher Education Academy.

Prosser, Michael, and Keith Trigwell. 1999. *Understanding Learning and Teaching: The Experience in Higher Education*. Buckingham, UK: SRHE/Open University Press.

Ramsden, Paul. 2005. *Learning to Teach in Higher Education*. London: RoutledgeFalmer.

Roxå, Torgny. 2005. "Pedagogical Courses as a Way to Support Communities of Practice Focusing on Teaching and Learning." Annual International Conference of the Higher Education Research and Development Society of Australasia, Sydney, Australia, July 3–6.

———. 2007. *Strategic Educational Development—Changing a Faculty's View on Teaching and Learning: A Theoretical Rationale and Case Study*. Southport: Griffith University, Queensland, Australia.

Roxå, Torgny, and Katarina Mårtensson. 2009a. "Significant Conversations and Significant Networks—Exploring the Backstage of the Teaching Arena." *Studies in Higher Education* 34 (5): 547–559.

———. 2009b. "Teaching and Learning Regimes from Within: Significant Networks as a Locus for the Social Construction of Teaching and Learning." In *The*

University and Its Disciplines: Teaching and Learning within and beyond Disciplinary Boundaries, edited by Carolin Kreber, 209–218. London: Routledge.
Roxå, Torgny, Katarina Mårtensson, and Mattias Alveteg. 2011. "Understanding and Influencing Teaching and Learning Cultures at University: A Network Approach." *Higher Education* 62: 99–111.
Roxå, Torgny, Thomas Olsson, and Katarina Mårtensson. 2008. "Appropriate Use of Theory in the Scholarship of Teaching and Learning as a Strategy for Institutional Development." *Arts and Humanities in Higher Education* 7 (3): 276–294.
Schön, Donald. 1983. *The Reflective Practitioner: How Professionals Think in Action*. Aldershot, England: Ashgate Publishing.
Senge, Peter. 2006. *The Fifth Discipline—the Art and Practice of the Learning Organisation*, 2nd edition. New York: Doubleday.
Stensaker, Bjørn. 2006. "Governmental Policy, Organisational Ideals and Institutional Adaptation in Norwegian Higher Education." *Studies in Higher Education* 31 (1): 43–56.
Stes, Ann, Mieke Clement, and Peter Van Petegem. 2007. "The Effectiveness of a Faculty Training Programme: Long-Term and Institutional Impact." *International Journal for Academic Development* 12 (2): 99–109.
Swedish National Agency for Higher Education. 2010. *Universitet och högskolor. Högskoleverkets årsrapport*. Stockholm: HSV.
Trowler, Paul. 2005. "Academic Tribes: Their Significance in Enhancement Processes." In Utvecklingskonferensen för högre utbildning, Karlstad, Sweden. Lund: Lund University.
———. 2008. *Cultures and Change in Higher Education: Theories and Practice*. Gordonsville, Virginia, U.S.: Palgrave.
———. 2009. "Beyond Epistemological Essentialism: Academic Tribes in the 21st Century." In *The University and Its Disciplines—within and beyond Disciplinary Boundaries*, edited by Carolin Kreber, 181–195. London: Routledge.
Trowler, Paul, and Roni Bamber. 2005. "Compulsory Higher Education Teacher Training: Joined-Up Policies, Institutional Architectures and Enhancement Cultures." *International Journal for Academic Development* 10 (2): 79–93.
Van Maanen, John, and Edgar Schein. 1979. "Toward a Theory of Organisational Socialization." *Research in Organisational Behaviour* 1: 209–264.
Watts, Duncan. 2003. *Small Worlds—the Dynamics of Networks between Order and Randomness*. NJ: Princeton University Press.
Wenger, Etienne. 1999. *Communities of Practice: Learning, Meaning, and Identity*. Cambridge: Cambridge University Press.
Willis, Paul. 1978. *Learning to Labour*. Aldershot, UK: Ashgate Publishing Group.

13 Instructional Development for University Teachers
Causes of Impact and Practical Implications

Ann Stes and Peter Van Petegem

INTRODUCTION

In recent years, increasing attention has been paid to the quality of teaching in higher education, which, in turn, has led universities and institutions of higher education, both in Belgium and abroad, to set up dedicated centres specifically tasked with organizing and supervising initiatives aimed at supporting the professional development of teachers. The instructional development of teachers has thus become an important challenge.

A perusal of the recent literature on instructional development reveals that, despite the importance attached to the effects of professional development initiatives, we know relatively little about what those effects actually are. Many instructional development programmes require reflective statements from participants, either with respect to individual sessions or the programme as a whole. These statements often give evidence of reflection and change. However, the conceptual and methodological underpinning of this evidence is often lacking in rigour.

A recent literature review (Stes et al. 2010) indicated that more attention should be given to studies researching behavioural outcomes, thereby drawing not only on the self-reports of participants, but also measuring actual changes in performance. Attempts to capture the effects at an institutional or student level also would be very worthwhile. There is a clear lack of systematic evaluations of the effect of professional development. Much insight could be gained from well-designed studies with a pre-test, a quasi-experimental character and/or using a mixed-method approach. Likewise, the long-term effects of instructional development remain a suitable terrain for future study (Stes et al. 2010). We need evidence of the impact of instructional development in order to help teaching support centre staff and those involved in making teaching policy to set up initiatives which help foster the professional development of teachers.

The purpose of this study is to fill that gap. Our central question is: what is the impact of instructional development programmes for teachers on their day-to-day teaching practice? We have investigated the effects, both at teacher level (does the teacher learn anything?) and at student level (do the students actually get any benefit from this in the end?). Finally, we have also looked at the impact at organisational level.

We start by describing the different levels of impact which can be identified and the context in which our research was carried out. We then go on to discuss the design and results of our three empirical impact studies. On the basis of these results we set out what can be learnt about the causes of impact at various levels. Finally, we explain the implications of the results for the support of the professional development of teachers as part of institutional policy.

LEVELS OF IMPACT

When discussing the effects of education or training, reference is often made to the model proposed by Kirkpatrick (1994). This model assumes four levels on which impact can be measured: (i) the general satisfaction of the participants with regard to education or training; (ii) the increase in the participants' knowledge and skills; (iii) changes in the participants' actual behaviour; and (iv) changes in the participants' broader professional context. With regard to the first level of satisfaction, other authors (e.g., Holton 1996; Weimer and Lenze 1998; Guskey 2000) have argued that this level ought not to be regarded as an impact level of training and education as such, but merely as an aspect of training and education that influences the effects on the other three levels. Measurements at the level of participants' satisfaction do not contribute to a clear picture of the ultimate impact of education or training, which is why we have excluded Kirkpatrick's first level (participants' satisfaction) from the present study.

Using existing overview studies of the effects of instructional development programmes in higher education (Levinson-Rose and Menges 1981; Weimer and Lenze 1998; McAlpine 2003; Prebble et al. 2004; Steinert et al. 2006) as a starting point, we went on to extend the Kirkpatrick model somewhat by including not only change in knowledge and skills but also change in attitude and/or conception at the second level of impact. With regard to changes in the broader professional context, we have made a distinction between changes which occur among students (in the area of their perceptions, study approach, or learning outcomes) and changes which do not relate to students. Table 13.1 gives an overview and brief description of the levels of impact covered in our present study.

It should be noted that Table 13.1 may not be read in a linear fashion, by which we mean that, for example, a change at the level of teacher learning does not constitute a necessary condition for a change at the level of behaviour. The way in which effects of instructional development are expressed at different levels is not determined in advance, but can differ from participant to participant and from situation to situation.

Table 13.1   Levels of Outcome as Distinguished in the Current Research

Level	Description
Change within teachers	
Learning	
Change in attitudes	Change in attitudes towards teaching and learning
Change in conceptions	Change in conceptions of teaching and learning
Change in knowledge	Acquisition of concepts, procedures, and principles
Change in skills	Acquisition of thinking/problem-solving, technical, and social skills
Behaviour	Transfer of learning to the workplace
Institutional impact	Wider changes in the organisation, attributable to the instructional development intervention
Change within students	
Change in perceptions	Change in students' perceptions of the teaching and learning environment
Change in study approaches	Change in students' approaches to studying
Change in learning outcomes	Change in students' performance

RESEARCH CONTEXT

In recent years conceptions of education in general and higher education in particular have undergone a fundamental change. Students are now regarded as being personally responsible for their learning process and it has become the teacher's job to create a learning environment that encourages active and cooperative learning and in which he or she acts as coach (Marton, Hounsell, and Entwistle 1997).

In response to this sea change in educational thinking, the University of Antwerp introduced a competency-oriented and student-centred vision of teaching in the academic year 2000–2001. The implementers of this plan realized that if this educational vision was to be applied in day-to-day teaching, careful thought would have to be given to the question of how best to provide support for academic staff. For this reason, in the years since 2000, the University of Antwerp has invested in a variety of instructional development initiatives, one of which is a one-year course for novice teachers. The characteristics of the unit responsible for the organisation of this course as well as the characteristics of the course itself are summarized below.

An Instructional Development Unit

The University of Antwerp (Flanders, Belgium) has approximately 13,000 students, which makes it the third largest university in Flanders. It consists of seven faculties and, in addition, there are three institutes at the university that have an autonomous status similar to that of a faculty. Each faculty or institute has its own unit (with a staff of two or three people) responsible for quality assurance of teaching. In addition to the faculty/institute units there is a small central unit, known as the Centre of Excellence in Higher Education, which organizes and designs the majority of instructional development initiatives. These initiatives encompass a one-year course for novice teachers; a semester-long training programme for junior teaching assistants; half-day workshops on specific instructional topics (e.g., portfolio assessment; teaching large groups); the electronic distribution of teaching tips and instructional support at a departmental level (e.g., regarding the introduction of a curriculum change). The head of the Centre of Excellence in Higher Education is a full professor of education; the other four members are teaching assistants, most of whom are either preparing or have finished a PhD on an instructional topic.

The fact that the centre of excellence is small and only recently established is not exceptional in the Flemish context. In most of the five other universities in Flanders, instructional development has also only recently been given systematic attention. Moreover, with regard to the status of the faculty developers—the majority of whom are not professors—the situation at the University of Antwerp is similar to that in other Flemish universities.

The One-Year Course for Novice Teachers

One of the instructional development initiatives offered by the Antwerp's Centre of Excellence in Higher Education is a one-year course for novice teachers. The course is run every two years. The target group consists of novice teachers (appointed as postdoctoral assistants or teachers in the past seven years). Registration is voluntary. The participant group is heterogeneous with regard to academic discipline and teaching experience and is restricted to a maximum of twenty-five participants.

The course sets out to help novice teachers bring their teaching conceptions and teaching practice into line with the University of Antwerp's educational vision (i.e., competency-oriented and student-centred education). The ultimate objective of the course is to arrive at improved learning outcomes among students. In terms of content, the course covers four subject areas: activating teaching methods; student assessment; using the Blackboard electronic learning environment; and curriculum development. Each subject area is taught in a competency-oriented and student-centred way so that participants have the opportunity to experience what this vision of education means in practice, for themselves, and from the perspective of being the student rather than the teacher.

The course alternates contact sessions and homework assignments. The contact sessions have a pronounced interactive emphasis and activating teaching methods are used, including discussions based on video or micro teaching fragments; case studies; supervised self-study; and group assignments. For each of the four subject areas referred to above, participants work on a homework assignment which encourages the transfer of what has been learned during the contact sessions to the teacher's own classroom practice. The details of the homework assignments are as follows:

- Describing a teaching environment; developing an activating teaching method; and preparing written study material that activates students' learning (subject area: activating teaching methods);
- Analysing the validity and reliability of a test or working out a design for an alternative assessment method (subject area: student assessment);
- Developing a discussion forum, learning route, or test in the Black-board electronic learning environment (subject area: Blackboard electronic learning environment);
- Analysing to what extent a particular course module is compatible with the course curriculum to which it belongs (subject area: curriculum development).

Participants are asked to base all their homework assignments around a single degree course module of their own choice, but which must be a module that they themselves teach. Attending the contact sessions and carrying out the homework assignments constitute a study load of 140 hours, spread over ten months.

In order to reward those taking part for their participation, teachers receive a certificate at the end of the course. To qualify for the award of a certificate, successful candidates are required to meet two criteria: to have participated in at least 75 percent of the contact sessions; and to have obtained a pass mark for each of the homework assignments. These conditions are imposed so as to make these certificates more valuable so that they will be recognized within the academic community, for example, when it comes to possible promotions.

ANALYTICAL FRAMEWORK

As stated above, the idea behind the one-year course was to help teachers bring their *teaching conceptions* into line with the University of Antwerp's own vision of teaching, that is, student-centred and competency-oriented education. It further sets out to bring the *teaching behaviour* of the participants more closely into line with this teaching concept and to improve the quality of their teaching. The ultimate objective of the course is to achieve an improvement in *learning outcomes among students*. In examining the impact of the one-year course, these three objectives (change in conceptions, change in behaviour, and improved learning outcomes among students) were explicitly taken into account and we have looked at how far these were actually achieved.

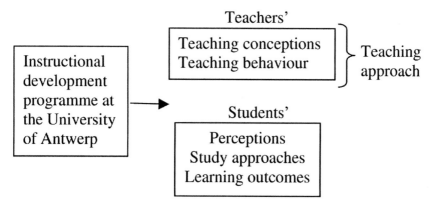

Figure 13.1 Framework for analysing the impact of the instructional development programme at the University of Antwerp.

Previous research (e.g., Trigwell and Prosser 1991) makes clear that students' learning outcomes are influenced by *students' perceptions of the teaching-learning environment* and by their *study approach*. If we consider teaching conceptions and teaching behaviour as one item, we can refer to them as the single variable *teachers' approach to teaching* (Trigwell and Prosser 1996). We have therefore taken these three variables (perceptions of students, their study approach, and the teachers' approach to teaching) into account in our analysis of the impact of the one-year course.

The resulting frame of reference which can now be used to examine the impact of the one-year course for novice teachers is given in Figure 13.1. The levels of impact described in Table 13.1 are: teachers' learning (the teacher's teaching conceptions), teachers' behaviour, and changes among students (student perceptions, study approach, and learning outcomes). These constitute the dependent variables in our study.

RESEARCH QUESTIONS

The present study looks at the impact of instructional development and focuses on the following research questions:

1. Do participants in an instructional development programme have a different conception of higher education (i.e., a more competency-oriented and student-centred vision) than prior to their participation? Do they differ in this regard from their colleagues who did not take part in the initiative?
2. Is their teaching perceived differently by their students (i.e., as more competency-oriented and student-centred)? Do their students exhibit a deeper study approach and better learning outcomes than prior

to their participation? Do their students differ in these areas from other students?

3. Is there a long-term effect of the instructional development programme? What is the relationship between the individual impact (in terms of change in teaching conceptions and behaviour) and the institutional impact (in terms of involvement in teaching matters at the level of the organisation)? Which factors, according to the participants, influence the long-term effect of the course?

We will now go on to discuss three studies which were carried out in order to provide an answer to these questions. For a more detailed description of each of the individual studies, see Stes (2008), Stes, Clement, and Van Petegem (2007), and Stes, Coertjens, and Van Petegem (2010).

THREE EMPIRICAL IMPACT STUDIES

Study One: Impact on Teachers' Approach to Teaching

In the first empirical study we looked at the impact of the one-year course for novice teachers offered at the University of Antwerp (described above) on their teaching approach. We opted for a quasi-experimental design: data were collected not only from the twenty teachers who had taken part in the course in 2005 (the experimental group), but also from twenty of their colleagues who were also teachers (the control group).

Quantitative data were collected using a translated version of the Approaches to Teaching Inventory (ATI) questionnaire (Trigwell and Prosser 1996), which we validated for use in our Flemish context (Stes, De Maeyer, and Van Petegem 2010). Both prior to the start of the one-year course (pre-test) and three months after the end of the course (post-test), the teachers taking part in the study filled out the ATI questionnaire with respect to one of the degree course modules which they taught. Those who took part in the one-year course focused their answers on the degree course module around which their work during the support course had been based. At the moment of the post-test, qualitative data were also collected by means of interviews conducted with a number of the teachers involved. In total, nineteen teachers from the experimental group and twelve teachers from the control group were asked about their teaching approach.

The quantitative analyses (paired t-tests and covariance analysis with the pre-test scores as covariate) indicate that there was some impact of the instructional development programme on participants' teaching approach, although a limited one. This finding was supported by the qualitative analysis of the interview data, in which the teaching approach of teachers from the experimental group (after the conclusion of their participation in the one-year course) was compared with the teaching approach of the control-group teachers. Our first research question was therefore answered in the affirmative: participants in an instructional development programme do indeed have a different conception of higher education (i.e., a more competency-oriented and student-centred vision) after the end of the course than prior to their participation, and they differ in this regard from colleagues who did not take part in the programme.

A recent study by Postareff et al. (2008) may provide a possible answer as to why we found only small effects. Their research revealed that some teachers' approaches to teaching are clearly either student- or teacher-focused. Profiles of other teachers consist of combinations of student- and teacher-focused approaches, making their profiles dissonant. Instructional development supporting teachers' development towards consonant student-focused profiles may cause dissonance before a consonant profile can be achieved (Postareff et al. 2008). It may be the case, therefore, that some of the teachers in our experimental group had a dissonant profile of teaching approach at the post-test, due to their participation in instructional development, which then evolved into a consonant, learning-focused approach later on.

In addition to the variable participation in the instructional development programme, it also appeared that the academic discipline which instructors teach is related to the way in which they approach their teaching. Above all, teachers who took part in the professional development route and who teach the so-called hard subjects (whether theoretical or applied), such as chemistry or medicine (Becher and Trowler 2001), exhibited a student-centred teaching approach at the end of the route.

Earlier studies (e.g., Lueddeke 2003; Lindblom-Ylänne et al. 2006) showed that teachers belonging to a hard discipline were less student-focused in their teaching approach than teachers belonging to a soft discipline. Our current study reveals that participants belonging to a hard discipline undergoing instructional development are particularly likely to exhibit a conceptual change/student-focused teaching approach at the end of their training. Previous research (Stes, Gijbels, and Van Petegem 2008) showed that at the moment of the pre-test the conceptual change/student-focused teaching approach of the participants in our study was not determined by academic discipline. It is therefore our hypothesis that instructional development has broken into the disciplinary academic tribes (Becher and Trowler 2001).

Study Two: Impact at the Student Level

A second empirical study focused on the impact of the one-year course at the student level. The impacts on students' perceptions of the teaching and learning environment, on students' study approach, and on their learning outcomes were all investigated with respect to a particular course. We looked at whether the impact of the one-year course depended on the number of students that teachers have and which year of the degree course these students are in (i.e., whether these are first-year students or not). As in study one, we opted for a quasi-experimental pre-test/post-test design. We used a multilevel approach allowing us to take into account individual differences between students (for example, arising out of differences in gender, age, intelligence,[1] expectations with regard to higher education, or preference for particular teaching formats).

Quantitative data were collected from around a thousand students, of whom about half were taught by a teacher who had taken part in the course (and so belonged to the experimental group) and the other half by a control group teacher (i.e., a teacher who belonged to the control group), both prior to the start of the one-year course (pre-test) and three months after the end of the course (post-test). We used the translated versions of three questionnaires, validated for the purposes of the Flemish teaching context: the experiences of teaching and learning questionnaire (ETLQ) part two (Entwistle 2005), the revised two-factor study process questionnaire (R-SPQ-2F) (Biggs, Kember, and Leung 2001), and the ETLQ part four (Entwistle 2005).

We estimated five models. Our initial basic model showed that teachers differ from each other with regard to their students' perceptions of the teaching and learning environment; their students' study approach; and the learning outcomes of their students. The differences between students of the same teacher were, however, greater than the differences between teachers.

A second model looked at the impact of the one-year course on students' perceptions, study approach, and learning outcomes without taking into account the influence of teacher characteristics (discipline, gender, academic position, number of years' teaching experience), context characteristics (size and which year of the degree course the students were in), and student characteristics (gender, age, total mark obtained in the previous academic year). With this gross model no significant effects of participation in the one-year course were found.

In a third model, the influence of teacher, student, and context characteristics was taken into account in order to establish the net impact of the one-year course. Both with regard to students' perceptions and with regard to students' study approach and learning outcomes, only limited effects of teacher participation in the one-year course were observed, which (interestingly) proved negative.

A fourth model examined the difference in impact of participation in the one-year course between teachers who taught first-year students and those who taught students from more senior years. Globally, the effects on students' perceptions, study approach, and learning outcomes appear slightly more positive for teachers of first-year students. Finally, a fifth model showed slightly more positive effects for teachers who taught larger groups of students than for teachers with smaller groups of students.

Thus, with regard to our second research question we can conclude that: (i) with respect to the teaching-learning environment provided by teachers who had taken part in the one-year course, very little difference was perceived by their students (in terms of a more competency-oriented and student-centred vision) and also that the scores their students obtain in terms of study approach and learning outcomes are almost the same as scores they obtained prior to their teachers' participation in the course; and (ii) that their students exhibit very little difference in these areas with respect to other students. The effect of the one-year course with regard to the perceptions of the teaching-learning environment, study approach, and learning outcomes of students appears slightly more positive for teachers who teach first-year students or who teach larger groups of students.

As mentioned above, in our first empirical study an effect of instructional development was indeed found on teachers' teaching approach, although this was neither strong nor very distinct. Thus, in this second study, we expected to find an impact on the teaching-learning environment as provided by the teachers. However, this impact was not found. As teachers' teaching approach is determined by teachers' conceptions of teaching, on the one hand, and teachers' teaching behaviour, on the other hand (Trigwell and Prosser 1996), it might be that the effect on teachers' teaching approach as found in the first empirical study is due to an effect on teachers' conceptions. That only weak effects on teachers' teaching approach were found might be due to the fact that there was no effect on teachers' teaching behaviour (in other words, on the way teachers provided the teaching-learning environment). Our results are thus in line with the findings of a study by Trigwell and Prosser (1996) in which inconsistencies were found between teaching intentions or conceptions, on the one hand, and teaching strategies on the other. The "mystery of higher education" (Murray and Macdonald 1997), whereby there is a disjunction between teachers' teaching conceptions and their daily teaching practice, seems also to be found in our studies.

We note that in the first study reported, teachers' teaching approach was measured on the basis of teachers' self-reporting (both quantitatively and qualitatively). It could be that teachers in the experimental group overestimated the student-centredness of their teaching approach; their participation in an instructional development programme that stressed the importance of a student-centred teaching approach might have resulted in their giving socially desirable answers (i.e., answers in line with the student-centred teaching concept as embraced by the university management). However, our second study investigated the way teachers provided the teaching-learning environment by using the perceptions of students. There is often a gap between the objective characteristics of a teaching-learning environment and students' perceptions of this environment (Ramsden 1997). It is possible that changes did indeed occur, but were not perceived by the students.

At all events, it is important to take students' perceptions into account as these are crucial with regard to the success of innovations (Ramsden 1997).

Entwistle (1998) stresses that it is not the teaching as such, but, specifically, the way students perceive the teaching they receive that affects student learning. A study by Lea, Stephenson, and Troy (2003) revealed that learning environments in higher education which are based on student-centred teaching have the potential to improve student learning outcomes. Our results clearly show that this potential was not realized. It is possible that, although—as the first study revealed—participants self-reported changes in their teaching approach, teachers did not actually gear their teaching-learning environment to the concept of student-centred teaching. On the other hand, it might be that this was simply not perceived by the students and therefore did not affect their study approach and there was, similarly, no increase in learning outcomes.

It is also possible that participants of an instructional development programme are willing and trying to take a more student-centred approach (impact on teaching approach, first study) at the end of the programme, but have difficulties in implementing this approach immediately in an accurate way (no impact on the teaching-learning environment as perceived by students, second study). It could be that more time is needed for a successful implementation in daily practice of what has been learned during instructional development. Follow-up research investigating the long-term impact of instructional development is described in study three.

Study Three: Long-Term Effects and Institutional Impact

The one-year course for novice teachers at the University of Antwerp aims to support participants in bringing their teaching conceptions into line with the student-centred and competency-oriented teaching vision established by the university. The intention is both to help them bring the teaching-learning environment they provide more into line with this teaching concept and to raise the quality of their teaching. The ultimate objective of the course, however, is to secure an improvement in student learning. In order to establish the impact of the one-year course, these three objectives (change in the teacher's conceptions; change in the teaching-learning environment they provide; and change in learning among students) were explicitly taken into account in the three studies referred to above.

However, previous research (Stes, Clement, and Nelissen 2002) has shown that—according to the participants—the one-year course also had an effect at the level of the organisation: after the course, participants got more involved in their department or faculty in the area of teaching and teaching policy. A third empirical study looked at whether this effect at organisational level could still be detected two years after the participants had finished the course. We also studied the long-term effects at the level of the individual teachers (in terms of change in teaching conceptions and teaching behaviour). Both types of impact were investigated by means of an exploratory study using a written questionnaire with open questions. Fourteen participants out of the total number of thirty teachers who took part in the one-year course organized in the academic year 2000–2001 filled out the questionnaire (a 47 percent response).

The results revealed that two years after the end of the one-year course, respondents still referred to the course as the reason for changes in their teaching and teaching conceptions. Moreover, effects were still mentioned at organisational level. The degree of change in teaching behaviour appeared to be related to the extent of changes in teaching conceptions. However, no unequivocal relationship was found between the degree of individual impact (in terms of changes in teaching conceptions and teaching behaviour) and institutional impact (in terms of involvement with teaching at organisational level).

It was primarily context characteristics that were experienced as factors which influence the long-term impact of the one-year course. A lack of consensus with colleagues was the factor most frequently mentioned as a negative-influencing element. Students were seen as another inhibiting factor: having too many students in class or their passive attitude were seen as making it difficult to apply the student-centred vision of teaching promoted during the course in day-to-day teaching practice. Other impediments to this were pressure of time and pressure to publish. The difficulty of maintaining the right balance between research and teaching and a lack of support (both practical support and support from policymakers) were also cited as elements which militate against genuine effects.

At the same time, however, colleagues and students were cited as the most important factors in promoting the application of what they had learned. If colleagues or students react enthusiastically to an innovation which teachers introduce in their teaching, this acts as a stimulus to the application of more ideas from the course. Working together with colleagues who had also taken part in the one-year course appeared to be particularly motivating.

We thus conclude (despite the fact that the study had an exploratory character and no quasi-experimental design or pre-test data were used) that the evidence found is encouraging with respect to the possibility of a long-term impact of instructional development.

CAUSES OF IMPACT: LESSONS LEARNT

The framework depicted in Figure 13.1 was used in our research for analysing the impact of the instructional development programme at the University of Antwerp. During our research, many new pathways and questions for future research emerged. In this section we will discuss some issues that are in need of further research. This will take us to the presentation of a new framework that takes into account the lessons learnt regarding the causes of impact on the basis of the University of Antwerp programme.

Influence of Intervening Variables

Our first study into the impact of instructional development on teachers' teaching approach did not take intervening variables into account. In the second study we used two interaction models to examine the interfering impact of the variables *student level* (first years or not) and *student numbers*. These two context variables were chosen to examine the interfering impact because earlier research (e.g., Clarke and Hollingsworth 2002; Trowler and Cooper 2002) stresses that the impact of training depends strongly on the subject's working context. In our third study the participants were explicitly asked about elements that might have influenced the long-term impact of the instructional development programme. Respondents spontaneously thought, in the first place, of contextual characteristics as influencing elements.

The results of a recent review study (Stes et al. 2010) revealed that characteristics of the instructional development itself, such as its duration and format (collective with a course-like character and/or an alternative format such as peer learning, action research, team teaching, or research grants regarding teaching), also influence the impact; whether an instructional development initiative is discipline-specific or not seemed to have no influence on the impact.

In addition to characteristics of the context and of the instructional development initiative, Baldwin and Ford (1988) distinguish teacher characteristics as a category influencing the transfer of what teachers learn during instructional development to their actual professional practice. Besides demographic teacher characteristics, characteristics such as teachers' satisfaction with the quality of the instructional development programme, the amount of instructional training teachers have received in general (apart from participation in the one-year programme for beginning faculty teachers), teachers' motivation for teaching, their perception of the degree to which teaching is valued within their institution (in comparison to research), or teachers' perception of teaching load can influence the impact of instructional development. These characteristics should be taken into account in future research. In order to get a better picture of the influence of different intervening variables, one possible approach might be, for example, a qualitative in-depth study into the impact of instructional development on individual participants.

In conclusion we feel that future research should explicitly look at the different sorts of conditions (regarding the characteristics of the context, the instructional development, and the participants) which encourage the impact of instructional development. With regard to the context, we observe that studies should not only take account of the specific context of individual teachers (e.g., whether they are teaching first years or not; whether they are teaching a small or larger number of students; and their teaching load); but that the broader institutional context in which teachers are working (e.g., a research-intensive university or not; teaching being amply valued or not) should also be considered.

Impact on Students

The second study looked at the impact of instructional development on students. However, students' perceptions of teaching are influenced by a large number of variables (Richardson 2006). Some of these, such as students' gender, age, and general academic level (in terms of global end mark obtained during the previous academic year), were controlled for in the net model of the multilevel analysis used in the study; but others, such as students' expectations with regard to higher education or their preferences with respect to teaching, were not taken into account. The fact that not all the individual differences between students were controlled for may have influenced our results regarding the impact of instructional development on students. Further research into student characteristics which influence the impact of teachers' instructional development on students is needed.

However, given that students' perceptions of the teaching-learning environment, their study approach, and learning outcomes are influenced by so many variables (Richardson 2006), it is by no means clear that we can expect the instructional development for teachers to achieve any significant impact at student level anyway.

Institutional Impact

The instructional development programme at the University of Antwerp is not explicitly aimed at changing the institutional culture. However, earlier research (Stes, Clement, and Nelissen 2002) revealed that—according to the participants—the programme does also exert some influence at institutional level, as participants try to make a contribution with regard to teaching culture and practices within their faculty. The third study showed that these effects at organisational level were still found two years after the end of the programme. We found no affirmation of the hypothesis that the extent of individual impact at the level of the teacher (teachers' change in conceptions and behaviour) coincides with the extent to which a participant is inclined to contribute to creating a new organisational teaching culture.

Further investigation of the elements that influence the occurrence or non-occurrence of institutional impact is needed. In this regard the results of the exploratory study with a select number of participants might be used to develop a questionnaire with items to be scored on a Likert scale. Such a questionnaire could be distributed on a large scale, and eventually in different institutions and/or countries. The quantitative data gathered in that way could be analysed in order to reveal more general findings regarding the institutional impact of instructional development in higher education.

Interrelationships between the Variables

The framework depicted in Figure 13.1 was used in our research to analyse the impact of the instructional development programme at the University of Antwerp. Further research might examine the interrelationships between different elements in the framework, of which only two examples are given here. Firstly, future research might look at whether the characteristics of teachers' students (such as students' study approach and learning outcomes) influence the impact of instructional development on teachers' teaching conceptions or behaviour or approach. In addition, teachers' teaching conceptions or behaviour or approach before participation in the instructional development programme might also influence the impact—at both teacher and student level. In other words: the dependent variables in our research may be considered as intervening variables as well. Further research might take their intervening influence into account.

A second area which might merit future research is the nature of the influence of instructional development on teachers' teaching conceptions and behaviour: is there first an impact on teachers' conceptions and then later an impact on teachers' behaviour or vice versa? Or is it more complex than this and could it be that both conceptions and behaviour are influenced at the same time and do they influence each other further? Earlier research has already gone into this topic, but the results have not always been compatible. Ho, Watkins, and Kelly (2001) showed that a change in teaching behaviour is possible if conceptions of teaching are addressed first. Trigwell and Prosser (1996) and Kember and Kwan (2000) stress that teachers' conceptions should be the primary focus of change as well. Guskey (2000), however, emphasises that a change in behaviour is a prerequisite to a change in conception.

As stated before, and in line with the research by Clarke and Hollingsworth (2002), we did not use a linear research framework. This also means that our research did not look at the question of which comes first: a change in conception or a change in behaviour. However, we did find some effects of instructional development on teachers' teaching approach (study one), although not on teachers' teaching behaviour, with respect to the way they provided the teaching-learning environment as perceived by students (study two). As we defined teachers' teaching approach as being determined by teachers' conceptions of teaching, on the one hand, and teachers' teaching behaviour on the other (Trigwell and Prosser 1996), it is possible that the effect on teachers' teaching approach as found in the first study is due to an effect on teachers' conceptions. The fact that we found only weak effects on teachers' teaching approach might be due to there being no effect on teachers' teaching behaviour (at least not in the short term). Follow-up research is needed to look at whether an effect on teaching behaviour is found in the longer term. If so, this would provide support to the idea that a change in teaching behaviour is more likely only after a change in teaching conceptions.

Outcomes outside the Scope of Teaching

It would also be worthwhile to investigate outcomes outside the scope of teaching as well, although these do not constitute explicit objectives of instructional development. Indeed, instructional development explicitly aims to help faculty members improve in terms of their role as teachers; whereas professional development, on the other hand, involves the entire career development of a faculty member and is not limited to teaching, but also considers research and services rendered to society (Centra 1989).

The research framework set out in Figure 13.1 ignores outcomes outside the scope of teaching. However, faculty members are probably more inclined to think in terms of their overall development as a person (professional development) than in terms of their development in a certain role (i.e., as a teacher; instructional development). We thus conclude that outcomes related to other roles that a faculty member plays besides his or her role as a teacher should also be given some place within the framework presented.

Resulting Frame of Reference

The frame of reference resulting from the five aspects that we have discussed above, which we will now present as a new framework for examining the impact of instructional development in future research, is given in Figure 13.2. It takes into account the lessons learnt about the causes of impact on the basis of the University of Antwerp programme.

We should point out that this framework can be used to examine the impact of instructional development in the short term as well as in the long term. The first two studies of our research investigated the impact of instructional development in the short term. This short-term evaluation revealed only minor effects on teachers and their students. Taking into account the idea that innovation takes a longer time period may be necessary in order to detect a clearer impact. The third study examined the long-term impact of instructional development. However, we only collected qualitative data as self-reported by the participants and no pre-test or quasi-experimental design was used; the study had a pronounced exploratory character and a more rigorous follow-up study would be worthwhile. A related area which merits further research is the relationship between the impact in the short and long terms. What participants learn while undergoing instructional development and what they implement in their teaching practice immediately afterwards might correlate with the degree of impact in the long term. Moreover, the relationship between what participants report will change as a result of instructional development and the final, real impact (in the short or long term) could also be explored (Rust 1998).

In line with the suggestions made by Gilbert and Gibbs (1999), the dependent variables in our first framework (see Figure 13.1) were determined on the basis of the intended outcomes of the instructional development

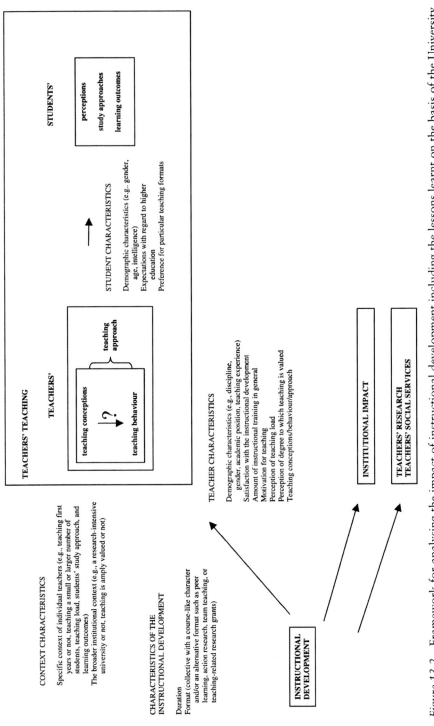

Figure 13.2 Framework for analysing the impact of instructional development including the lessons learnt on the basis of the University of Antwerp programme.

programme at the University of Antwerp, that is, outcomes which fitted the teaching concept as embraced by the university management. The question remains, however, as to whether it might not be better to have the intended outcomes (and thus also the way impact of instructional development is interpreted) defined by the participants themselves (or at least in collaboration with them). It is probably teachers themselves (and not the university management or the instructional developers) who are best placed to determine not only what is needed in order to ensure that the teaching concept of competence-based and student-centred teaching is put into practice, but also how this can be achieved.

With respect to our new framework (Figure 13.2), we suggest participants should be given the opportunity to give the framework a personal interpretation by asking them at the start of their instructional development which goals they want to achieve. Examining the impact of instructional development thus becomes an investigation of to what extent the outcomes, as initially stated by the participants themselves, are achieved.

IMPLICATIONS FOR INSTRUCTIONAL DEVELOPMENT IN HIGHER EDUCATION

Our research not only provides new pathways and questions for future research, but also has implications for the practice of instructional development in higher education. We will now go on to discuss these implications, focusing on the following aspects: (i) the specific design of an instructional development programme; (ii) the role of teaching policy and institutional structures with regard to the professional development of teachers; and (iii) the target group of instructional development programmes.

The Specific Design of an Instructional Development Programme

Our impact study clearly shows that instructional development programmes in higher education do not automatically lead to effects in day-to-day teaching practice. The particular one-year course which is the subject of the present study set out explicitly to bring the participants' teaching more closely into line with a competency-oriented and student-centred vision of education. In future, in order to improve the chances of success, it might be worth considering making the course more practical. For example, while up to now the homework assignments have mainly been written exercises of a somewhat academic nature, these could be transformed into practical, hands-on tasks such as coaching each other with regard to teaching or carrying out a small-scale action research based on the teacher's own classroom practice. The standard to which assignments have to be completed should then be adjusted accordingly. An assessment should be made as to whether teachers show evidence of having raised their professional

252 Ann Stes and Peter Van Petegem

standards in practice rather than whether on paper they seem to be able to do so, as has been mainly the case up until now.

McAlpine et al. (2006) suggest that instructional development programmes should focus on the four distinct zones of thinking which teachers employ: (i) the conceptual zone, relating to general teaching conceptions; (ii) the strategic zone, relating to broad but specific teaching activities, such as designing a course module; (iii) the tactical zone, relating to a specific teaching activity, such as the preparation of a particular lesson; and (iv) the in-action zone, relating to decisions which teachers take when supervising a specific class activity. The one-year course for novice teachers at the University of Antwerp mainly concentrates on the first three zones, but the fourth zone also needs to be addressed.

As stated before, we feel that it is a good idea to establish the specific objectives of the course in consultation with the participants (at least in part). In this way the course would be of a more needs-oriented nature.

Regarding the intended outcomes of instructional development, we note, as stated before, that it is by no means certain that we can expect to achieve any significant impact at student level, given that students' perceptions of teaching and their learning are influenced by multiple variables, such as gender, age, general academic level, expectations with regard to higher education, and preferences with respect to teaching (Richardson 2006).

In line with the results of other studies (e.g., Clarke and Hollingsworth 2002; Trowler and Cooper 2002), our research reveals that the impact of instructional development is influenced by the context in which the participants teach. It would therefore be worthwhile, as a complement to any central professional development route, to develop decentralized, context-specific initiatives at the level, for example, of the different faculties—an idea which has already been implemented at the University of Antwerp. Initiatives of this kind would make it easier to discuss inhibiting context characteristics and would also help encourage collaboration between direct colleagues.

The Role of Teaching Policy and Institutional Structures

Responding to the context in which teachers work is one way of taking into account the influence of contextual factors on the effects of instructional development. It is also important that both the policy and the structures of the institution should support and value the creation of powerful teaching environments as well as participation in instructional development, for example, when considering appointments or promotions. There is also a need for cooperation between universities in this regard. This is the case, for example, in the Netherlands, where the so-called Basic Teaching Qualification has been in use in all universities since 2008. What this means in practice is that every teacher at a Dutch university is required to demonstrate that he or she possesses a certain number of basic competencies in the area of teaching. Any gaps or weaknesses in these competencies can be addressed by participation in a support and supervision route, the precise format and content of which may differ from university to university. However, universities recognize each other's qualifications so that a teacher who has a qualification from one university and then goes to work at a different institution does not need to repeat the professional development route and/ or qualification course.

The instructional development programmes offered in a particular institution need to be explicitly tailored so that they are compatible with other initiatives that support curriculum and organisational development and with initiatives aimed at the professional development of teachers in the areas of research and broader services to society. A coherent body of development-oriented initiatives needs to be worked out at institutional level (the so-called educational development; Taylor and Rege Colet [2010]) in order to maximize the impact of sub-initiatives, such as instructional development activities.

The Target Group

The target group of the one-year course at the University of Antwerp that we have examined here consisted of novice teachers. This is in line with a general tendency to focus instructional development activities primarily on novice professionals, which, in turn, stems from two assumptions: (i) that novice teachers have no (or very little) teaching experience and that, consequently, their teaching is of an inferior quality to that of more experienced teachers; and (ii) that novice teachers do not yet enjoy tenure and it is thus easier to get them to agree to take part in a professional development initiative (Weimer and Lenze 1998).

We have to ask the question, however, as to whether these assumptions are correct and whether the most suitable moment for teachers to undergo instructional development really is at the start of their teaching careers. The net models in our second study have already shown that teachers with more than five years' teaching experience on average scored lower than teachers with a maximum of five years' experience with regard to student perceptions of good-quality teaching-learning environments and with regard to their students exhibiting a deep study approach and good learning outcomes. This finding suggests that it is not only novice teachers, but also teachers with more teaching experience, who ought to be considered as a potential target group for instructional development.

Whether changes in the design or target group of the instructional development programme and/or in institutional policies and structures might enhance its impact would be a very worthwhile area to explore in future research.

NOTES

1. Specified in terms of global end mark obtained the previous academic year.

BIBLIOGRAPHY

Baldwin, Timothy T., and Kevin J. Ford. 1988. "Transfer of Training: A Review and Directions for Future Research." *Personnel Psychology* 41: 63–105.
Becher, Tony, and Paul Trowler. 2001. *Academic Tribes and Territories: Intellectual Enquiry and the Cultures of Disciplines*, 2nd edition. Buckingham, UK: SRHE/Open University Press.
Biggs, John, David Kember, and Doris Y. P. Leung. 2001. "The Revised Two-Factor Study Process Questionnaire: R-SPQ-2F." *British Journal of Educational Psychology* 71: 133–149.
Centra, John A. 1989. "Faculty Evaluation and Faculty Development in Higher Education." In *Higher Education: Handbook of Theory and Research*, edited by John C. Smart, 155–179. New York: Agathon Press.
Clarke, David, and Hilary Hollingsworth. 2002. "Elaborating a Model of Teacher Professional Growth." *Teaching and Teacher Education* 18: 947–967.
Entwistle, Noel J. 1998. "Improving Teaching through Research on Student Learning." In *University Teaching: International Perspectives*, edited by James J. F. Forest, 73–112. New York: Garland.
———. 2005. "Enhancing Teaching-Learning Environments in Undergraduate Courses in Electronic Engineering: An Introduction to the ETL Project." *International Journal of Electrical Engineering Education* 42: 1–7.
Gilbert, Alan, and Graham Gibbs. 1999. "A Proposal for an International Collaborative Research Programme to Identify the Impact of Initial Training on University Teachers." *Research and Development in Higher Education* 21: 131–141.
Guskey, Thomas R. 2000. *Evaluating Professional Development*. Thousand Oaks, CA: Corwin Press.
Ho, Angela, David Watkins, and Mavis Kelly. 2001. "The Conceptual Change Approach to Improving Teaching and Learning: An Evaluation of a Hong Kong Staff Development Programme." *Higher Education* 42: 143–169.
Holton, Elwood F. III. 1996. "The Flawed Four-Level Evaluation Model." *Human Resource Development Quarterly* 7 (1): 5–21.
Kember, David, and Kam-Por Kwan. 2000. "Lecturers' Approaches to Teaching and Their Relationship to Conceptions of Good Teaching." *Instructional Science* 28: 469–490.
Kirkpatrick, Donald L. 1994. *Evaluating Training Programs: The Four Levels*. San Francisco: Berrett-Koehler Publishers.
Lea, Susan J., David Stephenson, and Juliette Troy. 2003. "Higher Education Students' Attitudes toward Student-Centred Learning: Beyond Educational Bulimia?" *Studies in Higher Education* 28 (3): 321–334.
Levinson-Rose, Judith, and Robert J. Menges. 1981. "Improving College Teaching: A Critical Review of Research." *Review of Educational Research* 51: 403–434.
Lindblom-Ylänne, Sari, Keith Trigwell, Anne Nevgi, and Paul Ashwin. 2006. "How Approaches to Teaching Are Affected by Discipline and Teaching Context." *Studies in Higher Education* 31: 285–298.
Lueddeke, George R. 2003. "Professionalizing Teaching Practice in Higher Education: A Study of Disciplinary Variation and Teaching Scholarship." *Studies in Higher Education* 28: 213–228.

Marton, Ference, Dai Hounsell, and Noel J. Entwistle, eds. 1997. *The Experience of Learning: Implications for Teaching and Studying in Higher Education.* Edinburgh: Scottish Academic Press.

McAlpine, Lynn. 2003. "Het belang van onderwijskundige vorming voor studentgecentreerd onderwijs." In *Dynamiek in het hoger onderwijs*, edited by Nathalie Druine, Mieke Clement, and Kim Waeytens, 57–71. Leuven, Belgium: Universitaire Pers.

McAlpine, Lynn, Cynthia Weston, Julie Timmermans, Denis Berthiaume, and Gail Fairbank-Roch. 2006. "Zones: Reconceptualizing Teacher Thinking in Relation to Action." *Studies in Higher Education* 31 (5): 601–615.

Murray, Kate, and Ranald Macdonald. 1997. "The Disjunction between Lecturers' Conceptions of Teaching and Their Claimed Educational Practice." *Higher Education* 33 (3): 331–349.

Postareff, Liisa, Nina Katajavuori, Sari Lindblom-Ylänne, and Keith Trigwell. 2008. "Consonance and Dissonance in Descriptions of Teaching of University Teachers." *Studies in Higher Education* 33 (1): 49–61

Prebble, Tom, Helen Hargraves, Linda Leach, Kogi Naidoo, Gordon Suddaby, and Nick Zepke. 2004. *Impact of Student Support Services and Academic Development Programmes on Student Outcomes in Undergraduate Tertiary Study: A Synthesis of the Research.* Report to the Ministry of Education, Massey University College of Education, New Zealand.

Ramsden, Paul. 1997. "The Context of Learning in Academic Departments." In *The Experience of Learning*, 2nd edition, edited by Ference Marton, Dai J. Hounsell, and Noel J. Entwistle, 198–216. Edinburgh: Scottish Academic Press.

Richardson, John T. E. 2006. "Investigating the Relationship between Variations in Students' Perceptions of Their Academic Environment and Variations in Study Behaviour in Distance Education." *British Journal of Educational Psychology* 76: 867–893.

Rust, Chris. 1998. "The Impact of Educational Development Workshops on Teachers' Practice." *International Journal for Academic Development* 3: 72–80.

Steinert, Yvonne, Karen Mann, Angel Centeno, Diana Dolmans, John Spencer, Mark Gelula, and David Prideaux. 2006. "A Systematic Review of Faculty Development Initiatives Designed to Improve Teaching Effectiveness in Medical Education: BEME Guide No. 8." *Medical Teacher* 28 (6): 497–526.

Stes, Ann. 2008. *The Impact of Instructional Development in Higher Education: Effects on Teachers and Students.* Gent, Belgium: Academia Press.

Stes, Ann, Mieke Clement, and Carla Nelissen. 2002. "Educational Innovation and Faculty's Professional Development: A Two-Way Link." Paper presented at the international ICED Conference, Perth, Australia.

Stes, Ann, Mieke Clement, and Peter Van Petegem. 2007. "The Effectiveness of a Faculty Training Programme: Long Term and Institutional Impact." *The International Journal of Academic Development* 12 (2): 99–109.

Stes, Ann, Liesje Coertjens, and Peter Van Petegem. 2010. "Instructional Development for Teachers in Higher Education: Impact on Teaching Approach." *Higher Education* 60 (2): 187–204.

Stes, Ann, Sven De Maeyer, and Peter Van Petegem. 2010. "Approaches to Teaching in Higher Education: Validation of a Dutch Version of the Approaches to Teaching Inventory." *Learning Environments Research: An International Journal* 13 (1): 59–73.

Stes, Ann, David Gijbels, and Peter Van Petegem. 2008. "Student-Focused Approaches to Teaching in Relation to Context and Teacher Characteristics." *Higher Education* 55 (3): 255–267.

Stes, Ann, Mariska Min-Leliveld, David Gijbels, and Peter Van Petegem. 2010. "The Impact of Instructional Development in Higher Education: The State-of-the-Art of the Research." *Educational Research Review* 5 (1): 25–49.

Taylor, Lynn, and Nicole Rege Colet. 2010. "Making the Shift from Faculty Development to Educational Development: A Conceptual Framework Grounded in Practice." In *Building Teaching Capacities in Universities: A Comprehensive International Model,* edited by Alenoush Saroyan and Mariane Frenay, 139–167. Sterling, VA: Stylus Publishing.

Trigwell, Keith, and Michael Prosser. 1991. "Relating Approaches to Study and the Quality of Learning Outcomes at the Course Level." *British Journal of Educational Psychology* 61: 265–275.

———. 1996. "Congruence between Intention and Strategy in University Science Teachers' Approaches to Teaching." *Higher Education* 32: 77–87.

Trowler, Paul, and Ali Cooper. 2002. "Teaching and Learning Regimes: Implicit Theories and Recurrent Practices in the Enhancement of Teaching and Learning through Educational Development Programmes." *Higher Education Research and Development* 21: 221–240.

Weimer, Maryellen, and Lisa F. Lenze. 1998. "Instructional Interventions: A Review of the Literature on Efforts to Improve Instruction." In *Effective Teaching in Higher Education: Research and Practice,* edited by Raymond P. Perry and John C. Smart, 205–240. New York: Agathon Press.

14 Evaluating the Impact of University Teaching Development Programmes

Methodologies that Ask Why There is an Impact

Keith Trigwell

INTRODUCTION

> I have had the good fortune of having exceptional mentors and world-class teachers . . . I become a student again in the Graduate Certificate and worked with two of the finest teachers I have ever encountered—X and Y. At the risk of sounding clichéd, this was not only a career-changing experience for me, but a life-changing one as well. (unsolicited email from senior lecturer, arts, University of Sydney, 2005)

There is little doubt that programmes on developing university teaching are having an impact. This one quote is typical of the response of at least one person in most of the programmes currently available in universities. This degree of individual impact is a major achievement for any intervention. The majority of the quantitative studies conducted on the outcomes of these programmes, using a variety of methods, also show a positive impact. Some of these studies are the subject of other chapters in this book and others are mentioned in the brief overview provided in the next section.

The purpose of this chapter is to build on this summary of how these programmes have been evaluated, and then to make a case for an additional form of evaluation: one in which we ask about the reasons why our programmes are having the effect that they have. Only by asking this *why* question will we be able to improve what it is that we provide. Only by asking why will we know the reasons some programmes work so successfully for some faculty and not so successfully for others. Only by asking why will we know whether successful programmes are transferable to other contexts. In the final section, both the how and the why contexts are presented through one case study looking at the relations between teaching programme development participation and the attainment of a teaching award in one university. This case study also contains further evidence of the positive impact of university teaching development programmes.

RESEARCH ON THE IMPACT OF FACULTY DEVELOPMENT

A range of activities are currently used in the development of university teaching. These include postgraduate certificate award courses, which normally involve study for one academic year part time, for example, programmes in the UK (McArthur, Earl, and Edwards 2004) and Australia (Ramsden 2003); workshop trainings, which are typically short-term courses, from a few hours to a few weeks long (e.g., Rust 1998; Weurlander and Stenfors-Hayes 2008); specific development activities like video feedback (e.g., Dalgaard 1982; Schreurs and Van Vilet 1998); or micro-teaching, as well as portfolio work as a means to foster faculty development (e.g., Jarvinen and Kohonen 1995). The training modality differs from formal to informal training (Sharpe 2004; Lomas and Nicholls 2005; Knight, Tait, and Yorke 2006; Viskovic 2006) and the purposes, from changing practice to changing conceptions.

According to Guskey's (2000) model of faculty development, the impact of the development tends to happen at five different levels, and therefore can be evaluated at these levels. The levels described are (i) academics' reaction to the development programme; (ii) academics' conceptual change (i.e., changes in teaching conceptions, intentions, knowledge of teaching, attitudes, motivations and self-efficacy); (iii) academics' behavioural change (i.e., use of teaching skills, techniques, and strategies); (iv) organisational support and changes; (v) changes in students' learning. This range is similar to that proposed in other evaluation models, for example, Chism and Szabó (1997) and Kirkpatrick (1998).

In evaluating programmes, the first question is whether it should be at some or all of these levels. The answer depends, in part, on the aims of the programmes. In some cases it might not appear to be appropriate to assess the impact of a programme that, while recognising that improvements in student learning are desirable, also recognises that this cannot be the responsibility of the programme, in the same way that how students behave in the workforce following graduation cannot be the responsibility of their undergraduate teachers. There is also the possibility of using proxies for student learning. While there is evidence from the literature on the use of evaluation methods to ascertain the impact on student learning (level five), and some evidence is included below, level five is not the main focus of this chapter. Here the focus is on levels two and three, and to a lesser extent level four.

As the number and range of evaluation studies increase, there is growing evidence of the positive impact of faculty development activities across this full range of levels, including positive changes in attitudes toward faculty development (e.g., Steinert et al. 2006). In studying changes of conceptions of teaching (level two), Hanbury, Prosser, and Rickinson (2008) used the Approaches to Teaching Inventory to monitor changes in self-reported approach to teaching of faculty completing teaching development courses in over thirty UK universities. Large effect sizes are reported for changes from less to more conceptual change/student-focused teaching approaches, and small to medium effect sizes for changes from more to less information transfer/teacher-focused approaches. Given that the changes to these approaches in these directions are associated with desirable changes in students' approaches to learning (Trigwell, Prosser, and Waterhouse 1999), these results are strong confirmation of the positive impact of the programmes across the UK.

Postareff, Lindblom-Ylänne, and Nevgi (2007) adopted a mixed research method combining both quantitative and qualitative analysis to examine the relation between the amount of pedagogical training and the changes of teaching conceptions. Two hundred lecturers at the University of Helsinki were categorized into four groups using the different amount of pedagogical training they had obtained. They found that teachers needed to reach a threshold of pedagogical training before there were increases in scores on the approaches to teaching that supported high-quality student learning. By analysing qualitative data obtained from twenty-three interviews with some of the participants, the researchers argued that shorter courses might increase degrees of uncertainty, and lower self-efficacy, whilst a longer course increased the teachers' self-efficacy, and supported conceptual changes (Postareff, Lindblom-Ylänne, and Nevgi 2007).

The relation between faculty development training and teachers' conception of teaching has also been shown to be bidirectional, with faculty development changing teachers' conceptions of teaching but teachers' initial state of teaching also influencing their perceptions of faculty development (Åkerlind 2003). Teachers with a teacher-focused conception of teaching often considered the faculty development programme as being about obtaining new knowledge and skills, while teachers with a student-focused conception of teaching saw development as a means to increase student learning. As suggested by Weurlander and Stenfors-Hayes (2008), teachers' initial conceptions of teaching might have an impact on the amount of gain from faculty development programmes.

The studies described above by Hanbury, Prosser, and Rickinson (2008) and Postareff, Lindblom-Ylänne, and Nevgi (2007) and Stes and Van Petegem (in this volume) have made use of the Approaches to Teaching Inventory (ATI) (Trigwell and Prosser 2004; Prosser and Trigwell 2006) in their evaluation. This instrument gives a score for each of two approaches to teaching, and as noted above, changes in scores on the two approach scales have been shown to be related to changes in students' approaches to learning (Trigwell, Prosser, and Waterhouse 1999). The ATI therefore provides evaluation data at Guskey's (2000) evaluation level two and also at level five by proxy.

The phenomenographic origins of the ATI mean that it does not capture the full range of the experience of teaching. A better proxy for change in student learning at Guskey's (2000) level five would therefore be a teaching engagement questionnaire that includes those additional aspects of teaching that development programmes are aiming to achieve, such as communication and scholarship, as well as an understanding of subject matter. At the present time no such questionnaire appears to exist, but if the scores on the teaching engagement dimensions of the inventory change in relation to changes in student learning scores, it will also constitute a suitable proxy indicator for evaluating teaching development programmes.

Other studies on conceptions include those by Donnelly (2008) and Ho, Watkins, and Kelly (2001) and on promotion of motivation (Lycke, Hoftvedt, and Holm 1998); and enhancement in self-efficacy and confidence (Donnelly 2008; Postareff, Lindblom-Ylänne, and Nevgi 2007). Finally, the conclusions in a report by Prebble et al. (2004), involving a systematic review of 150 studies, noted that teaching development programmes underpinned by conceptual change models can be effective in changing teachers' beliefs from a teacher- to student-focused approach.

At level three, quality of teaching practice, Steinert et al.'s (2006) synthesis of research on faculty development in medical education from 1980–2002 stated that participants often reported self-perceived changes in teaching behaviour, use of new educational initiatives and designs after the faculty development intervention. In addition, increased gains in specific teaching strategies and skills (i.e., assessing learners' needs, using a more learner-centred approach) were also described.

Ho and associates (2001) used a longitudinal design to initiate a conceptual change paradigm in faculty development and examined the influence of such training on teaching practice as measured by Ramsden's (1991) Course Experience Questionnaire (CEQ). In order to control the context-dependent factors in teaching (Samuelowicz and Bain 2001; Singer 1996), the same course was evaluated for the same lecturer before and after the training programme year. The results indicated that teachers with changed conceptions of teaching received gains on their teaching practices from students, whereas teachers without conceptual change did not show any improvement in evaluation of their teaching practices rated by their students (Ho, Watkins, and Kelly 2001).

In a survey study which examined the effectiveness of a faculty development programme known as SUCCEED (Southeastern University and College Coalition for Engineering Education), Brawner and colleagues (Brawner et al. 2002) found that over half of the respondents employed more effective teaching methods, such as using active and team-based learning, which they attributed to their participation in faculty development workshops and seminars.

There is less research on the level-four impact (organisational changes). While being more community than organisationally based, the interventions described by Roxå and Mårtensson in this volume suggest that there may be positive effects of development programmes at this level. Stes and Van Petegem (in this volume) report some impact at the institutional level.

Brew and Ginns (2008) document a positive relationship between engagement in the scholarship of teaching (including graduate certificate courses) and students' course experience at the department/faculty level. Where a department/faculty was highly engaged in the scholarship of teaching, students in that faculty/department described experiencing higher quality courses. The Scholarship Index (SI) used to measure scholarly engagement is a measure of a variety of activities involved in university teaching, such as university teaching qualification, teaching awards, publications, and presentations on university teachings. Because it is not purely devoted to measuring faculty development, teachers who have not received any faculty development training can still actively reflect their own teaching practice. Stes, Clement, and Van Petegem (2007) found that while novice teachers in Belgium were able to attribute changes in elements of their teaching to the programme, there was little if any institutional impact.

It is difficult to attribute changes in student learning outcomes as resulting from faculty development programmes (level five), but both Gibbs and Coffey (2004) and Ho, Watkins, and Kelly (2001) use students' self-report of their approaches to learning as a proxy (based on the many studies that show positive relations between deep approaches to learning and higher quality learning outcomes, e.g., Marton and Säljö 1976; Prosser and Trigwell 1999). Ho, Watkins, and Kelly's (2001) study described above also included the impact of faculty development on students' approaches to learning. By distributing the revised version of the Approaches to Studying Inventory to students (Entwistle and Tait 1994), the researchers found that those teachers with a confident perception of their conceptual change in teaching exerted a positive impact on their students' studying approaches, with a shift from more surface approaches of students in their pre-programme teaching towards adopting deeper approaches in their post-programme teaching. However, whether faculty development also has an impact on changes of students' perceptions of their learning experience has not been established.

While most of these reported impacts are positive, it has been noted (Stes, Clement, and Van Petegem 2004) that while the effects may be felt by individuals, there is little impact institutionally. In another study, McArthur, Earl, and Edwards (2004) observe that no differences in teaching methods are found between teachers who completed a postgraduate certificate and those who did not, but they still concluded with a positive attitude towards such training programmes by pointing out that they at least "enable less experienced faculty to develop teaching and learning attitudes and methods more quickly than they would without undertaking the postgraduate certificate" (p. 10). Other possible explanations were also identified, such as "it may take time for them to be able to introduce their preferred teaching methods into established courses" (p. 6). This suggestion aligns with those from other researchers. For instance, Healey (2000) suggested that it is possible that teaching skills go backwards as a result of training since a teacher might be confused by new knowledge. Both these conclusions raise the issue of what it is that is being evaluated. This is the topic of the next section.

WHY ARE TEACHING DEVELOPMENT PROGRAMMES HAVING AN IMPACT?

The sections above, and many of the other chapters in this book, provide compelling evidence that teaching development programmes are having an impact. The methods that can be used to provide this evidence are also described in this literature. The most common methods being used are quantitative and involve comparing mean scores before and after interventions. The scores being compared can be from surveys of students, from the teachers' self-reports, and from peers. Other methods include measures of student performance in assessment (e.g., Norton, Norton, and Shannon in this volume) or on approaches to learning inventories; and of teachers' performance in receiving awards and grants (see below), or in promotions; and finally, comparisons between programmes using a variety of outcomes such as student satisfaction, student learning, teachers' performance, and teachers' reflections.

While the positive outcomes achieved in almost all these studies are welcomed by the university policymakers, the shortcomings of the approaches adopted are (i) that the programmes being compared may not have the same aims and are therefore not comparable; (ii) that the performance indicators used may not be appropriately aligned with programme aims (for example, using teaching awards as an indicator of success, as will be shown in the next section, is not appropriate in some continental European universities where the programme aims are not oriented towards scholarly teaching outcomes); and (iii) that the programmes may be run in quite different contexts and of quite different forms. Many types of programmes are on offer, and they vary in length, content, and mode of presentation. They also cater for quite different groups of faculty. Analyses that aggregate results from these different programmes may also mask the impact that individual programmes, or even elements of programmes, may be having. The questions for this section are how do we know what sorts of programmes, or parts of programmes, are effective, and what are not, and why are they more or less effective? Or, what works for whom in what circumstances?

A qualitative method is almost always required if the evaluation is to be informative with respect to improvement or transfer to a different context. As McArthur, Earl, and Edwards (2004) show, quantitative studies alone can lead to misleading conclusions. In their study at one UK institution, the differences between a sample of faculty who had completed a graduate certificate, and one who had not, on a range of measures, were very small. When the qualitative data were investigated, some of the more subtle distinctions between the groups became more apparent.

In his descriptions of the research methods used in higher education research, Tight (2003) lists eight methods in common use (though some are used more frequently than others). They are: documentary analysis; comparative analysis; interviews; surveys and multivariate analyses; conceptual analysis; phenomenography; critical and feminist perspectives; and auto/biographical and observational studies. All are similarly available for evaluation studies, and the methods chosen, as in any research approach, will depend on the question being addressed.

What is not available through most of these methods and what is needed in the evaluation of all interventions are the answers to our questions: why it is that the programmes are having any impact, whether that impact is subtle or obvious. To do this effectively requires an approach that involves an investigation of the mechanisms of change. One such approach has been described as realistic evaluation (Pawson and Tilley 1997) and elements of this approach are used in the next two sections to answer the why questions.

Realistic evaluation seeks to understand the relations between context, mechanism, and outcome. For teaching development programmes this means finding out what actions lead to what outcomes for what people. It is aimed at finding out why there is an impact rather than whether there is an impact, and to do so, an articulation of the change theory or mechanism being employed to achieve the proposed development is required. If possible, what the evaluation may need to do is to find out how the programme enters the teachers' reasoning. To do so requires the use of qualitative methods as well as the quantitative approaches in most common use. It then does not matter what method(s) are used as long as what is used provides information about what it is that is trying to be achieved, and that the method(s) selected are used appropriately.

The evaluation questions then become "What is it about an intervention that might work for certain people in certain circumstances?" rather than (say) whether the overall score for teaching practice is improved by this intervention. To answer this question what is needed is (i) a hypothesis of the relations between context, mechanism of change, and outcome; (ii) an investigation of these relations; and (iii) a revised hypothesis based on the data obtained. Such an approach is rarely adopted in teaching development programme evaluation, or indeed in most teaching/learning contexts. The difficulty is hypothesising the reasons why the programme aims are expected to be achieved (i.e., what is the causal "theory" underlying the approach taken to achieve those aims?).

In summarising their idea of realistic evaluation, Pawson and Tilley (1997, 214–219) provide eight rules that define their approach. These are reproduced below with illustrative examples from teaching development programme evaluation for six of them. It should be noted that rigorous realistic evaluation is very complex and time-consuming and is unlikely to be fully implemented in practice. However, the benefits of planning an evaluation using this approach are that factors often not considered are brought to the fore, and without the inclusion of the core elements of realistic evaluation, assessments of programme transferability are not possible. The first two rules are more about this broad planning element than about the practice of realistic evaluation. The final two rules focus on using the outcomes of the evaluation process, and are presented as brief headings only.

Rule One: generative causation. Evaluators need to attend to how and why social programmes have the potential to cause change. For most programme coordinators, achieving change through the provision of teaching development programmes is a given and is not usually the subject of evaluation. The fact is that we know very little about why the programmes provided are successful, or why the success is moderate, and for this reason generative causation should be included. The capacity for change of natural and social phenomena is only triggered in conducive circumstances. The evaluator of teaching development programmes needs to understand the conditions required for the programme's causal potential to be released and whether this has been released in practice.

Rule Two: ontological depth. Evaluators need to penetrate beneath the surface of observable inputs and outputs of a programme. This rule is what separates realistic evaluation from the majority of evaluations described in this book. It requires that causes and effects other than those measured in before-and-after studies are included. It acknowledges that programmes are always embedded in a range of attitudinal, individual, institutional, and societal processes, and thus programme outcomes are generated by a range of micro and macro forces. These include rewards for teaching development, competition from research, career prospects, tenure requirements, status of teaching, and many other forces.

Rule Three: mechanisms. Evaluators need to focus on how the causal mechanisms which generate social and behavioural problems are removed or countered through the alternative causal mechanisms introduced in a social programme. Teaching development programmes aim to remove or counter the problem of poor university teaching. If any causal mechanism is proposed in programme evaluation, it is usually a learning or change theory. In his study of the ways academic developers explain their actions, Land (2001) described thirteen different models or mechanisms, including teachers experiencing and practising effective teaching methods through the application of programme ideas to their own teaching (a disjointed incrementalism model); or development that occurs through provision of designed pathways and critical "stepping stones," and engagement with those who have already travelled this path (a diffusion model—Land 2001).

Rule Four: contexts. Evaluators need to understand the contexts within which problem mechanisms are activated and in which programme mechanisms can be successfully fired. For whom in what circumstance does a programme work? A programme that aims to produce teachers who teach more effectively may have an effective mechanism to achieve such an outcome for teachers who intend to improve their teaching and raise their student feedback rating. But if other teachers doing the same programme are doing it to receive a teaching qualification to assist career advancement and academic mobility, the programme may not be seen as successful if looked at through the feedback from students.

Rule Five: outcomes. Evaluators need to understand what the outcomes of an initiative are and how they are produced. All programmes have multiple outcomes. Outcomes are not inspected simply in order to see if programmes work, but are analysed to discover if the conjectured mechanism/context theories are confirmed. Outcomes will include those related to aims, such as more effective teaching and enhanced student learning, but might also include enhanced teacher self-efficacy, more scholarly practice, teaching leadership, teaching-research congruence, policy enhancement, and so on.

Rule Six: context-mechanism-outcome configurations. In order to develop transferable and cumulative lessons from research, evaluators need to orient their thinking to context-mechanism-outcome pattern configurations. This rule is at the core of realistic evaluation. The conjectured context-mechanism-outcome configuration is the starting point for the evaluation and the refined context-mechanism-outcome configuration is the finding of an evaluation. It is the process that enables refinement or development of a programme and, in understanding the nature of the context-mechanism-outcome configuration, enables a decision to be made regarding transferability of the intervention. A mechanism to achieve an outcome of teachers having learned to think about teaching from students' perspectives might involve teachers experiencing variation between their current conceptions of teaching and the desired student-focused conceptions of teaching through the use of interview transcripts and the research literature, with the power of reason (an empirical-rational strategies model—Land 2001).

A quantitative analysis using a before-and-after study of changes in conceptions of teaching using the ATI might show, on average, that this aim has been achieved (i.e., the mean conceptual change/student-focus scale score for the group has risen, and the mean score for the information transfer/teacher-focus approach scale score has dropped). While the mean score may mask individual variation, even looking at change in scores of individual teachers will not inform the evaluator as to whether this mechanism is the cause of the observed outcomes. Do some teachers not achieve the desired outcome because their reasons for doing the programme do not involve a change to their conceptions? Do some teachers achieve the desired outcomes through a different context-mechanism-outcome configuration? These questions form the basis of the refined context-mechanism-outcome configuration and the next iteration of the evaluation.

Rule Seven: teacher-learner processes. In order to construct and test context-mechanism-outcome pattern explanations, evaluators need to engage in a teacher-learner relationship with programme policymakers, practitioners, and participants.

Rule Eight: open systems. Evaluators need to acknowledge that pro-grammes are implemented in a changing and permeable social world, and that programme effectiveness may thus be subverted or enhanced through the unanticipated intrusion of new contexts and new causal powers.

There will be variation in how teachers respond to evaluation instruments, how students perceive the teaching of those teachers, how teachers prepare applications for awards or grants, or any other method used to evaluate the programme. In other words there will be a variety of contexts to be considered. What is therefore needed is a greater depth of analysis of the quantitative results from survey instruments through, for example, an accompanying qualitative approach. Some of the variation in the reasons that aims may or may not be achieved can be found, for example, through interviews with participants, through programme document analysis, through focus-group discussions, or through analyses of assessment items such as reflective statements or teaching portfolios. Elements of such an approach are described in the case study in the next section.

A CASE STUDY: USING REALISTIC EVALUATION IDEAS AND TEACHING AWARDS IN EVALUATING PROGRAMME IMPACT

The Graduate Certificate in Educational Studies (Higher Education) (Grad Cert) offered by the Institute for Teaching and Learning (ITL) at the University of Sydney in Australia is one of the main faculty development strategies provided by the university. It is available for any academic faculty member whose responsibilities include teaching. Rather than focusing on instructional strategies, techniques, or methods, the Grad Cert emphasizes the enhancement of student learning through a focus on teacher thinking, and one mechanism through which teachers may develop their teaching is through the scholarship of teaching. The programme endows university teachers with opportunities to reflect on educational theory and student learning research from the perspective of their own teaching experiences.

One of the aims of the programme is therefore the development of a scholarly approach to teaching, and in traditional evaluation terms it follows that one way to evaluate the success of the programme is to see whether indicators of the scholarship of teaching show higher scores for people who have completed the programme than for those who have not. An important aspect of a successful University of Sydney application for a teaching award is an evidence-based description of exemplary teaching practice, but what is also required (and what makes it scholarly) is an account of why the adopted teaching practice was used, and why it might have been successful. Receiving a teaching award at the University of Sydney may therefore be an indicator of the ability of faculty to make use of the scholarship of teaching in a teaching award application, and therefore an indicator of whether a

Table 14.1 Relations between Completion of Grad Cert in University Teaching and Receipt of University Teaching Awards

	All faculty (n)	%	Awards (n)	%
Completed Grad Cert	334	15*	24	31
Not completed Grad Cert	1866*	85*	54	69
Total (n)	2200*	100	78	100

*Approximate numbers only as total faculty numbers change from year to year.

programme designed to enhance the use of the scholarship of teaching has been successful.

If the faculty who have completed the Grad Cert make up a higher proportion of those receiving a teaching award than for the same group in the whole population, this might suggest that the programme has been successful, for some faculty at least, in enhancing their scholarship of teaching. Table 14.1 uses data from the university records of faculty who have completed the Grad Cert programme and those in receipt of a teaching award, in the last ten years.

Table 14.1 shows that approximately 15 percent of university teaching faculty at the University of Sydney have completed the Grad Cert (percentage in column three) but that this group of completing faculty constitute over 30 percent of the successful applicants for university teaching awards (percentage in column five). In a simplistic interpretation of these results, this year-long programme built around the development of teaching to foster scholarly approaches to teaching would appear to be successful. If the programme were having no effect, the proportion of those completing the programme who received awards would also be at around 15 percent.

This conclusion is overly simplistic, as the outcomes may be due to other factors. For example, participation in the Grad Cert programme is voluntary for most university faculty, so it could be argued that those who volunteer to do a programme on teaching are interested in teaching, and are therefore more likely to be those who will receive teaching awards. Further analysis of the data shows that this is unlikely.

In three faculties (of sixteen in the university) the Grad Cert programme is compulsory. If the argument proposed above is the reason for the results in Table 14.1, the proportion of faculty from the "compulsory" faculties would be expected to be similar to the proportion in the overall population (as they are unlikely to be more interested in teaching than the general population). As Table 14.2 shows, the proportions of faculty receiving awards from the "compulsory" faculties (at over 30 percent) are more in line with the proportions from the voluntary faculties (and to the whole of

Table 14.2   Teaching Reward Recipients from Facilities for Whom the Grad Cert Is Compulsory/Voluntary and Who Have Completed/Not Completed the Programme

	Compulsory GC faculties	%	Voluntary GC faculties	%
Completed Grad Cert (GC)	5	38	19	29
Not completed Grad Cert	8	62	46	71
Total	13	100	65	100

the completion group) than to the proportions who have not done the programme (15 percent), indicating that even when faculty do not volunteer to do the programme, they are likely to benefit from it in their application for a teaching award.

This simple study conducted using existing data indicates that faculty who have completed the Graduate Certificate in Educational Studies (Higher Education) at the University of Sydney are much more likely to be successful in receiving a teaching award from that institution than those who do not do the programme. It may therefore be concluded that the programme is the most likely cause of the variation in the percentages between columns three and five in Table 14.1, and is therefore achieving the aim of developing the scholarship of teaching. Because the numbers in Table 14.2 are so small, it is not possible to draw conclusions regarding the advantages of voluntary or compulsory programmes, but as an approach to, and a measure of the success of the programme, the study indicates that the programme is successful (for some) in achieving the particular aim of enhancing the scholarship of teaching.

Most of the programme evaluations described in this book and in the literature stop at this point. They do tell us that the programmes are a useful developmental resource, but they are not realistic evaluations. They do not tell us anything about why some participants in the programme do not develop the scholarship of teaching, or whether this type of programme could be used successfully to develop the scholarship of teaching in other contexts. Similarly, this quantitative study cannot indicate how the programme could be improved. To do this, what is needed is a realistic evaluation that asks the reasons why some teachers do not develop their scholarship of teaching, and therefore in what situations the programme is successful or not. In other words, the evaluation question becomes "What is it about the intervention that might work for certain people in certain circumstances?"

A realistic evaluation requires the development and testing of a context-mechanism-outcome configuration. For this programme aim (to develop the scholarship of teaching), the configuration can be hypothesised as the outcomes being achieved through the teachers gathering ideas/practice for a scholarly portfolio through the provision of resources, experts, examples, and literature (a continuous improvement causation model—Land 2001). The evaluation question then becomes: in what contexts, and for which people, is this configuration achieved? Interviews conducted in one of the faculties where the programme was compulsory were used to explore this further. The interviews were conducted by management staff in the academic unit as part of a process of deciding whether to continue to require new teaching faculty to do the programme. The key questions asked of faculty who had previously completed the programme were whether it was useful and why they thought it was or wasn't useful. For this case study we focus here on the responses related to scholarship, and report two quite different types of comments.

For more than half of the interviewees, the programme was considered to have been useful, as it led to a more reflective approach to teaching, more confidence in teaching, more orientation towards the students and their needs, and acknowledgement of scholarly approaches to teaching. Two comments illustrate this outcome:

> I am better equipped to reflect on my teaching and implement changes to my teaching on a yearly basis.
>
> Through the Grad Cert I have learned that I can improve my teaching practices with the help of colleagues and students. I've become aware that research can be done in teaching and this could be extremely useful in refining our teaching practice.

But for some, the programme was not considered to be useful and this scholarship aim was seen to be one of the reasons why it was not. The causal mechanism did not work for these people—the literature was not considered to be helpful (and in one case it was considered to be not readable), the portfolio approach was considered cumbersome, and the examples were not relevant. These views give some insight into why the programme was not successful for some participants: it did not match their needs or expectations and there was no continuous improvement.

> The set texts required a lot of reading time and effort for very little return and I found many of the articles consisted largely of unsupported opinion often criticising previous articles for promoting ideas and theories that were unsupported. This made the current approaches seem even more like ephemeral fashions rather than sound advice based on scientific evidence.
>
> Most of us really didn't see the point of studying the scholarship of teaching unless you were interested in getting out of research in your own discipline.

Responses of this sort give the programme designers some insight into what might be changed to make the programme more effective. For example, the first of the last set of quotes led to a review of the nature of the literature provided to participants. The second quote, and ones like it, came from people who were not aiming to achieve the scholarship of teaching because they felt it was an alternative to doing research in their own discipline. A failure on the part of the programme design team to distinguish between the scholarship of teaching and the scholarship of discovery (discipline research) was part of the reason why these teachers did not aim to develop the scholarship of teaching. But knowing of this intention, it is possible to consider new mechanisms, such as helping the participants use the programme to develop a way to combine their teaching and research *or* to create more time for research in their discipline by developing a more strategic approach to teaching.

Despite the explanatory feedback described above, the development of teaching in this faculty has been considerable, and is measurable in the increasingly positive response by students to their learning environment (Trigwell, Caballero Rodriguez, and Han 2011). This evidence suggests that in the next cycle of context-mechanism-outcome hypothesis and testing, other mechanisms may need to be considered. In this faculty, a culture of teaching development had extended beyond the teaching development programmes available to faculty. A study of the international contexts of effective university teaching leadership completed in 2009 (Gibbs, Knapper, and Piccinin 2009) included a case study of this faculty. One extract from that case study notes that:

> many faculty members were becoming knowledgeable about teaching, for example by taking the Graduate Certificate programme offered by ITL. . . . These faculty members in turn passed on their expertise to colleagues, often informally through mentoring, team teaching, and classroom visits, but also by offering workshops on new teaching and assessment processes. (Gibbs, Knapper, and Piccinin 2009, 52)

This evidence suggests that Grad Cert "success" may be enhanced for some by a supportive context in the faculty, and reduced for some through a mismatch of programme and participant intentions. The success of this programme in other faculties, or in other university contexts, may not be so clear, and has to be taken into account when assessments are made on replicating/transferring the intervention.

CONCLUSION

The methods used to evaluate the programmes designed to develop university teaching include a wide range of higher education research methods, though the methods dominating the literature are quantitative before-and-after studies (Kreber and Brook 2001). This research suggests that most programmes are, on average, successful in achieving their aims. What is less well known is why the programmes are successful, and therefore (i) whether the successes in one context are transferable to other contexts, and (ii) what is needed to improve the programme. This chapter has used some of the ideas of realistic evaluation (Pawson and Tilley 1997) to illustrate how that information might be attained. Realistic evaluation is a somewhat idealistic approach, but it does provide a framework for what needs to be considered in effective evaluation. Where changes are experienced, more qualitative investigations are required to establish whether the proposed cause of the change has indeed been the actual cause of the change, and in what contexts that, or any other cause, has been effective.

BIBLIOGRAPHY

Åkerlind, Gerlese S. 2003. "Growing and Developing as a University Teacher: Variation in Meaning." *Studies in Higher Education* 28 (4): 375–390.

Brawner, Catherine E., Richard M. Felder, Rodney Allen, and Rebecca Brent. 2002. "A Survey of Faculty Teaching Practices and Involvement in Faculty Development Activities." *Journal of Engineering Education* 91 (4): 393–396.

Brew, Angela, and Paul Ginns. 2008. "The Relationship between Engagement in the Scholarship of Teaching and Learning and Students' Course Experiences." *Assessment & Evaluation in Higher Education* 33 (5): 535–545.

Chism, Nancy Van Note, and Borbála Szabó. 1997. "How Faculty Development Programmes Evaluate Their Services." *Journal of Faculty, Programme and Organisation Development* 15 (2): 55–62.

Dalgaard, Kathleen A. 1982. "Some Effects of Training on Teaching Effectiveness of Untrained University Teaching Assistants." *Research in Higher Education* 17 (1): 39–50.

Donnelly, Roisin. 2008. "Lecturers' Self-Perception of Change in Their Teaching Approaches: Reflections on a Qualitative Study." *Educational Research* 50 (3): 207–222.

Entwistle, Noel J., and Hilary Tait. 1994. *The Revised Approaches to Studying Inventory.* Edinburgh: Centre for Research into Learning and Instruction, University of Edinburgh.

Gibbs, Graham, and Martin Coffey. 2004. "The Impact of Training of University Teachers on Their Teaching Skills, Their Approach to Teaching and the Approach to Learning of Their Students." *Active Learning in Higher Education* 5 (1): 87–100.

Gibbs, Graham, Christopher Knapper, and Sergio Piccinin. 2009. *Departmental Leadership of Teaching in Research-Intensive Environments.* Research and Development Series. London, UK: Leadership Foundation for Higher Education.

Guskey, Thomas R. 2000. *Evaluating Professional Development.* Thousand Oaks, CA: Corwin Press.

Hanbury, Andria, Michael Prosser, and Mark Rickinson. 2008. "The Differential Impact of UK Accredited Teaching Development Programmes on Academics' Approaches to Teaching." *Studies in Higher Education* 33 (4): 449–483.

Healey, Mick. 2000. "Developing the Scholarship of Teaching in Higher Education: A Discipline-Based Approach." *Higher Education Research & Development* 19 (2): 169–189.

Ho, Angela, David Watkins, and Mavis Kelly. 2001. "The Conceptual Change Approach to Improving Teaching and Learning: An Evaluation of a Hong Kong Staff Development Programme." *Higher Education* 42: 143–169.

Jarvinen, Annikki, and Viljo Kohonen. 1995. "Promoting Professional Development in Higher Education through Portfolio Assessment." *Assessment & Evaluation in Higher Education*, 20 (1): 25–36.

Kirkpatrick, Donald L. 1998. *Evaluating Training Programmes*, 2nd edition. San Francisco: Berrett-Koehler.

Knight, Peter, Jo Tait, and Mantz Yorke. 2006. "The Professional Learning of Teachers in Higher Education. *Studies in Higher Education* 31 (1): 319–339.

Kreber, Carolin, and Paula Brook. 2001. "Impact Evaluation of Educational Development Programmes." *The International Journal for Academic Development* 6 (2): 96–108.

Land, Ray. 2001. "Agency, Context and Change in Academic Development." *The International Journal for Academic Development* 6 (1): 4–20.

Lomas, Laurie, and Gill Nicholls. 2005. "Enhancing Teaching Quality through Peer Review of Teaching." *Quality in Higher Education* 11 (2): 137–149.

Lycke, K. H., B. O. Hoftvedt, and H. A. Holm. 1998. "Training Educational Supervisors in Norway." *Medical Teacher* 20 (4): 337–340

Marton, Ference, and Roger Säljö. 1976. "On Qualitative Differences in Learning: I—Outcome and Process." *British Journal of Educational Psychology* 46 (1): 4–11.

McArthur, Jan, Shirley Earl, and Vivien Edwards. 2004. Impact of Courses for University Teachers." Paper presented at the Australian Association for Research in Education, Melbourne, Australia.

Pawson, Ray, and Nicholas Tilley. 1997. *Realistic Evaluation*. London: Sage.

Postareff, Liisa, Sari Lindblom-Ylänne, and Anne Nevgi. 2007. "The Effect of Pedagogical Training on Teaching in Higher Education." *Teaching and Teacher Education* 23: 557–571.

Prebble, Tom, Helen Hargraves, Linda Leach, Kogi Naidoo, Gordon Suddaby, and Nick Zepke. 2004. *Impact of Student Support Services and Academic Development Programmes on Student Outcomes in Undergraduate Tertiary Study: A Synthesis of the Research. A Report to the Ministry of Education, New Zealand.* Palmerston North, NZ: Massey University College of Education.

Prosser, Michael, and Keith Trigwell. 1999. *Understanding Learning and Teaching: The Experience in Higher Education.* Buckingham, UK: SHRE/Open University Press.

———. 2006. "Confirmatory Factor Analysis of the Approaches to Teaching Inventory." *British Journal of Educational Psychology* 76 (2): 405–419.

Ramsden, Paul. 1991. "A Performance Indicator of Teaching Quality in Higher Education: The Course Experience Questionnaire." *Studies in Higher Education* 16 (2): 129–150.

———. 2003. *Learning to Teach in Higher Education*, 2nd edition. London: Routledge Falmer.

Rust, Chris. 1998. "The Impact of Educational Development Workshops on Teachers' Practice." *The International Journal for Academic Development* 3 (1): 72–80.

Samuelowicz, Katherine, and John D. Bain. 2001. "Revisiting Academics' Beliefs about Teaching and Learning." *Higher Education* 41 (3): 299–325.

Schreurs, Marie-Louise, and Jedidja Van Vilet. 1998. The Improvements of Students' Skills in a Problem-Based Curriculum. In *Improving Student Learning:*

Improving Students as Learners, edited by Chris Rust, 154–159. Oxford: Oxford Centre for Faculty and Learning Development.

Sharpe, Rhona. 2004. "How Do Professionals Learn and Develop? Implications for Faculty and Educational Developers." In *Enhancing Faculty and Educational Development*, edited by David Baume and Peter Kahn, 132–153. London: Routledge Falmer.

Singer, Ellen R. 1996. "Espoused Teaching Paradigms of College Faculty." *Research in Higher Education* 37 (6): 659–679.

Steinert, Yvonne, Karen Mann, Angel Centeno, Diana Dolmans, John Spencer, Mark Gelula, and David Prideaux. 2006. "A Systematic Review of Faculty Development Initiatives Designed to Improve Teaching Effectiveness in Medical Education: BEME Guide No. 8." *Medical Teacher* 28 (6): 497–526.

Stes, Ann, Mieke Clement, and Peter Van Petegem. 2007. "The Effectiveness of a Faculty Training Programme: Long-Term and Institutional Impact." *International Journal for Academic Development* 12 (2): 99–109.

Tight, Malcolm P. 2003. *Researching Higher Education.* Maidenhead, UK: Open University Press.

Trigwell, Keith, Katia Caballero Rodriguez, and Feifei Han. 2011. "Assessing the Impact of a University Teaching Development Programme." *Assessment & Evaluation in Higher Education*, First published on 05/05/2011. DOI:10.1080/02602938.2010.547929.

Trigwell, Keith, and Michael Prosser. 2004. "Development and Use of the Approaches to Teaching Inventory." *Educational Psychology Review* 16 (4): 409–424.

Trigwell, Keith, Michael Prosser, and Fiona Waterhouse. 1999. "Relations between Teachers' Approaches to Teaching and Students' Approaches to Learning." *Higher Education* 37: 57–70.

Weurlander, Maria, and Terese Stenfors-Hayes. 2008. "Developing Medical Teachers' Thinking and Practice: Impact of a Faculty Development Course." *Higher Education Research and Development* 27 (2): 143–153.

Viskovic, Alison. 2006. "Becoming a Tertiary Teacher: Learning in Communities of Practice." *Higher Education Research & Development* 25 (4): 323–339.

15 Creating Successful Teacher Development Programmes

Eszter Simon and Gabriela Pleschová

In this concluding chapter, the main findings of the book are summarized and lessons about what is necessary to create successful teacher development programmes are drawn. Here, a programme is deemed as "successful" if it achieves its desired outcomes, which—as is discussed below—can be many. This chapter discusses programme effects that are not published elsewhere and goes through the classification of existing models, different ways to measure impact as well as the comparability of programmes. Aside from this, this chapter summarizes the factors that have been shown to have an effect on teacher development programmes in this book, and brings forward suggestions for newly established programmes. Moreover, it proposes recommendations for managers who are engaged in the (re-) design of teacher development programmes together as well as an agenda for future research.

FACTORS INFLUENCING PROGRAMME SUCCESS

This book reaffirms the role of many variables that have been associated with the success of trainings in various studies. Some of the variables that are expected to impact teaching are linked to characteristics of individuals. First, people more open to change and less satisfied with their current teaching are easier to impact (Karm, Remmik, and Haamer). An important conceptual barrier both in England (Norton, Norton, and Shannon) and in Canada (Knapper) is the belief that teachers are born not made and, therefore, that training is futile. This might discourage attendance or, in cases where attendance is compulsory, it could increase the difficulty with which instructional developers succeed in triggering changes in the beliefs and practices of those attending the course (Chng and Soong). These types of change tend to be more marked in teachers coming from the hard sciences than in teachers coming from other fields of expertise (Stes and Van Petegem).

Shifts in teachers' beliefs and attitudes do not always translate into changes in their teaching practices. Prior socialization towards a teacher-centred approach to teaching in a participant's discipline tends to hinder change in his or her teaching practice (Karm, Remmik, and Haamer; Gibbs and Coffey 2004). Many young teachers often lack confidence in their skills in teaching and in their own knowledge in relation to their field of specialization. This hinders change in their teaching practices, despite the fact that change has clearly occurred in their thinking toward a more student-centred approach to teaching (Norton, Norton, and Shannon; Stes and Van Petegem). In addition, when teachers adopt a student-centred approach to teaching, students often perceive them as lacking authority, and this may especially discourage young, inexperienced teachers, who can have difficulty asserting their authority, to put these types of new skills into practice (Norton, Norton, and Shannon).

The gap between change in beliefs and in behaviour has also been linked to course content and institutional factors. If the theoretical background of instructional development courses is not clearly explicated (Karm, Remmik, and Haamer), an attitudinal change is possible to achieve but it will not spill over into classroom behaviour. In addition, if the aim of a course is to change teachers' classroom behaviour, it necessarily has to include components of practical training, which tends to be what teachers value most (Chng and Soong; Renc-Roe and Yarkova), at least in the short term (Nevgi). Similarly, courses covering too much information or requiring too much change in teachers may also fail to achieve their goals. If trainees are left to question everything they have done so far, they can feel as though they have no foundations to build on and become doubtful of their own capacities, which can make the task of improving practices appear insurmountable, thusly discouraging innovation and change (Postareff, Lindblom-Ylänne, and Nevgi 2007). This is an important challenge, and Norton, Norton, and Shannon in this book identify self-doubt as a hindrance to behavioural change.

Compulsory training ensures that those who need the training most participate, even though they may often be those that are the least likely to attend these types of events. The fact of training people who are disinterested, however, is likely to limit the degree of success of the programme (Chng and Soong). On the other hand, the fact of training only teachers who volunteer to participate runs the risk of attracting those who are already quite good at teaching, because they are most likely to be interested in the topic. Because of this, the impact of teacher development programmes may be less the result of the training itself than of the characteristics of the training group (Trigwell).

Most evidence supports the assertion that longer programmes are more effective than shorter ones. Karm, Remmik, and Haamer confirm this finding. Time appears to be a limiting factor in other respects. What is valued about a training course in the short term (i.e., immediately following the training) is not quite the same as what appears valuable in the long term. Practical or survival skills are particularly useful in the short term, but the appreciation for changes in beliefs, theoretical understandings, or membership in a community of teachers increases over time (Nevgi). Thus, it is worth considering long-term effects as these are the ones that may attract teachers to come back for more training. This relates to a suggestion by Stes et al. (2010) that the long-term impact of teacher development programmes should be studied, as well as changes in the strength of this impact over time.

One of the most important points brought up by this book is researchers' repeated affirmation of the importance of institutional and systemic factors in influencing success in teacher development programmes. These factors seem to play a more significant role in influencing behavioural changes than conceptual factors do. It is futile to change teachers' concepts about teaching, if institutional change is impossible in the short or medium term, for example, because of rigid accreditation and quality assurance practices, or departmental inflexibility (Norton, Norton, and Shannon; Quinlan and Berndtson). In this case, instead of maintaining and developing enthusiasm for teaching, training will leave teachers frustrated at the fact that structural factors limit their ability to bridge the gap between their current practices and improved teaching methods. This is particularly troubling because it does not only limit the effects of current training, but also discourages trainees to attend instructional development courses in the future. Because quality assurance measures are bureaucratic, they bring about inflexibility in universities (Norton, Norton, and Shannon), thusly favouring the *status quo*. While this prevents negative change from occurring, for example, the worsening of teaching practices, it also hinders the implementation of further quality enhancement measures.

Student-centred teaching methods require more time to be spent on teaching in general. However, if this approach to teaching is used in classrooms with many students, results may be difficult to achieve (Norton, Norton, and Shannon; Stes and Van Petegem). Indeed, the current trends of not only having more students in classrooms but also of including a greater diversity in students' skill levels are discordant with the pursuit of more student-centred teaching approaches and better quality teaching.

According to Ishiyama et al., neither enhanced job placement nor career achievements, as can be seen through winning teaching awards, are a consequence of teacher-training. They have also found that research universities in the U.S. are better at producing both good researchers and good teachers. Taken together, Ishiyama et al.'s results about the superiority of research universities in training good teachers, as well as Quinlan and Berndston's arguments considering quality assurance, confirm earlier findings on higher education in the European Union (Pleschová and Simon 2009).

At the institutional level, the difficulty in influencing departments, disciplinary cultures, and prior socialization are particularly serious problems (Karm, Remmik, and Haamer; Knapper). Social pressure from colleagues for lack of change can quickly terminate any effort towards innovation

(Norton, Norton, and Shannon; Roxå and Mårtensson). Roxå and Mårtensson suggest that this type of challenge can be addressed by creating a community or network of those interested in teaching, which can serve as a support base for members in case their departments or faculties are not receptive to new ideas in teaching.

One of the major conclusions of this book is that PhD students are unlikely to apply what they have learnt through teacher development training in a way that can bring about an impact at the institutional level. On the one hand, this is because many PhD students do not remain in academia, and so training them can constitute a waste of resources (Knapper). Knapper's study also suggests that in educational systems with no compulsory teacher-training in higher education (HE) and in which schools do not hire back their own PhD students, the education system as a whole could profit from training, but the home university that took the burden of training upon itself may not. Because of their limited institutional influence, PhD students and young professors cannot be expected to be successful in applying and diffusing what they have learnt through training in their departments. In other words, when only PhD students are trained, staff developers entrust the least influential or powerful faculty members the role of being agents of change (Roxå and Mårtensson).

Training for PhD students is usually based on the assumption that they would be most open to ideas about teaching, while experienced faculty members would be hostile toward the idea of changing their practices and taking instructional development courses. This is an assumption that may need to be re-examined, especially in light of findings that experienced teachers scored better in terms of change achieved in their conceptions of teaching as a result of attending an instructional development course (Stes and Van Petegem; Stes et al. 2010). Table 15.1 summarizes the factors mentioned in this book to have a proven positive effect on teacher development courses.

So far, the research programme has identified many factors that have an impact on programme success. Individual level factors have been examined more thoroughly than institutional variables. The effect of institutional factors is often confirmed as a side effect of individual studies (e.g., Norton, Norton, and Shannon) but is rarely the focus of studies. Accordingly, it is advocated for here that more attention be paid to the institutional and systemic factors that affect success in instructional development programmes. Furthermore, in the future, the type of research that is most needed is not exploratory research, but rather research testing the impact of certain identified factors and qualifying that impact. Without identifying such factors, the capacity of impact research to inform practice is limited (Trigwell). Theory-driven studies are also rare, and in this respect, Roxå and Mårtensson's study is welcomed, because it attempts to draw hypotheses from literature in the field of psychology.

Table 15.1   Factors Discussed in This Book That Are Proven to Have a Positive
Impact on Instructional Development Programmes

Trainee characteristics	• Academic background/discipline • Authority issues in the classroom • Beliefs about teaching • Openness to change • Degree of self-satisfaction/self-doubt with own teaching • Previous learning experience • Previous teaching experience
Student characteristics	• Previous learning experience • Diligence • Socioeconomic status
Factors related to the instructional development course	• Breadth of content to be transmitted • Practicality of training methods used (mentoring, tutoring, scholarship of teaching and learning [SOTL], peer/group learning etc.) • Whether the training is compulsory of voluntary • Heterogeneity or homogeneity in the academic backgrounds of participants • Training length • Role of participants in formulating training aims and strategies • Time between the end of the training and data collection
Factors relating to the home environment of trainee	• Students' reaction to changes in teaching • Departmental or disciplinary colleagues' reaction to changes in teaching • Teaching traditions in each particular discipline • Teachers' workload • Time constraints • Class size • Managerial attitudes to teaching • Promotion practices • Ease of changing course content and teaching methods
National policies	• Quality assurance • Availability of funding for teacher development • Incentives for quality teaching

MEASURING IMPACT

The Outcomes of Instructional Development

Instructional development can bring about outcomes on many levels. The authors included in this book examine outcomes by using various criteria, many of which echo choices made in the literature. Most studies deal with changes in teachers (Nevgi; Norton, Norton, and Shannon; Karm, Remmik, and Haamer; Davies and Maguire) and, to a lesser extent, students (e.g., Stes and Van Petegem). Reflections on outcomes at the institutional level are much rarer (Stes and Van Petegem) and are often brought up indirectly in studies focusing on teachers and students (Norton, Norton, and Shannon; Davies and Maguire).

This can also be seen in studies by Kirkpatrick (1994), Guskey (2000), Smith (2004), and Stes et al. (2010), where research outcomes are considered in great detail in relation to students and teachers, while outcomes related to institutions are added only as an afterthought. Contrarily to this, Roxå and Mårtensson use Bauer et al.'s (1999) and Hannah and Lester's (2009) model, which categorizes outcomes according to micro, meso, and macro levels. Unlike other ways of considering the outcomes of teacher development programmes, the latter categorization is helpful because it treats these levels with equal weight.

These different approaches can be unified to serve as a more complete conceptual framework for analysing the outcomes of teacher development programmes, as has been done in Table 15.2. In creating this new conceptual framework, it was considered that the division of outcomes into the micro, meso, and macro levels was closest to a conventional understanding of the levels of analysis as levels of abstraction (see e.g., Singer 1961; Hudson and Vore 1995). For example, four of Guskey's (2000) five categories fall into the individual or micro level, only his fourth category falls to the meso level, and he does not consider macro-level factors at all (see Table 15.2).

First of all, upon identifying the level of analysis that is considered by a particular study, it is possible to determine what micro-, meso-, or macro-level entities the programme studied was seeking to affect change in. The most obvious answers at the micro level are students and teachers; however, it is important to consider whether managers should be included into this category. Indeed, institutional level change is unlikely to happen without managers' individual recognition of the importance of teacher development. In this book, Murphy comes closest to considering the influence of managers; however, in her study, she includes them as a means to examine institutional reactions to teacher development programmes. While it is important to include managers as a group representing their institution, it is also essential that studies consider managers' influence as individuals.

Once these entities are identified, it is possible to name the types of change that a programme is expected to bring about in these entities. "Change," here, is mostly seen in terms of conceptual/attitudinal and behavioural transformation; however, other types of change have also been considered. For example, in Nevgi's chapter in this book, a category was included that had as yet seldom been considered for looking at change in teachers, namely personal development and personal growth. Also, other authors in this book (Norton, Norton, and Shannon; Karm, Remmik, and Haamer, and Davies and Maguire; Murphy) consider teachers' enthusiasm for learning.

Table 15.2   Levels of Analysis and the Outcomes of Instructional Development Programmes with Examples from the Literature

	Type of Entity (Change in whom)?	Types of change (Change of what?)	Examples of change	Examples from literature
Micro Level	Teachers • PhD students • Young teachers • Experienced teachers	*Concepts, Attitudes, Perceptions*	Acceptance of the usefulness of student-centred approaches to teaching	Stes, Clement, and Van Petegem; Ho 2000; Postareff et al. 2007
			Self-efficacy beliefs	Postareff et al. 2007
			Commitment to scholarship of teaching and learning	Hubball and Burt 2006
		Behaviour	Classroom teaching	Gibbs and Coffey 2004; Ho 2000; Shannon, Twale, and Moore 1998
			Reflection on self, personal growth	Nevgi in this volume
			Enthusiasm	Skef et al. (1998)
			Reflection on teaching	Renc-Roe and Yarkova in this volume
			Research on teaching	Hubball and Burt 2006
		Future	Employability	N/A
			Promotion	N/A
			Authority in the classroom	Norton, Norton, and Shannon in this volume

		Concepts, Attitudes, Perceptions	Perceptions of teaching and learning environment	Stes et al. 2011b
	Students • Freshmanvs. senior • Socioeconomic Background	*Behaviour*	Approach to learning (deep-learning which can bring about better grades)	Gibbs and Coffey 2004; Ho 2000
			Learning outcomes	Stes et al. 2011a
		Future	Employability	Ishiyama et al. in this volume
			Appreciation of the need for further training and lifelong learning	N/A
	Managers including chairs and senior staff	*Concepts, Attitudes, Perceptions*	Acknowledgment of the importance of teacher development	Haydn 2005
		Behavior	Support for teacher development (i.e., the creation and sustaining of programs)	Haydn 2005
		Future	Becoming a stakeholder	N/A
	Informal • Significance networks • Workgroup	*Concepts, Attitudes, Perceptions*	Untrained members' conception of change	N/A
			Group views of teaching and learning as a whole	N/A
Meso Level		*Behaviour*	Attitude toward trained members	N/A
			Interaction between group members	N/A
			Interaction with outside groups (lobbying)	N/A
		Future	Group survival	N/A

Table 15.2   (continued)

Type of Entity (Change in whom)?	Types of change (Change of what?)	Examples of change	Examples from literature
	Concepts, Attitudes, Perceptions	Untrained group members' conception of change	N/A
		Group views of teaching and learning as a whole	N/A
		Attitude toward trained members (level of acceptance)	Harnish and Wild 1993; Haydn 2005
Formal • Academic discipline • Department • Faculty	Behaviour	Quality of teaching	Olsson and Roxå (2008)
		Interaction between group members (cooperation in teaching)	Stes, Coertjens, and Van Petegem (2010)
		Interaction with outside groups (lobbying, cooperation in advocacy for improved teaching)	N/A
	Future	Reputation	N/A
		Popularity among students (e.g., number of applications)	N/A

Level	Category	Dimension	Item		Reference
Macro Level	Institution as a whole	Concepts, Attitudes, Perception	Views of management (as a group) about teaching	N/A	
		Behaviour	Institutional strategy		Barrie, Ginns, and Prosser 2005
			Promotional practices	N/A	
			Relationship between teaching and research	N/A	
			Consistency of teacher development with other initiatives promoting quality education	N/A	
		Future	Reputation	N/A	
			Popularity among students (e.g., number of applications)	N/A	
	National educational system	Concepts, Attitudes, Perceptions	View on the role of teaching	N/A	
		Behaviour	Policies affecting the importance attributed to quality in teaching	N/A	
		Future	Reputation at home and abroad	N/A	
	Regional educational system	Concepts, Attitudes, Perception	View on the role and importance of quality teaching	N/A	
		Behaviour	Policies affecting the appreciation of quality in teaching	N/A	
		Future	Community outreach	N/A	
			Economic Potential	N/A	

Furthermore, over and above traditional considerations of conceptual, perceptual, attitudinal, and behavioural changes, Ishiyama and colleagues consider change in future prospects. At the individual level, these can be understood as, for example, improved career prospects such as employability (Ishiyama et al.) or promotion practices. Changes in teachers' authority in the classroom are another type of individual change that was examined by Norton, Norton, and Shannon.

While knowledge on entities at the meso and macro levels is much less developed than that on the micro level, this conceptualization appears to work well at all levels. For example, it places informal groups such as significant networks, workgroups, and formalized groups such as departments, disciplines, and schools at the meso level.[1] When it comes to the macro level, entities involved can include, for example, institutions, educational systems, and higher education areas beyond the nation-state.

It may appear farfetched to expect that instructional development courses could impact, for example, the economic potential of the European Union. However, if educational policies at the European level are increasingly framed in terms of making Europe the world's number one economy, then the policymakers can ask if teacher development contributes to this in any way. It is not suggested here that this impact is direct or appears in the short term.

In addition to studying impact at various levels, in various entities, and in terms of type of change, it is a worthy research task to investigate how impacts at different levels are linked together. The implementation of this type of research could begin by studying each level separately, and subsequently analyse the way in which different levels and factors interact. The gap between change in beliefs and change in behaviour is of great interest to better understand (Norton, Norton, and Shannon; Stes and Van Petegem), as is the relation between teacher behaviour and student learning. However, such interaction complicates research exponentially. The fact that a dependent variable on one level is often an independent or intervening variable on another makes it a challenge to entangle the relationship between variables.

All the outcomes listed in Table 15.2 are arguably valid measures of success, which suggests that Gibbs and Coffey's (2004) appeal to focus on student learning represents a very restrictive view about educational development. The impact of teacher development programmes on student learning is affected by many factors, the study of which can bring us to a better understanding of student learning. An important first step, however, is for researchers to take a step back in selecting their variables more precisely and rigorously.

Operationalizing Impact Variables

The impact of teacher development programmes on individual teachers is currently the most developed and commonly measured out of all different types of impacts that programmes can bring about. Standard questionnaires are validated and used across countries for this particular type of impact measurement (Stes and Van Petegem; Trigwell). Interviews are equally common research tools and are designed to measure change in teaching conceptions or behaviour. Indeed, the majority of contributors in this book have conducted their research partially or entirely through the use of interviews (e.g., Murphy; Nevgi; Karm, Remmik, and Haamer). Aside from this, some researchers collect data that is more objective than teachers' self-assessments; for example, teaching portfolios, teachers' coursework, or focus-group discussions (Renc-Roe and Yarkova).

Other conceptualizations of the individual-level dependent variable are not as well defined. For example, the measure of impact on students is particularly challenging. Indeed, because students commonly attend classes with different instructors at different stages of their university education, it is not possible to implement a pretest/posttest design with professors on the same sample of students (Knapper). Moreover, as has been discussed by earlier research, students' approach to studying and their learning outcomes depend more on their perception of their learning context than on the learning context itself. Furthermore, this perception of students on their learning environment tends to be determined by their previous learning experiences (Prosser and Trigwell 1999). However, the greater problem is that the operationalization of teacher development programmes on the national and institutional level is at an embryonic state, as is the state of research at these levels.

One of the main elements brought up by this book is a questioning of the usefulness of using student perceptions as a measure of success of teacher development programmes. Firstly, this is because the process of obtaining students' perceptions demands too much from students. For example, students are expected to reflect on the process they are subjects to, and are asked to deduce changes in teaching, but without knowing that different teaching styles and methods exist or that change has been effected in them (Karm, Remmik, and Haamer). As a result, it is difficult to be certain that, for example, Stes and Van Petegem found no change in students' learning environment because there actually was none, or because students were unable to perceive it. That is to say, asking students to identify change carries with it the risk of becoming a victim to type II errors, that is, the rejection of positive results even when they are present. While relying on student perceptions can prove itself a useful method when the aim is to identify drastic changes, teacher development courses typically yield small-scale impacts, at least in the short term (Stes and Van Petegem).

Data Collection and Analysis

Certain limitations of current data collection methods being used to study the impact of teacher development programmes are expected to fade away in the long term. Indeed, the fact that many studies use small convenience samples, which can limit their generalizability, is likely to change as programmes become better established, because researchers will then be able to use bigger samples. Until then, it is recommended to follow Murphy's and Renc-Roe and Yarkova's choice of collecting information from multiple sources, preferably including more objective evidence on instructors' thinking or behaviour. Otherwise, the choice made by Ishiyama et al. to limit their examination to a smaller group of teachers, that is, tenure track faculty, is recommended. This does not only ease the burden of data collection, but also allows for the detection of certain subtleties that would otherwise remain undetected, for example, in this case, differences between tenure-track and temporary faculty members. While this comes at the price of limiting the applicability of findings, we argue that rigorous results about a limited phenomenon or group of people can be more useful than more generalizable, but perhaps less clear and focused, findings.

It is argued here that the imprecision in methods of data analysis is a greater problem than are challenges related to data collection. This is of particular concern in relation to qualitative studies, but can more easily be solved than data collection problems. Ishiyama et al.; Norton, Norton, and Shannon; and Murphy can serve as good models for their use of clear methods for data analysis. This is particularly important in studies that aim at theory building and theory testing, which are advocated for in this book. This type of study requires the use of both quantitative and qualitative methods, and so a mixed-methods approach is considered as the most appropriate for carrying them out (see, e.g., Stes and Van Petegem). Indeed, while statistical methods can ascertain which variables have a significant influence, qualitative methods are essential to qualify the relationship between variables.

COMPARING PROGRAMMES

A very interesting conclusion that stems from studies in this book is that programme developers and training participants face very similar problems. These include obstacles created by the institutional context where training takes place, difficulties related to transforming conceptual change into behavioural change in teachers, and the impatience of new teachers, in that they seek out "quick-fix" solutions to their challenges. At the beginning of this book, it was mentioned that cross-national studies were unwise because they operated in such differing contexts. This does not imply that there is nothing common in these programmes. However, problems common to different contexts may need contextualized solutions in relation to each particular culture and programme, because different mechanisms can be at play in connecting the same independent and dependent variables across contexts. While some variables may be universally influential in affecting the impact of teacher development programmes, it is recommended that comparisons between programmes in different countries or at different institutions be done through methodologically sound case selection. It can be argued that the statement made by Stes and colleagues (2010) on the importance of standardized practices for the operationalization of research would only partially solve methodological problems.

Below is a list of dimensions that were taken from this book that, depending on each study's research questions and hypotheses, are potentially important in categorizing programmes. These categorizations may potentially assist case selection for comparative research studies. While the combination of these dimensions, especially that of the first six on the list, can describe existing models well, further work is needed in order to arrive at more precise categories.

- Programme aims

Table 15.1 showed the categorization of objectives that programmes can set out to influence. It is only fair to compare programmes on the basis of the goals they set out to achieve, and to hold the programmes responsible for these.

- Programme structure

A programme's structure can first of all be characterized by its length. Programmes may last from a few days to a year or more. Many PhD students are typically trained in the course of short programmes, while teachers may opt for programmes lasting a year or more in countries where degrees are also offered in instructional development (Murphy; Davies and Maguire; Nevgi). Programmes may adopt different formats; for example, they can take the form of workshops or be delivered as semester-long courses. Alternately, they can be informal as are some mentorship programmes or discussion groups, through which teachers can study the effectiveness of their own teaching. Finally, programmes may be offered in a combination of traditional and non-traditional learning environments, be offered in parallel to the classes that trainees teach in a given semester, or be offered independently from these.

- Programme history

The history of instructional development at an institution is usually important in informing the kinds of effects we might expect from them. For example, we cannot expect young programmes to produce a significant impact on student learning, and so perhaps it is irrelevant to examine this connection.

- Programme content

First of all, programmes may be general in that they discuss all aspects of teaching in HE, or specialized, offering, for example, training about one or a few aspects of teaching such as assessment practices or the use of IT. A given programme's content may also be categorized on the basis of whether it teaches skills, theories and concepts, or a combination of both. Finally, programmes can be characterized in terms of whether their content relates to a specific discipline or not.

- Target group

Programmes most often target PhD students (Renc-Roe and Yarkova) and sometimes involve inexperienced professors (Karm, Remmik, and Haamer). Some programmes are open to all faculty members (e.g., University of Northern Ireland; see Davies and Maguire), while a few target experienced faculty members.

- Institutional incentives

Institutional policies can create an environment that positively supports instructional development, that hinders it, or that has no effect on its implementation. Indeed, institutions can offer incentives at departmental, faculty, or university levels, which can influence the impact of a programme in different ways. For example, some institutions decide to make teacher development programmes compulsory to follow, while others insist for teachers to participate on a voluntary basis. While making programmes compulsory is not a particularly strong incentive to attract teachers' participation (Chng and Soong), many factors can attract interest towards them nonetheless. Such incentives can be formal, for example, if they offer participating teachers concrete rewards like a promotion, or informal, for example, general appreciation of taking a course that can bring forward positive feeling in teachers and empower them in relation to their teaching. Another informal factor that can incentivize teachers' participation in these programmes is that participating teachers can influence the future of their institutions by actively spreading their newly acquired knowledge.

- Characteristics of the host institution

One obvious way to categorize institutions is according to whether they are most focused on teaching or on research. Also, institutions can be categorized in relation to whether they are private or public, or with regards to the kind of degrees that they offer (BA, MA, and/or PhD; part-time or full-time, etc.). These categorizations can serve as important determinants of an institution's practice and culture.

- Characteristics of the educational system

Educational systems can be characterized by their degree of centralization (i.e., the extent to which universities are independent in their capacity to act in response to their own needs and of lobbying which needs to occur with national-level policymakers in order to foster lasting change with regards to teaching-related issues within it). The educational system is decentralized in Canada (Knapper) and in the U.S. (Ishiyama et al.), while control over educational policies and practice occurs in a more centralized way in the UK (Davies and Maguire; Norton, Norton, and Shannon) and Ireland (Murphy). This is important because varying degrees of centralization and possibly differing country sizes can determine an educational system's level of resistance to change, and help to inform best strategies for managers to pursue in bringing about change. In relation to this, it is worth noting that change can likely occur more easily in smaller states, where political and academic elites are often closely or directly linked.

Hiring practices may also be important in categorizing educational systems. While some systems encourage universities to hire their own PhD students to continue on as teachers, others explicitly forbid such practice.[2]

NEW PROGRAMMES

It is crucial for the designers of new instructional development programmes to take their cultural and institutional context into account, as was done by Karm, Remmik, and Haamer. Indeed, these three programme developers started off with an understanding that teaching practices and attitudes toward teaching in Estonia were closely linked to the Communist past of their country. However, it was only after running their programme that they realized the extent of those influences—for example, because discussions about teaching had long been taboo in that they had been seen to imply incompetence in teachers, attempts at them were largely unsuccessful. In light of this knowledge, they opted for the creation of discussion forums and of teaching communities as interventions to achieve programme aims. Because of its sensitivity to the local context, this intervention became one of the best-received elements of their programme.

In their study, Davies and Maguire also pay attention to local needs, but identify them in institutional terms. To be specific, they show that programme aims not only have to take into account the priorities of academic developers and teachers, but it is also important that they be in harmony with their institutional context. This example can serve as indirect support for Roxå and Mårtensson's theoretical argument that teacher development needs to become a process that operates simultaneously in top-down and bottom-up directions. Students and teachers should participate in policy formulation, but in a way that is considerate of institutional factors as well as national policy objectives.

New or recent programmes that are not well embedded into their institutional context can ensure their own survival in two ways. First, they must be able to teach useful things to their students, and second, they must manage to preserve and spread the enthusiasm of young professors in a way that does not question the teaching expertise of more established professors. Also, practical training (Chng and Soong; Karm, Remmik, and Haamer) is particularly useful in the short term as well as in the long term for new programmes. In the short term, they can enhance the reputation of a programme among its participants, and in the long term, practical exercises that encourage teachers to document or reflect upon their own teaching can bring about changes in their beliefs about teaching.

Different strategies exist to assist teachers in implementing lessons learnt in teacher development programmes in their everyday practice. One strategy is to involve experienced teachers as mentors, which can also attenuate their doubts about the programmes and turn them into key stakeholders as well as important agents of change. Alternately, teacher developers can show teachers how to research the relationship between their teaching practice and student learning (Norton, Norton, and Shannon), which can help trainees to assess and understand the effects of their changed teaching practices.

FUTURE AREAS OF RESEARCH

One of the most important contributions of this book is that it presents studies that identify many hypotheses that had not yet been explored, as well as assumptions that require further testing. While there are too many to discuss them exhaustively, the most important of these are focused on below.

Examining the role of time in influencing impacts of teacher development programmes, as is done through longitudinal studies, can be particularly instructive. For example, while it is known that the length of a training programme tends to relate positively to its effects (Shannon, Twale, and Moore 1998), some studies also present the success of short-term programmes (Ho 1998, 2000). Aside from looking at the relationship between the length of programmes and their impacts, longitudinal studies should also look into other questions. For example, Nevgi uses a longitudinal approach to show that the aspects of teacher development programmes that are most valued by teachers are different immediately following the training than a few years after it has taken place. Also using a longitudinal approach, Stes and Van Petegem suggest that the impact of such programmes is strongest immediately, and that it fades as time goes by. Given that it is relatively easy to change teachers' conceptions about teaching, but that it is much more difficult to turn this conceptual change into behavioural change, it can be assumed that changes in these two spheres happen sequentially. Similarly, affecting change in teachers appears easier than affecting changes at the institutional level, let alone development in students' learning. It may be unreasonable, however, to expect any kind of changes to occur in the very short term, that is to say, immediately following the first training session. Indeed, expecting too much change too quickly from teachers can make them feel inadequate (Karm, Remmik, and Haamer), as was also found by

Postareff, Lindblom-Ylänne, and Nevgi (2007) as well as by Stes, Coertjens, and Van Petegem (2010).

Aside from this, Chng and Soong documented evidence that teachers tend to prefer training sessions that include practical elements and alternative training formats. This is probably because the transition from understanding the teaching and learning process to adapting one's teaching practice so that it is informed by that understanding is very challenging for participants (McAlpine et al. 2009, 268). However, of all existing formats and structures for teacher development programmes, it is as of yet unclear which has the most favourable impact on teaching, on learning, and on the acceptance and development of programmes. Also, insight is lacking as to what particular format of training is best suited for achieving select impacts. For example, Roxå and Mårtensson as well as Knapper question the merit of training PhD students as the best strategy to achieve institutional impact. While it is possible that training PhD students is not justified, no empirical evidence has been gathered to support or reject this suggestion.

It has been found that changes in the beliefs and behaviour of teachers coming from the hard sciences tend to be more marked when they go through teacher development programmes; however, the reasons for this are as of yet unknown (Stes and Van Petegem). A possible explanation is that because hard sciences tend to be taught in a way that is more teacher-centred, and that change is accordingly more difficult to achieve, when change does occur in these teachers, it is very visible. It is important to understand these types of findings. If, for example, this possible explanation were proven to be accurate, it would mean that teachers from the hard sciences could be particularly good subjects on whom to research the effects of teacher development programmes, for two main reasons. Firstly, they can serve as good subjects on whom to apply a pretest/posttest experimental research design because, as a pretest group, they have not yet been introduced to student-centred teaching. Consequently, the observable change sought out would be more pronounced, and thus easier to identify.

It is possible to note a shift toward discipline-specific teacher development training in some settings, for example, in the UK, where units increasingly work with and through specific department or academic faculties rather than offering university-wide, generic courses for all teachers (Baume and Kahn 2004, 190; Gossling 2009). While some programme participants may prefer sessions to be organized in this way, there is no clear evidence as to what they are more effective at achieving than general trainings that are open to teachers from all disciplines. While the former may have a greater impact at the institutional level, the latter may be better at having each teacher explain and discuss their own teaching style (Karm, Remmik, and Haamer) and building a cross-disciplinary community of teachers on a university campus.

Research questions and hypotheses are also abundant on how different meso- and macro-level factors affect the impact of teacher development programmes, and these deserve greater attention. First of all, how does quality assurance affect teachers' behaviour in the classroom? Or, in more general terms, what level of top-down interventions and what form of support yield the largest impacts on programmes? The authors in this book suggest that quality assurance does not seem to bring about change in terms of improved teaching (Quinlan and Berndtson; Norton, Norton, and Shannon). It may also be that some of the rigidities that are held against quality assurance are related instead to the overbureaucratization of universities in general. Aside from this, further questions of interest relate to how different educational systems and hiring practices influence change in teachers' attitude and behaviour. Finally, it is also worthwhile to investigate the hiring practices that are most effective for training PhD students.

According to Ishiyama et al., research schools produce better teachers who are more likely to win teaching awards. While the reason for this is as of yet unclear, possible hypotheses include that perhaps these schools are very rigorous in selecting well-rounded candidates for their doctoral programmes. Alternately, it may also be that certain conditions within these types of institutions itself favour the improved performance of teachers. Also, the fact of completing a teacher development course does not seem to improve a teacher's employability, perhaps because HE institutions, even those more focused on teaching, consider research achievements as most important in their hiring decisions.

In their study, Quinlan and Berndtson reflect on the dynamic and ever-changing nature of HE, and the demands it poses to faculty members. New challenges constantly appear. For example, as a result of the Bologna Process, exchange programmes for students and teachers demand for both teachers to begin offering courses in a foreign language, and for students to learn in another language as well. According to these authors, teaching and learning in a foreign language are very different from education in one's mother tongue. New studies are needed to generate a better understanding of the difference between teaching and learning in one's mother tongue and in a foreign language, in the context of HE. A clearer understanding of specific demands on teachers as a result of increases in student and teacher exchanges can help to inform the content of instructional development courses, so that it assists teachers in coping with these challenges.

Finally, it is important to understand how the success of teacher development programmes is being measured at primary and secondary levels in the education system. In contexts where teachers adopt a teacher- or subject-centred approach in lower levels of the educational system, the achievement of positive results in student learning is made more difficult at the tertiary level. This can be explained by the fact that in these contexts, students are socialized to teacher-centred learning environments from an early age (Prosser and Trigwell 1999). Stes and Van Petegem share a similar view in their study, in affirming that prior socialization indeed informs the impact of programmes on student learning; for example, they found that the attitudes of first-year students are easier to mould than that of students who are more advanced in their studies.

LESSONS FOR MANAGERS

This book offers advice for managers supporting teacher development initiatives in a way that shows institutional support, an essential component to their success. One of a manager's most important roles is to work in alignment with bottom-up initiatives for teacher development and to participate in their creation (Norton, Norton, and Shannon; Karm, Remmik, and Haamer; Knapper). While their responsibilities in this respect are numerous, three major areas of contribution can be highlighted as priority: managers should participate in defining the goals of teacher development programmes so that they fit within the institution's strategy for education; managers should create formal incentives to encourage efforts on behalf of teachers to improve their teaching; and managers should create an institutional environment in which quality in teaching is valued. This is consistent with what Gibbs (2000, 3) recommends to developers of teacher-training programmes: that they focus on designing strategies for quality teaching at their universities, and that they increasingly preoccupy themselves with the implementation of policy than with the development of policy. A manager's role is to facilitate this change because, as Gosling (2001, 76) warns, "educational development must occur throughout the institution if it is to impact on organisational change."

The remainder of this chapter will be dedicated towards offering advice with regards to the definition of a programme's aims. First, trainings that are tailored to specific academic disciplines appear better at bringing about behavioural change in teachers on the basis of conceptual change. Also, while teachers value the cross-disciplinary, community-building nature of trainings that are open to teachers from different fields, these general programmes are unable to teach content that can specifically refer to teaching a specific discipline (Karm, Remmik, and Haamer; Davies and Maguire). Studies have found, however, that such general programmes allow participants to discuss the practices that are traditionally associated with their discipline, and can assist them in challenging their assumptions whilst presenting them with new approaches (Cooper 2004, 56).

Communities that facilitate discussion around teaching-related issues can improve teachers' continuous enthusiasm for teaching and strengthen their identities as teachers. It is important to generate enthusiasm amongst participating teachers in order for a programme to yield an impact (Norton, Norton, and Shannon; Davies and Maguire; Murphy), and thus it is suggested for introductory courses to be designed generally, and for the content of advanced courses to be tailored to specific disciplines. This choice is based on findings by Jenkins (1996) that while courses tailored to a specific discipline have greater long-term effects, general programmes have a strong impact on a few individuals, who tend to continue to act as change agents in their discipline and institution.

Second, teachers also value the practical aspect of introductory courses that give them quick solutions to problems encountered in the classroom (Nevgi; Chng and Soong; Renc-Roe and Yarkova). For this, alternative ways of teaching and learning appear particularly useful, for example, through such interventions as a mentorship programme, as was done in Singapore (Chng and Soong), or with the implementation of a colleague-to-colleague follow-up activity to the teacher-training course, as was introduced in Estonia (Karm, Remmik, and Haamer). These strategies can be tremendously effective, for example, for inexperienced teachers that doubt their own abilities (Nevgi). The mentorship programme also constitutes an interesting means by which to involve experienced faculty members into a teaching community, which could increase their interest in teaching-related issues, for their own benefit and that of their mentees.

Third, the fact of making attendance to trainings compulsory can be associated with participants' early withdrawal from the course, and can thus limit the achievement of change in teachers (Chng and Soong). Yet, when teachers are trained on a voluntary basis, those most motivated, and perhaps better at teaching, are those most likely to participate, rather than those who may need to improve their teaching practices the most. It is recommended here that institutions starting to offer teacher development programmes do so on a voluntary basis, in order to avoid the creation of obstacles before the value of instructional development becomes known and appreciated.

Fourth, one clear message from this book is that more trainings should target well-established faculty members. As noted previously, some authors doubt (e.g., Knapper; Roxå, and Mårtensson) the cost-effectiveness of teaching PhD students. Others, however, have questioned this claim because they have noted that there is a great demand coming from PhD students to be trained (Trigwell and Millan 2006; Pleschová and Simon 2009). Indeed, doctoral candidates value these courses because they help them to become more effective instructors when they are employed as teaching assistants.

Some universities, including some in the UK, are trying to solve this dilemma by offering different courses for PhD candidates and for newly hired teachers without a teaching qualification. Programmes for doctoral students usually last one semester, while programmes for young professors generally consist of several modules spanning over a longer time period. Faculty members can also follow instructional development courses that last several semesters and allow participants recognition for their participation in the form of a certificate or a diploma. In light of these findings, it is recommended that courses for PhD students be kept voluntary, and that training for academics employed as teachers be made compulsory.

Fifth, local cultural and institutional contexts need be taken into account in order to run successful teacher development programmes (Karm, Remmik, and Haamer; Davies and Maguire). Here, Murphy's finding, that some directors of accredited programmes are starting to question the usefulness of "one-size-fits-all" teacher development programmes in Ireland, is noteworthy. For the same reason, we also caution against the homogenization of HE across borders (Quinlan and Berndtson).

The role of the managers, including department chairs, is equally important in providing incentives for faculty members to attend training; for example, by making teacher development a promotion requirement. It is not recommended, however, that attendance at teacher development courses be asked of teachers over and above already existing research and administrative requirements, since it will hardly endear faculty to instructional development (Evans and Abbott 1999). We propose it is done as part of a process that redefines promotion practices as a whole. Finally, managers can also promote teaching by creating an open and positive atmosphere as well as developing forums where such issues can be discussed within and across academic units. A key strategy for managers is to tap into the enthusiasm of motivated faculty members who have the capacity to become important agents of change (Norton, Norton, and Shannon; Davies and Maguire).

NOTES

1. We primarily relied upon chapters by Roxå and Mårtensson, Murphy, and Quinlan and Berndtson in the delineation of possible meso-level and macro-level entities and changes. A more systematic discussion of the meso and macro levels is difficult until a greater number of research specifically targets this level.
2. Hiring practices may be determined at the institutional level in decentralized education systems.

BIBLIOGRAPHY

Barrie, Simon, Paul Ginns, and Michael Prosser. 2005. "Early Impact and Outcomes of an Institutionally Aligned, Student Focused Learning Perspective on Teaching Quality Assurance." *Assessment & Evaluation in Higher Education* 30 (6): 641–656.
Bauer, Marianne, Berit Askling, Susan Gerard Marton, and Ference Marton. 1999. *Transforming Universities: Changing Patterns of Governance, Structure and Learning in Swedish Higher Education.* London: Jessica Kingsley Publishers.
Baume, David, and Peter Kahn. 2004. "How Shall We Enhance Staff and Educational Development?" In *Enhancing Staff and Educational Development*, edited by Peter E. Kahn and David Baume, 185–194. New York: RoutledgeFalmer.
Cooper, Alice. 2004. "Leading Programmes in Learning and Teaching." In *Enhancing Staff and Educational Development*, edited by Peter E. Kahn and David Baume, 56–80. New York: RoutledgeFalmer.

Evans, Linda, and Ian Abbott. 1999. *Teaching and Learning in Higher Education.* London and New York: Cassell.

Gibbs, Graham. 2000. "Learning and Teaching Strategies: The Implications for Educational Development." *Educational Developments* 1 (1): 1–5.

Gibbs, Graham, and Martin Coffey. 2004. "The Impact of Training of University Teachers on their Teaching Skills, Their Approach to Teaching and the Approach to Learning of Their Students." *Active Learning in Higher Education* 5 (1): 87–100.

Gosling, David. 2001. "Educational development units in the UK—what are they doing five years on?" *International Journal for Academic Development* 6 (1): 74–90.

Guskey, Thomas R. 2000. *Evaluating Professional Development.* Thousand Oaks, CA: Corwin Press.

Hannah, Sean T., and Paul B. Lester. 2009. "A Multilevel Approach to Building and Leading Learning Organisations." *The Leadership Quarterly* 20: 34–48.

Harnish, Dorothy, and Lynn A. Wild. 1993. "Peer Mentoring in Higher Education: A Professional Development Strategy for Faculty." *Community College Journal of Research and Practice* 17 (3): 271–282.

Haydn, Mathias. 2005. "Mentoring on a Programme for New University Teachers: A Partnership in Revitalizing and Empowering Collegiality." *International Journal for Academic Development* 10 (2): 95–106.

Ho, Angela. 1998. "A Conceptual Change Staff Development Program: Effects as Perceived by the Participants." *The International Journal for Academic Development* 3 (1): 24–38.

———. 2000. "A Conceptual Change Approach to Staff Development: A Model for Programme Design." *The International Journal for Academic Development* 5 (1): 30–41.

Hubball, Harry T., and Helen Burt. 2006. "Scholarship of Teaching and Learning: Theory-Practice Integration in Faculty Certificate Programs." *Innovative Higher Education* 30 (5): 327–344.

Hudson, Valerie, and Christopher Vore. 1995. "Foreign Policy Analysis Yesterday, Today and Tomorrow." *Mershon International Studies Review* 39: 209–238.

Jenkins, Alan. 1996. "Discipline–Based Educational Development." *International Journal for Academic Development* 1 (1): 50–62.

Kirkpatrick, Donald. L. 1994. *Evaluating Training Programs: The Four Levels.* San Francisco: Berrett-Koehler Publishers.

McAlpine, Lynn, Cheryl Amundsen, Mieke Clement, and Greg Light. 2009. "Rethinking Our Underlying Assumptions about What We Do and Why We Do It: Academic Development as a Case." *Studies in Continuing Education* 31 (3): 261–280.

Olsson, Thomas, and Torgny Roxå. 2008. "Evaluating Rewards for Excellent Teaching—a Cultural Approach." Engaging Communities Proceedings of the 31st HERDSA Annual Conference, Rotorua, NZ, 1–4 July, 261–272.

Pleschová, Gabriela, and Eszter Simon. 2009. "Teaching Training for Political Scientists Ph.D.s Students in Europe. Determinants of a Tool for Enhanced Teaching in Higher Education." *Journal of Political Science Education* 5 (3): 233–249.

Postareff, Liisa, and Sari Lindblom-Ylänne and Anne Nevgi. 2007. "The Effect of Pedagogical Training on Teaching in Higher Education." *Teaching and Teacher Education* 23: 557–571.

Prosser, Michael, and Keith Trigwell. 1999. Understanding Learning and Teaching. Buckingham, UK: SRHE/Open University Press.

Shannon, David M., Darla J. Twale, and Matthew S. Moore. 1998. "TA Teaching Effectiveness: The Impact of Training and Teaching Experience." *The Journal of Higher Education* 69 (4): 440–466.

Singer, J. David. 1961. "The Level of Analysis Problem in International Relations." *World Politics* 14 (1): 77–92.

Skeff, Kelley M., Georgette A. Stratos, Merlynn R. Bergen, and Donald P. Regula, Jr. 1998. "A Pilot Study of Faculty Development for Basic Science Teachers." *Academic Medicine* 73 (6): 701–704.

Smith, Holly. 2004. "The Impact of Staff Development Programmes and Activities." In *Enhancing Staff and Educational Development*, edited by Peter E. Kahn and David Baume, 96–116. New York: RoutledgeFalmer.

Stes, Ann, Mieke Clement, and Peter Van Petegem. 2007. "The Effectiveness of a Faculty Training Programme: Long-Term and Institutional Impact." *International Journal for Academic Development* 12 (2): 99–109.

Stes, Ann, Liesje Coertjens, and Peter Van Petegem. 2010. "Instructional Development for Teachers in Higher Education: Impact on Teaching Approach." *Higher Education* 60: 187–204.

Stes, Ann, Sven De Maeyer, David Gijbels, and Peter Van Petegem. 2011a. "Instructional Development for Teachers in Higher Education: Effects on Students' Learning Outcomes." *Teaching in Higher Education* 16: 1–14, iFirst Article.

———. 2011b. "Instructional Development for Teachers in Higher Education: Effects on Students' Perceptions of the Teaching–Learning Environment." *British Journal of Educational Psychology* 102: 1–22.

Stes, Ann, Mariska Min-Leliveld, David Gijbels, and Peter Van Petegem. 2010. "The Impact of Instructional Development in Higher Education: The State-of-the-Art of the Research." *Educational Research Review* 5: 25–49.

Trigwell, Keith, and Elena Millan. 2006. "Monitoring the Progress of Preparation for Academic Practice for Postgraduate Research Students." Oxford Learning Institute, University of Oxford, http://www.learning.ox.ac.uk/files/Monitoring%20the%20Progress%20of%20Preparation%20for%20AP.pdf, accessed 10/06/2008.

Contributors

Erkki Berndtson is Senior Lecturer in Political Science at the University of Helsinki. His recent publications in the field of higher education policy include "Public Space, Architecture and Democracy: Teaching Politics to Students from Different Cultures" (with Henri Goverde in *European Political Science*) and "Education Policy and the Harmonization of Political Science as a Discipline" in *Education in Political Science: Discovering a Neglected Field*.

Huang Hoon Chng is Associate Professor in the Department of English Language and Literature, National University of Singapore. She teaches and researches feminist theory. Her recent publications include "Gender, Space, and Discourse across Borders: Talking Gender in Cyberspace" (with Janemaree Maher in *Feminist Teacher*) and "Negotiating Crisis in a Feminism Classroom: The Politics of Representation" (with Chitra Sankaran in *Australian Feminist Studies*). She is the author of the book *Separate and Unequal: Judicial Rhetoric and Women's Rights*. She is currently Director of the Centre for Development of Teaching and Learning.

Alexandra Cole is Associate Professor of Political Science at California State University, Northridge. Her research interests include political parties and European political party systems. She is also interested in the assessment of student learning and curriculum development in political science.

Vicky Davies is Staff Development Adviser at the University of Ulster. She began her career as a language lecturer and worked on the design and development of a number of European and UK-based Computer-Assisted Language Learning (CALL) projects. Since 2003 she has been a module tutor on the university's Postgraduate Certificate in Higher Education Practice, and joint course director since 2010. She has presented at numerous conferences in the UK and Europe on the pedagogy-technology nexus and its attendant development issues for higher education practice. She is a member of the SEDA-PDF committee and an external reviewer for institutions seeking SEDA recognition.

Anu Haamer is Lecturer of University Pedagogy at the University of Tartu, Estonia. She is a PhD student in semiotics and her research interests include development of reflective practice and identity of academics.

Kerstin Hamann is Professor of Political Science at the University of Central Florida. Her research focuses on Spanish politics, comparative political economy (Western Europe), and comparative industrial relations as well as the scholarship of teaching and learning. She is the author of *The Politics of Industrial Relations: Labor Unions in Spain* and the co-editor of *Assessment in Political Science*. Her research has also been published in edited volumes and journals, including *Comparative Political Studies, British Journal of Industrial Relations, Industrial and Labor Relations Review*, and the *Journal of Political Science Education*.

John Ishiyama is Professor of Political Science at the University of North Texas. His research interests include democratization and political parties in post-Communist Russian, European and Eurasian, and African (especially Ethiopian) politics, ethnic conflict and ethnic politics, and the scholarship of teaching and learning. He is the author of six books and over 100 journal articles and book chapters, appearing in journals such as the *American Political Science Review, Comparative Politics, Comparative Political Studies, Political Research Quarterly*, and *Party Politics*. Currently, he serves as editor in chief of the *Journal of Political Science Education*.

Mari Karm is Staff Developer and Lecturer of University Pedagogy at the University of Tartu, Estonia. She holds a PhD in education and her research interests include professional identity and professional learning of academic staff. She has published in numerous journals including *Studies for Learning Society, Journal for Estonian Educational Publications*, and the *International Journal for Academic Development*.

Christopher Knapper has been a professional educational developer for over thirty-five years. He was founding director of two Canadian educational development centres, first at the University of Waterloo and later at Queen's University, where he is currently Professor Emeritus of Psychology. He was the first president of the Society for Teaching and Learning in Higher Education. He has written many books and articles on university teaching, and was editor of the *International Journal for Academic Development* between 1994 and 2003. As a consultant on university pedagogy, he has worked with universities in twenty-two different countries and on five continents.

Sarah Maguire is Staff Development Adviser at the University of Ulster. She had taught environmental science and geography before moving into staff and educational development. As a developer, she has supported a range of staff in a diversity of ways. She has looked for new ways to engage a broader base of staff in developing their own professional practice to enhance the learner experience. Most recently she has led a team re-accrediting the institution's postgraduate certificate in Higher Education Practice. Her recent publications focus on development opportunities for learning support staff and enhancing professional practice through peer review.

Kimberly A. Mealy is the Director of Educational, Professional, and Diversity Programs of the American Political Science Association (APSA). Prior to joining the APSA staff, she was teaching fellow and visiting assistant professor in the Political Science Department at Wellesley College. At APSA, she directs APSA's diversity programming, the annual APSA Teaching and Learning Conference, Civic Education and Engagement projects, and the Mentoring Initiative. Her research areas include political participation, voting rights, African American political behaviour, religion and politics, civic engagement, and teaching and learning.

Jennifer Murphy is Manager of the Irish National Academy for Integration of Research, Teaching and Learning (NAIRTL). Her research interests relate to issues of higher education management and teaching and learning. She is currently pursuing a doctorate of business administration in higher education management and has previously completed a master's in ICT in education and a postgraduate diploma in educational administration. She is co-author of "From Dry Ice to Plutarch's Fire—the Integration of Research and Teaching and Learning" in *Medical Education: The State of the Art*, and co-editor of *Research-Teaching Linkages: Practice and Policy*.

Katarina Mårtensson is an academic developer at the Centre for Educational Development, Lund University, Sweden. Her main research interest is in strategic educational development. Her recent publications include articles (e.g., in *Studies in Higher Education*) and a book chapter (in *The University and Its Disciplines: Teaching and Learning within and beyond Disciplinary Boundaries*) about significant networks; and articles about network approaches to influencing teaching and learning cultures at university (in *Higher Education*) and promoting scholarship of teaching and learning as a way to develop a quality culture in university (in *Higher Education Research and Development*).

Anne Nevgi holds a PhD in education and is University Lecturer at the Centre for Research and Development of Higher Education, University of Helsinki, Finland. Her recent publications include co-authored articles

such as "University Teachers' Approaches to Teaching and Their Pedagogical Use of ICTs: A Comparative Case Study of Finland, Japan and
India" (in *Journal of US-China Educational Review*), and "Disciplinary
and Gender Differences among Higher Education Students in Self-Regulated Learning Strategies" (in *Educational Psychology*).

Angela D. Nichols is a graduate student at the University of North Texas.
Her current research focuses on the processes of transitional justice in
post-conflict societies and their impact on peace duration, as well as the
onset and prevention of geno/politicides.

Bill Norton is Honorary Research Associate at Liverpool Hope University and since 2001 has researched a wide range of learning and
teaching issues, practices, and initiatives in higher education including blended learning, information literacy, academic writing, and student transition and retention. He has published a number of papers
and reports and given presentations at conferences, both national and
international. In recent years, a main research interest has been lecturers' perceptions, beliefs, and approaches to assessment, marking,
and feedback.

Lin Norton is Emeritus Professor of Pedagogical Research at Liverpool
Hope University, where she formerly worked as the Dean of Learning
and Teaching. Her research interests include pedagogical action research
and her most recent book is *Action Research in Teaching and Learning:
A Practical Guide to Conducting Pedagogical Research in Universities*.
She has also published extensively in journals and books in assessment,
meta-learning, and lecturers' beliefs and behaviours.

Gabriela Pleschová is responsible for a teacher development programme
at the Institute of Physics, Slovak Academy of Sciences, Bratislava. As
a political scientist, she also teaches at the Department of East Asian
Studies at Comenius University in Bratislava. Since 2004, she has been
coordinating development activities for beginner teachers in higher education. She also serves as a member of the editorial board of the *Journal of Political Science Education*, and is currently pursuing a graduate
degree in education at the University of Oxford.

Kathleen M. Quinlan is the Head of Educational Development at the University of Oxford and research fellow in the Department of Education
at Oxford. She has held educational development positions at the Australian National University and the Cornell Veterinary College and has
published on teaching portfolios, peer review of university teaching, academics' beliefs about teaching in history and engineering, and problem-
based learning in higher education.

Marvi Remmik is Staff Developer at the University of Tartu, Estonia, and PhD student at the University of Turku, Finland. Her research interests include professional identity and professional development of academics. She has published in the *Estonian Journal of Educational Publications* and the *International Journal for Academic Development*.

Joanna Renc-Roe is Development Manager of the Curriculum Resource Centre at Central European University, Hungary. She received her PhD in education from Keele University, UK. She has organised a range of training workshops for visiting academics from many post-socialist countries, and has developed the Teaching in Higher Education course for doctoral students. Her current research interests include educational policy and practice, internationalisation and academic identity, academic teaching practices, and the scholarship of teaching and learning.

Torgny Roxå is an academic developer in the Faculty of Engineering, Lund University, Sweden. His main research interest is in strategic educational development. Recent publications include articles (e.g., in *Studies in Higher Education*) and a book chapter (*The University and Its Disciplines: Teaching and Learning within and beyond Disciplinary Boundaries*) about significant networks; articles about network approaches to influencing teaching and learning cultures at university (in *Higher Education*) as well as about promoting scholarship of teaching and learning as a way to develop a quality culture in university (in *Higher Education Research and Development*).

Lee Shannon is Project Officer for the Hope Forum for Professional Ethics and is a former Write Now CETL researcher based at Liverpool Hope University. Lee is currently completing a PhD on the psychology of conceptual metaphor. His research interests include exploring lecturers' views on assessment, marking, and feedback, the pedagogical value of examinations, and the student/tutor relationship. He has presented research at national and international conferences and has co-authored a number of journal articles in the pedagogical field.

Eszter Simon is Adjunct Professor of Political Science at the University of Szeged in Hungary and Recurring Visiting Professor at the Center of North American Studies of the Economics University in Bratislava. Her research interest includes counterinsurgency, foreign policy analysis, American foreign policy, Central European politics, and teacher development in higher education. Currently, she is a staff development advisor at the Institute of Physics, Slovak Academy of Sciences. She is the co-author of "Teacher Training for Political Science Ph.D. Students in Europe: Determinants of a Tool for Enhancing Teaching in Higher Education" (in the *Journal of Political Science Education*).

Alan Soong Swee Kit is a senior education specialist at the Centre for Development of Teaching and Learning (CDTL), National University of Singapore. He has been working in the area of professional development in higher education since 2002. He conducts staff and student workshops on various pedagogy and learning issues, and carries out research for CDTL on various aspects of pedagogy and effective teaching. He recently co-authored the book *Integrating Blended-Scaffolded Learning Design into Curriculum: The SCBC Model, Singapore: Pearson Education*, 2009 (with Santhakumari Thanasingam).

Ann Stes is a postdoctoral assistant at the University of Antwerp's Centre of Excellence in Higher Education. Her recent publications include the book *The Impact of Instructional Development in Higher Education: Effects on Teachers and Students* and several articles such as "Effects of Teachers' Instructional Development on Students' Study Approaches in Higher Education" (in *Studies in Higher Education*), and "Instructional Development for Teachers in Higher Education: Effects on Students' Perceptions of the Teaching-Learning Environment" (in *British Journal of Educational Psychology*).

Keith Trigwell is Professor of Higher Education at the Institute for Teaching and Learning (ITL) at the University of Sydney. He was previously director of the ITL and of the Oxford Centre for Excellence in Preparing for Academic Practice at the University of Oxford. His research interests include investigating qualitative differences in university teaching and students' learning experiences, including development of the Approaches to Teaching Inventory. He has published more than 100 journal articles, conference papers, and books. He is a former co-president of the International Society for the Scholarship of Teaching and Learning, and a recipient of the Society's Lifetime Achievement Award (Leadership).

Peter Van Petegem is full professor at the Institute for Education and Information Sciences of the University of Antwerp, Head of Department of ECHO, and chairs the research group EduBRON. He is editor in chief of *Studies in Educational Evaluation*. His recent publications include "The Development of Learning Patterns of Student Teachers: A Cross-Sectional and Longitudinal Study" (in *Higher Education*), "Learning Pattern Development throughout Higher Education: A Longitudinal Study" (in *Learning and Individual Differences*), and "Changing Students' Approaches to Learning: A Two Year Study within a University Teacher Training Course" (in *Educational Studies*).

Tatiana Yarkova is Senior Program Manager of the Special and Extension Programs at Central European University, Hungary. She teaches course design and student assessment for CEU doctoral students, and facilitates workshops for visiting scholars. She holds an MA in Sociology from CEU and Lancaster University, and a PhD from the Graduate School for Social Research, Poland. Her research interests include sociology of education and sociology of knowledge and science, specifically academic cultures and academic socialization, academic networks, and the power/knowledge nexus in institutions and systems of higher education.

Index

A

academic developer, 89, 90, 93, 99, 100, 204, 237, 251, 305
academic development, 10, 21, 29, 32, 57, 110, 193, 227, 258–261. *See also* educational development; faculty development; instructional development; pedagogical development; professional development; teacher development; teacher-training; teaching development
academic practice, 109, 115, 119 155, 161, 162, 164, 165, 166, 167, 206
accredited programme, 59, 60151, 153, 154, 155, 156, 157, 162, 163, 164, 165, 166, 167, 168, 193, 295
action research, 191, 204, 205, 206, 207, 246, 251
adult learners, 88
American Political Science Association 35–36, 61
analytical framework, 238
Anglo-Saxon countries, 2, 9, 10, 21
approach to teaching, 7, 21, 25, 28–29, 30, 58, 62, 63, 64, 65, 66, 90, 95,108, 239, 240–241, 243–244, 246, 248, 259, 267, 269, 274, 275, 276
Approaches to Teaching Inventory (ATI), 4, 240, 258–259, 265
Assessment Design Inventory (ADI), 203
assessment, 1, 6, 8 19, 22, 24–25, 28–32, 35, 37, 78, 93, 107, 108, 113, 122, 151, 153, 155, 156, 159, 160, 161, 166, 193, 197, 206 237, 238, 251. *See also* grading; marking. Emotional issues of, 194, 195, 200, 201, 203; design, 140, 202, 203; pedagogy, 203; philosophy, 140, 198, 204; practice, 54, 58, 60, 61, 140–141, 191, 192, 194, 195, 196, 199, 200, 201, 203, 204, 205, 207, 288; purpose, 140, 192, 195, 196
attitudinal change. *See* change (attitudinal)
Australia, 2, 3, 8, 1455, 56, 59, 61, 65, 67, 137–138, 143, 258, 266
award winning teachers, 34, 43, 50, 261–262, 266–268. *See also* teaching award(s)

B

Baylor University, 36, 41
Belgium, 1, 9, 10, 135, 139, 234, 236, 237
Bologna process, 17, 129–137, 140, 152, 171, 292
Browne review, 106, 138–139, 141

C

Canada, 2, 11, 53–68, 129, 274, 289
Carnegie Academy for the Scholarship of Teaching and Learning (CASTL), 145
Carnegie Classification System, 44, 50
Carnegie Foundation for the Advancement of Teaching, 32
Central and Eastern Europe, 32, 86, 135
Central European University (CEU), 11, 19–22, 31–33

Centre for Excellence in Higher Education (University of Antwerp), 236–237
change agent, 121, 165, 227, 294
change catalyst, 152
change enabler, 153
change: attitudinal, 3, 4, 6, 7, 9, 60, 61–63, 64, 90, 235–236, 275, 284; conceptual, 9, 220, 241, 254, 259, 260, 261, 265, 286, 290, 293; in beliefs (*see* change (attitudinal)); in teaching behaviour, 5, 6, 9, 11, 60, 62–63, 235, 236, 238, 240, 244–245, 247, 248, 275, 276, 279, 284, 285, 286, 290, 293
cognitive barrier. *See* conceptual barrier
community of practice, 59–60, 61, 63, 91–92, 99–101, 121, 219
compulsory training, 64, 67, 213, 274, 275, 277, 278, 288, 294
conceptions, 7, 90, 174, 182, 184, 205, 214, 219, 220, 222, 236, 238, 240, 244–245, 247, 248, 258–260, 265, 285, 290, 277
conceptual barrier,166, 274
conceptual change. *See* change (conceptual)
constraints, 82, 117, 166, 191, 194, 195, 196, 197, 199, 203, 278
constructive alignment, 24, 28, 122, 175
context: course, 242, 245, 246, 252, 285, 286, 289, 292; cultural, 6, 88, 289, 295; institutional, 20–23, 105, 144, 246, 286, 289, 295; local, 9, 13, 143–145, 166, 213, 214, 215, 229, 236–237, 246, 252, 289, 295
continuing professional development (CPD). *See* professional development
Council of Europe, 130
course design, 19, 22, 25, 30–31, 42, 50, 93–95, 117, 152, 156
cultural differences, 136, 140–141, 145
cultural orientation, 141, 144–145
cultural perspective ,141, 144–145217, 218, 224, 228,
curriculum, 2 19, 32, 35, 41, 55, 56, 59, 73, 108, 114, 118, 122, 130, 136–137, 143, 145–146, 152, 156, 159, 164, 165, 171, 173, 174–176, 193, 206, 237, 238, 253

D
data analysis, 4, 12, 39, 42, 240, 285–286
data collection, 4, 5, 6, 12, 39, 42, 76, 134, 240, 242, 247, 249, 285–286, 279
Dearing report, 106, 137, 141, 192, 202
departmental influence, 13, 58, 244, 276, 277, 278,
disciplinary culture, 13, 58, 65, 146, 241, 276
disciplinary differences, 98, 142–143, 145–146, 203, 204, 241, 246
disciplinary influence, 141, 242, 274, 278, 293–294
discipline (academic), 8, 26–27, 28, 29, 31, 35, 42, 58, 65, 87, 92, 95, 98, 101, 105, 108, 116, 117, 120, 121, 136, 137, 139, 139, 141–143, 145–146, 159, 160, 161, 173, 186, 193, 196, 203–204, 205–207, 214, 217–219, 237, 241, 246, 270, 274, 284, 288, 291, 293–294
doctoral education, 32, 50, 58, 59, 60, 67, 131. *See also* graduate education
doctoral programmes, 32, 50, 292
doctoral students, 1, 11, 19–22, 31, 32, 34–42, 50, 58, 59, 60, 67, 277, 280, 287, 288, 289, 291, 292, 294

E
Education International Pan-European Structure, 131
educational development, 2, 8, 10, 14 23, 30, 53, 55–60, 63–64, 65, 66, 74, 141–144, 253, 258–261, 284, 293. *See also* academic development
Erasmus exchange programme, 135–136, 144
established professors, 289
Estonia, 11, 86–104, 289, 294
European Association for Quality Assurance in Higher Education (ENQA), 130, 134, 140

European Association of Institutions in Higher Education (EURASHE), 130–131

European Commission, 129–132, 136, 139, 144–145, 147

European Credit Transfer and Accumulation System (ECTS),130, 132, 134, 136, 147, 156, 157, 158, 160, 161

European Higher Education Area (EHEA), 129–131, 133–134, 140

European Research Area (ERA), 131, 133–134

European Students' Union (ESU), 130

European Union (EU), 86, 88, 89, 131, 132, 127, 151, 276, 284

European University Association (EUA), 130, 132

evaluation, 2, 6, 12 19–20, 22–23, 26, 55, 56, 60, 61, 63–64, 72, 76–77, 84–85, 96, 107, 116, 121, 140, 151, 156, 160, 193, 206, 234, 249, 257–273

excellent teaching, 27–28, 82, 86

external priorities, 114

F

faculty attitudes, 9, 60, 61–62, 64, 65, 137, 235–236, 277, 294, 295

faculty development, 3, 25, 33, 249258–261. *See also* academic development

feedback, 2, 4, 8 22–24, 26, 28, 30–31, 60, 76, 81–84, 96, 99, 107, 113, 116, 117, 122, 163, 192–195, 198, 199, 200–203, 206

flexible learning paths, 134, 136

follow-up study ,58, 171, 180, 244, 248, 249

formal training, 61, 65, 74, 194, 201, 202, 204

future research, 14, 27, 50, 234, 245–251, 253, 290–292

G

grading: systems, 136, 140. *See also* assessment; marking

graduate education, 32–33, 34–36, 56, 57–58, 59, 61, 65–66, 71, 144. *See also* doctoral education

H

hard sciences, 241, 274, 291

Higher Education Academy (HEA), 1, 105, 106, 107, 110, 13, 118, 121, 139, 145, 192

higher education: policy, 21–22, 27, 162; practice, 111, 112, 113, 114, 116, 120, 121, 122; research, 22, 33, 263

Hix Rankings, 38–39

Humboldtian university, 170–172, 173, 174, 175, 176, 179, 186, 187

Hungary, 11, 19, 135

I

identity, 20, 23, 26, 133, 197214, 216, 217, 219, 221, 223, 224, 227

impact 1, 2, 5, 6, 7, 8, 9, 10, 11, 12, 13, 14, 19, 24–25, 30, 63–64, 66, 72–73, 75, 76, 84, 105, 110, 117, 121, 151, 154, 155, 162, 163, 164, 165, 166, 167, 172, 173, 174, 179, 186, 221, 227, 229. *See also* programme impact; programme success. Causes of, 234, 235, 245, 249, 262–263, 266–270, 274–278; levels of (*see* levels of analysis; levels of impact); measurement of, 63–64, 234–256, 266–268, 274, 284–285; of pedagogical courses, 63–64, 66, 95–99; of programmes (*see* programme impact); of university teaching programs, 2, 3, 5, 6, 10, 11, 13 90, 95, 98, 191,192, 194, 196, 203, 204, 206, 207; on individuals, 9, 10, 12, 179–186, 240–241, 244–245, 246, 247, 257, 274, 277; on teachers, 7, 9, 10, 179–186, 235–236, 238–239, 240–241, 244–245, 248–251, 266–268, 274 -276, 277, 278, 279, 284

improving university teaching, 8, 14, 53, 55, 63–64, 65176–179, 205, 206, 207, 237, 238, 244, 249, 251

individual level factors/variables, 10, 194, 203, 242, 246, 247279, 284, 285

inexperienced teachers, 289, 294. *See also* new faculty members; young teachers

innovative teaching, 28, 31, 140, 165, 201
institutional incentives, 54, 65, 139, 252–253, 288, 293, 295
institutional influence, 1, 8, 9, 11, 13, 194, 196, 197, 277, 279, 285, 289, 293
institutional level factors and variables, 1, 8, 9, 39–41, 105, 107, 108, 109, 111, 191, 194, 205, 207, 234, 236, 240, 244–245, 246–247, 275, 276, 277, 279, 290, 291, 295
institutional structures, 252–253
instructional development, 11, 13, 14, 71, 129, 135, 137–147, 170–174, 176–179, 180, 181, 182–184, 186, 234–253, 275, 277, 278, 284, 287–289, 292, 294, 295. *See also* academic development
Integrated Postsecondary Education Data System (IPEDS), 37, 51
intervening variables, 11, 246, 248, 284
Ireland, 1, 105, 111, 135, 151–169, 288, 289, 295

J
job placement, 11, 36–42, 276
joint degrees, 134

L
learning outcomes, 6, 7, 9 23–24, 32, 62, 64, 78, 94–95, 140,151–169, 152, 153, 155, 156, 158, 160, 161, 167, 192, 235–239, 241–244, 248, 249, 251–252, 281, 285
levels of analysis, 9, 242, 279, 280–283. *See also* levels of impact
levels of impact, 8, 10, 235–236, 239, 247, 258–262. *See also* levels of analysis
lifelong learning, 75, 131–133, 135, 281
Lisbon strategy, 129, 132, 147
Liverpool Hope University, 193, 205, 206, 207
long-term effect, 10, 191, 204234, 244–245, 248, 249, 275, 276, 286, 290, 294

M
macro level, 9, 191, 203215, 217, 223, 224, 225, 226, 227, 229, 279, 283, 284, 292, 295

management, 9, 73, 78, 114, 166221, 224, 225, 227, 229, 251, 283
managers, 13, 113, 114, 115, 117, 118215, 216, 217, 222, 225, 227, 229, 278, 279, 281, 289, 293–295
marking, 192, 194, 195, 197, 198, 199, 200, 201, 202. *See also* assessment; grading
mentoring, 35, 36, 278, 101, 160, 270
mentors, 6, 8, 75, 83–84, 94–95, 142, 182, 183, 193, 257, 290
mentorship, 6, 8, 71–72, 76, 79, 81–84, 287, 294
meso level, 9, 191, 203, 213, 215, 217, 218, 219, 221, 222, 223, 224, 225, 226, 227, 228, 229, 279, 281, 284, 292, 295
Miami University of Ohio, 41, 50
micro level, 9, 13, 191215, 217, 218, 222, 223, 225, 227, 279, 280, 284
mixed research method, 234, 240, 259, 286

N
National Center for Education Statistics (U.S.), 51
National University of Singapore, 11, 72–73
natural sciences. *See* hard sciences
new faculty members, 8, 11, 53, 55, 57, 58–61, 63, 64–66, 75, 237. *See also* inexperienced teachers; young teachers. Support for, 236
Nordic countries, 1, 9, 10 21, 53, 59, 135
Northern Europe, 21, 129
Northern Ireland, 111, 135, 288
Norway, 135

O
organisation, 6, 107, 152214, 215, 216, 217, 218, 219, 223, 224, 225, 226, 227, 228, 229, 293
organisational level, 236, 244–245, 247, 253

P
pedagogical action research. *See* action research
pedagogical course, 6, 7 89, 93–95, 96, 101 171, 181, 182, 183, 229. *See also* pedagogical development (course); professional

development (programme); teacher-training; university teaching programme
pedagogical development, 21, 171, 174, 177, 178, 179, 181, 187. *See also* academic development. Course, 180, 181, 186 (*see also* pedagogical course; professional development (programme); teacher-training; university teaching programme
pedagogical philosophy, 191, 194, 195, 196, 198, 201, 204
peer observation, 93, 94, 95, 99, 100
PhD students. *See* doctoral students
postgraduate certificate, 105, 106, 108, 111, 112, 113, 121, 122, 193, 206, 238, 257, 266, 268, 270
postgraduate diploma, 154, 158, 160, 206, 294
power relations, 199, 200, 201, 220, 223, 277
practical implications, 251–253
practicum, 72, 75–76, 79–84, 174–175, 180
practitioner experience, 207
Preparing Future Faculty program (U.S.), 49
primarily undergraduate institutions, 41, 44–49
professional development, 3, 21–22, 29, 62–63, 66, 71–72, 74–77, 79, 81, 84, 93, 101, 105, 108, 109, 111, 112, 118, 120, 122, 154–156, 158, 160, 201, 205, 207, 214, 234, 235, 249, 251, 253, 258–261. *See also* academic development. Accredited, 57, 60, 66, 105; continuing, 62, 66, 74, 105, 106, 108–113, 116, 118–122, 157, 194, 201, 205, 207; programme, 71–72, 74–75, 77, 106, 241, 252, 253 (*see also* pedagogical course; pedagogical development (course); teacher-training; university teaching programme)
Professional Standards Framework, 105, 106, 118, 138–141, 193
professional standards, 106, 109, 118, 119, 138–141
programme aim, 7, 13, 21, 25, 138–141, 237 262, 263, 268, 287, 289

programme content, 8, 237–238, 287
programme evaluation, 263, 264, 268, 287
programme history, 287
programme impact, 4–12, 19, 95–99, 179–187, 266–270
programme length, 8, 90, 100, 238, 278, 287, 290
programme redesign, 251–252
programme structure, 11, 73, 76, 174–176, 237–238, 287
programme success, 2, 8, 9, 10, 13, 274–278. *See also* impact; programme impact

Q
Quality Assurance Agency, 197
quality assurance, 2, 19, 55, 66, 73 130, 132, 134, 140–141, 196, 276, 278, 292
quality of teaching, 1, 2, 7, 86, 89, 100, 166, 202, 216, 238, 260

R
rankings of political science departments, 36, 38–39
realistic evaluation, 263–265, 268, 271
reflection, 91, 96, 99, 100, 101, 141–142
reflective practice, 25,141–142
reflexive teaching, 141–142
research intensive universities, 19, 44–48, 247
research methods, 3, 4, 5, 10, 12, 161, 285; problems with, 277, 279, 284, 285–287, 291

S
scholarly teaching, 19, 23, 29–31, 60
scholarship of teaching and learning (SOTL), 22, 32–33, 56, 101,152, 155, 158, 201, 202, 205, 214, 278
self-doubt, 200, 275, 278, 294
significant networks, 217, 218,219, 220,221, 222, 223, 224, 225, 227, 228, 284
Singapore, 11, 71, 73–74, 164, 294
social dimension, 131, 133, 135, 140
Southern Europe, 129
staff developer. *See* academic developer
staff mobility, 130, 134–135, 139–140, 144
strategic students, 196, 197

student: diversity of, 135–138, 144, 197; doctoral (*see* doctoral students); employability of, 38, 131–133, 135, 137, 140, 280, 281, 284, 292; mobility of, 130, 132, 134–136, 139, 146; perceptions, 7, 91, 99, 200, 235–236, 239, 241–244, 247, 252, 253, 285; learning of, 4–9, 11–14, 19, 21, 25–27, 30, 53, 60, 62–65, 66, 80, 107, 122, 159, 162, 166, 167, 193–196, 201, 205, 207, 213–215, 221, 222, 224, 235–239, 241–244, 247, 248, 252, 253, 284, 287, 290, 292, 293

student-centred teaching, 6, 7, 89, 90, 91, 121, 122, 236, 237, 238, 241, 251, 275, 276, 291. *See also* student-focused teaching

student-focused teaching, 7, 90, 192, 241, 259, 260, 265. *See also* student-centred teaching

study approach, 6, 7, 9, 63–64, 235–236, 239, 241–244, 247, 248, 253

Sweden, 1, 9, 135, 223, 224,

systemic level factors and variables, 276, 277

T

target group, 11, 21, 237, 253, 288

teacher development, 1–13 19, 74, 151, 179, 180, 181–185, 186–187, 241, 258–261. *See also* academic development

teacher qualification, 176, 238, 252–253

teacher-centred teaching, 131, 138. *See also* teacher-focused teaching

teacher-focused teaching, 192, 241, 259. *See also* teaching centred teaching

teacher-training, 3, 4, 6, 10, 11, 12, 14, 56, 57, 58–60, 61, 62–66, 71, 73, 84, 89, 98, 106, 108, 213, 214, 215, 218, 219, 221, 222, 223, 224 227, 228, 229, 234–255. *See also* academic development; pedagogical course; pedagocial development (course); professional development (programme); university teaching programme. For graduate students, 13, 34–36

teaching assistants, 56, 57–59, 74, 107, 237

teaching award(s), 6, 42–45, 48, 19, 163, 165, 167, 257, 261–262, 266–268, 276, 292. *See also* award winning teachers

teaching career, 19–20, 82, 249, 253

teaching development, 44–50, 73, 76, 137–146, 153, 258–261275, 277, 279, 284, 285, 287- 295. *See also* academic development

teaching effectiveness, 142

teaching experiment, 75, 81

teaching policy, 234, 244, 245, 252

teaching portfolios, 6, 22, 28–30, 32, 56, 59, 60–61, 67, 142, 152, 285

teaching skills, 3, 8 23–24, 30, 44–50, 88, 117, 152, 157, 172–173, 175, 178, 184, 185, 186, 202, 214; development of, 24, 86, 89, 92, 95, 101, 195, 201, 235–236

tertiary teacher education, 292

training course, 3, 22, 89, 95, 275, 294

transferability, 91, 236, 238, 246

transformative learning, 142

type II error, 285

U

U.S. Federal Department of Education, 37

U.S., 7, 8, 14, 19–20, 35–50, 53, 54, 56, 57, 61, 64, 65, 67, 129, 137–138, 141, 145, 152, 166, 276, 289

UK, 1, 2, 4, 8, 53, 54, 56, 57, 60, 61, 65, 66, 67, 105–126, 129, 135, 137–141, 143, 145, 152, 166, 191–207, 258–259, 262, 289, 291, 294

UNESCO's European Centre for Higher Education, 130

unity of research and teaching, 171–173, 185

University of Antwerp, 7, 9, 236–239, 245, 249–250, 252

University of Helsinki, 170, 171–172, 175, 176–178, 179, 183, 185–186

University of Nottingham, 2

University of Sydney, 2, 257, 266–268

University of Tartu, 87, 89, 92, 95, 101

University of Ulster, 105, 106, 110, 111, 112, 115, 116

university pedagogy, 62, 63171, 172–173, 174, 174–176, 178,

179, 180, 181, 182, 183, 185,
185–186
university teaching programme,
191, 192, 193, 195, 196, 202,
203, 204, 206, 207. *See also*
pedagogical course; pedagogical
development (course); professional development (programme); teacher-training
US News and World Report Rankings,
38, 45

V

Visible effects, 214, 217, 219, 220, 221,
222, 228, 229

voluntary training, 5, 93, 237

W

workgroup, 152, 214, 215, 217,
218,219, 220,221, 222, 223,
224, 225, 227, 228, 229, 284
Write Now Centre for Excellence
in Teaching and Learning
(CETL—Liverpool Hope Uni-
versity), 191

Y

young teachers, 237, 253, 275, 277,
288. *See also* inexperienced
teachers; new faculty members